Microsoft® SQL Server™ 2005 Stored Procedure Programming in T-SQL & .NET, Third Edition

Dejan Šunderić

McGraw-Hill

New York   Chicago   San Francisco
Lisbon   London   Madrid   Mexico City   Milan
New Delhi   San Juan   Seoul   Singapore   Sydney   Toronto

The McGraw·Hill Companies

The McGraw-Hill Companies
160 Spear Street, Suite 700
San Francisco, California 94105
U.S.A.

To arrange bulk purchase discounts for sales promotions, premiums, or fund-raisers, please contact **McGraw-Hill** at the above address.

Microsoft® SQL Server™ 2005 Stored Procedure Programming in T-SQL & .NET, Third Edition

1234567890 DOC DOC 019876

ISBN 0-07-226228-1

Acquisitions Editor	Wendy Rinaldi
Project Editor	Mark Karmendy
Acquisitions Coordinator	Alex McDonald
Technical Editor	Karl Hilsmann
Copy Editor	Mark Karmendy
Proofreader	Paul Tyler
Indexer	Claire Splan
Composition	International Typesetting and Composition
Illustration	International Typesetting and Composition
Series Design	Peter F. Hancik, Lucie Ericksen, Elizabeth Jang
Cover Series Design	Pattie Lee

This book was composed with Adobe® InDesign®.

Writing a book isn't easy, but living with someone who is writing a book can be, at times, even harder. I would like to thank my wife Mirjana and my son Nikola for their patience, understanding, support, and inspiration.

About the Author

Dejan Šunderić, MCDBA, is the principal consultant at Trigon Blue, Inc. (www.trigonblue.com), and the president of the Toronto SQL Server User Group (www.tssug.ca). He specializes in database and application development on the SQL Server platform.

Projects that he has been involved with cover B2C and B2B e-commerce, financial, medical, document-management, mortgage, asset-management, insurance, real-estate, IT supply chain, process control, communication, data warehouse, and OLAP systems. Dejan has worked as a database architect, database and application developer, database administrator, team leader, project manager, writer, and technical trainer.

He is the author of *SQL Server 2000 Stored Procedure Programming* (www.trigonblue .com/stored_procedure.htm), and co-author of *Windows 2000 Performance Tuning and Optimization* and four other books, as well as numerous technical articles for several computer and professional publications.

His career started in Belgrade, Yugoslavia, where he graduated from the Faculty of Electrical Engineering. In 1995 he moved to Toronto, Canada, then in 2001 to Pittsburgh, PA. He is now back in Toronto working on a multi-terabyte database and leading a local organization of SQL Server professionals.

Dejan can be contacted via the book's web site (www.trigonblue.com/ clr_stored_procedure).

Contents at a Glance

Contents

Acknowledgments

I wish to thank all the people who helped to make this book a reality, and in particular:

- **Olga Baranova**, who created several examples for Chapters 11, 12, 13, 14, 18, and 21.
- **Tom Woodhead**, for straightening the winding course of my writings.

Introduction

Welcome to *Microsoft SQL Server 2005 Stored Procedure Programming in T-SQL & .NET*. This book identifies and describes the key concepts, tips, techniques, and best practices the professional developer needs to master in order to take full advantage of stored procedures using SQL Server's native Transact-SQL and .NET compatible programming languages.

Microsoft SQL Server is the relational database management system (RDBMS) of choice for a growing number of business organizations and professional database and application developers. The reasons for this growing popularity are quite simple:

► **Integration**   No other RDBMS integrates as fully and cleanly with applications and integrated development environments (IDEs) designed to run on the ubiquitous Microsoft Windows platform.

► **Ease of use**   SQL Server provides a suite of tools to allow DBAs to design, develop, deploy, and manage database solutions. These interfaces automate repetitive tasks and provide simple ways to perform complex operations. SQL Server integrates seamlessly with development tools such as Visual Studio to allow developers to design and develop client/server or Internet solutions rapidly.

► **Flexibility**   You can use different features within SQL Server to achieve similar results. (Of course, with flexibility comes choice, and choice means that the developer is responsible for choosing the most appropriate means of achieving an end. This book will help you make those choices.)

► **Power**   SQL Server makes large amounts of data available to large numbers of concurrent users while maintaining the security and integrity of the data.

When I began working with SQL Server, reference materials relating to the development and deployment of stored procedures were rare and not particularly helpful. These materials described basic concepts, but the examples presented were often trivial and not complex enough to be applied to real-world situations in which aspects such as error handling, debugging, naming conventions, and interfaces to other applications are critical. As the legions of application developers and development DBAs migrated from Microsoft Access to SQL Server, and as SQL Server became the leading database for mission-critical application and decision support systems development, the need for more advanced work on SQL Server stored procedures became even more critical.

Who Should Read This Book

This book has been written to fill this gap, and thus it has been written with a wide audience in mind. Ideally, it will be neither the first nor the last book you read on SQL Server, but it may be the one you refer to and recommend the most. Above all, this book has been written to help professional developers get the most out of SQL Server stored procedures in both Transact-SQL and .NET and to produce quality work for their clients.

If you are an experienced SQL Server developer, you will find this book to be an essential reference text full of tips and techniques to help you address the development issues you encounter in the course of your day-to-day development activities.

If you have some experience with SQL Server development but substantially more in other programming environments such as Visual Basic or C#, you will find this book useful as a tool to orient yourself with the SQL Server environment and become proficient more quickly with SQL Server stored procedure and CLR integration concepts and methods. You will be able to incorporate effective, swift Transact-SQL stored procedures (and other database objects) into client or middleware code and also produce CLR methods (and classes) that will be compiled into CLR stored procedures (and other database objects). If you are a novice SQL Server developer, the concepts, tips, and techniques you will learn in reading this book and working through the exercises will help you attain the knowledge, skills, and good habits that will help you become an accomplished professional.

I hope that this book remains close to your workstation for a long time. Indeed, in the course of this book's useful life, you may in turn be all three of the users just described.

What You Will Find in This Book

Each chapter in this book will provide conceptual grounding in a specific area of the SQL Server development landscape. The first ten chapters are dedicated to Transact-SQL stored procedure programming. Chapters 11 to 14 cover development of stored procedures (and other database objects) in .NET languages such as Visual Basic .NET and C#. The rest of the book is focused on advanced topics such as security, debugging, deployment, performance issues, and the interaction of Transact-SQL code with environments.

Chapter 1, "The SQL Server 2005 Environment and Tools," is a quick introduction to tools that are part of SQL Server 2005 and that will be used through the rest of the chapters.

Chapter 2, "Stored Procedure Design Concepts," explores Transact-SQL stored procedure design in greater detail, with particular attention paid to the different types of stored procedures, their uses, and their functionality.

Chapter 3, "Basic Transact-SQL Programming Constructs," describes Transact-SQL, the ANSI SQL-92–compliant programming language used to write scripts in SQL Server. This chapter summarizes data types, variables, flow control statements, and cursors in the context of SQL Server 2005.

Chapter 4, "Functions," describes the extensive set of built-in functions available in SQL Server 2005 and how to use them in various common situations.

Chapter 5, "Composite Transact-SQL Constructs: Batches, Scripts, and Transactions," describes the various ways in which you can group Transact-SQL statements for execution.

Chapter 6, "Error Handling," provides a coherent strategy for handling errors as they occur.

Chapter 7, "Special Types of Stored Procedures," describes user-defined, system, extended, temporary, global temporary, and remote stored procedures.

Chapter 8, "Views," presents all types of views—standard SQL views, indexed views, INFORMATION_SCHEMA views, and local and distributed partitioned views.

Chapter 9, "Triggers," presents Transact-SQL triggers—After triggers and Instead-of triggers.

Chapter 10, "User-defined Functions," describes the design and use of Transact-SQL scalar and table-valued user-defined functions.

Chapter 11, "Fundamentals of .NET Programming in SQL Server 2005," introduces architecture, concepts, and techniques for coding SQL Server 2005 programmatic database object in .NET-compatible programming languages.

Chapter 12, "Fundamentals of CLR Stored Procedure Development," focuses on the development and management of stored procedures in C# and Visual Basic .NET and usage of ADO.NET to implement database access.

Chapter 13, "CLR Functions and Triggers," focuses on the development and management of managed user-defined functions and triggers in C# and Visual Basic .NET.

Chapter 14, "CLR Database Objects Advanced Topics," starts with the development and management of managed user-defined types and managed aggregate functions.

Then it covers implementing transactions in all types of CLR database objects. The end of the chapter is dedicated to architectural guidelines for justifiable uses of managed database objects.

Chapter 15, "Advanced Stored Procedure Programming," introduces some advanced techniques for coding stored procedures, such as dynamically constructed queries, optimistic locking using timestamps, and nested stored procedures.

Chapter 16, "Debugging," presents tools and methods for debugging both Transact-SQL and .NET database objects in Visual Studio .NET and SQL Server Management Studio.

Chapter 17, "Source Code Management," demonstrates how you can manage Transact-SQL source code in a repository such as Visual SourceSafe.

Chapter 18, "Database Deployment," demonstrates how you can manage and deploy Transact-SQL source code from development to the test and production environments. It explains and demonstrates two alternative approaches—one using Visual Studio .NET and the other, more traditional, using scripts developed in Transact-SQL, VBScript, or .NET.

Chapter 19, "Security," starts with a description of security-related features and concepts in SQL Server 2005. It later describes typical security architectures and implementation on SQL Server.

Chapter 20, "Stored Procedures for Web Search Engines," presents an example of how to use stored procedures in a web application that queries the database system. Several optimization techniques are used to avoid typical design problems and improve the performance.

Chapter 21, "Interaction with the SQL Server Environment," focuses on the ways in which you can use system stored procedures, functions, and commands to interact with the SQL Server environment, and also discusses the ways in which user-defined stored procedures can help you leverage the existing functionality of various elements within the SQL Server environment.

Appendix A, "Naming Conventions," provides you with a suggested naming convention for database objects that you can use on SQL Server projects.

Appendix B, "Stored Procedure Compilation, Storage, and Reuse," explains how to manage and process Transact-SQL stored procedures in SQL Server.

Appendix C, "Data Types in SQL Server 2005," provides you with a list of data types in use in SQL Server 2005, their sizes, ranges, and sample constants.

Requirements

To make full use of this book, you will need access to a server running one of the following editions of SQL Server 2005 (with either 32-bit or 64-bit support):

- ► **Enterprise Edition**   Supports all features and scales to enterprise level

- ► **Standard Edition**   Scales to the level of departmental servers; supports up to four CPUs

- ► **Workgroup Edition**   Scales to the level of workgroup server; limited to usage of two CPUs and database size of up to 3GB

- ► **Evaluation Edition**   Supports all features of Enterprise Edition; use is limited to 120 days; available for download over the Web

- ► **Developer Edition**   Supports all features of Enterprise Edition but has a different licensing policy

Stored Procedure Programming Requirements

You can also perform most of the stored procedure programming–oriented activities described in this book using a stand-alone PC with Windows 2000 Professional or Windows XP Pro to run one of the following versions of Microsoft SQL Server 2000:

- ► **Express Edition**   Designed for mobile or stand-alone users and applications; does not support some advanced features, such as fail-over clustering, Web Services, Integration Services, or Full-Text Search; it can utilize only a single CPU; size of individual database is limited to 1GB; its licensing supports free distribution as part of your custom systems and applications.

- ► **Developer Edition**   Licensed to be used only as a development and test server, although it supports all features of Enterprise Edition.

Although Express Edition is compatible with all other versions of SQL Server 2005 and thus makes an excellent development tool in a stand-alone environment, the absence of administrative tools such as SQL Server Management Studio means that some of the information you find in this book will not be usable right away. I recommend that you obtain some other version (such as Developer Edition or Evaluation Edition) or buy a Server/Per-Seat Client Access License (CAL) that will allow you to use administrative tools against Express Edition.

NOTE

Microsoft has released SQL Server Management Studio Express that could be used to manage Express Edition instances, but it is too simple and inconvenient. You should upgrade.

.NET Programming Requirements

To explore and use .NET programming features, you need to install and use the following:

- ▶ Any version of SQL Server 2005
- ▶ .NET Framework 2.0

Installation of Visual Studio 2005 .NET is recommended but not required.

Sample Database and Other Resources

You may have noticed that this book does not include a CD. SQL Server development is a dynamic field, as you will see if you compare the first, second, and third editions of the book. Rather than increase the cost of the book by adding a CD, which would be out of date almost before it hit the bookstore, the publisher and I have chosen to make additional resources available for download via the Web. In addition to the sample database (more information on that in just a bit) that I have created and will use through most of this book, other resources available include these:

- ▶ **Several tools for source code management and database deployment**   Set of T-SQL, VBScript, and .NET tools for generating, managing, and deploying code of database objects.

- ▶ **Sample SQLCLR code**   Visual Studio .NET sample projects for demonstrating development of database objects in Visual Basic .NET and C#.

- ▶ **Periodic updates**   As noted earlier, SQL Server development is a dynamic field, and thus a book on SQL Server needs to be dynamic to meet the evolving needs of its audience. Reader feedback is important to me. Check my web site (www.trigonblue.com) for periodic updates on issues raised by readers.

- ▶ **Author's web site**   Aside from being the source of the sample database and periodic update downloads, the Trigon Blue web site provides a wealth of excellent reference materials and links. Visit the site often for SQL Server and e-business news. While you're there, have a look at the many articles and white papers, and check out Trigon Blue's many product and service offerings.

Sample Database

The subject of the Asset5 sample database created for this book is an asset-management system within a fictional organization. Although the database is based on real-world experience within financial institutions, it is also applicable in many other environments.

The main purpose of the database is to track assets. Assets are defined as equipment, and all variations in their content, attributes, and shape are recorded as values of properties. The Inventory table tracks location, status, leasing information, and who is currently using each asset. To transfer an asset from one location to another, to assign assets to a different owner or department, to request maintenance, or to request upgrades or new assets, users of the database use orders and order items. Activities performed to complete the order are recorded in the charge log and interdepartmental invoices are generated. There are lookup tables used to track provinces, lease frequencies, statuses, and other details.

Sample Database Installation

You should download this database and install it on your server before you begin to read the rest of this book. To download and install the sample Asset5 database:

1. Visit **www.trigonblue.com**/stored_procedures_2005

2. Click the Download Sample DB link.

3. Click the Asset5 sample database link to start the download. When prompted, opt to save the file to disk. Remember the location where you saved the file.

4. Unzip the contents of the Zip file into the Data folder of the machine on which SQL Server is installed (usually \Program Files\Microsoft SQL Server\ MSSQL.1\MSSQL\Data).

5. Make sure that SQL Server is running. If necessary, go to Control Panel | Administrative Tools | Services, find the SQL Server service in the list, and make sure that its status is Started.

6. Run SQL Server Management Studio (Start | Programs | Microsoft SQL Server 2005).

7. You will be prompted to connect to SQL Server. Make sure that Server Type is set to Database Engine and that Server Name is set to the name of the machine (network) name on which you installed SQL Server. If you have specified the name of an instance of SQL Server 2005 during the installation, you must specify the instance name in the field as well with backslash (\) as a delimiter. In the screen shown here, the machine name is LG and the instance name is RC.

8. If your Windows login is a member of the Administrators local group, you can leave Authentication set to Windows Authentication and click OK. If you are one of the local administrators, you can ask an administrator to give you such access or ask a database administrator to create a SQL server login for you. In that case you would need to change Authentication to SQL Server Authentication and then specify a login and password to connect to the server.

9. Management Studio will appear on the screen with Object Browser connected to the server in the left side of the window.

10. Click the New Query button on the toolbar to open a new query window. Management Studio opens a query window pointing to the *master* database.

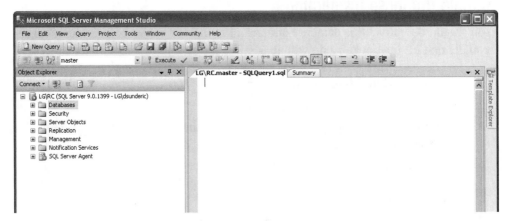

11. Type the following text in the query window:

```
EXEC sp_attach_db 'Asset5',
'C:\Program Files\Microsoft SQL Server\MSSQL.1\MSSQL\Data\Asset5.mdf',
'C:\Program Files\Microsoft SQL Server\MSSQL.1\MSSQL\Data\Asset5_log.ldf'
```

12. If the location of the folder containing the Asset5 database file is different from the one shown in the command, change the command.

13. To attach the database, select Query | Execute from the menu bar. SQL Server attaches the database. The database is now ready for use.

Purpose and Design of the Sample Database

The Asset5 database is designed to track and manage assets within an organization. This database allows users to

▶   Track features of assets

▶   Search for assets with specific features

- ▶ Record the current location and status of an asset

- ▶ Track the person and organizational unit to which the asset is assigned

- ▶ Note how an asset is acquired and the cost of the acquisition

- ▶ Keep parameters concerning leases (for example, lease payments, lease schedules, and lease vendors used to obtain assets)

- ▶ Identify assets for which lease schedules have expired

- ▶ Record orders to departments in charge of services such as acquisition, disposal, servicing, and technical support

- ▶ Monitor the processing of orders

- ▶ Manage the costs associated with actions taken on order items

Database Diagram

Figure 1-1 shows the physical implementation of the Asset5 entity relationship diagram.

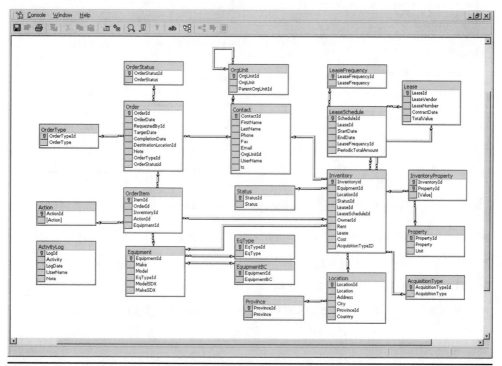

Figure 1-1   *A database diagram of the Asset5 database*

Description of Assets

The following illustration shows the tables involved in the description of each asset. Detailed information about deployed equipment and their features is essential for the proper management of current inventory as well as future upgrades and acquisitions.

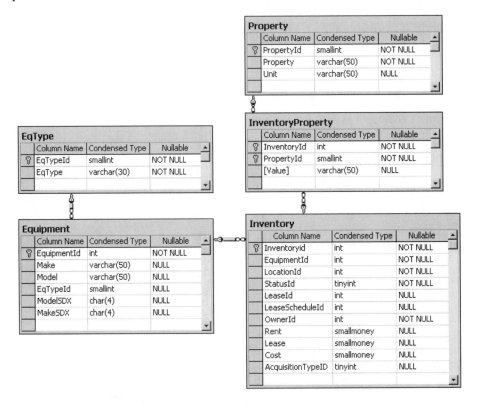

Information in these asset description tables allows users to

▶ Manage a list of standard equipment deployed within the organization

▶ Manage a list of attributes (properties) that can be used to describe assets

▶ Manage a list of attributes for each asset

▶ Obtain a summary of equipment deployed within the organization

▶ Make decisions about the deployment of a software package based on the capabilities of existing equipment in the field

▶ Find obsolete pieces of equipment that need to be disposed of and replaced with new equipment

Inventory   The central table in the Asset5 database is the Inventory table. It is designed to track the assets currently deployed within an organization. The most important information about an asset indicates what kind of equipment it is. This table also stores information about the asset's current location and its status, as well as the way in which the asset was acquired and the cost of acquisition.

Equipment   The Equipment table stores the make and model of each type of asset. Each piece of equipment with a unique make and model has a separate record in this table. It groups equipment by equipment type.

EqType   This table lists types of equipment. For example, equipment types include notebook, printer, monitor, keyboard, mouse, scanner, and network hub.

Property   Each asset in the database can be described with a set of attributes listed in the Properties table. This table also records a unit used to store the value of the property. For example, the properties (and units of measure) of a monitor are size (inch), resolution (pixel), and type, while an external hard disk has properties (and units) such as capacity (GB), size (inch), and adapter.

InventoryProperty   Each asset in the Inventory table has a set of properties. The InventoryProperty table stores the values of each property (except for make and model, which are recorded in the Equipment table).

For example, a Toshiba (Make) Protégé 7020 (Model) notebook (EqType) assigned to an employee has 64 (value) MB (unit) of RAM (property), 4.3 (value) GB (unit) of HDD capacity (property), a Pentium II 333 (value) processor (property), and so on. Another employee is using an upgraded version of the same equipment with 128 (value) MB (unit) of RAM (property), 6.4 (value) GB (unit) of HDD capacity (property), a Pentium II 366 (value) processor (property), and so on.

Deployment of Assets

This following set of tables keeps track of the location in which an asset is deployed and the person and organizational unit to which the asset is assigned.

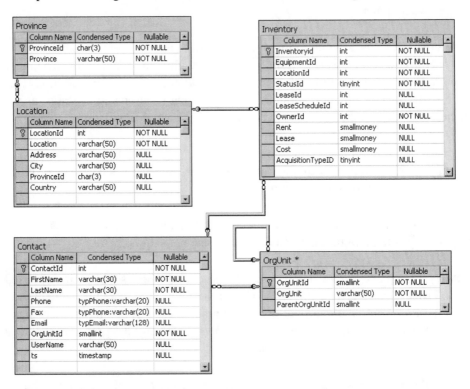

The information in these asset deployment tables allows users to

▶   Manage a list of locations within an organization

▶   Manage a list of persons working within an organization

▶   Retrieve contact information about persons to whom assets are assigned

▶   Generate reports about assets deployed by province and organizational unit

▶   Retrieve a list of assets assigned to a particular person

▶   Manage relationships between organizational units

▶   Assign person(s) to organizational units

Location   The Location table stores information about the physical location of the deployed asset. Each location has a name and an address as attributes.

Province   This table contains a list of provinces and states. The primary key is the abbreviation of the province/state. The presence of this table is essential for reports, which will aggregate asset deployment by location, province/state, and country.

Contact   This table contains a list of persons involved in the asset management process. It includes persons with assets assigned to them, persons completing and approving orders, and persons performing maintenance and support.

OrgUnit   Each contact is assigned to some organizational unit within the organization. The OrgUnit table records relationships among companies, cost centers, departments, and the like. This table is designed as a recursive table: an organizational unit can be part of some other organizational unit. This quality also reflects the need for rapid changes in today's work environment due to change of ownership, restructuring, and so on.

Leasing Tables

An important aspect of asset management is the tracking of lease information. It helps management avoid payment of penalties associated with late returns or the failure to return leased assets to the leasing vendor:

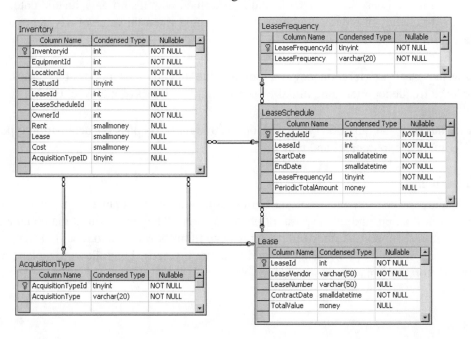

The information in the lease tables allows users to

▶ Keep track of the assets associated with each lease

▶ Manage lease schedules to keep track of the start, end, and duration of lease periods

▶ Identify assets that need to be returned to a lease vendor

▶ Generate reports on assets deployed by lease schedule and lease contract

▶ Retrieve a list of assets obtained from a particular lease vendor

▶ Retrieve the total value of lease payments, lease schedules, and lease contracts

Lease   The Lease table contains information about lease contracts. It records the name of the lease vendor, the number of the lease that the vendor is using to track the contract, the date the contract was signed, and the total value of assets assigned to the lease.

LeaseSchedule   Assets obtained through one lease contract might not be received on the same date. An asset might also be under a different payment regime and lease duration. Therefore, each lease contains a set of lease schedules. Each schedule is recorded in the LeaseSchedule table and is described with a start date, an end date, and the frequency of payments. This table also tracks the total value of payments per lease term.

LeaseFrequency   LeaseFrequency is a lookup table that contains all possible values for lease frequency including monthly, semimonthly, biweekly, and weekly.

AcquisitionType   AcquisitionType is a lookup table that lists possible acquisition types including lease, purchase, and rent.

Order Tables

Orders are the primary means of managing assets within the organization. Users can request new assets and the disposal of obsolete assets. They can request maintenance and technical support. Authorized personnel can monitor orders and react to them, associate a cost with their execution, and generate invoices. The following tables are used to store information about orders:

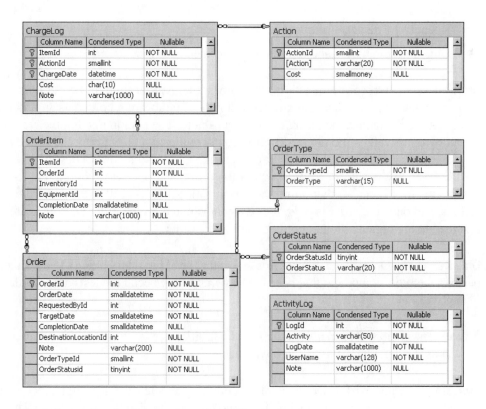

The information in these order tables allows users to

► Request new equipment

► Request technical support

► Request maintenance

► Execute scheduled maintenance

► Track the status of orders

► Assign a staff member to execute the order

► Approve the execution of orders

► Manage a list of actions and the default costs associated with them

► Track costs associated with each activity

► Generate interdepartmental invoices

► Request the transfer of assets

► Request the disposal of obsolete assets

► Generate summaries and reports on performed activities

Order   Users can record requests in the Order table. At that time, the order date and target date are recorded. General request requirements are recorded as an order type, and special requirements are recorded as a note. The person making the request is recorded, as well as the person approving the request and assigning the order for execution. If the order is a transfer request, the table also records a destination for the asset. Users can track the status of the order, and once it is completed, its completion date is set. At that point, one organizational unit is billed for performed actions, and once the order is paid, the payment is noted on the order and funds are assigned to the organizational unit completing the order.

OrderItem   The OrderItem table records assets that need the intervention of authorized personnel or new equipment that needs to be purchased. Special requests are recorded in the Note field.

Action   The Action table manages the list of activities needed to complete a request as well as the default cost associated with each.

ChargeLog   Actions performed on an order item to complete an order will be recorded in the ChargeLog table. This table will be used to generate an invoice after completion of the order.

OrderStatus   The OrderStatus table is used as a lookup table to manage the status of orders. It contains statuses such as

► Ordered

► In-process

► Canceled

► Deferred

► Completed

OrderType   The OrderType table is used as a lookup table to store the general requirements of the order. It contains values such as

► Requisition

► Transfer

► Support

► Scrap

► Repair

ActivityLog   This table is not related specifically to the recording of orders. Rather, it is a repository for audit trail information. Most of the time it is populated by a trigger associated with some specific database change.

CHAPTER

1

The SQL Server 2005 Environment and Tools

IN THIS CHAPTER

SQL Server 2005 Tools

Basic Operations in Management Studio

Y ou already know that SQL Server 2005 is a full-featured and powerful database management system. You may also be experienced in some or many aspects of this system. But before you proceed to become an expert in application development using SQL Server stored procedures, we should probably take a step back and look at the big picture to ensure that we share the same conceptual grounding.

To attain this conceptual grounding, I will start with a 30,000-ft. overview that will cover the following topics:

▶   A brief introduction to SQL Server 2005 tools

▶   A quick overview of stored procedure and table design

I have written this overview to enable people who are in a hurry to learn the basics and then get down to developing complex stored procedures to retrieve, manipulate, update, and delete data, and to address a variety of business problems. I am going to assume that you have already had an opportunity to work with SQL as a language for making queries on SQL Server or some other database system, and that you understand common database concepts. The purpose of this overview is to define the terminology that you will use as the foundation on which to build your knowledge of programming in the SQL Server environment. If you need a more in-depth conceptual grounding than that offered here, I direct you to *SQL Server 2005: A Beginner's Guide* by Dušan Petković (McGraw-Hill/Osborne, 2005).

NOTE

To those of you who find the material in this chapter excessively basic, I offer my apologies and suggest you skip ahead to the next chapter. However, if you have any doubts about whether you should skip ahead, don't. The information presented in the following pages may be basic, but it is extremely important that you have a full understanding of the fundamentals before you tackle the more complex topics built upon those basics.

SQL Server 2005 Tools

All versions of SQL Server 2005 (except SQL Server 2005 Express) are delivered with this set of management tools:

▶   SQL Server Configuration Manager

▶   SQL Server Management Studio

- ▶ Database Engine Tuning Advisor
- ▶ DTS Import and Export Wizard
- ▶ SQL Server Profiler
- ▶ SQL Server Books OnLine (BOL)
- ▶ Replication Monitor (sqlmonitor.exe)
- ▶ SQLCMD
- ▶ osql
- ▶ SQL Server Error and Usage Reporting
- ▶ SQL Server Surface Area Configuration

There are also many tools that are not related to the relational database engine:

- ▶ Business Intelligence Development Studio
- ▶ Analysis Services | Deployment Wizard
- ▶ Analysis Services | Migration Wizard
- ▶ Analysis Services | Instance Rename
- ▶ Notification Services Command Prompt
- ▶ Reporting Services Configuration

The following sections discuss some of these tools.

SQL Server Configuration Manager

SQL Server Configuration Manager is a new tool in SQL Server 2005. You can use it to manage SQL Server 2005 services and connections. It has been developed as a Microsoft Management Console (MMC) plug-in application (see Figure 1-1), so we can safely ignore its trivial menu and toolbar content. Its window is divided into a Console tree (left pane) and a Details pane. You can manage SQL Server services and connection configurations by navigating objects in the Console tree.

Managing Services

SQL Server 2005 is implemented as the following services:

- ▶ SQL Server
- ▶ SQL Server Agent

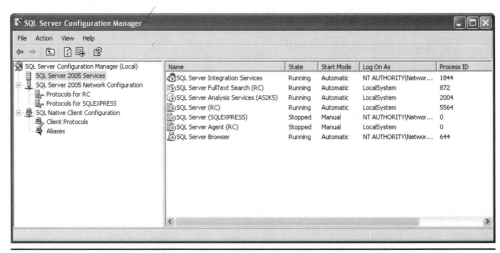

Figure 1-1   *SQL Server Configuration Manager*

- ► SQL Server Browser
- ► SQL Server Integration Services
- ► SQL Server Analysis Services
- ► SQL Server FullText Search
- ► Reporting Services

There are also several support services that can be reached through SQL Server Management Studio and Business Intelligence Studio, such as

- ► Notification Services
- ► Distributed Transaction Coordinator (MSDTC)
- ► Database Mail

The relational database server is implemented as the *SQL Server* service. It receives queries from users, executes them, sends responses to calling applications, and manages data in database files. Most of this book is dedicated to programming and interaction with this service.

SQL Server Agent is an automation service that manages the scheduled execution of tasks and notifies administrators of problems that occur on the server.

Analysis Services is a service that implements infrastructure for OnLine Analytical Processing (OLAP) and data mining.

Reporting Services is a system for design and delivery of relational and OLAP reports that works on top of SQL Server and IIS.

FullText Search allows users to create word-oriented queries against string data stored in relational table columns.

Notification Services is a platform for alerting users to changes in databases.

The *Distributed Transaction Coordinator (MSDTC)* is a service that manages *two-phase commit* transactions spanned over multiple servers. This service ensures that changes that need to be made to data stored on different servers complete successfully.

Integration Services provide ETL (extract, transform, and load) functionality that replaces Data Transformation Services (DTS) from previous versions of SQL Server. Users can create packages for extracting, transforming, and loading data from one data source to another.

Database Mail is used to send and receive e-mail. It is possible to configure SQL Server to perform tasks such as receiving requests and returning result sets through e-mail to notify administrators of the success status of scheduled tasks and of errors encountered.

Services listed in SQL Server Configuration Manager can be started, stopped, and paused using the pop-up menu that opens when you right-click the particular service (that is, on each node of the tree). The SQL Server service must be running if you want to work on relational databases as described in this book.

Managing Connections

SQL Server and client tools can use different protocols to communicate with SQL Server:

- ▶ Shared Memory
- ▶ Named Pipes
- ▶ TCP/IP
- ▶ VIA

Shared Memory is a protocol designed to allow users to connect only locally— from the machine on which SQL Server is running. After installation, it is possible to communicate with SQL Server using only Shared Memory. *TCP/IP* and *Named Pipes* are protocols designed to allow users to access and manage SQL Server from networked workstations. The *VIA* protocol is used on legacy (mainframe) networks.

From SQL Server Configuration Manager, you can control how your server connects to the network using SQL Server 2005 Network Configuration. This node contains separate subnodes for each instance of the database server (see Figure 1-2).

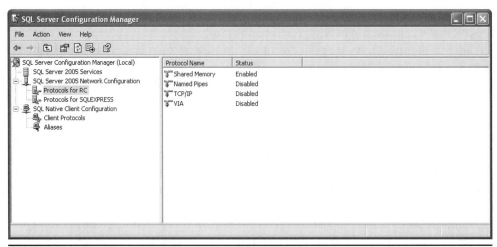

Figure 1-2 *Network configuration in SQL Server Configuration Manager*

NOTE

Unless your network administrator tells you differently, you should probably enable the TCP/IP and Named Pipes protocols to allow users on the LAN to connect to it. However, if you are installing SQL Server on a computer that is connected directly to the Internet and which will typically be used by clients installed locally (as would be the case on your home computer), you should accept the default network configuration (only Shared Memory enabled).

In SQL Native Client Configuration | Client Protocols node you can set how client programs on the local machine (such as Management Studio or SQLCMD) connect to servers. In SQL Native Client Configuration | Aliases node you can set new names (aliases, pseudonyms) and connection parameters for servers on the network.

SQL Server Management Studio

This tool, shown in Figure 1-3, is a new feature in SQL Server 2005. It replaces Enterprise Manager and Query Analyzer from earlier versions. It has been developed using a Visual Studio shell as a base.

It follows the paradigm of Visual Studio, in which most tools are organized as tabbed, dockable, or floating windows.

The Registered Servers pane lets you view and manage parameters for connecting to your servers. Its toolbar allows you to select a server (service) type—SQL Server,

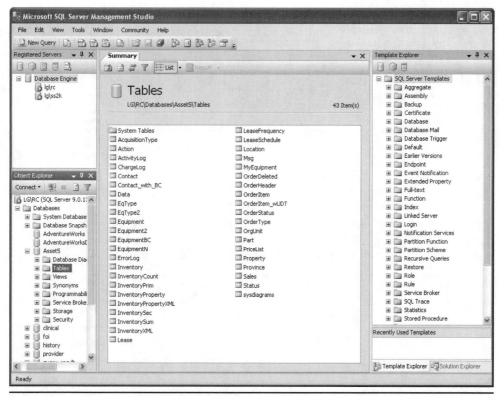

Figure 1-3   *SQL Server Management Studio*

Analysis Services, Reporting Services, SQL Server Mobile, or Integration Services.
This book focuses on using SQL Server.

NOTE

When you install SQL Server, you can connect only to local servers. You need to add (register) other servers to see them listed here.

The Object Explorer pane displays database and server objects in a hierarchy
designed for easy navigation (see Figure 1-4). It works in the same way as any other
GUI tree object. You can click the + symbol next to any node on the tree or press the
RIGHT ARROW key on the keyboard to expand the node. When you right-click a node,
a context-sensitive menu is displayed. Unlike previous versions, system objects
(such as databases, tables, and stored procedures) are grouped together in a special

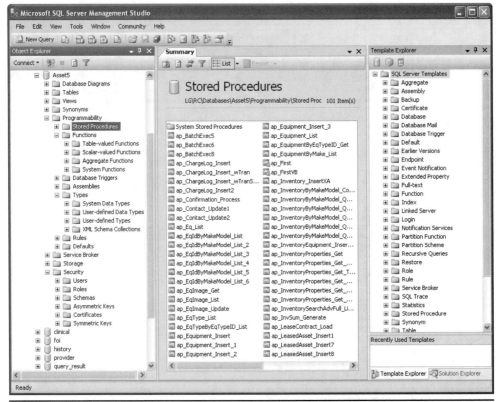

Figure 1-4 *Object Explorer*

folder and not mixed with user-defined objects. Users can check for the existence of a database object; explore its contents (that is, view records in a table); execute and debug objects such as stored procedures; view the structure and dependencies of an object; view and edit extended properties of the object; and drag the name of a database object to the Query window or create a script of an object in a new Query window, file, or Clipboard.

The Summary page shows details of the node (object) selected in the Console tree. If the user selects a folder with tables or stored procedures, the Summary page lists the tables or stored procedures in the current database and shows other significant information related to selected objects.

When you open the Properties sheet of an object or start some operation that requires additional information, Management Studio opens a window that is resizable and nonmodal (see Figure 1-5). Users can switch back to the Object Browser and/or

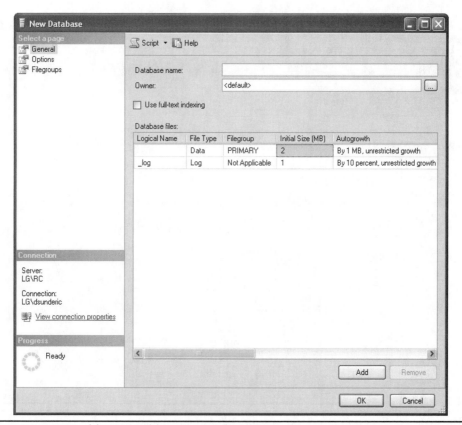

Figure 1-5   *Resizable, scriptable, nonmodal window*

open another window to get additional information needed to complete the first window. When required information is entered, you can choose to execute the change immediately, schedule it for later, or save the script file that will be used to implement the change later.

SQL Server Management Studio supports relational (SQL), Analysis Services (MDX, DMX, XMLA), and SQL Mobile queries. When you open a Query window (see Figure 1-6), you can type in the query and execute it (Query | Execute).

If you need assistance with your SQL queries you can choose Query | Design Query in Editor and Management Studio will open a Query Designer window with panes for adding and joining tables and selecting output columns.

Management Studio treats queries the same way Visual Studio treats other documents with source code—they can be saved as script files and organized within

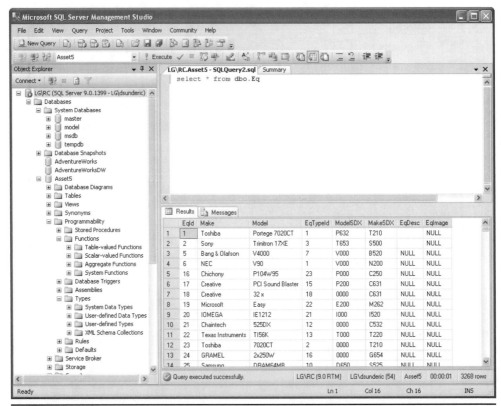

Figure 1-6   *Script and project management in Management Studio*

projects and solutions. Script files are central objects for designing, debugging, and executing Transact-SQL (T-SQL) statements (such as queries) against a SQL Server database.

Template Explorer is a window with a useful set of script templates for managing how database and server objects are organized (see Figure 1-7). You just drag a template to your script window and replace parameter placeholders with your custom values. Placeholders have < and > as delimiters and name, data type, and default values as parameters. Alternatively, you can choose Query | Specify Values for Template Parameters and Management Studio will prompt you to set them.

TIP

If the parameter that you need is a database object, you can also drag it from the Object Browser to a query or script, instead of typing it.

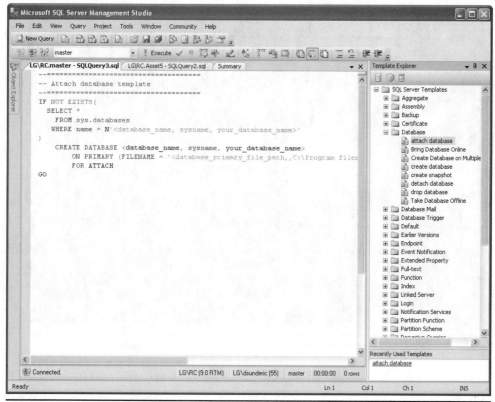

Figure 1-7   *Template Explorer*

SQLCMD Utility

Before graphical utilities (such as Management Studio in SQL Server 2005 and Query Analyzer and ISQL for Windows in earlier SQL Server versions), DBAs used command line utilities such as *isql* and *osql* to run Transact-SQL statements against the server. Such tools are reminiscent of UNIX environments and they are seldom used now that GUI applications, such as Management Studio, are available.

SQLCMD uses OLE DB to execute Transact-SQL batches, while Management Studio uses .NET SqlClient. This difference sometimes leads to different behavior when the same scripts are executed in them.

Figure 1-8 shows the utility's parameters, as well as a couple of Transact-SQL batch commands.

```
SQLCMD                                                                      - □ ×
C:\Program Files\Microsoft SQL Server\90\Tools\Binn>sqlcmd/?
Microsoft (R) SQL Server Command Line Tool
Version 9.00.1399.01 NT INTEL X86
Copyright (c) Microsoft Corporation.  All rights reserved.

usage: Sqlcmd           [-U login id]           [-P password]
  [-S server]           [-H hostname]           [-E trusted connection]
  [-d use database name] [-l login timeout]     [-t query timeout]
  [-h headers]          [-s colseparator]       [-w screen width]
  [-a packetsize]       [-e echo input]         [-I Enable Quoted Identifiers]
  [-c cmdend]           [-L[c] list servers[clean output]]
  [-q "cmdline query"]  [-Q "cmdline query" and exit]
  [-m errorlevel]       [-V severitylevel]      [-W remove trailing spaces]
  [-u unicode output]   [-r[0|1] msgs to stderr]
  [-i inputfile]        [-o outputfile]         [-z new password]
  [-f <codepage> | i:<codepage>[,o:<codepage>]] [-Z new password and exit]
  [-k[1|2] remove[replace] control characters]
  [-y variable length type display width]
  [-Y fixed length type display width]
  [-p[1] print statistics[colon format]]
  [-R use client regional setting]
  [-b On error batch abort]
  [-v var = "value"...] [-A dedicated admin connection]
  [-X[1] disable commands, startup script, enviroment variables [and exit]]
  [-x disable variable substitution]
  [-? show syntax summary]

C:\Program Files\Microsoft SQL Server\90\Tools\Binn>sqlcmd -SLG\RC
1> use Asset5
2> go
Changed database context to 'Asset5'.
1> select top 5 * from dbo.Eq
2> go
```

Figure 1-8   *SQLCMD command line utility*

SQL Server Profiler

Profiler is a component of SQL Server designed to monitor activities on servers and in databases (see Figure 1-9).

You can use this utility to capture queries against a database, the activities of a particular user application, login attempts, failures, errors, and transactions. It is often used to improve the performance of a system, and you can also use it to troubleshoot and debug stored procedures and Transact-SQL scripts.

The Help Subsystem and SQL Server Books OnLine

Traditionally, due to the nature of the environment, SQL Server client tools have been light on context-sensitive help, but SQL Server has a subsystem that is a great tool for browsing through its documentation—*SQL Server Books OnLine (BOL)*. This subsystem contains the complete set of SQL Server Reference documents—which used to be delivered on paper—in the form of an online, searchable, and indexed hierarchy of documents.

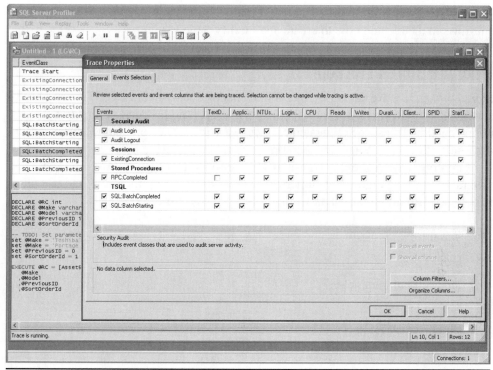

Figure 1-9   *SQL Server Profiler*

You can start SQL Server Books OnLine from Start | Programs | Microsoft SQL Server 2005 | Documentation and Tutorials. You can also launch it using Management Studio's Dynamic Help feature: Just highlight a keyword in a query and select the Help | Dynamic Help menu to open the pane.

In the Contents tab, you can browse through the hierarchy of the material, as in Windows Explorer, or you can switch to either the Index tab to see a list of keywords or to the Search tab to define search criteria. The Help Favorites tab enables you to bookmark pages that you want to refer to later.

Basic Operations in Management Studio

This section will serve as a primer to introduce you to the concepts of executing, creating, and editing stored procedures. I will walk through the usage of the most important SQL Server client tools. Since Transact-SQL is just another programming language, I will follow a tradition first established by an unknown programmer and start with a trivial Hello World example. Finally, I will show you how to view and edit rows in a table and how to create and modify table structure.

What Are Stored Procedures?

Stored procedures are database objects that encapsulate collections of Transact-SQL statements on the server for later repetitive use. Although stored procedures use nonprocedural Transact-SQL statements, they are in essence procedural. They define algorithms that determine how operations should be performed.

Stored procedures are the Transact-SQL equivalents of subroutines in other programming languages. Developers of custom database applications can use all major programming constructs while building stored procedures:

- ▶ Variables
- ▶ Data types
- ▶ Input/output parameters
- ▶ Return values
- ▶ Conditional execution
- ▶ Loops
- ▶ Comments

SQL Server includes a set of *system stored procedures* designed for administering the system. Their role is to provide information, set configuration, control the environment, manage user-defined objects, and schedule and run custom tasks.

Execution of Stored Procedures in Management Studio

The execution of stored procedures in Management Studio is very simple. Let's try it using the system stored procedure sp_who, which lists all users and processes connected to the system.

1. Run Management Studio (Start | Programs | Microsoft SQL Server 2005 | SQL Server Management Studio).

2. The Management Studio application prompts you for a server, username, and password, as shown on Figure 1-10. If the application is unable to connect to the server, you should check whether the SQL Server service is running and whether you correctly typed the name of the server and/or your username and password.

Figure 1-10   *Connect to Server dialog box*

TIP

If you are a SQL Server or local administrator, you can use Windows Authentication. SQL Server will use your Windows login to authorize your access to database and server objects. If you have set SQL Server to work in mixed mode during installation and you know the sa (system administrator) login and password, you can switch to SQL Server Authentication. The name of your machine is the name of the SQL Server. If you are working on the machine that has SQL Server installed, you can always use "(local)" or a simple dot "." to refer to the current machine as the server to which you want to connect. If you have created a named instance of SQL Server, you will have to reference it after a backslash "\" character.

3. Once you have logged in successfully, Management Studio displays a tree of server objects in the Object Browser.

4. Open the Query window by clicking New Query | New SQL Server Query. You are prompted to confirm connection parameters.

5. In the Query pane, type the following code:

```
exec sp_who
```

NOTE

Management Studio uses different colors to distinguish keywords, variables, comments, and constants.

6. To run the stored procedure, you can select Query | Execute, click the Execute button on the toolbar, or press CTRL-E. The application will split the screen to display both query and results (see Figure 1-11). This stored procedure lists active processes on the current server as well as the login names of the users who started them.

7. You can click the Messages tab to see whether SQL Server has returned any messages along with the result (such as the number of records, a warning, or an error).

8. Select Query | Results To | Results to Text and then execute the query again (Query | Execute). The window displays the result set in the form of text. Messages are mixed with result sets in this case.

NOTE

Before we continue, please ensure that you have installed the sample Asset5 database. If you have not already installed it, review the download and installation instructions in the Introduction.

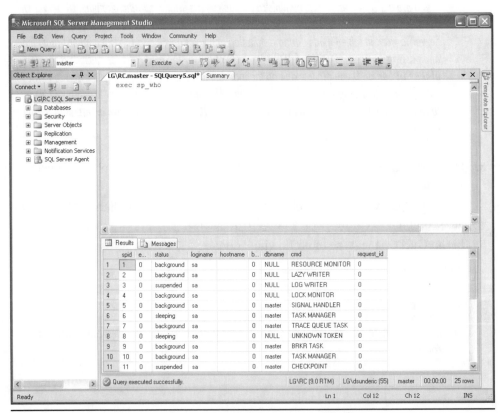

Figure 1-11 *Executing a stored procedure in Management Studio*

Editing Stored Procedures

I will now lead you through the process of editing stored procedures.

1. Open the Object Browser.

2. Expand Databases | Asset5 | Programmability | Stored Procedures and the program will display a list of stored procedures.

3. In this list, find a stored procedure named ap_Equipment_List, and right-click it. When you right-click an object, a context-sensitive menu appears with options to let you perform operations such as deleting and renaming the stored procedure or creating a new stored procedure.

4. Select Modify on the pop-up menu. The application opens a window to allow you to view and edit the stored procedure (see Figure 1-12).

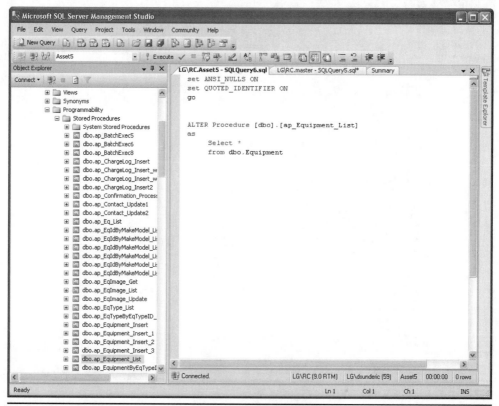

Figure 1-12 *A window for modifying a stored procedure*

Creating Stored Procedures

To create a stored procedure, follow these steps:

1. Right-click any stored procedure or the Stored Procedures node in the Object Browser and select New Stored Procedure from the pop-up menu. Management Studio displays a window with a template for the stored procedure (see Figure 1-13).

2. Replace the existing Select statement with the following code after the As keyword:

```
Select 'Hello world'
Select * from dbo.EqType
```

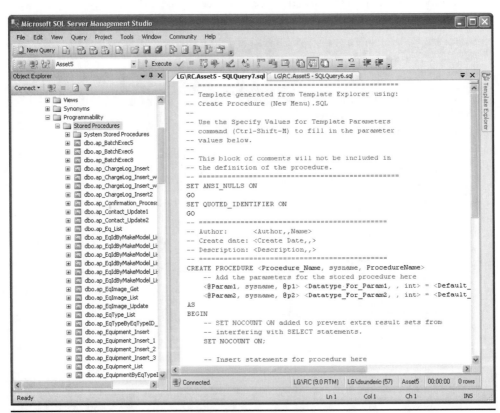

Figure 1-13 *Creating new stored procedures*

3. Set the name of the procedure to ap_Hello and drop placeholders for parameters (between Create Procedure and As). Alternatively, you can delete everything in the Query window and simply type the following:

```
Create Procedure ap_Hello
as
    Select 'Hello world'
    Select * from dbo.EqType
return
GO
```

4. Click Query | Parse on the main menu to verify the syntax of the procedure.

5. Click OK.

6. Select Query | Execute from the menu. The procedure is compiled and stored in the database. Unfortunately, you will not be able to see it in the list of stored procedures in the Object Browser. You have to refresh it by right-clicking the Stored Procedure node and selecting Refresh from the context menu.

I will now show you how to execute this stored procedure without typing code:

1. Display the context-sensitive menu for the procedure (right-click it in the Object Browser).

2. Choose Script Stored Procedure As | Execute To | New Query Editor Window. Management Studio generates code for executing the stored procedure.

3. Choose Query | Execute (or press CTRL-E). Management Studio returns two result sets in this case, since we have two Select statements in our stored procedure (see Figure 1-14).

Editing Stored Procedures in the Query Window

Before Enterprise Manager and Management Studio, administrators used scripts to manage database objects. Traditionally, DBAs included the code for deleting (dropping) the original stored procedure and then re-creating the stored procedure (with the changed code):

1. Open a new Query window (click New Query | New SQL Server Query).

2. Confirm connection parameters.

3. Type the following code in the Query pane:

```
DROP PROCEDURE ap_Hello
GO

CREATE PROCEDURE ap_Hello
```

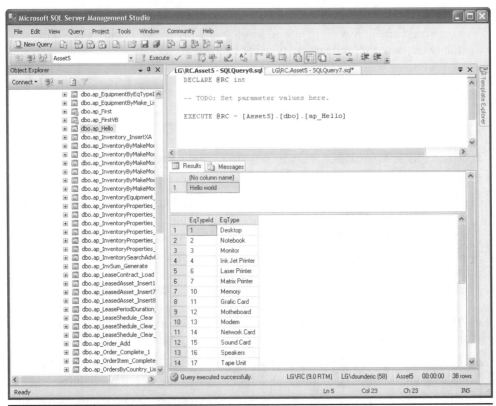

Figure 1-14 *Execution of stored procedure with two result sets*

```
AS
    SELECT 'Hello World'
    SELECT * from dbo.Inventory
return
GO
```

4. If you haven't changed the default settings for your login, Management Studio opens a Query window against the master database. Use the Available Database drop-down list box in the toolbar to switch to the Asset5 database (see Figure 1-15). Alternatively, you can add the following code at the top of the query:

```
USE Asset5
GO
```

5. Execute the code by selecting Query | Execute (CTRL-E).

NOTE

Alternatively, you could have generated this code using Script Stored Procedure As | Drop To | New Query Window and Script Stored Procedure As | Create To | Clipboard.

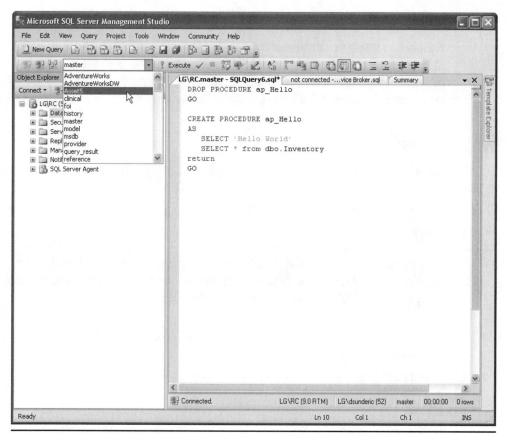

Figure 1-15 *Available databases*

SQL Server first deletes the existing stored procedure and then re-creates it (with the new code). The trouble with this method (dropping and then re-creating) is that you also drop some attributes associated with the stored procedure (such as permissions), which also affects other dependent objects. Since Microsoft SQL Server 7.0, it has been possible to use the Alter Procedure statement to modify an existing stored procedure without affecting permissions and other dependent objects:

```
ALTER PROCEDURE ap_Hello
AS
    SELECT 'Hello World again!'
    SELECT * from dbo.Inventory
return
GO
```

NOTE

You may have noticed the Go command in the previous two examples. This command is not a SQL statement. It is not even part of the Transact-SQL language. It is a signal to the Query window in Management Studio (and to some other tools, such as SQLCMD) to treat the SQL statements as one set—a batch. All statements in a batch are compiled and executed together.

Syntax Errors

Sooner or later you will make a typo, and the server will react with an error. Let's deliberately cause a problem to see how the server reacts. We will create an error by commenting out a required part of the code.

NOTE

There are two ways to type comments in the Transact-SQL language. If you type two dashes (- -), the rest of that line will be ignored by the server. Code stretched over multiple lines can be commented out by using / and */ as delimiters at either end of the comment.*

1. Right-click Procedure_1 and choose Script Stored Procedure As | Alter | New Query Window.

2. Comment out the second line (the keyword As):

```
Alter Procedure Procedure_1
--As
    Select 'Hello World again!'
    Select * from dbo.Inventory
return
Go
```

3. As soon as you execute this code, the server reports an error (see Figure 1-16). Keep in mind that SQL Server is not a perfect compiler. Some error messages that it reports may not contain sufficient details or may even be misleading. The rule of thumb is simple: Check your basic syntax first.

TIP

If you double-click the error message in the Results pane, Query Analyzer will try to return the cursor to the line containing the error in the Query pane (actually, to the first line that appears after the last statement that executed correctly). This feature is very useful when you are executing a long batch.

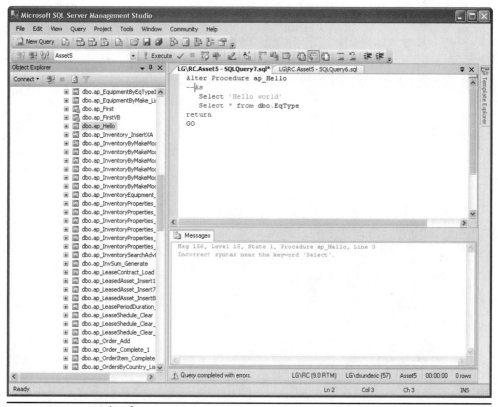

Figure 1-16 *Example of syntax error*

Another advantage the Alter statement has over the drop/create approach is that the stored procedure remains intact after an unsuccessful attempt such as we produced in this example.

Viewing and Editing Tables

I will now demonstrate how to view, edit, and change tables in Management Studio.

1. Open Management Studio.
2. Expand Databases | Asset5 | Tables.
3. Find the dbo.EqType table in the list and right-click it to open its context-sensitive menu.
4. Select Open Table and the program will open its records in a grid (see Figure 1-17).

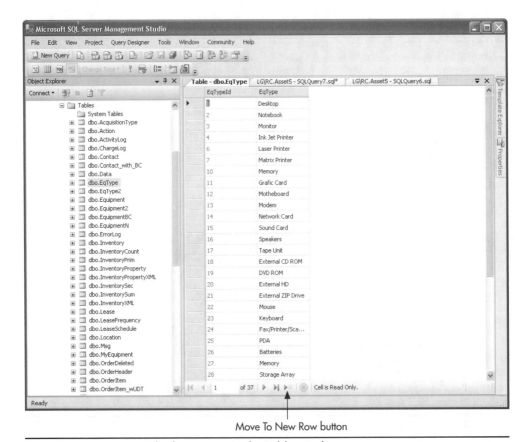

Move To New Row button

Figure 1-17 *Viewing and editing rows in the Table window*

You can now use the buttons at the bottom of the grid or the cursor keys to navigate. The record that contains the cursor (that is, the current record) has a little arrow at the left border of the grid. To add records to the table, move the cursor below the last row of the grid (or press the Move To New Row button). If you want to modify one of the existing records, position your cursor on it and press the F2 key. To delete a record, you can click its left border to display a context-sensitive menu and then select the Delete command.

TIP

Naturally, you can view tables and perform table modifications using SQL statements (Select, Insert, Update, and Delete) from the Query window. In fact, that is the preferred way.

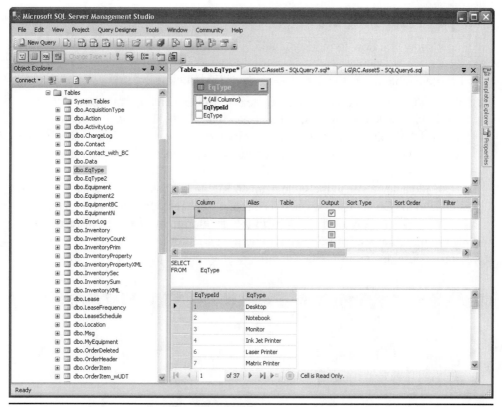

Figure 1-18 *A Query window for editing tables*

The Table window, shown in Figure 1-18, is in fact a special form of the Query window. Its context-sensitive menu contains a Pane submenu that contains Diagram, Criteria, SQL, and Results options. They work as switches to open panes for managing the query. The Diagram pane provides a visual means of managing tables that participate in the query and their links. The Criteria pane allows you to specify columns in the result set and criteria for selecting records. The SQL pane displays the SQL query statement that corresponds to the settings in the Diagram and Criteria panes. If you edit the content of the SQL pane, Management Studio will update the Diagram and Criteria panes and vice versa. The Results pane shows the result of the query specified in the SQL pane or the Diagram and Criteria panes. You can also edit rows in this pane if your query is simple enough (based on a single table). You can issue statements other than Select in this window. You can use Change Type to switch to the Insert, Update, or Delete statements. The window is similar to the Query Design window in Microsoft Access and Visual Studio, so I will not spend any more time describing it here.

Changing Table Structure

I will now show you how to modify a table's structure:

1. Locate a table in the Object Browser and right-click it.
2. When you select Modify from the context-sensitive menu, the program will open a new window to display its structure (see Figure 1-19). The top half of the window is a grid that you can use to add and modify table columns. The bottom half of the window shows the properties of the column that is selected in the top grid.

You can add a new table in the same manner. Right-click in an existing table or on the Tables node in the Object Browser, and then select New Table from the pop-up menu.

Now you have made your first steps in the development of stored procedures and managing tables in Transact-SQL. The next chapter explores SQL Server stored procedure design in greater detail.

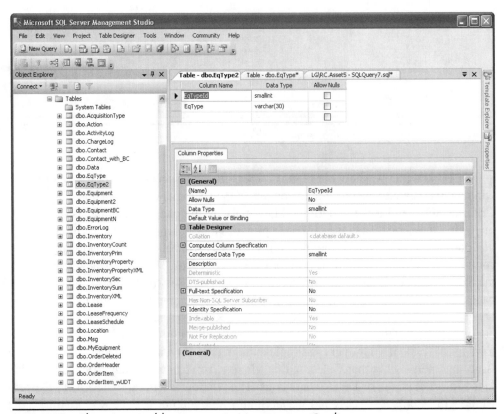

Figure 1-19 *Changing a table structure in Management Studio*

Stored Procedure Design Concepts

IN THIS CHAPTER

Anatomy of a Stored Procedure
Types of Stored Procedures
Managing Stored Procedures
The Role of Stored Procedures in the Development of Database Applications

A *stored procedure* is a set of Transact-SQL (T-SQL) statements that is compiled and stored as a single database object for later repetitive use. It is the equivalent of a subroutine and a function in other programming languages. Upon completion of this chapter, you will be able to do the following:

- ► Create a stored procedure
- ► Explain the elements of a stored procedure
- ► List ways to return information from a stored procedure
- ► Pass input parameters to a stored procedure
- ► Receive output parameters from a stored procedure
- ► Receive a return value from a stored procedure
- ► Explain where stored procedures are stored on SQL Server
- ► Explain the compilation and reuse of stored procedures

Anatomy of a Stored Procedure

We can describe a stored procedure in terms of

- ► Composition
- ► Functionality
- ► Syntax

Composition

Logically, a stored procedure consists of

- ► A *header* that defines the name of the stored procedure, the input and output parameters, and some miscellaneous processing options. You can think of it as an API (application programming interface) or declaration of the stored procedure.
- ► A *body* that contains one or more Transact-SQL statements to be executed at runtime.

Creating Stored Procedures

Let's look at the simplified syntax for implementing the core functionality of stored procedures:

```
CREATE PROC[EDURE] procedure_name
    [ {@parameter data_type} [= default] [OUTPUT] ] [,...n]
AS
    sql_statement [...n]
```

The following is an example of a stored procedure:

```
Create Procedure ap_Equipment_Get
    @chvMake varchar(50)
as
    Select *
    from dbo.Equipment
    where Make = @chvMake
```

This Transact-SQL statement creates a stored procedure named ap_Equipment_Get with one input parameter. During execution, ap_Equipment_Get returns a result set containing all records from the Equipment table having a Make column equal to the input parameter.

Please, be patient and do not create the procedure in the Asset5 database yet. If you try to create a stored procedure that already exists in the database, SQL Server will report an error. You can reproduce such an error if you run the same statement for creating a stored procedure twice. For example:

```
Msg 2714, Level 16, State 3, Procedure ap_Equipment_Get, Line 4
There is already an object named 'ap_Equipment_Get' in the database.
```

As I have shown in Chapter 1, one way to change a stored procedure is to drop and re-create it. There are two ways to prevent the error just described. One way is to use an Alter Procedure statement to change the stored procedure. I will explain this technique in the next section. The traditional way to prevent this error is to delete a stored procedure (using the Drop Procedure statement) and then create it again:

```
Drop Procedure ap_EquipmentByEqTypeID_Get
go

Create Procedure ap_EquipmentByEqTypeID_Get
    @intEqTypeId int
as
    Select *
    from dbo.Equipment
    where EqTypeId = @intEqTypeId
GO
```

If you are not sure whether a stored procedure exists, you can write a piece of code to check for its existence. If you do not, SQL Server will report an error when you try to drop a stored procedure that does not exist. This code takes advantage of the fact that SQL Server records each database object in sys.objects system view. It also uses programming constructs I have not yet introduced in this book. For now, do not worry about the details. All will become clear later.

```
if  exists (select *
    from sys.objects
    where object_id = object_id(N'[dbo].[ap_EquipmentByEqTypeID_Get]')
    and type in (N'P', N'PC'))
DROP PROCEDURE [dbo].[ap_EquipmentByEqTypeID_Get]
GO
CREATE PROCEDURE [dbo].[ap_EquipmentByEqTypeID_Get]
    @intEqTypeId [int]
AS
    Select *
    from dbo.Equipment
    where EqTypeId = @intEqTypeId
GO
```

NOTE

Most of the stored procedures in this book already exist in the database. If you just try to create them, SQL Server will complain with error 2714. If you are sure that the code that you have typed is correct, you can drop the original stored procedure and put yours in its place. Or you can alter the original stored procedure and use your code instead.

It is much better to rename your stored procedure. All stored procedures in the Asset5 database start with the ap_ prefix. You could start yours, for example, with up_ (for user procedure).

I follow a similar practice when I create several versions of the same stored procedure to illustrate a point or a technique. I merely change the stored procedure's suffix by adding a version number (for instance, _1, _2, and so on).

Altering Stored Procedures

The other way to change a stored procedure is to use the Alter Procedure statement:

```
Alter Procedure [dbo].[ap_Equipment_Get]
    @chvMake varchar(50)
as
Select *
    from dbo.Equipment
    where Make = @chvMake
go
```

The syntax of this statement is identical to the syntax of the Create Procedure statement (except for the keyword). The main reason for using this statement is to avoid undesirable effects on permissions and dependent database objects. For more details about permissions, see Chapter 18.

The Alter Procedure statement preserves all aspects of the original stored procedure. The object identification number (id column) of the procedure from the sys.objects system view remains the same, and all references to the stored procedure are intact. Therefore, it is much better to use the Alter Procedure statement than to drop and re-create the procedure. For more details about the sys.objects table and the object identification number (id column), see "Storing Stored Procedures" in Appendix B.

Limits

When you are creating or changing a stored procedure, you should keep in mind the following limits:

▶ The name of the procedure is a standard Transact-SQL identifier. The maximum length of any identifier is 128 characters.

▶ Stored procedures may contain up to 2,100 input and output parameters.

▶ The body of the stored procedure consists of one or more Transact-SQL statements. The maximum size of the body of the stored procedure is 128MB.

Functionality

Stored procedures can be used to

▶ Return information to the caller

▶ Modify data in databases

▶ Implement business logic in data tier

▶ Control access to data

▶ Improve performance of the system

▶ Reduce network traffic

▶ Perform other actions and operations (such as process e-mail, execute operating system commands and processes, and manage other SQL Server objects)

There are four ways to receive information from a stored procedure:

- ▶ Returning result sets
- ▶ Using input and output parameters
- ▶ Using return values
- ▶ Global cursor

The first three will be explained in this chapter, while the fourth one will be skipped as not recommended.

Returning Result Sets

To obtain a result set from a stored procedure, insert a Transact-SQL statement that returns a result set into the body of the stored procedure. The simplest way is by using a Select statement, but you could also call another stored procedure.

It is also possible to return several result sets from one stored procedure. Such a stored procedure will simply contain several Select statements. You should note that some client data-access methods (such as ADO.NET) can access all result sets, but others will receive just the first one or possibly even report an error.

Using Input and Output Parameters

Let's add a new procedure to the Asset5 database:

```
Create procedure dbo.ap_EqIdByMakeModel_List
     @chvMake varchar(50),
     @chvModel varchar(50)
as
     select EqId
     from dbo.Equipment
     where Make = @chvMake
     and Model = @chvModel
GO
```

This is a very simple stored procedure. It uses two input parameters to receive the make and model, and returns identifiers of equipment that matches the specified make and model.

Physically, the stored procedure encapsulates just one Select statement. The header and body of the procedure are divided by the keyword As. The header of the stored procedure contains a list of parameters delimited with a comma (,) character. Each parameter is defined with an identifier and a data type. Parameter identifiers must begin with the at sign (@).

You can use the following statement to execute the stored procedure:

```
Execute dbo.ap_EqIdByMakeModel_List 'Toshiba', 'Portege 7020CT'
```

The keyword Execute is followed by the name of the stored procedure. Since the stored procedure requires two parameters, they are provided in the form of a comma-delimited list. In this case they are strings, so they must be delimited with single quotation marks.

The keyword Execute is not needed if the stored procedure is executed in the first statement of a batch:

```
dbo.ap_EqIdByMakeModel_List 'Toshiba', 'Portege 7020CT'
```

However, I recommend you use it. It is a good habit that leads to clean code. You can use its shorter version (Exec) to save keystrokes:

```
Exec dbo.ap_EqIdByMakeModel_List 'Toshiba', 'Portege 7020CT'
```

In any case, the execution will return a result set containing just one value in one record:

```
EquipmentId
-----------
1

(1 row(s) affected)
```

Stored procedures can return output parameters to the caller. To illustrate, we will create a stored procedure similar to the previous one, but having one critical difference: This new stored procedure contains an additional parameter. The direction of the parameter is controlled by including the keyword Output after the data type:

```
Create procedure dbo.ap_EqIdByMakeModel_List_2
    @chvMake varchar(50),
    @chvModel varchar(50),
    @intEqId int output
as
    select @intEqId = EquipmentId
    from dbo.Equipment
    where Make = @chvMake
    and Model = @chvModel
```

The Select statement does not return a result set, as the previous one did. Instead, it assigns an output parameter, @EqId, with the selected value.

NOTE

This stored procedure is not perfect. It may seem correct at first glance, but there is a potential problem with it. More than one piece of equipment (that is, more than one record) could correspond to the criteria. I will address this issue in detail in the chapters to follow.

In this case, we require a more complicated batch of Transact-SQL statements to execute the stored procedure. We must define the variable that will receive the output value. The parameter must be followed by the Output keyword to indicate that a value for the parameter will be returned by the procedure. At the end of the batch, the result of the stored procedure is displayed using the Select statement:

```
Declare @intEqId int
Execute dbo.ap_EqIdByMakeModel_List_2 'Toshiba',
                                      'Portege 7020CT',
                                      @intEqId OUTPUT
Select @intEqId 'Equipment Identifier'
```

The batch returns the value of the variable as an output parameter:

```
Equipment Identifier
-------------------
1

(1 row(s) affected)
```

NOTE

A typical error is to forget to mark parameters in Execute statements with Output. The stored procedure will be executed, but the value of the variable will not be returned.

Using Return Values

An alternative way to send values from a stored procedure to the caller is to use a *return value*. Each stored procedure can end with a Return statement. The statement can be followed by an *integer* value that can be read by the caller. If the return value is not explicitly set, the server will return the default value, zero (0).

Because return values are limited to int data types, they are most often used to signal an error status or error code to the caller. We will examine this use later. First, let's explore its functionality in some unorthodox examples.

In the following example, the value returned by the procedure will be assigned to the local variable and finally returned to the caller:

```
Create Procedure [dbo].[ap_EqIdByMakeModel_List_3]
    @chvMake varchar(50),
    @chvModel varchar(50)
as

Declare @intEqId int

Select @intEqId  = EquipmentId
from dbo.Equipment
where Make = @chvMake
and Model = @chvModel

Return @intEqId
```

The same functionality could be achieved even without a local variable, since a Return statement can accept an integer expression instead of an integer value:

```
Create Procedure dbo.ap_EqIdByMakeModel_List_4
    @chvMake varchar(50),
    @chvModel varchar(50)
as
   Return (select EqId
           from dbo.Equipment
           where Make = @chvMake
           and Model = @chvModel)
```

To execute the stored procedure and access the returned value, we require the following lines of code:

```
Declare @intEqId int
Execute @intEqId = ap_EqIdByMakeModel_List_3 'Toshiba', 'Portege 7020CT'
Select @intEqId 'Equipment Identifier')
```

Notice the difference in assigning a value. The local variable must be inserted before the name of the stored procedure. The result of the batch is the returned value:

```
Equipment Identifier
--------------------
1

(1 row(s) affected)
```

This solution, however, is not a perfect way to transfer information from a stored procedure to a caller. In the first place, it is limited by data type. Only integers can be returned this way (including `int`, `smallint`, and `tinyint`). This method was often used in old versions of SQL Server to return status information to the caller:

```
Create Procedure dbo.ap_EqIdByMakeModel_List_5
    @chvMake varchar(50),
    @chvModel varchar(50),
    @intEqId int output
as
    select @intEqId = EqId
    from dbo.Equipment
    where Make = @chvMake
    and Model = @chvModel
Return @@error
```

In this example, the stored procedure will potentially return an error code. @@error is a scalar function that contains an error number in the case of failure or a zero in the case of success. To execute the stored procedure, use the following code:

```
Declare    @intEqId int,
           @intErrorCode int
Execute @intErrorCode = dbo.ap_EqIdByMakeModel_List_5
                               'Toshiba',
                               'Portege 7020CT',
                               @intEqId output
Select @intEqId result, @intErrorCode ErrorCode
```

The result will look like this:

```
result        ErrorCode
-----------   -----------
1             0

(1 row(s) affected)
```

An ErrorCode of 0 indicates the stored procedure was executed successfully without errors.

Default Values

If the stored procedure statement has parameters, you must supply values for the parameters in your Exec statement. If a user fails to supply them, the server reports an error. It is possible, however, to assign default values to the parameters so that the user is not required to supply them. Default values are defined at the end of a parameter definition, behind the data types. All that is needed is an assignment (=) and a value:

```
create Procedure dbo.ap_EqIdByMakeModel_List_6
    @chvMake  varchar(50) = '%',
    @chvModel varchar(50) = '%'
as
    Select *
    from dbo.Equipment
    where Make Like @chvMake
    and Model Like @chvModel
```

The procedure is designed as a small search engine that accepts T-SQL wild cards. You can execute this stored procedure with normal values:

```
Execute dbo.ap_EqIdByMakeModel_List_6 'T%', 'Portege%'
```

The result set will consist of records that match the criteria:

EqId	Make	Model	EqTypeId
1	Toshiba	Portege 7020CT	1
34	Toshiba	Portege 7021CT	1

(2 row(s) affected)

If one parameter is omitted, as follows, the procedure will behave, since the value that was defined as a default has been supplied:

```
Execute dbo.ap_EqIdByMakeModel_List_6 'T%'
```

The server will return the following result set:

EqId	Make	Model	EqTypeId
1	Toshiba	Portege 7020CT	1
34	Toshiba	Portege 7021CT	1

(2 row(s) affected)

Even both parameters may be skipped:

```
Execute dbo.ap_EqIdByMakeModel_List_6
```

The server will return all records that match the default criteria:

```
EqId          Make                    Model                     EqTypeId
-----------   ---------------------   -----------------------   --------
1             Toshiba                 Portege 7020CT            1
2             Sony                    Trinitron 17XE            3
. . .
```

Passing Parameters by Name

You do not have to follow parameter order if you pass parameters by name. You must type the name of the parameter and then assign a value to it. The parameter name must match its definition, including the @ sign.

This method is sometimes called *passing parameters by name.* The original method can be referred to as *passing parameters by position.* In the following example, the server will use T% for the second parameter and a default value, %, for the first one:

```
Execute dbo.ap_EqIdByMakeModel_List_6 @Model = 'T%'
```

The result of the search will be the following:

```
EqId          Make                    Model                       EqTypeId
-----------   ---------------------   -------------------------   --------
449           Compaq                  TP DT ACMS ALL LPS Pers Use 3
855           Compaq                  TP DT BCMS ALL LPS Pers Use 3
. . .
```

The opportunity to skip parameters is just one reason for passing parameters by name. Even more important is the opportunity to create a method that makes code more readable and maintainable. And, if a developer makes a mistake and assigns a value to a nonexistent parameter, the error will be picked up by SQL Server.

TIP

Although passing parameters by position can be a little faster, passing parameters by name is preferable.

Syntax

The following is the complete syntax for the creation of a stored procedure:

```
CREATE PROC[EDURE] schema.procedure_name [;number]
    [
        {@parameter schema.data_type} [VARYING] [= default] [OUTPUT]
    ]
    [,...n]
[WITH {   RECOMPILE
        | ENCRYPTION
        | EXECUTE AS { CALLER | SELF | OWNER | 'user_name' }
      }
]
[FOR REPLICATION]
AS
    sql_statement [...n]
```

When you create a stored procedure using With Encryption, the code of the stored procedure is encrypted and then saved in the database. SQL Server will be able to use the encrypted version of the source code to recompile the stored procedure when needed, but none of the users (not even the system administrator) will be able to obtain it.

NOTE

That was the theory. In reality, you should not count on SQL Server encryption to protect your code. It is possible to find on the Internet the means to defeat SQL Server encryption. Copyright and good support are much better protection for the company's interests when you deploy stored procedures on the server of your client.

Keep in mind that you will not be able to change a stored procedure if you create the procedure using With Encryption. You must preserve its code somewhere else (ideally, in a source-code management system like Visual SourceSafe, described in Chapter 16). For more details about storage and encryption of stored procedures, see "Storing Stored Procedures" in Appendix B.

As a developer, you might decide to recompile a stored procedure each time it is used. To force compilation, you should create the stored procedure using With Recompile. Recompiling for each use may improve or degrade the performance of the stored procedure: Although the compilation process is extra overhead when you are executing the stored procedure, SQL Server will sometimes recompile the stored procedure differently (and more economically) based on the data it is targeting. You will find more details about compilation and reasons for recompiling a stored procedure later in this chapter.

[;*number*] is an optional integer value that can be added to the name of a stored procedure. In this way, a user can create a group of stored procedures that can be deleted with a single Drop Procedure statement. Procedures will have names such as these:

► ap_Equipment_List;1

► ap_Equipment_List;2

► ap_Equipment_List;3

Numbering of stored procedures is sometimes used during development and testing, so that all nonproduction versions of a procedure can be dropped simultaneously and quickly.

Stored procedures that include the For Replication option are usually created by SQL Server to serve as a filter during the replication of databases.

An output parameter for a stored procedure can also be of the `cursor` data type. In such a case, the structure of the result set contained by the cursor might vary. The [Varying] option will notify SQL Server to handle such cases. But it is too early to talk about cursors. We will return to cursors in the next chapter.

The Execute As clause is introduced in SQL Server 2005. It allows a developer to specify an execution context of a stored procedure (and other programmatic database objects). A developer can specify which user SQL Server should use to validate permissions on database objects referenced by the stored procedure. You can find more information about this in Chapter 19.

All of these options involve rarely used features. Some of them will be covered in more detail later in this book, but some are simply too esoteric.

Types of Stored Procedures

There are many types of stored procedures:

► User-defined

► System

► Extended

► Temporary

► Global temporary

► Remote

► CLR

There are also database objects, which are very similar in nature:

▶ Triggers

▶ Views

▶ User-defined functions

As you can infer from the name, *user-defined stored procedures* are simply plain, stored procedures assembled by administrators or developers for later use. All the examples we have discussed so far in this chapter have been such stored procedures.

Microsoft delivers a vast set of stored procedures as part of SQL Server. They are designed to cover all aspects of system administration. Internally, *system stored procedures* are just regular stored procedures. Their special features result from the fact that they are stored in system databases (*master* and *msdb*) and they have the prefix sp_. This prefix is more than just a convention. It signals to the server that the stored procedure should be accessible from all databases without putting the database name as a prefix to fully qualify the name of the procedure. For example, you can use sp_spaceused to examine usage of the current database, such as disk space for data and indexes.

We will examine all types of stored procedures in more detail in Chapter 6.

Managing Stored Procedures

Microsoft SQL Server Management Studio is the primary tool that you will use to control the environment and manage stored procedures. We will review the ways that you can use it to

▶ List stored procedures

▶ View code of stored procedures

▶ Rename stored procedures

▶ Delete stored procedures

▶ List dependent and depending objects

Listing Stored Procedures

The easiest way to list stored procedures in a database is to view them from Management Studio. All you need to do is to expand in the Object Browser the following nodes: *server* | Databases | *database* | Programmability | Stored Procedures. We have demonstrated that in the previous chapter.

The alternative is the traditional way based on Transact-SQL. SQL Server is delivered with the system stored procedure sp_stored_procedures.

```
Exec sp_stored_procedures
```

The stored procedure sp_stored_procedures retrieves a list of stored procedures from the sys.objects system view in the database. If you want to see the sys.objects table's contents, execute the following statement:

```
Select *
from sys.objects
```

You can see the results in Figure 2-1.

To see just user-defined stored procedures, you need to filter the database objects with Type set to 'P':

```
Select *
from sys.objects
where type = 'P'
```

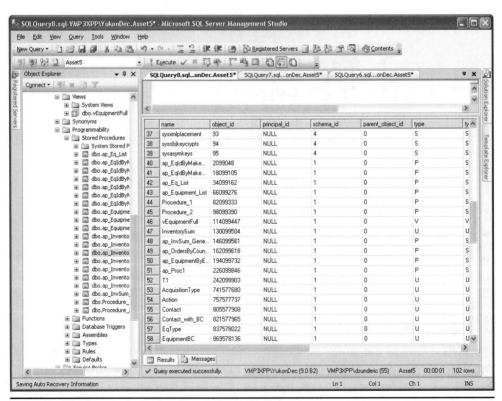

Figure 2-1   *Objects in sys.objects*

It might look like overkill to list stored procedures this way and you may be right. However, it is useful to know how SQL Server stores and manages stored procedures, because sooner or later you will need to open a back door to automate something in the environment.

NOTE

In earlier versions of SQL Server, a list of database objects was stored in dbo.sysobjects. In SQL Server 2005, this system table was replaced by two system views — sys.sysobjects and sys.objects. Tables are similar, but not identical. You can see in BOL or when you execute it, that there is a couple of columns that are different. Microsoft plans to keep sys.objects, while sys.sysobjects is in this version for compatibility, just in case the code that you are porting from earlier versions to SQL Server 2005 contains references to dbo.sysobjects.

Viewing Code of Stored Procedures

I have already shown you in the previous chapter how to display code of a stored procedure in Management Studio. You can choose either the Modify option from the context-sensitive menu of a stored procedure or Script Stored Procedure As | Alter To | New Query Editor Window.

It is a little bit more difficult to display a stored procedure in the traditional way using Transact-SQL. You need to use the sp_helptext system stored procedure. The database that contains the stored procedure must be the current database, and you must supply the name of the stored procedure as a parameter:

```
exec sp_helptext 'dbo.ap_EqIdByMakeModel_List'
```

NOTE

You can also use sp_helptext to view the code of other database objects such as triggers, views, defaults, and rules.

If you now want to save the code of the stored procedure, you can copy it through the Clipboard to your Query pane, or you can save the contents of the Results pane in a text file:

1. From the main menu, choose Query | Results To | Results to Text.
2. Execute sp_helptext.
3. Select File | Save Results As and specify a name for the file. Verify that the File Format is set to ANSI.

The result will be saved to an ANSI file, which you can edit in any text editor, such as Notepad.

Renaming Stored Procedures

There are several ways to change the name of a stored procedure. If you use sp_rename or a command of Management Studio, SQL Server will change the name of the object in the sys.sysobjects view but it will not affect the code of the stored procedure:

```
Exec sp_rename 'Procedure2', 'Procedure_2'
```

When you open the procedure with the Modify option from the context-sensitive menu, everything will look normal. But you might receive unexpected results when you try to execute the Create Procedure statement or the Alter Procedure statement after that. You will clearly see the problem if you generate the script of the stored procedure:

```
USE [Asset5]
GO
/****** Object:  StoredProcedure [dbo].[Procedure_2]
Script Date: 02/13/2005 19:14:04 ******/
SET ANSI_NULLS ON
GO
SET QUOTED_IDENTIFIER ON
GO
create proc Procedure2
as
select 'Hello world'
select * from dbo.EqType
GO
SET ANSI_NULLS OFF
GO
SET QUOTED_IDENTIFIER OFF
GO
```

Although the window name and comment refer to the new stored procedure name, the old stored procedure name is referenced in the only place that matters—in the Create Procedure statement.

   sp_rename was designed to change the names of all database objects (including tables, views, columns, defaults, rules, and triggers). In fact, the versatility of this stored procedure is the reason the code is not changed in the previous example. The stored procedure is designed to change only the names of objects in the sys.sysobjects view.

Database objects with code such as stored procedures, views, and user-defined functions require a different strategy. It is better to drop them and create them again. Again, do not forget to change all associated objects, such as permissions, at the same time. The Alter Procedure statement cannot help us in this case, since we need to change the name of the stored procedure.

NOTE

This operation is not something that you should perform very often. It could be problematic if you were to do it on a production server. SQL Server contains a procedure cache — a part of the memory where it keeps compiled versions of stored procedures. You should flush the procedure cache to force all dependent stored procedures (which refer to the stored procedure by its old name) to recompile. You can use the DBCC FREEPROCCACHE command or you can simply restart SQL Server (service) and the procedure cache will be emptied.

Deleting Stored Procedures

To delete a stored procedure from Management Studio, right-click the name of the stored procedure in the list and select Delete. Drop Procedure is a Transact-SQL statement for deleting a stored procedure. To use it, you must supply the name of the stored procedure as a parameter:

```
DROP PROCEDURE dbo.Procedure_1
```

Objects that are referencing the stored procedure that has been dropped will not be able to run properly after this.

Listing Dependent and Depending Objects

If you plan to perform some dramatic action, such as deleting or renaming a database object, you should first investigate which objects will be affected by the action. Microsoft SQL Server keeps a list of dependencies between objects in the sys.sysdepends system view in each database. To view this list in Management Studio:

1. Right-click the name of the database object in the Object Browser.
2. Select View Dependencies, and SQL Server will display a dialog box with a list of dependencies.
3. You can also switch between the "Objects that depend on…" and "Objects on which … depends" choices.

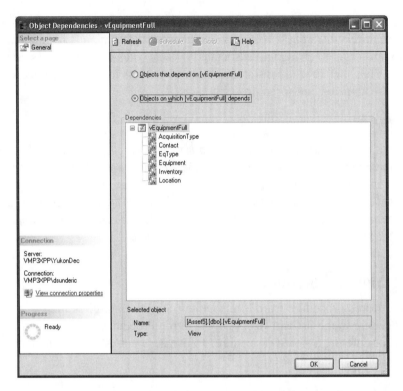

The system stored procedure sp_depends has a similar function. It can also return one or two result sets—one for dependent objects and one for depending objects. If you execute the following statement in the Query window,

```
exec sp_depends ap_Equipment_Full
```

you will see a result like that shown in Figure 2-2.

NOTE

Unfortunately, you cannot completely rely on SQL Server to get a list of dependencies. It does not update the content of the sys.sysdepends view in all cases. You can reproduce and observe this behavior when, for example, you drop and re-create a table. However, in that case, SQL Server will warn you that it cannot properly update dependencies.

This problem has been a known issue since version 4.21, but since SQL Server 7.0, the problem is even more difficult to manage because of deferred name resolution (it is possible to compile some objects such as stored procedures before all objects that they reference are defined in the database). Therefore, if SQL Server displays an empty list, you should open the source code and check it!

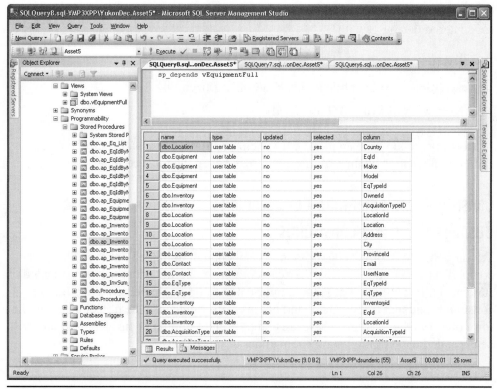

Figure 2-2   *Results of sp_depends*

Neither of these methods will show you dependencies between objects outside of the current database.

The Role of Stored Procedures in the Development of Database Applications

To properly design and use stored procedures in the development of applications, it is critical to understand their role and advantages.

Enforcement of Data Integrity

The most important task for each DBA is to maintain the data integrity of the database that he or she is managing. If a DBA is not almost fanatical about data integrity, the results for the database will be potentially disastrous. During my career, I have encountered databases with

- ▶ 106 different provinces of Canada (one of them was France)
- ▶ An Address column filled with "Guest had frozen Fish."
- ▶ Nine ways to write HP LaserJet III…

Stored procedures are an ideal tool to help you standardize and control data entry, and to implement validation of information and even the most complex constraints.

Consistent Implementation of Complex Business Rules and Constraints

Transact-SQL stored procedures are powerful enough to implement even the most complex business rules because they can combine both procedural and set-oriented statements. Everything that is too complicated to be implemented using other constraints and that is procedural and not just set-oriented can be implemented in the form of a stored procedure. These are complex and important considerations and will be expanded upon throughout the remainder of this book.

NOTE
Naturally, stored procedures are not the only way to implement business logic on the server. Three-tier architecture envisions implementation of business services on a middleware server.

Modular Design

Stored procedures allow developers to encapsulate business functionality and provide callers with a simple interface. Stored procedures behave like a black box. The caller does not have to know how they are implemented, just what they do, what input is required, and what output will be generated. From a development standpoint, this also reduces the complexity of the design process. You do not need to know how a stored procedure is implemented. You just need to reference it in your application or your own procedures.

Maintainability

System design is a cyclic process. Every system needs to be reviewed, changed, and improved. By hiding database structure details behind stored procedures, database administrators can reduce or hopefully eliminate the need to change all other components (that is, client applications and middleware components) of the system whenever they change the database structure.

Microsoft has achieved the same goal with system stored procedures and system tables. Although you can use the contents of system tables directly in your applications, you should base your code on system stored procedures because Microsoft reserves the right to change tables from version to version but has promised to keep the interface and functionality of stored procedures intact.

Another advantage is that stored procedures are implemented on the server and can be maintained centrally. If the business logic is implemented in the client application, a huge effort will be needed to deploy changes.

Reduced Network Traffic

One of the major disadvantages of file-server architecture is high network traffic due to the fact that entire files are being transferred across the network. If a client/server system is well designed, the client will receive just the information it needs, which is usually just a slight portion of the database, thus significantly reducing the network traffic.

If a client/server system is implemented with even more of the processing/business logic on the server (that is, using stored procedures), even less data will be transferred back and forth through the network.

Faster Execution

Stored procedures have several performance advantages over ad hoc queries. Stored procedures are cached in a compiled form on the database server, so when they need to be used, the server does not have to parse and compile them again.

A developer can optimize a stored procedure's code so that every user will use the best possible method to perform an action.

Enforcement of Security

One sign of a well-designed database system is that it prevents users from directly accessing the tables and forces them to use stored procedures to perform specific functions. It is also easier to manage a set of stored procedures by functionality than to manage table- and column-level permissions.

Basic Transact-SQL Programming Constructs

A ll modern relational database management systems are based on an implementation of SQL (Structured Query Language). Most vendors have extended SQL into a more sophisticated programming language. The ANSI committee has standardized the language several times, of which ANSI SQL-92 is the latest specification. Unfortunately (or fortunately—depending on your point of view), each vendor has created its own version of this specification to extend ANSI SQL.

The language in use in Microsoft SQL Server is called Transact-SQL (T-SQL). It complies with the ANSI SQL-92 standard, and you can use this ANSI SQL–compliant language to select, update, insert, and delete records from tables.

T-SQL Identifiers

All databases, servers, and database objects in SQL Server (such as tables, constraints, stored procedures, views, columns, and data types) must have unique names, or *identifiers*. They are assigned when an object is created, and used thereafter to identify the object. The identifier for the object may, if needed, be changed.

The following are the rules for creating identifiers:

▶ Identifiers may have between 1 and 128 characters. There are exceptions to this rule: certain objects are limited (for instance, temporary tables can have identifiers up to only 116 characters long). Before Microsoft SQL Server 7.0, identifiers were limited to 30 characters.

▶ The first character of the identifier must be a letter, underscore (_), at sign (@), or number sign (#). The first letter must be defined in the Unicode 2.0 standard. Among other letters, Latin letters a–z and A–Z can be used as a first character. Some characters (@ and #) have special meanings in T-SQL. They act as signals to SQL Server to treat their carriers differently.

▶ Subsequent characters must be letters from the Unicode 2.0 standard, or decimal digits, or one of the special characters @, #, _, or $.

▶ SQL Server reserved words should not be used as object identifiers.

▶ Identifiers cannot contain spaces or other special characters except for @, #, _, or $.

TIP

You can check which identifiers are valid by using the system stored procedure sp_validname.

If the identifier does not comply with one of the previous rules, it is referred to as a *delimited identifier,* and it must be delimited by double quotes (" ") or square brackets ([ ]) when referenced in T-SQL statements. You can change the default behavior if you use the Set Quoted_Identifier Off statement. The role of single and double quotes will be reversed. Single quotes will delimit identifiers, and double quotes will delimit strings.

As an interim migration aid, you can specify the compatibility mode in which SQL Server will run using the system stored procedure sp_dbcmptlevel. Changing the compatibility mode will affect the way in which SQL Server interprets identifiers. You should check Books OnLine for more information if you are running in any compatibility mode other than 80.

NOTE

The designers of Microsoft SQL Server have created a special system data type called `sysname` to control the length of identifiers. You should use it—instead of `nvarchar(128)`—for variables that will store database object identifiers. Before SQL Server 7, this type was a synonym for `varchar(30)`. If Microsoft again changes the way identifiers are named, procedures using `sysname` will automatically be upgraded.

The following are valid identifiers:

- Cost
- Premium36
- prCalcCost
- idx_User
- @@Make
- #Equipment
- [First Name]
- "Equipment ID"
- [User]
- [User.Group]

NOTE

Although delimiters can be used to assign identifiers that are also keywords (such as User) to objects, this practice is not recommended. You will save a substantial amount of time if you use regular identifiers.

Database Object Qualifiers

The complete name of a database object consists of four identifiers, concatenated in the following manner:

```
[[[server.][database].][schema].]database_object
```

Each of these identifiers must comply with the rules described in the previous section. *Server, database,* and *schema* are often referred to as *database object qualifiers*. The complete name of the object is often referred to as the *fully qualified name,* or *four-part name.*

Schema is a part of the name that is used to logically group database objects. You can also think of them as a *namespace.* Two database objects can have the same name as long as they belong to different namespaces. SQL Server 2005 databases by default have a couple of namespaces: dbo (as default schema), INFORMATION_SCHEMA (defined by SQL-92 Standard for system views that provide metadata information), sys (for system tables and views), and guest.

In SQL Server 2005, a user can create database objects that belong to any schema. If a user does not specify the schema, SQL Server 2005 will make it part of the default dbo schema. It is possible to define another schema and assign it as a default schema to any user. You can find more details about schemas in BOL.

NOTE

Before SQL Server 2005, schemas were tied with users that created objects. If the object was created by the user who created the database (or any member of the db_owner *fixed database role or* sysadmin *server role), SQL Server will record the owner as* dbo. *In other cases, the username of whoever created the object will be assigned as the object owner. Therefore, this segment of object name used to be called* owner.

When you are referencing the object, if you do not specify the name of the schema, SQL Server will first try to find the object in the sys schema. If such an object does not exist, SQL Server will try to locate it in the schema named the same as the user. If it does not exist there either, SQL Server will attempt to find it in the dbo schema. For example, to resolve the stored procedure name ap_Eq_List specified by using dsunderic without a schema name, SQL Server 2005 will try to find it as:

► sys.ap_Eq_List

► dsunderic.ap_Eq_List

► dbo.ap_Eq_List

TIP

To avoid this waste of time, always try to explicitly specify the schema.

Server and *database* are (naturally) the names of the server and the database in which the object is stored.

You do not have to use all the qualifiers all the time. You can omit the server name and/or the database name if the database object is located in the current database and/or on the current server. You can also omit using the schema name when referencing a database object in one of the default schemas. For example, when you are connected to the Asset5 database on the SQLBox server, instead of typing

```
SQLBox.Asset5.dbo.ap_Eq_List
```

you can use any of the following:

```
ap_Eq_List
dbo.ap_Eq_List
Asset5.dbo.ap_Eq_List
Asset5..ap_Eq_List
SQLBox.Asset5..ap_Eq_List
SQLBox...ap_Eq_List
SQLBox..dbo.ap_Eq_List
```

NOTE

You can also use consecutive periods to skip qualifiers.

But the real advantage of a schema is that you can use it to group database objects such as those in the Object Browser (see Figure 3-1).

Data Types

Data types specify the type of information (such as number, string, picture, date) that can be stored in a column or a variable.

SQL Server recognizes 28 *system-defined data types*. Apart from these data types, you can create *user-defined data types* in T-SQL and in .NET to fulfill specific needs.

The following are the categories of system-defined data types:

▶ Character strings
▶ Unicode character strings

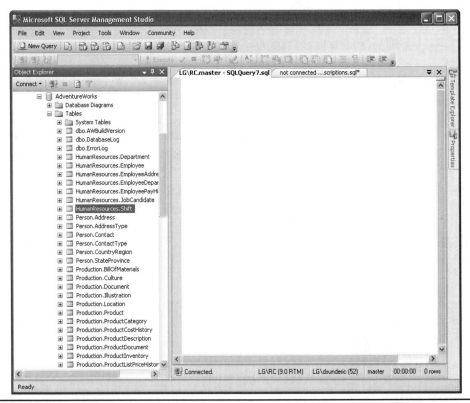

Figure 3-1　*Grouping objects using a schema in the Object Browser*

- ▶ Date and time
- ▶ Approximate numeric
- ▶ Exact numeric
- ▶ Integer numbers
- ▶ Monetary
- ▶ Binary
- ▶ Special

NOTE

In some cases, you can use different identifiers to refer to a data type in T-SQL code. For example, the `char` data type can be referenced as `character`, and `varchar` can be referenced as `character varying`. Some of these synonyms are based on ANSI SQL-92 standard requirements.

Character Strings

Character data types store character strings. The four different character types vary in length and storage characteristics:

- ► char
- ► varchar
- ► varchar(max)
- ► text

The char data type is used to store strings of fixed size. As noted earlier, the maximum size of this data type is 8,000 characters, which is a significant increase over the 255-character limit in early versions. When a variable or a table column is assigned with a string that is shorter than its nominal size, it is padded with trailing spaces to fill the specified field length.

The varchar data type stores strings of variable size up to 8,000 characters long. When a character value whose length is less than the nominal size is assigned to the column or variable, SQL Server does not add trailing spaces to it, but records it as is. varchar data types occupy two additional bytes in order to record the length of the string.

NOTE

Maintenance of this information requires some additional computation during I/O operation, but that time is usually countered by savings in the space required. A record using such columns occupies less space, and more records fit into a single page. Therefore, SQL Server reads more records when accessing data, and it is more likely that a single page contains the information that the user is looking for.

The text data type is used to store huge amounts of data. One field can store up to 2GB ($2^{31} - 1$ bytes) of information. Only a 16-byte pointer to this data is stored in the table. Therefore, additional processing overhead is involved with the use of text columns. There are special functions for processing text values.

NOTE

You should avoid using this data type because Microsoft plans to remove it in future versions of SQL Server. You should use the new varchar(max) *data type instead.*

Varchar(max) looks and operates like the varchar data type, but it is by internal structure and functionality actually much more like the text data type.

It is also designed to store large strings (up to 2GB). The string is stored in special data pages, not in the data page with the rest of the record. Its biggest advantage is that most string operating functions that work with `varchar` also work with `varchar(max)`; however, there are a few new functions for additional functionality. The following command creates a table with four fields using different character string data types:

```
Create table Contacts(ContactId char(8),
                      Name varchar(50),
                      Note text,
                      Resume varchar(max))
```

Character constants are delimited from the rest of the Transact-SQL code with quotes. For example, the following statement inserts contact information:

```
insert into Contacts (ContactId, Name, Note, Resume)
values ('CO-92-81', 'Tom Jones', 'Tom@trigon.com', 'N/a')
```

Unicode Character Strings

Microsoft SQL Server 2005 has four character data types for storing Unicode data—using non-ASCII character sets. They are equivalent to the `char`, `varchar`, `varchar(max)`, and `text` data types and are called

▶ `nchar`

▶ `nvarchar`

▶ `nvarchar(max)`

▶ `ntext`

The main difference between these new data types and the older character data types is that the new data types can hold Unicode characters, which occupy 2 bytes per character. Therefore, the maximum string length that they can store is half that of the corresponding older data types (4,000 for `nchar` and `nvarchar`).

The following statement creates the same table as the previous example but uses Unicode data types:

```
Create table Contacts_2(ContactId nchar(8),
                        Name nvarchar(50),
                        Note ntext,
                        Resume nvarchar(max))
go
```

Unicode character constants are also delimited with quotes but are prefixed with N':

```
insert into Contacts_2 (ContactId, Name, Note, Resume)
values (N'CO-92-81', N'Tom Jones', N'Tom@trigonblue.com', N'N/a')
```

This N' prefix might look a little odd, but you will get used to it. Microsoft documentation is full of samples with Unicode constants. It was some time before I discovered the reason Microsoft uses N' as a prefix. It stands for "National." In fact, acceptable alternative identifiers for these data types are

- ▶ National char
- ▶ National char varying
- ▶ National char varying(max)
- ▶ National text

TIP

Typically, it is not a problem if you omit the N' prefix on constants. SQL Server automatically converts the string to its Unicode equivalent. Naturally, it is better to insert it whenever you are dealing with Unicode columns or variables, but it is not a big problem. The CPU will just have to perform a couple of extra cycles to make the conversion.

However, there are cases in which it becomes a problem. When your string constant is part of a query criterion, then the presence of the N' prefix might significantly affect execution of the query. If the column is defined as a non-Unicode string and the criterion is specified with the N' prefix, SQL Server converts every row of the table to compare it with the Unicode constant. As a result, the query performs a table scan instead of using an index.

Date and Time Data Types

SQL Server supports two T-SQL data types for storing date and time:

- ▶ datetime
- ▶ smalldatetime

The main difference between these two data types is in the amount of space they occupy. datetime occupies 8 bytes and smalldatetime only 4 bytes. Other differences between the two types are the precision of the date stored and the range of dates that can be used. The precision of smalldatetime is one minute, and it covers dates from January 1, 1900, through June 6, 2079, which is usually more than enough. The precision of datetime is 3.33 ms, and it covers dates from January 1, 1753, to December 31, 9999.

Date and time constants are written in Transact-SQL with quote delimiters (as are character strings):

```
update Contacts_2
Set DateOfBirth = '2/21/1965 10:03 AM'
where ContactId = 'CO-92-81'
```

TIP

SQL Server supports many different date and time formats. The Convert() function accepts a parameter that controls the format of date and time functions (explained in detail in Chapter 4).

If time is not specified in a constant, SQL Server automatically assigns a default value—12:00 A.M. (midnight). You should keep in mind that SQL Server always records time as a part of these data types. Thus, if you want to select all contacts born on a particular day, you should *not* use something like this:

```
select *
from Contacts_2
where DateOfBirth = '2/21/1965'
```

This statement would extract records with DateOfBirth set to midnight of that day. Such a solution might be acceptable if all other applications recording values in the field also make the same mistake. A proper solution would be

```
select *
from Contacts_2
where DateOfBirth >= '2/21/1965' and DateOfBirth < '2/22/1965'
```

Integer Numbers

Integers are whole numbers. SQL Server supports 1- , 2- , 4- , and 8-byte integers. The `bit` data type is used to store 1 or 0, to represent logical true and false values. The following table lists integer data types, their storage size, and range of values.

Data Type	Storage Size	Minimum	Maximum
int	4 bytes	−2,147,483,648 (−2G)	2,147,483,647 (2G − 1)
smallint	2 bytes	−32768 (−32K)	32767 (32K − 1)
tinyint	1 byte	0	255 (2^8 − 1)
bigint	8 bytes	−9,223,372,036,854,775,808 (-2^{63})	9,223,372,036,854,775,807 ($2^{63}-1$)
bit	1 bit	0	1

The great thing about the int data types is that they can store huge numbers in a small space. For this reason, they are often used for key values. If the data type of the primary key is int, the table can store up to four billion records, which is typically enough for any purpose. Therefore, if you are not sure about the size of your table, use int as its primary key.

TIP

However, we are starting to see computers with billions of records—both OLTP and data warehousing systems are getting bigger and bigger, and there are also some implementations of distributed databases that can use integers higher than two billion. In those cases you could use big int *for primary keys.*

Integer constants do not need delimiters:

```
update Inventory
Set StatusId = 3,
    Operational = 0
Where InventoryId = 3432
```

Approximate Numbers

Decimal numbers are often stored in real and float data types, also known as *single* and *double precision.* Their advantage is that they do not occupy much space but they can hold large ranges of numbers. The only trouble is that they are not exact. They store a binary representation of the number that is often approximately, but not exactly, equal to the original decimal number.

Precision is the number of significant digits in the number, and *scale* is the number of digits to the right of the decimal point. For example, the number 123456.789 has a precision of 9 and a scale of 3. The precision of real numbers is up to 7 digits, and the precision of float numbers is up to 15 digits. For this reason, they are ideal for science and engineering (where, for example, you may not care about a couple of meters when you are measuring the distance between the Earth and the Moon), but they are not adequate for the financial industry (where a company budget has to be exact to the last cent).

To record the number 234,000,000,000 in mathematics, you can use 234×10^9, and in Transact-SQL, you can use 234E9. This is known as *scientific notation.* The number after E is called the *exponent,* and the number before E is called the *mantissa.* This notation can be used to store small constants, too. In mathematics, 0.000000000234 can be written as 0.234×10^{-9}, and in Transact-SQL, it can be written as 0.234E-9.

SQL Server uses the IEEE 754 standard to store these numbers. When a `float` or `real` variable or column is assigned a number, SQL Server first converts the decimal number to its binary representation. This conversion is the reason these values are approximately, but not exactly, equal to the decimal version. This is why they are referred to as *approximate numbers.* Therefore, you should not rely on the equivalence of two such numbers. You should limit their use in Where clauses to < and > operators and avoid the use of the = operator.

Exact Numbers

The `decimal` or `numeric` data type does not use approximations when storing numbers. Unfortunately, it requires much more space than the `real` and `float` data types. When a `decimal` column or a variable is defined, you have to specify its scale and precision.

SQL Server can store `decimal` numbers with a maximum precision of 38. Scale can be less than or equal to the precision.

In the next example, Weight and Height columns have precision 5 and scale 2—the columns can have up to two digits after the decimal point and up to three digits before.

```
Create table Patient (PatientId int,
                      FullName varchar(30),
                      Weight decimal(5,2),
                      Height decimal(5,2),
                      ADP smallint,
                      BDZ tinyint)
go
```

`decimal` constants do not need delimiters either:

```
insert into Patient (PatientId, FullName, Weight, Height, ADP, BDZ)
values (834021, 'Tom Jones', 89.5, 188.5, 450, 11)
```

Monetary Data Types

The `money` and `smallmoney` data types are a compromise between the precision of `decimal` numbers and the small size of `real` numbers. `smallmoney` occupies 4 bytes and uses the same internal structure as `int` numbers. The data can have up to four digits after the decimal point. For this reason, you can store numbers ranging from –214,768.3648 to 214,768.3647 in the `smallmoney` data type. The `money` data type uses the same structure for storing information as the `bigint` data type. It occupies 8 bytes for storage, so its values must range from –922,337,203,685,477.5808 to +922,337,203,685,477.5807.

Monetary constants can be preceded by $ or one of 18 other currency symbols (listed in SQL Server Books OnLine):

```
update Inventory_2
Set Rent = $0,
LeaseCost = $119.95
Where InventoryId = 3432
```

Binary Data Types

Binary data types are used to store strings of bits. SQL Server supports four basic binary data types, the attributes of which are similar to character data types:

- ▶ `binary`
- ▶ `varbinary`
- ▶ `varbinary(max)`
- ▶ `image`

The `binary` and `varbinary` data types can store up to 8,000 bytes of information, and `image` and `varbinary (max)` can store up to 2GB of data. The following example creates a table that has two binary columns:

```
CREATE TABLE MyTable (
    Id int,
    BinData varbinary(8000),
    Diagram varbinary(max))
go
```

Binary constants are written as hexadecimal representations of bit strings and prefixed with 0x (zero and x):

```
Update MyTable
Set BinData = 0x82A7210B
where Id = 121131
```

A cool, new feature of SQL Server 2005 is the OPENROWSET() function with the new BULK OLE DB provider to read a file and load it as a rowset to a `varbinary (max)` column:

```
UPDATE dbo.MyTable
SET Diagram = (SELECT *
               FROM OPENROWSET(BULK 'C:\My Pictures\desktop.bmp',
                        SINGLE_BLOB) AS a )
where Id = 121131
```

Special Data Types

The following sections cover the special data types.

timestamp

The `timestamp` data type is not designed to store date or time information, but rather is a binary value that serves as a version number of the record. The value is updated every time the record is updated, and the value is unique in the database. It is used to implement optimistic locking. You can find more details about this subject in "Optimistic Locking Using `timestamp` Values" in Chapter 15. Only one field in a table can be defined as the `timestamp` value. It occupies 8 bytes.

uniqueidentifier

The `uniqueidentifier` data type stores 16-byte binary values. These values are often called *globally unique identifiers (GUIDs).* When a system generates a new GUID value, it is guaranteed that the same value cannot be produced again, neither on the same computer nor on any other computer in the world. GUIDs are generated using the identification number of the network card and a unique number obtained from the computer's clock. Manufacturers of network cards guarantee that the identification number of a network card will not be repeated in the next 100 years.

A `uniqueidentifier` constant is usually presented as

- ▶ **Character string**   '{BB7DF450-F119-11CD-8465-00AA00425D90}'
- ▶ **Binary constant**   0xaf16a66f7f8b31d3b41d30c04fc96f46

However, you will rarely type such values. In Transact-SQL, GUIDs should be generated using the NEWID function. There is also a Win32 API function that a client application can use to produce a GUID value.

`uniqueidentifier` values are used relatively often for implementations of web applications and distributed database systems. In web applications, designers might use the `uniqueidentifier` data type to generate a unique identifier before the record is sent to the database. In distributed systems, this data type serves globally unique identifiers.

xml

The `xml` data type is a major new feature of SQL Server 2005. Before it was introduced, users were storing XML documents as strings or binary data. The new data type allows SQL Server to parse an XML document stored in an XML column and verify that it is compliant with the schema that the user associated with the column.

It is also useful in that a user can issue queries (in the XQuery language) against data in `xml` columns (for example, to find rows that contain XML documents that have specified values in specified attributes or elements). It is very exciting that it is possible to index `xml` columns and their attributes and elements, so that the engine does not have to do table and column scans.

However, apart from additional features, the `xml` data type is based on the `varchar(max)` data type and it is therefore limited to 2GB. The following example creates a table that has an `xml` column:

```
Create table dbo.Eq2(
            EqId int,
            EqCompList xml)
```

You should use quotes as delimiters around XML constants:

```
INSERT INTO dbo.Eq2(EqId, EqCompList)
VALUES(123,'<CompList><CZ101/><AZ401/><BZ407/></CompList>')
```

sql_variant

The `sql_variant` data type is based on the same idea as the `variant` data type in Visual Basic. It is designed to allow a single variable, column, or parameter to store values in different data types. Internally, variant objects record two values:

▶   The actual value

▶   The metadata describing the variant: base data type, maximum size, scale, precision, and collation

The following statement creates a lookup table that can store values of different types:

```
Create table Lookup(
   LookupGroupId tinyint,
   LookupId smallint,
   LookupValue sql_variant)
Go
```

Before SQL Server 2000, more than one field was needed to store lookup values of different data types.

The following statements illustrate how you can insert different types of values in one column:

```
Insert Lookup (LookupGroupId, LookupId, LookupValue)
Values (2, 34, 'VAR')
Insert Lookup (LookupGroupId, LookupId, LookupValue)
```

```
Values (3, 22, 2000)
Insert Lookup (LookupGroupId, LookupId, LookupValue)
Values (4, 16, '1/12/2000')
Insert Lookup (LookupGroupId, LookupId, LookupValue)
Values (4, 11, $50000)
```

A sql_variant object can store values of any data type *except these:*

▶ text

▶ ntext

▶ image

▶ varchar(max)

▶ nvarchar(max)

▶ varbinary(max)

▶ timestamp

▶ sql_variant

▶ any user-defined data types

But there are more serious restrictions on their use:

▶ sql_variant columns are limited to 8,016 bytes.

▶ sql_variant columns *can* be used in *indexes* and *unique keys* if the total length of the data in the key is shorter than 900 bytes. However, this is not a limitation of the sql_variant data type. Indexes cannot be based on columns that are larger than 900 bytes in total.

▶ sql_variant columns *cannot* have an identity property.

▶ sql_variant columns *cannot* be part of a computed column.

▶ *You must use functions for converting data types* when assigning values from sql_variant objects to objects of other data types.

▶ The comparison of sql_variant values has complex rules and is prone to errors.

▶ sql_variant values are automatically converted to nvarchar(4000) when accessed from client applications using OLE DB Provider for SQL Server 7.0 or the SQL Server ODBC Driver from SQL Server 7.0. If stored values are longer than 4,000 characters, SQL Server will return just the first 4,000 characters.

▶ sql_variant values are automatically converted to varchar(255) when accessed from client applications using the SQL Server ODBC Driver from SQL Server 6.5 or earlier, or using DB-Library. If stored values are longer than 255 characters, SQL Server will return just the first 255 characters.

▶ sql_variant columns are not supported in the Like predicate.

▶ sql_variant columns do not support full-text indexes.

▶ sql_variant objects cannot be concatenated using the + operator, even if the stored values are strings or numeric. The proper solution is to convert values before concatenation.

▶ Some functions—Avg(), Identity(), IsNumeric(), Power(), Radians(), Round(), Sign(), StDev(), StDevP(), Sum(), Var(), VarP()—do not support sql_variant parameters.

TIP

You should be very conservative in using the sql_variant *data type. Its use has serious performance and design implications.*

table

The table data type is used to store a recordset for later processing. In some ways, this data type is similar to a temporary table. You cannot use this type to define a column. It can only be used as a *local variable* to *return the value of a function.*

NOTE

You will find more information about table *variables in the "Table Variables" section later in this chapter, and more information about table-valued functions in Chapters 4 and 9.*

The Cursor Data Type

This is a special kind of data type that contains references to cursors. You will see in the "Cursors" section later in this chapter that cursors are programming constructs that are designed to allow operations on records one at a time. It is not possible to define a column of this type. It can be used only for variables and stored procedure output values.

Transact-SQL User-defined Data Types

You can define custom data types in a database. Traditional user-defined data types are defined in Transact-SQL. We will describe them in this segment of the book.

In SQL Server 2005, it is possible to define user-defined data types in .NET as well. We will describe the .NET user-defined data types in Chapter 13.

These new types are based on system-defined data types and are accessible only in the database in which they are defined. You can define them from Enterprise Manager or using the system stored procedure sp_addtype:

```
Exec sp_addtype Phone, varchar(20), 'NOT NULL'
Exec sp_addtype typPostalCode, varchar(7), 'NULL'
```

The first parameter is the name of the new data type, the second parameter is the system-defined data type on which it is based, and the third parameter defines the nullability of the new data type. When the command is executed, the server adds the type to the sys.systype system view of the current database.

New types can be based on any system-defined type except timestamp.

TIP

A fascinating aspect of user-defined data types is that you can change them in one step across the database. For example, if you decide that decimal(19,6) is not big enough for your monetary values, you can replace it with decimal(28,13). You can simply run the script that first changed the data type and then re-create all database objects that are referencing it. This feature is very useful during the development stage of a database. Unfortunately, when a database is already in the production phase, tables contain data, and this feature becomes a lot more complicated.

The designers of Microsoft SQL Server have included one special data type with the server—sysname. It is used to control the length of Transact-SQL identifiers. When the server is working in default mode, the length of this type is set to 128 characters. When the compatibility level is set to 65 or 60, the length is shortened to 30 characters. You should use it to define columns and variables that will contain Transact-SQL identifiers.

Variables

Variables in Transact-SQL are the equivalent of variables in other programming languages, but due to the nature of the Transact-SQL language, their use and behavior are somewhat different.

SQL Server 2005 (and 2000) documentation recognizes only *local variables* and *table variables*. Documentation in SQL Server 7 and earlier versions was also referring to *global variables*. In SQL Server 2005 (and 2000) global variables are considered to be functions.

Local Variables

The scope of local variables is a batch (a set of T-SQL statements that is sent to SQL Server and executed simultaneously). This restriction implicitly includes a single stored procedure (because stored procedures are defined in a batch). This is a significant limitation. However, several workarounds can be used as solutions to this problem.

A stored procedure cannot access variables defined in other stored procedures. One way to pass values to and from stored procedures is to use parameters. Keep in mind that you are passing only the values associated with the variables, not references, as you can in some other programming languages.

Another way to transfer value between stored procedures or between batches is the use of more permanent database objects such as tables or temporary tables.

Let's review basic operations with local variables.

Declaring Variables

Before you can do anything with a local variable, you need to declare it. Declaration consists of the reserved word Declare and a list of variables and their respective data types.

The names of variables must comply with the rules for identifiers with one exception—they must begin with @:

```
Declare @LastName varchar(50)
```

It is possible to define several variables in a single Declare statement. You just need to separate them with commas:

```
Declare    @LastName varchar(50),
           @FirstName varchar(30),
           @BirthDate smalldatetime
```

NOTE

One stored procedure or a batch can have up to 10,000 local variables.

You can define variables based on user-defined data types:

```
Declare @OfficePhone phone
```

NOTE

You cannot define the nullability of the variable, as you can with table columns. This does not mean that variables cannot contain null values. In fact, before assignment, the value of each variable is null. It is also possible to explicitly set the value of each variable to null.

Assigning Values with the Select Statement

There are several ways to assign a value to a local variable. In early versions of
SQL Server, the only way to do this was to use a modification of the Select statement:

```
Select @LastName = 'Smith'
```

It is also possible to assign several variables in the same statement:

```
Select   @LastName = 'Smith',
         @FirstName = 'David',
         @BirthDate = '2/21/1965'
```

> **NOTE**
>
> *It is necessary to assign a value of an appropriate data type to the variable; however, there are
> some workarounds. In some cases, the server will perform an implicit conversion from one data
> type to another. SQL Server also includes a set of functions for explicit conversion. Convert() and
> Cast() can be used to change the data type of the value (see Chapter 4). Some data types are not
> compatible, so explicit conversion is the only solution.*

Quite often, variables are assigned values from the result set of the Select statement:

```
Select   @Make = Equipment.Make,
         @Model = Equipment.Model,
         @EqType = Equipment.EqType
From EqType INNER JOIN Equipment
     ON EqType.EqTypeId = Equipment.EqTypeId
Where EqId = 2
```

There are some potential problems associated with this approach. How will the
server assign values if the result set contains multiple records, or no records?

If more than one record is returned in the result set, a variable will be assigned the
values from the *last* record. The only trouble is that we cannot predict which record
will be the last, because this position depends on the index that the server uses to
create the result set.

It is possible to create workarounds to exploit these facts (that is, to use hints to
specify an index or use minimum and/or maximum functions to assign extreme values).
The recommended solution, however, is to narrow the search criteria so that only one
record is returned.

The other behavior that might cause unexpected results is the case in which
a result set does not return any records. It is a common belief and expectation of

many developers that the variable will be set to null. This is absolutely incorrect. The content of the variable *will not be changed* in this case.

Observe the following example, or try to run it against the Asset5 database:

```
Declare    @make varchar(50),
           @model varchar(50),
           @EqType varchar(50)

Select     @Make = 'ACME',
           @Model = 'Turbo',
           @EqType = 'cabadaster'

Select     @Make = make,
           @Model = Model,
           @EqType = EqType.EqType
From EqType INNER JOIN Equipment
     ON EqType.EqTypeId = Equipment.EqTypeId
Where EqId = -1

Select @make make, @model model, @EqType EqType
```

Since the Equipment table does not have a record with the identifier set to –1, the variables will keep their original values.

```
make                      model                      EqType
----------------------    --------------------------  --------------
ACME                      Turbo                      cabadaster
(1 row(s) affected)
```

Only if the values of the variables were not previously set will they continue to contain a null value.

The variable can be assigned with any Transact-SQL expression such as a constant or a calculation, or even a complete Select statement that returns a single value:

```
Select     @Make = Make,
           @Model = Model,
           @EquipmentName = Make + ' ' + Model,
           @EqType = (select EqType
                      from dbo.EqType EqType
                      where EqType.EqTypeId = Equipment.EqTypeId)
From dbo.Equipment
Where EqId = 2
```

There is one combination of statements and expressions that will result in a syntax error. It is not possible to return a result set from the Select statement and to assign a variable in the same Select statement:

```
Select    Make,
          @Model = Model     -- wrong
From dbo.Equipment
Where EqId = 2
```

Assigning Values with the Set Statement

In SQL Server 7.0, the syntax of the Set statement has been expanded to support the assignment of local variables. In earlier versions, it was possible to use the Set statement only to declare cursor variables. Today, Microsoft is proclaiming this as a preferred method for assigning variables:

```
Set @LastName = 'Johnson'
```

Use of the Set statement is preferable, since it makes code more readable and reduces the opportunity to make a mistake (assign a variable and return a result set at the same time).

There is just one problem with the Set statement—it is not possible to assign several values with one statement. You will be forced to write code like this:

```
Set      @Make = 'ACME'
Set      @Model = 'Turbo'
Set      @EqType = 'cabadaster'
```

Assigning Values in the Update Statement

The ability to set the values of local variables in an Update statement is a feature that is buried deep in the oceans of SQL Server Books OnLine. It is an element that was designed to solve concurrency issues when code needs to read and update a column concurrently:

```
Update Inventory
Set @mnsCost = Cost = Cost * @fltTaxRate
Where InventoryId = @intInventoryId
```

Displaying the Values of Variables

The value of a variable can be displayed to the user by using a Select or a Print statement:

```
Select @LastName
Print @FirstName
```

It is possible to include a local variable in a result set that will be returned to the user:

```
Select    make "Selected make",
          Model "Selected Model",
          @Model "Original model"
From Equipment
Where EqId = 2
```

Global Variables

Global variables constitute a special type of variable. The server maintains the values in these variables. They carry information specific to the server or a current user session. They can be examined from anywhere, whether from a stored procedure or a batch. In the SQL Server 2005 documentation, Microsoft refers to them as *scalar functions,* meaning that they return just one value. Since you can still find references to global variables in some documentation and since I would like to use some of them in this chapter, I will review them both here and in the next chapter, which is dedicated to functions.

Global variable names begin with an @@ prefix. You do not need to declare them, since the server constantly maintains them. They are system-defined functions and you cannot declare them.

Let's review the principal global variables/scalar functions.

@@identity

This is a function/global variable that you will use frequently. It is also a feature that generates many of the questions on Usenet newsgroups.

One column in each table can be defined as the Identity column, and the server will automatically generate a unique value in it. This is a standard technique in Microsoft SQL Server for generating *surrogate keys* (keys whose values are just numbers and do not carry any information). Usually, such columns will be set to assign sequential numbers:

```
Create table Eq (EqId int identity(1,1),
                 Make varchar(50),
                 Model varchar(50),
                 EqTypeId int)
```

The @@identity global variable allows you to get the last identity value generated in the current session. It is important to read the value as soon as possible (that is, in the next Transact-SQL statement). Otherwise, it might happen that you initiate, for example, another stored procedure or a trigger that inserts a record to a different table with an Identity column. In such a case, SQL Server overwrites the number stored in @@identity with the new value. In the following example, a record will be inserted and a new identifier will immediately be read:

```
Declare @intEqId int
Insert into Eq(Make, Model, EqTypeId)
Values ('ACME', 'Turbo', 2)
Select @intEqId = @@identity
```

If one Transact-SQL statement inserts several records into a table with an Identity column, @@identity will be set to the value from the last record:

```
Declare @intEqId int
Insert into Equipment(Make, Model, EqTypeId)
    Select Make, Model, EqTypeID
    From NewEquipment
Select @intEqId = @@identity
```

You will use this function very often. One of the most common types of stored procedures that you will write will just insert a record and return its new key to the caller.

@@error

After each Transact-SQL statement, the server sets the value of this variable to an integer value:

▶ **0** If the statement was successful

▶ **Error number** If the statement has failed

This global variable is the foundation of all methods for error handling in the Microsoft SQL Server environment. It is essential to examine the value of this variable before any other Transact-SQL statement is completed, because the value of @@error will be reset. Even if the next statement is only a simple Select statement, the value of the @@error variable will be changed after it. In the following example, let's assume that an error will occur during the Update statement. @@error will contain the error code only until the next statement is executed; even the command for reading the @@error value will reset it. If it was completed successfully, SQL Server will set @@error to 0. The only way to preserve the @@error value is to immediately read it and store it in a local variable; then it can be used for error handling.

```
Update Equipment
Set EqTypeId = 3
```

```
Where EqTypeId = 2
Select @intErrorCode = @@error
```

If it is necessary to read more than one global variable immediately after a statement, all such variables should be included in a single Select statement:

```
Declare    @intEqId int,
           @intErrorCode int
Insert into Equipment(Make, Model, EqTypeId)
Values ('ACME', 'Turbo', 2)
Select     @intEqId = @@identity,
           @intErrorCode = @@Error
```

The @@error variable will be set to an error number only in the case of errors, not in the case of warnings. Supplementary information that the server posts regarding errors or warnings (that is, severity, state, and error messages) are not available inside a stored procedure or a batch. Only the error number is accessible from a stored procedure or a batch. Further components of error messages can be read only from the client application.

You will find more details about use of the @@error function in the "Error Handling based on @@Error" section in Chapter 6.

@@rowcount

After each Transact-SQL statement, the server sets the value of this variable to the total number of records affected by it. It can be used to verify the success of selected operations:

```
select Make, Model, EqTypeid
into OldEquipment
from Equipment
where EqTypeid = 2

if @@rowcount = 0
  Print "No rows were copied!"
```

NOTE

Certain statements (like the If statement) will set @@rowcount to 0, and certain statements (like Declare) will not affect it.

Rowcount_big() is a function introduced in SQL Server 2000. It returns the number of affected records in the form of a `bigint` number.

TIP

When you try to update an individual record, SQL Server will not report an error if your Where clause specifies a criterion that does not qualify any records. SQL Server will not update anything, and you might, for example, think that the operation was successful. You can use @@rowcount to identify such cases.

Table Variables

Table variables are objects similar to temporary tables and were introduced in SQL Server 2000. A table variable is declared using the `table` data type. A statement declaring a table variable initializes the variable as an empty table with a specified structure. As a table definition, such a statement includes definitions of columns with their data type, size, precision, and optional constraints (primary key, identity, unique, and check constraints). All elements have to be defined during the declaration. It is not possible to alter or add them later.

The following batch declares a table variable, inserts rows, and returns them to the user:

```
Declare @MyTableVar table
     (Id int primary key,
      Lookup varchar(15))

Insert @MyTableVar values (1, '1Q2000')
Insert @MyTableVar values (2, '2Q2000')
Insert @MyTableVar values (3, '3Q2000')

Select * from @MyTableVar
Go
```

Because of their nature, table variables have certain limitations:

▶ Table variables can only be part of the Select, Update, Delete, Insert, and Declare Cursor statements.

▶ Table variables can be used as a part of the Select statement everywhere tables are acceptable, except as the destination in a Select...Into statement:

```
Select LookupId, Lookup
Into @TableVariable       -- wrong
From Lookup
```

▶ Table variables can be used in Insert statements except when the Insert statement collects values from a stored procedure:

```
Insert into @TableVariable    -- wrong
    Exec prMyProcedure
```

▶ Unlike temporary tables, table variables always have a *local scope.* They can be used only in the batch, stored procedure, or function in which they are declared.

▶ Table variables are considered to be nonpersistent objects, and therefore they will not be rolled back after a Rollback Transaction statement.

TIP

If possible, use table variables instead of temporary tables. Table variables have less locking overhead and therefore are faster.

Flow-control Statements

Flow-control statements from T-SQL are rather rudimentary compared to similar commands in other modern programming languages such as Visual Basic and C#. Their use requires knowledge and some skill to overcome their lack of user friendliness. However, on a positive note, they allow the creation of very complex procedures.

This section covers the use of the following Transact-SQL statements and programming constructs:

▶ Comments

▶ Statement block

▶ If...Else

▶ While...Break

▶ Break

▶ Continue

▶ GoTo

▶ WaitFor

▶ Begin...End

Comments

You can include comments inside the source code of a batch or a stored procedure; these comments are ignored during compilation and execution by SQL Server. It is a common practice to accompany source code with remarks that will help other developers to understand your intentions.

Comments can also be a piece of Transact-SQL source code that you do not want to execute for a particular reason (usually while developing or debugging). Such a process is usually referred to as *commenting out* the code.

Single-line Comments

There are two methods to indicate a comment. A complete line or part of the line can be marked as a comment if the user places two hyphens (--) at the beginning. The remainder of the line becomes a comment. The comment ends at the end of the line:

```
-- This is a comment. Whole line will be ignored.
```

You can place the comment in the middle of a Transact-SQL statement. The following example comments out the last column:

```
Select LeaseId, LeaseVendor --, LeaseNumber
From dbo.Lease
Where ContractDate > '1/1/1999'
```

This type of comment can be nested in another comment defined with the same or a different method:

```
-- select * from dbo.Equipment -- Just for debugging
```

This commenting method is compatible with the SQL-92 standard.

Multiline Comments: /* ... */

The second commenting method is native to SQL Server. It is suitable for commenting out blocks of code that can span multiple lines. Such a comment must be divided from the rest of the code with a pair of delimiters—(/*) and (*/):

```
/*
This is a comment.
All these lines will be ignored.
*/

/* List all equipment. */
select * from Equipment
```

Comments do not have a length limit. It is best to write as much as is necessary to adequately document the code.

Single-line comments can be nested inside multiline comments:

```
/*
-- List all equipment.
Select * from Equipment
*/
```

SQL Server 2005 also supports the nesting of multiline comments. Earlier versions of SQL Server had problems with that. In different versions and in different tools, the following may or may not generate a syntax error:

```
/* This is a comment.
/* Query Analyzer in SQL Server 2000 will understand the following
delimiter as the end of the first comment. However, it will work fine
in SQL Server 2005 Management Studio.*/
   This will generate a syntax error in some cases. */
Select * from dbo.Equipment
```

In Chapter 5 where I discuss batches, I will illustrate the restriction that multiline comments cannot span more than one batch.

Documenting Code

Again, your comments will be of benefit to other developers who read your code; your comments will be better still if you make their presence in the code as obvious as possible. It is a favorable, although not required, practice to accompany comment delimiters with a full line of stars, or to begin each commented line with two stars:

```
/****************************************************************
** File: ap_Equipment_Insert.sql
** Name: ap_Equipment_Insert
** Desc: Insert equipment and equipment type
**       (if not present).
**
** Return values: ErrorCode
**
** Called by:    middleware
**
** Parameters:
** Input                                   Output
** ----------                              ----------
```

```
** Make                                    EqId
** Model
** EqType
**
** Auth: Dejan Sunderic
** Date: 1/1/2005
**********************************************************************
** Change History
**********************************************************************
** Date:           Author:      Description:
** --------        --------      ------------------------------------
** 11/1/2005       DS           Fixed:49. Better error handling.
** 11/2/2005       DS           Fixed:36. Optimized for performance.
**********************************************************************/
```

Inserting two stars at the beginning of each line serves two purposes:

▶ They are a visual guide for your eye. If you comment out code this way, you will not be in doubt whether a piece of code is functional or commented out.

▶ They force SQL Server to report a syntax error if somebody makes an error (for example, by nesting comments or by spanning comments over multiple batches).

The preceding example is based on part of a SQL script for creating a stored procedure generated by Visual InterDev. It is very useful to keep track of all these items explicitly, especially Description and Change History. It is a personal choice to be more elaborate in describing stored procedures, but if you are, your comments can be used as instant design documentation.

Occasionally, developers believe that this type of header is sufficient code documentation, but you should consider commenting your code throughout. It is important to comment not *how* things are being done, but *what* is being done. I recommend that you write your comments to describe what a piece of code is attempting to accomplish, and then write the code itself. In this way, you create design documentation that eventually becomes code documentation.

Statement Blocks: Begin...End

The developer can group several Transact-SQL statements by using Begin...End statements in a logical unit. Such units are then typically used in flow-control statements to execute a group of Transact-SQL statements together. Flow-control statements, such as If and While, can incorporate a single statement or a statement block to be executed when certain conditions are met.

```
Begin
     Transact-SQL statements
End
```

There must be one or more Transact-SQL statements inside a block. If there is only one statement inside, you could remove the Begin and End keywords. Begin and End must be used as a pair. If a compiler does not find a matching pair, it will report a syntax error.

Begin and End can also be nested, but this practice is prone to errors. However, if you are cautious and orderly, there should not be a problem. An excellent way to avoid such problems is to indent the code:

```
Begin

     Insert Order(OrderDate, RequestedById,
                     TargetDate, DestinationLocation)
     Values(@OrderDate, @ContactId,
            @TargetDate, @LocId)

     Select    @ErrorCode = @@Error,
               @OrderId = @@Identity

     if @ErrorCode <> 0
     begin
          RaiseError('Error occurred while inserting Order!', 16,1)
          Return @@ErrorCode
     end
End
```

Conditional Execution: The If Statement

The If statement is the most common flow-control statement. It is used to examine the value of a condition and to change the flow of code based on the condition. First, let us review its syntax:

```
If boolean_expression
     {Transact-SQL_statement | statement_block}
[else
     {Transact-SQL_statement | statement_block}]
```

When the server encounters such a construct, it examines the value of the Boolean expression. If this value is True (1), it executes the statements or the statement block that follows it. The Else component of the statement is optional.

It includes a single statement or a statement block that will be executed if the Boolean expression returns a value of False (0).

The following code sample tests the value of the @ErrorCode variable. If the variable contains a 0, the server inserts a record in the Order table and then records the value of the identity key and any error that may have occurred in the process.

```
If @ErrorCode = 0
Begin
    Insert dbo.Order(OrderDate,  RequestedById,
                     TargetDate, DestinationLocation)
    Values(@dtOrderDate,  @intContactId,
           @dtTargetDate, @intLocId)

    Select   @intErrorCode = @@Error,
             @intOrderId = @@Identity
End
```

Let us take a look at a more complex case. The following stored procedure inserts a record in the Equipment table and returns the ID of the record to the caller. The stored procedure accepts the equipment type, make, and model as input parameters. The stored procedure must then find out if such an equipment type exists in the database and insert it if it does not.

```
Create Procedure dbo.ap_Equipment_Insert_1
-- Store values in Equipment table.
-- Return identifier of the record to the caller.
    (
        @chvMake varchar(50),
        @chvModel varchar(50),
        @chvEqType varchar(30)
    )
As
declare   @intEqTypeId int,
          @intEqId int


-- read Id of EqType
Select @intEqTypeId = EqTypeId
From dbo.EqType
Where EqType = @chvEqType
-- does such eqType already exists in the database
If  @intEqTypeId IS NOT NULL
    --insert equipment
    Insert dbo.Equipment (Make, Model, EqTypeId)
    Values (@chvMake, @chvModel, @intEqTypeId)
Else
```

```
    --if it does not exist
    Begin
        -- insert new EqType in the database
        Insert dbo.EqType (EqType)
        Values (@chvEqType)

        -- get id of record that you've just inserted
        Select @intEqTypeId = @@identity

        --insert equipment
        Insert dbo.Equipment (Make, Model, EqTypeId)
        Values (@chvMake, @chvModel, @intEqTypeId)
    End
Select @intEqId = @@identity


-- return id to the caller
return @intEqId
```

There are a few items that could be changed in this stored procedure, but the importance of this example is to illustrate a use of the Else statement.

One item that could be improved upon is the process of investigating the EqType table with the Exists keyword. Its use here is similar to its use in the Where clause. It tests for the presence of the records in the subquery:

```
If [NOT] Exists(subquery)
    {Transact-SQL_statement | statement_block}
[else
    {Transact-SQL_statement | statement_block}]
```

The stored procedure prInsertEquipment can be modified to use the Exists keyword:

```
    . . .
If  Exists (Select EqTypeId From dbo.EqType Where EqType = @chvEqType)
    . . .
```

Naturally, if you use the Not operator, the encapsulated statement will be executed if the subquery does not return records:

```
Create Procedure ap_Equipment_Insert_2
-- Store values in equipment table.
-- Return identifier of the record to the caller.
    (
        @chvMake varchar(50),
        @chvModel varchar(50),
        @chvEqType varchar(30)
    )
```

```
As
declare    @intEqTypeId int,
           @intEqId int


-- does such eqType already exist in the database
If  Not Exists (Select EqTypeId From dbo.EqType Where EqType = @chvEqType)
    --if it does not exist
    Begin
          -- insert new EqType in the database
          Insert dbo.EqType (EqType)
          Values (@chvEqType)

          -- get id of record that you've just inserted
          Select @intEqTypeId = @@identity
    End
else
    -- read Id of EqType
    Select @intEqTypeId = EqTypeId
    From dbo.EqType
    Where EqType = @chvEqType

--insert equipment
Insert dbo.Equipment (Make, Model, EqTypeId)
Values (@chvMake, @chvModel, @intEqTypeId)

Select @intEqId = @@identity

-- return id to the caller
Return @intEqId
```

Both If and Else statements can be nested:

```
alter Procedure ap_Equipment_Insert_3
-- Store values in equipment table.
-- Return identifier of the record to the caller.
    (
          @chvMake varchar(50),
          @chvModel varchar(50),
          @chvEqType varchar(30)
    )
As
declare @intEqTypeId int,
        @ErrorCode int,
        @intEqId int
```

```
-- does such eqType already exist in the database
If  Not Exists (Select EqTypeId From dbo.EqType Where EqType = @chvEqType)
    --if it does not exist
    Begin
        -- insert new EqType in the database
        Insert dbo.EqType (EqType)
        Values (@chvEqType)

        -- get id of record that you've just inserted
        Select @intEqTypeId = @@identity,
            @ErrorCode = @@Error
        If @ErrorCode <> 0
            begin
                Select 'Unable to insert Equipment Type. Error: ',
                    @ErrorCode
                Return -1
            End
    End
Else
    Begin
        -- read Id of EqType
        Select @intEqTypeId = EqTypeId
        From dbo.EqType
        Where EqType = @chvEqType

        Select @ErrorCode = @@Error

        If @ErrorCode <> 0
            begin                             .

                Select 'Unable to get Id of Equipment Type. Error: ',
                    @ErrorCode
                Return -2
            End
    End

--insert equipment
Insert dbo.Equipment (Make, Model, EqTypeId)
Values (@chvMake, @chvModel, @intEqTypeId)

-- return id to the caller
Select @intEqId = @@identity,
    @ErrorCode = @@Error
```

```
If @ErrorCode <> 0
    Begin
        Select 'Unable to insert Equipment. Error: ', @ErrorCode
        Return -3
    End


Return @intEqId
```

There is no limit to the number of levels. However, this capability should not be abused. The presence of too many levels is a sure sign that a more in-depth study should be made concerning code design.

Looping: The While Statement

Transact-SQL contains only one statement that allows looping:

```
While Boolean_expression
    {sql_statement | statement_block}
    [Break]
    {sql_statement | statement_block}
    [Continue]
```

If the value of the Boolean expression is True (1), the server will execute one or more encapsulated Transact-SQL statement(s). From inside the block of statements, this execution can be controlled with the Break and Continue statements. The server will interrupt the looping when it encounters a Break statement. When the server encounters a Continue statement, it will ignore the rest of the statements and restart the loop.

NOTE

Keep in mind that loops are primarily tools for third-generation languages. In such languages, code was written to operate with records one at a time. Transact-SQL is a fourth-generation language and is written to operate with sets of information. It is possible to write code in Transact-SQL that will loop through records and perform operations on a single record, but you pay for this feature with severe performance penalties. However, there are cases when such an approach is necessary.

It is not easy to find bona fide examples to justify the use of loops in Transact-SQL. Let us investigate a stored procedure that calculates the factorial of an integer number:

```
Create Procedure ap_CalcFactorial
-- calculate factorial
-- 1! = 1
```

```
-- 3! = 3 * 2 * 1
-- n! = n * (n-1)* . . . 5 * 4 * 3 * 2 * 1
    @inyN tinyint,
    @intFactorial bigint OUTPUT
As


Set @intFactorial = 1

while @inyN > 1
begin
    set @intFactorial = @intFactorial * @inyN
    Set @inyN = @inyN - 1
end

return 0
```

Another example could be a stored procedure that returns a list of properties assigned to an asset in the form of a string:

```
alter Procedure ap_InventoryProperties_Get
/**************************************************************
Return comma-delimited list of properties that are describing asset.
i.e.: Property = Value Unit;Property = Value Unit;Property = Value
 Unit;Property = Value Unit;Property = Value Unit;...

test:
declare @p varchar(max)
exec ap_InventoryProperties_Get 5, @p OUTPUT, 1
select @p
**************************************************************/
    (
        @intInventoryId int,
        @chvProperties varchar(max) OUTPUT,
        @debug int = 0
    )


As

declare @intCountProperties int,
        @intCounter int,
        @chvProperty varchar(50),
        @chvValue varchar(50),
        @chvUnit varchar(50)
```

```
Create table #Properties(
        Id int identity(1,1),
        Property varchar(50),
        Value varchar(50),
        Unit varchar(50))

-- identify Properties associated with asset
insert into #Properties (Property, Value, Unit)
    select Property, Value, Unit
    from dbo.InventoryProperty InventoryProperty
        inner join dbo.Property Property
        on InventoryProperty.PropertyId = Property.PropertyId
    where InventoryProperty.InventoryId = @intInventoryId

if @debug = 1
    select * from #Properties

-- set loop
select @intCountProperties = Count(*),
       @intCounter = 1,
       @chvProperties = ''
from #Properties

-- loop through list of properties
while @intCounter <= @intCountProperties
begin
    -- get one property
    select @chvProperty = Property,
        @chvValue = Value,
        @chvUnit = Unit
    from #Properties
    where Id = @intCounter

    -- assemble list

    set @chvProperties = @chvProperties + '; '
                        + @chvProperty + '='
                        + @chvValue + ' ' +  ISNULL(@chvUnit, '')

    -- let's go another round and get another property
    set @intCounter = @intCounter + 1
end
```

```
if Substring(@chvProperties, 0, 2) = '; '
    set @chvProperties = Right(@chvProperties, Len(@chvProperties) - 2)

drop table #Properties
return 0
```

Unconditional Execution: The GoTo Statement

The GoTo statement forces the server to continue the execution from a *label*:

```
GoTo label
...
label:
```

The *label* has to be within the same stored procedure or batch. It is not important whether the *label* or the GoTo statement is defined first in the code. The *label* can even exist without the GoTo statement. On the contrary, the server will report an error if it encounters a GoTo statement that points to a nonexistent label.

The following stored procedure uses the GoTo statement to interrupt further processing and display a message to the user when an error occurs:

```
Create Procedure dbo.ap_Lease_Close
-- Clear Rent, ScheduleId, and LeaseId on all assets associated
-- with specified lease.
    @intLeaseId int
As
    -- delete schedules
    Update dbo.Inventory
    Set Rent = 0,
        LeaseId = null,
        LeaseScheduleId = null
    Where LeaseId = @intLeaseId
    If @@Error <> 0 Goto PROBLEM_1

    -- delete schedules
    Delete from dbo.LeaseSchedule
    Where LeaseId = @intLeaseId
    If @@Error <> 0 Goto PROBLEM_2

    -- delete lease
    Delete from dbo.Lease
    Where LeaseId = @intLeaseId
    If @@Error <> 0      Goto PROBLEM_3
    Return 0
```

```
PROBLEM_1:
    Select 'Unable to update Inventory!'
    Return 50001
PROBLEM_2:
    Select 'Unable to remove schedules from the database!'
    Return 50002
PROBLEM_3:
    Select 'Unable to remove lease from the database!'
Return 50003
```

NOTE

The stored procedure is only an academic example. It would be better to use transactions and rollback changes in case of errors. I will describe transactions in Chapter 5.

Scheduled Execution: The WaitFor Statement

There are two ways to schedule the execution of a batch or stored procedure in SQL Server. One way is based on the use of SQL Server Agent. The other way is to use the WaitFor statement. The WaitFor statement allows the developer to specify the time when, or a time interval after which, the remaining Transact-SQL statements will be executed:

```
WaitFor {Delay 'time' | Time 'time'}
```

There are two variants to this statement. One specifies the delay (time interval) that must pass before the execution can continue. The time interval specified as a parameter of the statement must be less than 24 hours. In the following example, the server will pause for one minute before displaying the list of equipment:

```
WaitFor Delay '00:01:00'
    Select * from Equipment
```

The other variant is more significant. It allows the developer to schedule a time when the execution is to continue. The following example runs a full database backup at 11:00 P.M.:

```
WaitFor Time '23:00'
    Backup Database Asset To Asset_bkp
```

There is one problem with this Transact-SQL statement. The connection remains blocked while the server waits to execute the statement. Therefore, it is much better to use SQL Server Agent than the WaitFor statement to schedule jobs.

Cursors

Relational databases are designed to work with sets of data. In fact, the purpose of the Select statement, as the most important statement in SQL, is to define a set of records. In contrast, end-user applications display information to the user record by record (or maybe in small batches). To close the gap between these conflicting requirements, RDBMS architects have invented a new class of programming constructs—*cursors.*

Many types of cursors are implemented in various environments using different syntax, but all cursors work in a similar fashion:

1. A cursor first has to be defined and its features have to be set.
2. The cursor must be populated.
3. The cursor has to be positioned (*scrolled*) to a record or block of records that needs to be retrieved (*fetched*).
4. Information from one or more current records is fetched, and then some modification can be performed or some action can be initiated based on the fetched information.
5. Optionally, steps 3 and 4 are repeated.
6. Finally, the cursor must be closed and resources released.

Cursors can be used on both server and client sides. SQL Server and the APIs for accessing database information (OLE DB, ODBC, DB-Library) all include sets of functions for processing cursors.

SQL Server supports three classes of cursors:

► Client cursors

► API server cursors

► Transact-SQL cursors

The major difference between Transact-SQL cursors and other types of cursors is their purpose. Transact-SQL cursors are used from stored procedures, batches, functions, or triggers to repeat custom processing for each row of the cursor. Other kinds of cursors are designed to access database information from the client application. We will review only Transact-SQL cursors.

Transact-SQL Cursors

Processing in Transact-SQL cursors has to be performed in the following steps:

1. Use the Declare Cursor statement to create the cursor based on the Select statement.
2. Use the Open statement to populate the cursor.
3. Use the Fetch statement to change the current record in the cursor and to store values into local variables.
4. Do something with the retrieved information.
5. If needed, repeat steps 3 and 4.
6. Use the Close statement to close the cursor. Most of the resources (memory, locks, and so on) will be released.
7. Use the Deallocate statement to deallocate the cursor.

NOTE

Transact-SQL cursors do not support processing blocks of records. Only one record can be fetched at a time.

It is best to show this process through an example. We will rewrite the stored procedure that we used to illustrate the use of the While statement. The purpose of this stored procedure is to collect the properties of a specified asset and return them in delimited format (Property = Value Unit;). The final result should look like this:

```
CPU=Pentium II;RAM=64 MB;HDD=6.4 GB;Resolution=1024x768;Weight=2 kg;
```

Here is the code for the new instance of the stored procedure:

```
Alter Procedure dbo.ap_InventoryProperties_Get_Cursor
/*****************************************************************
Return comma-delimited list of properties that are describing asset.
Property = Value unit;Property = Value unit;Property = Value unit;...

Output:      @chvProperties
Return:      n/a

             Name          Date         Description
Created by:  Dejan Sunderic 2005.04.18
Modified by:
```

```
test:
declare @p varchar(max)
exec dbo.ap_InventoryProperties_Get_Cursor 5, @p OUTPUT, 1
select @p

*********************************************************************/
    (
        @intInventoryId int,
        @chvProperties varchar(max) OUTPUT,
        @debug int = 0
    )

As

declare   @intCountProperties int,
          @intCounter int,
          @chvProperty varchar(50),
          @chvValue varchar(50),
          @chvUnit varchar(50)

Set @chvProperties = ''

Declare @CrsrVar Cursor

Set @CrsrVar = Cursor For
    select Property, Value, Unit
    from dbo.InventoryProperty InventoryProperty
        inner join dbo.Property Property
        on InventoryProperty.PropertyId = Property.PropertyId
    where InventoryProperty.InventoryId = @intInventoryId

Open @CrsrVar

Fetch Next From @CrsrVar
Into @chvProperty, @chvValue, @chvUnit

While (@@FETCH_STATUS = 0)
Begin

    Set @chvUnit = Coalesce(@chvUnit, '')

    If @debug <> 0
```

```
            Select @chvProperty Property,
                   @chvValue [Value],
                   @chvUnit [Unit]


        -- assemble list
        Set @chvProperties = @chvProperties + @chvProperty + '='
                           + @chvValue + ' ' +  @chvUnit + '; '
        If @debug <> 0
            Select @chvProperties chvProperties

        Fetch Next From @CrsrVar
        Into @chvProperty, @chvValue, @chvUnit

End

Close @CrsrVar
Deallocate @CrsrVar

Return 0
```

The stored procedure will first declare a cursor:

```
Declare @CrsrVar Cursor
```

The cursor will then be associated with the collection of properties related to the specified asset:

```
Set @CrsrVar = Cursor For
    Select Property, Value, Unit
    From dbo.InventoryProperty InventoryProperty
        inner join dbo.Property  Property
        On InventoryProperty.PropertyId = Property.PropertyId
    Where InventoryProperty.InventoryId = @intInventoryId
```

Before it can be used, the cursor needs to be opened:

```
Open @CrsrVar
```

The content of the first record can then be fetched into local variables:

```
Fetch Next From @CrsrVar
Into @chvProperty, @chvValue, @chvUnit
```

If the fetch was successful, we can start a loop to process the complete recordset:

```
While (@@FETCH_STATUS = 0)
```

After the values from the first record are processed, we read the next record:

```
    Fetch Next From @CrsrVar
    Into @chvProperty, @chvValue, @chvUnit
```

Once all records have been read, the value of @@fetch_status is set to −1 and we exit the loop. We need to close and deallocate the cursor and finish the stored procedure:

```
Close @CrsrVar
Deallocate @CrsrVar
```

Now, let's save and execute this stored procedure:

```
Declare @chvRes varchar(max)
Exec ap_InventoryProperties_Get_Cursor 5, @chvRes OUTPUT
Select @chvRes Properties
```

SQL Server will return the following:

```
Properties
--------------------------------------------------------------------
CPU=Pentium II ; RAM=64 MB; HDD=6.4 GB; Resolution=1024x768 ; Weight
=2 kg; Clock=366 MHz;
```

Cursor-related Statements and Functions

Let's review statements and functions that you need to utilize to control cursors.

The Declare Cursor Statement

The Declare Cursor statement declares the Transact-SQL cursor and specifies its behavior and the query on which it is built. It is possible to use syntax based on the SQL-92 standard or native Transact-SQL syntax. I will display only the simplified syntax. If you need more details, refer to SQL Server Books OnLine.

```
Declare cursor_name Cursor
For select_statement
```

The name of the cursor is an identifier that complies with the rules set for local variables.

The Open Statement

The Open statement executes the Select statement specified in the Declare Cursor statement and populates the cursor:

```
Open { { [Global] cursor_name } | cursor_variable_name}
```

The Fetch Statement

The Fetch statement reads the row specified in the Transact-SQL cursor:

```
Fetch    [    [ Next | Prior | First | Last
                | Absolute {n | @nvar}
                | Relative {n | @nvar}
            ]
            From
        ]
{ { [Global] cursor_name } | @cursor_variable_name}
[Into @variable_name[,...n] ]
```

This statement can force the cursor to position the current record at the Next, Prior, First, or Last record. It is also possible to specify the Absolute position of the record or a position Relative to the current record.

If the developer specifies a list of global variables in the Into clause, those variables will be filled with values from the specified record.

If the cursor has just been opened, you can use Fetch Next to read the first record.

@@ fetch_status

@@fetch_status is a function (or global variable) that returns the success code of the last Fetch statement executed during the current connection. It is often used as an exit criterion in loops that fetch records from a cursor.

Success Code	Description
0	Fetch was completely successful.
−1	The Fetch statement tried to read a record outside the recordset (last record was already read) or the Fetch statement failed.
−2	Record is missing (for example, somebody else has deleted the record in the meantime).

@@cursor_rows

As soon as the cursor is opened, the @@cursor_rows function (or global variable) is set to the number of records in the cursor (you can use this variable to loop through the cursor also).

When the cursor is of a dynamic or keyset type, the @@cursor_rows function will be set to a negative number to indicate it is being asynchronously populated.

The Close Statement

The Close statement closes an open cursor, releases the current recordset, and releases locks on rows held by the cursor:

```
Close { { [Global] cursor_name } | cursor_variable_name }
```

This statement must be executed on an opened cursor. If the cursor has just been declared, SQL Server will report an error.

The Deallocate Statement

After the Close statement, the structure of the cursor is still in place. It is possible to open it again. If you do not plan to use it anymore, you should remove the structure as well, by using the Deallocate statement:

```
Deallocate { { [Global] cursor_name } | @cursor_variable_name}
```

Problems with Cursors

Cursors are a valuable but dangerous tool. Their curse is precisely the problem they are designed to solve—the differences between the relational nature of database systems and the record-based nature of client applications.

First of all, cursors are procedural and thus contradict the basic idea behind the SQL language—that is, to define what is needed in a result, not how to get it.

Performance penalties are an even larger problem. Regular SQL statements are set-oriented and much faster. Some types of cursors lock records in the database and prevent other users from changing them. Other types of cursors create an additional copy of all records and then work with them. Both approaches have performance implications.

Client-side cursors and API server cursors are also not the most efficient way to transfer information between server and client. It is much faster to use a "fire hose" cursor, which is actually not a cursor at all. You can find more details about "fire hose" cursors in *Hitchhiker's Guide to Visual Basic and SQL Server,* 6th edition, by William Vaughn (Microsoft Press, 1998).

The Justified Uses of Cursors

The rule of thumb is to avoid the use of cursors whenever possible. However, in some cases, such avoidance is not possible.

Cursors can be used to perform operations that cannot be performed using set-oriented statements. It is acceptable to use cursors to perform processing based on statements, stored procedures, and extended stored procedures, which are designed to work with one item at a time. For example, the sp_addrolemember system stored procedure is designed to set an existing user account as a member of the SQL Server role. If you can list users that need to be assigned to a role, you can loop through them (using a cursor) and execute the system stored procedure for each of them.

Excessive processing based on a single row (for example, business logic implemented in the form of an extended stored procedure) can also be implemented using a cursor. If you implement such a loop in a stored procedure instead of in a client application, you can reduce network traffic considerably.

Another example could be the export of a group of tables from a database to text files using bcp. The bcp utility is a command-prompt program that can work with one table at a time. To use it within a stored procedure, you need to execute it using the xp_cmdshell extended stored procedure, which can run just one command at a time:

```
Alter Procedure util.ap_Tables_BcpOut
--loop through tables and export them to text files
     @debug int = 0
As

Declare    @chvTable varchar(128),
           @chvCommand varchar(255)

Declare @curTables Cursor

-- get all USER-DEFINED tables from current database
Set @curTables = Cursor FOR
    select name
     from sysobjects
     where xType = 'U'

Open @curTables

-- get first table
Fetch Next From @curTables
Into @chvTable

-- if we successfully read the current record
While (@@fetch_status = 0)
```

```
Begin

    -- assemble DOS command for exporting table
    Set @chvCommand = 'bcp "Asset5..[' + @chvTable
                    + ']" out D:\backup\' + @chvTable
                    + '.txt -c -q -Sdejan -Usa -Pdejan'
    -- during test just display command
    If @debug <> 0
        Select @chvCommand chvCommand

    -- in production execute DOS command and export table
    If @debug = 0
        Execute master.dbo.xp_cmdshell @chvCommand, NO_OUTPUT

    Fetch Next From @curTables
    Into @chvTable

End

Close @curTables
Deallocate @curTables

Return 0
```

If you execute this stored procedure (without specifying the @debug parameter), SQL Server will execute the following sequence of command-prompt commands to export tables:

```
bcp "Asset5..[InventorySum]" out D:\backup\InventorySum.txt -c -q
-Sdejan -Usa -Pdejan
bcp "Asset5..[EqType]" out D:\backup\EqType.txt -c -q
-Sdejan -Usa -Pdejan
bcp "Asset5..[AcquisitionType]" out D:\backup\AcquisitionType.txt -c -q
-Sdejan -Usa -Pdejan
bcp "Asset5..[Action]" out D:\backup\Action.txt -c -q -Sdejan -Usa -Pdejan
bcp "Asset5..[Contact]" out D:\backup\Contact.txt -c -q
-Sdejan -Usa -Pdejan
bcp "Asset5..[Contact_with_BC]" out D:\backup\Contact_with_BC.txt -c -q
-Sdejan -Usa -Pdejan
bcp "Asset5..[EquipmentBC]" out D:\backup\EquipmentBC.txt -c -q
-Sdejan -Usa -Pdejan
bcp "Asset5..[Inventory]" out D:\backup\Inventory.txt -c -q -Sdejan
-Usa -Pdejan
```

```
bcp "Asset5..[InventoryProperty]" out D:\backup\InventoryProperty.txt
-c -q -Sdejan -Usa -Pdejan
bcp "Asset5..[InventoryXML]" out D:\backup\InventoryXML.txt -c -q
-Sdejan -Usa -Pdejan
...
```

TIP

In Chapter 15, in the "A While Loop with Min() or Max() Functions" section, I will demonstrate another method for looping through a set of records using the While statement. Personally, I seldom use cursors; I prefer to use the method demonstrated in Chapter 15 for operations that cannot be implemented with set operations.

CHAPTER
4

Functions

IN THIS CHAPTER

Using Functions

Types of Functions

Microsoft has done a fantastic job providing database administrators and developers with an extensive set of built-in functions for SQL Server. Since SQL Server 2000, you are also able to create your own T-SQL functions. In SQL Server 2005 it is possible to design functions in .NET languages as well. We will cover the design of T-SQL user-defined functions in detail in Chapter 10 and .NET functions in Chapters 11 to 14, and focus here on the uses of functions and their attributes.

Using Functions

Functions are T-SQL elements that are used to evaluate zero or more input parameters and return data to the caller. The syntax for calling a function is

```
Function_name ([parameter] [,...n])
```

For example, the Sin() function has the following syntax:

```
Sin(float_expression)
```

So, to display the sine of 45 degrees, you would use

```
SELECT Sin(45)
```

Some functions accept more than one parameter, and some do not require parameters at all. For example, the GetDate() function, which returns the current date and time on the system clock to the caller, accepts no parameters. We will use the GetDate() function to illustrate the most common ways to use functions in T-SQL.

In Selection and Assignment

Functions can be used to represent a value or a part of a value to be assigned or selected in a Set or Select statement. In the following example, two variables are populated using values stored in the selected record and a third variable is populated using a function:

```
Select  @chvMake = Make,
        @Model = Model,
        @dtsCurrentDate = GetDate()
from dbo.Equipment
where EquipmentID = @intEqId
```

As previously noted, this use is not limited to the Select statement. Values can be assigned in the Set statement, displayed in the Print statement, stored in a table using Update and Insert, or even used as parameters for other functions:

```
Create Procedure dbo.ap_Schedule_Insert
    @intLeaseId int,
    @intLeaseFrequencyId int
As


Insert dbo.LeaseSchedule(LeaseId, StartDate,
                            EndDate, LeaseFrequencyId)
Values (@intLeaseId, GetDate(),
      DateAdd(Year, 3, GetDate()), @intLeaseFrequencyId)


Return
```

This procedure inserts the current date using the GetDate() function in the StartDate column. The EndDate column is calculated using the DateAdd() function, which accepts the GetDate() function as one parameter. It is used to set the end date three years from the current date. This was just an example of the usage of functions; you will be able to see more details about GetDate() and DateAdd() in the "Date and Time Functions" section of this chapter.

As Part of the Selection Criteria

Functions are often used in the Where clause of T-SQL statements:

```
SELECT Inventory.InventoryId
FROM LeaseSchedule INNER JOIN Inventory
    ON LeaseSchedule.ScheduleId = Inventory.LeaseScheduleId
WHERE (LeaseSchedule.EndDate < GetDate())
AND (Inventory.Rent <> 0)
```

This Select statement selects the lease schedules that have reached the end of the term by comparing EndDate to the current date.

In Expressions

You can also use functions anywhere you can use an expression, such as in an If statement, which requires a Boolean expression to determine further execution steps:

```
If @dtmLeaseEndDate < GetDate()
    Begin
        ...
    end
```

As Check and Default Constraints

Functions can also be used to define Check and Default constraints:

```
ALTER TABLE [dbo].[Order] (
    [OrderId] [int] IDENTITY (1, 1) NOT null ,
    [OrderDate] [smalldatetime] NOT null ,
    [RequestedById] [int] NOT null ,
    [TargetDate] [smalldatetime] NOT null ,
    [CompletionDate] [smalldatetime] null ,
    [DestinationLocationId] [int] null
) ON [PRIMARY]

GO

ALTER TABLE [dbo].[Order] WITH NOCHECK ADD
   CONSTRAINT [DF_Order_OrderDate] DEFAULT (GetDate()) FOR [OrderDate],
   CONSTRAINT [PK_Order] PRIMARY KEY  CLUSTERED
 (
   [OrderId]
 )  ON [PRIMARY]
GO
```

In this case, the Order table will automatically set the OrderDate field to the current date if a value is not supplied.

Instead of Tables

Because SQL Server has a `table` data type, it is also possible for a function to return a recordset. Such functions are referred to as *table-valued functions.* These functions can be used in T-SQL statements anywhere tables are expected. In the following example, the result of the function is joined with a table (dbo.EqType) to produce a new result set:

```
declare @dtmLastMonth datetime
set @dtmLastMonth = DateAdd(month, -1, GetDate())
Select *
from dbo.fnNewEquipment (@dtmLastMonth) NewEq
inner join dbo.EqType  EqType
on NewEq.EqTypeId = EqType.EqTypeId
```

To reference any user-defined function including a table-valued function, you must specify the object owner along with the function name (*owner.function*).

The only exception to this rule is in the use of built-in table-valued functions. In this case, you must place two colons (::) in front of the function name. For example, the fn_ListExtendedProperty() function lists properties of the database object (see Figure 4-1). For more details about extended properties, see Chapter 15.

Types of Functions

Based on the type of result that is returned, there are two primary groups of built-in functions:

▶ Scalar

▶ Rowset

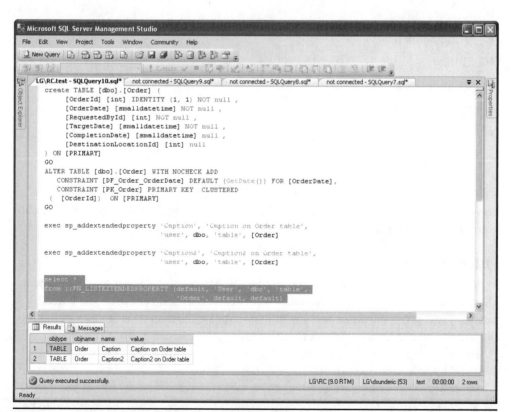

Figure 4-1   *Using table-valued user-defined functions*

Scalar Functions

Most of the time when we refer to functions, we are thinking of the scalar type. The name of this type refers to the fact that these functions return only one value.

Based on their functionality (although not necessarily their return values), we can divide scalar functions into the following groups:

- ▶ System
- ▶ Date and time
- ▶ String
- ▶ Mathematical
- ▶ Metadata
- ▶ Security
- ▶ Cryptographic
- ▶ Text and image
- ▶ Cursor
- ▶ Configuration
- ▶ System statistical
- ▶ Aggregate
- ▶ Ranking

We will not be able to cover in detail all the built-in functions available in SQL Server, but we will discuss the key functions that you will use most frequently. You can find complete documentation of all built-in functions in SQL Server Books OnLine.

System Functions

System functions return information related to the Microsoft SQL Server environment. They are used to return object names and identifiers, the current user, the current database, session, application, and login; to investigate the data type of an expression; and to perform conversions between data types.

Let's examine some of the system functions that are likely to be more frequently used and look at some examples.

Conditional Expression: Case   In other programming languages, Case is considered to be a flow-control programming construct. In earlier versions of SQL Server documentation,

Case was classified as an expression. Since SQL Server 7.0, it is classified as a function, which is mathematically more correct. However, all of these classifications are more or less true.

The Case function/expression enables the user to evaluate an expression and to return the value associated with the result of the expression. For example, the Case function/expression in the following stored procedure returns the approximate number of days associated with a leasing schedule:

```
Create Procedure dbo.ap_LeasePeriodDuration_Get
-- return approximate number of days associated with lease frequency
    @inyScheduleFrequencyId tinyint,
    @insDays smallint OUTPUT
As
Declare @chvScheduleFrequency varchar(50)

Select @chvScheduleFrequency = ScheduleFrequency
From dbo.ScheduleFrequency
where ScheduleFrequencyId = @inyScheduleFrequencyId
select @insDays =
    Case @chvScheduleFrequency
         When 'monthly' then 30
         When 'semi-monthly' then 15
         When 'bi-weekly' then 14
         When 'weekly' then 7
         When 'quarterly' then 92
         When 'yearly' then 365
    END
return
```

The Case function/expression works much like a Select statement with nested If statements. In fact, most of the time, you can write equivalent code using nested If statements.

There are two types of Case functions/expressions:

▶ Simple Case functions/expressions

▶ Searched Case functions/expressions

A simple Case function/expression has the following syntax:

```
Case input_expression
    WHEN when_expression THEN result_expression
        [...n]
```

```
    [
        ELSE else_result_expression
    ]
END
```

The previous example used this kind of Case function/expression. SQL Server attempts to match the *input_expression* with one of the *when_expression*s. If it is successful, it returns the *result_expression* associated with the first matching *when_expression*. An Else clause is also part of the Case function/expression. If the value of the *input_expression* is not equal to either of the *when_expression*s, the function returns the value of the *else_result_expression*.

A searched Case function/expression is very similar. The only difference is that it does not have an *input_expression*. The complete criteria are inside the When clause in the form of a Boolean expression:

```
Case
    WHEN Boolean_expression THEN result_expression
        [...n]
    [
        ELSE else_result_expression
    ]
END
```

SQL Server returns the *result_expression* associated with the first *Boolean_expression*, which is true. If all *Boolean_expression*s are false, SQL Server returns the *else_result_expression*.

In the following example, a searched Case function/expression has to be used because the *Boolean_expression*s have different operators (= and Like):

```
Create Procedure dbo.ap_LeaseInfo_List
-- list all lease contract information
As

Select LeaseVendor [Lease Vendor],
        LeaseNumber [Lease Number],
        Case -- some vendors have id of sales reps
            -- incorporated in lease numbers
            When LeaseVendor = 'Trigon FS'
                Then Substring(LeaseNumber, 5, 12)
            When LeaseVendor Like 'EB%'
                Then Substring(LeaseNumber, 9, 8)
            When LeaseVendor Like 'MMEX%'
                Then Substring(LeaseNumber, 7, 6)
```

```
                When LeaseVendor = 'DAFS'
                        Then Substring(LeaseNumber, 8, 11)
                Else 'Unknown'
        end [Lease Agent],
    ContractDate [Contract Date]
from dbo.Lease
```

TIP

Although both examples use Case functions/expressions as a part of the Select statement, keep in mind that you can use them anywhere that you can place an expression. This flexibility might come in very handy in some situations.

Getting Information About Data   You can use numerous functions to return information about expressions, the most important of which are the following:

► IsDate()

► IsNumeric()

► DataLength()

► Binary_CheckSum()

IsDate() is a function that is used to determine whether an expression is a valid date. It is particularly useful when you need to read data from text files. If the result of this function is 1 (true), SQL Server guarantees that you will be able to convert the data to the `datetime` data type. IsDate() uses the following syntax:

```
IsDate(expression)
```

In the following stored procedure, SQL Server verifies that Lease Data (received as a string) can be converted to a `datetime` value. It then stores this result with the rest of the parameters in the Lease table.

```
Create Procedure dbo.ap_LeaseContract_Load
-- insert lease contract information and return id of lease
        @chvLeaseVendor varchar(50),
        @chvLeaseNumber varchar(50),
        @chvLeaseDate varchar(50),
        @intLeaseId int OUTPUT
As
Declare @intError int

-- test validity of date
```

```
if IsDate(@chvLeaseDate) = 0
begin
     Raiserror ('Unable to Convert to date.', 16, 1)
     return -1
end

insert into dbo.Lease(LeaseVendor, LeaseNumber, ContractDate)
values (@chvLeaseVendor, @chvLeaseNumber,
        Convert(smalldatetime, @chvLeaseDate))

select @intLeaseId = Scope_Identity()

return
```

You can use the IsNumeric() function to determine whether it is possible to convert a character value or expression into one of the numeric data types (`int`, `smallint`, `tinyint`, `real`, `float`, `money`, `smallmoney`, `decimal`, or `numeric`). IsNumeric() uses the following syntax:

```
IsNumeric(expression)
```

The DataLength() function returns the number of bytes used to store or display an expression. This information is particularly useful when processing variable-length character data types.

NOTE

DataLength() returns the number of bytes used to store the expression, not the number of characters, as does the Len() function. For example, each character in the `nvarchar` data type (or any of the Unicode data types) uses 2 bytes.

The DataLength() function uses the following syntax:

```
DataLength(expression)
```

If you assign a string value to a variable and that value is too long, SQL Server will not report an error. It will simply truncate the value and assign it. You can use this function to prevent such behavior:

```
If DataLength(@Select) + DataLength(@From) + DataLength(@Where) <= 8000
    Select @SQL = @Select + @From + @Where
```

This example was critical on SQL Server 2000 and SQL Server 7. On SQL Server 2005 it is possible to define string variables using `varchar(max)` or `nvarchar(max)`.

SQL Server 2000 introduced the Binary_CheckSum() function, which calculates the binary checksum of a specified expression or set of table columns. It is designed to detect changes in a record. This function uses the following syntax:

```
Binary_CheckSum(*|expression[,...n])
```

TIP

Binary_CheckSum() is a much-needed tool for data warehousing projects. It allows DBAs to detect and handle the problem of "slowly changing dimensions" types 2 and 3.

The following stored procedure compares the binary checksum of columns containing new information with the checksum of columns already stored in the table; if the values do not match, the new data will be inserted into the table:

```
CREATE Procedure ap_Equipment_Update
-- Check if values were changed in the meantime
-- Update values in equipment table.
        @intEqId int,
        @chvMake varchar(50),
        @chvModel varchar(50),
        @intEqTypeId int,
        @debug int = 0
As
declare @intNewEqBC int

set @intNewEqBC = Binary_CheckSum(@chvMake,
                                  @chvModel,
                                  @intEqTypeId)
if @debug <> 0
    Select @intNewEqBC NewBC
if @debug <> 0
    select EqBC OldBC
    from EquipmentBC
    where EqId = @intEqId

if not exists (Select EqBC
              from EquipmentBC
              where EqId = @intEqId)
    insert EquipmentBC (EqId, EqBC)
        select @intEqId,
            Binary_CheckSum(Make, Model, EqTypeId)
        from Equipment
        where EqId = @intEqId
```

```
-- Check if values were changed in the meanwhile
if @intNewEqBC <> (Select EqBC
                        from EquipmentBC
                        where EqId = @intEqId)
begin
    if @debug <> 0
        select 'Information will be updated.'

    -- update information
    update Equipment
    Set  Make = @chvMake,
         Model = @chvModel,
         EqTypeId = @intEqTypeId
    where EqId = @intEqId

    if exists(select EqId
              from    EquipmentBC
              where   EqId = @intEqId)
        update EquipmentBC
        Set EqBC = @intNewEqBC
        where EqId = @intEqId
    else
        insert EquipmentBC (EqId, EqBC)
        values (@intEqId, @intNewEqBC)
end
return
```

Binary_CheckSum() is case-sensitive. It evaluates columns/expressions differently depending on the case (uppercase/lowercase) used in the column or expression. This might seem unusual since most SQL Server behavior depends on the code page that you select during installation. If the default is selected, SQL Server ignores the case of characters when matching them. The nature of the algorithm used to implement the Binary_CheckSum() function is such that it cannot work that way. Fortunately, SQL Server contains a CheckSum() function that ignores the case of the characters in arguments.

These functions are also valuable for comparing and indexing long string columns. Instead of creating an index on such column, you can add a column based on the checksum or binary checksum of the value in the string column and index it instead. This type of index is typically called a *hash index*. SQL Server will find matching records by comparing int values instead of comparing long strings, which might provide significant performance improvement.

Functions for Handling null Values   SQL Server is equipped with a set of three functions to help ease the pain of using null in your database system:

```
NullIf(expression, expression)
IsNull(check_expression, replacement_value)
Coalesce(expression [,...n])
```

NullIf() returns null if two expressions in the function are the same value. If the expressions are not equivalent, the function returns the value of the first expression.

This function can be useful when calculating the average of columns that accept null values. For example, let's assume that the author of the Asset database has created constraints or stored procedures such that a user can leave the value of the Inventory .Rent column as either null or zero when equipment is not leased. In this case, the Avg() function for calculating the average of the column will eliminate records containing null from the average but keep records with zero. It is not that the Avg() function is implemented improperly, but rather that our design can be improved. It is possible to implement a workaround using the NullIf() function:

```
select    AVG(Rent) [average without nulls],
          AVG(NullIf(Rent, 0)) [average without nulls and zeros]
from Inventory
```

An average calculated in this way will be different from an average calculated in the standard way:

```
average without nulls average without nulls and zeros
-------------------- ------------------------------
100.0000                150.0000
(1 row(s) affected)
```

```
Warning: Null value eliminated from aggregate.
```

The IsNull() function examines the *check_expression*. If its value is null, the function returns the *replacement_value*. If the value of the *check_expression* is not null, the function returns the *check_expression*.

Let's suppose you want to calculate an average based on the total number of computers in the Inventory table. You can use the IsNull() value to replace null values during the calculation:

```
select AVG(Rent) [Eliminating nulls],
       AVG(ISNULL(rent, 0)) [with nulls as zeros]
from Inventory
```

The average price of computers which counts nulls as zeros is less than the average that ignores computers with the price set to null:

```
Eliminating nulls  with nulls as zeros
-----------------  --------------------
100.0000              75.0000


(1 row(s) affected)

Warning: Null value eliminated from aggregate.
```

The last line is a warning that refers to the fact that null values are excluded when Avg() is calculated.

NOTE

The name of this function is confusing, especially if you are a Visual Basic programmer. It cannot be used to test whether the value of an expression is null. You should use these operators instead:

```
If expression IS null
If expression IS NOT null
```

The Coalesce() function is often used to coalesce (unite) values that are split into several columns. The result of the function is the first non-null expression. This function uses the following syntax:

```
COALESCE(expression [,...n])
```

In the following example, we coalesce values from three columns (Rent, Lease, and Cost) into one value (Acquisition Cost). Coalesce() evaluates the input expressions and returns the first non-null value.

```
SELECT Inventory.Inventoryid,
       Equipment.Make + ' ' + Equipment.Model Equipment,
       AcquisitionType.AcquisitionType,
       COALESCE(Inventory.Rent, Inventory.Lease, Inventory.Cost) [Cost]
FROM Inventory INNER JOIN AcquisitionType ON
     Inventory.AcquisitionTypeID = AcquisitionType.AcquisitionTypeId
             INNER JOIN Equipment
        ON Inventory.EquipmentId = Equipment.EquipmentId
```

The result contains just one column, showing the cost of acquisition:

```
Inventoryid Equipment                           AcquisitionType Cost
----------- ------------------------------      --------------- ---------
5           Toshiba Portege 7020CT              Purchase        1295.0000
6           Toshiba Portege 7020CT              Rent             200.0000
8           Toshiba Portege 7020CT              Lease             87.7500
10          Toshiba Portege 7020CT              Lease             99.9500
```

Conversion Functions   The Cast() and Convert() functions are used to explicitly convert the information in one data type to another specified data type. There is just one small difference between these two functions: Convert() allows you to specify the format of the result, whereas Cast() does not. Their syntax is

```
Cast(expression AS data_type)
Convert(data_type[(length)], expression [, style])
```

In this case, *expression* is any value or expression that you want to convert, and *data_type* is the new data type. The following statement concatenates two strings and an error number and returns them as a string:

```
Select "Error ["+Cast(@@Error as varchar)+"] has occurred."
```

The result is an error number integrated with a sentence, which might be useful in an error handling situation:

```
-----------------------------------------------------
Error [373] has occurred.
```

In the Convert() function, *style* refers to the formatting style used in the conversion of date and time (datetime, smalldatetime) or numeric (money, smallmoney, float, real) expressions to strings (varchar, char, nvarchar, nchar). The following command displays the current date in the default and German style:

```
select GetDate() standard, Convert(varchar, GetDate(), 104) German
```

The result is

```
standard                      German
----------------------------  ------------------------------
2003-07-11 11:45:57.730       11.07.2003
```

Style with Two-digit Year	Style with Four-digit Year	Standard	Format
–	0 or 100	Default	mon dd yyyy hh:miAM (or PM)
1	101	USA	mm/dd/yy
2	102	ANSI	yy.mm.dd
3	103	British/French	dd/mm/yy
4	104	German	dd.mm.yy
5	105	Italian	dd-mm-yy
6	106	–	dd mon yy
7	107	–	mon dd, yy
8	108	–	hh:mm:ss
–	9 or 109	Default + milliseconds	mon dd yyyy hh:mi:ss:mmmAM (or PM)
10	110	USA	mm-dd-yy
11	111	Japan	yy/mm/dd
12	112	ISO	yymmdd
-	13 or 113	Europe default + milliseconds	dd mon yyyy hh:mm:ss:mmm(24h)
14	114	–	hh:mi:ss:mmm(24h)
–	20 or 120	ODBC canonical	yyyy-mm-dd hh:mi:ss(24h)
–	21 or 121	ODBC canonical (with milliseconds)	yyyy-mm-dd hh:mi:ss.mmm(24h)
–	130	Kuwaiti	dd/mm/yyyy hh:mi:ss.mmmAM
–	131	Kuwaiti	dd mm yyyy hh:mi:ss.mmmAM

Table 4-1   *Formatting Styles for* `datetime` *Information*

Table 4-1 lists formatting styles that you can use when converting `datetime` to character or character to `datetime` information.

The following table lists formatting styles that you can use when converting monetary values to character information:

Value	Output
0 (default)	Two digits behind decimal point No commas every three digits Example: 1234.56
1	Two digits behind decimal point Commas every three digits Example: 1,234.56
2	Four digits behind decimal point No commas every three digits Example: 1234.5678

In the following example, we format a monetary value:

```
Select    $12345678.90,
          Convert(varchar(30), $12345678.90, 0),
          Convert(varchar(30), $12345678.90, 1),
          Convert(varchar(30), $12345678.90, 2)
```

The result is

```
-------------- -------------- ---------------- --------------
12345678.9000 12345678.90    12,345,678.90    12345678.9000
```

Value	Output
0 (default)	In scientific notation, when needed; six digits maximum
1	Eight digits always in scientific notation
2	Sixteen digits always in scientific notation

TIP

Microsoft recommends using the Cast() function whenever the formatting power of Convert() is not required because Cast() is compatible with the ANSI SQL-92 standard.

When you specify the target data type of variable length as a part of the Cast() or Convert() functions, you should include its length, too. If you do not specify length, SQL Server assigns a default length of 30. Therefore, the previous example could be written as

```
Select    $12345678.90,
          Convert(varchar, $12345678.90, 0),
          Convert(varchar, $12345678.90, 1),
          Convert(varchar, $12345678.90, 2)
```

You need to use conversion functions when you do any of the following:

▶ Supply a Transact-SQL statement or function with a value in a specific data type

▶ Set the format of a date or number

▶ Obtain a value that uses an exotic data type

In some cases, SQL Server automatically (that is, behind the scenes) converts the value if the required data type and the supplied data type are compatible. For example, if some function requires a `char` parameter, you could supply a `datetime` parameter and SQL Server will perform an *implicit conversion* of the value. In the opposite direction, you must use an *explicit conversion*—that is, you must use conversion functions. If it is not possible to convert the expression to the specified data type, SQL Server raises an error.

TIP

SQL Server Books OnLine includes a table that lists which data types can be converted to other data types and which kind of conversion (explicit or implicit) is required.

Information About the Current Session   The following functions return information associated with the current session (for instance, how you logged on to the server, your username in the database, the name of the server, the permissions you have in the current database, and so on):

Function	Description
App_Name()	Name of the application that opened the session.
Host_Id()	ID of the computer hosting the client application.
Host_Name()	Name of the computer hosting the client application.
Permissions()	Bitmap that specifies permissions on a selected column, a database object, or the current database.
Current_User	Name of the database user, same as User_Name().
Session_User	Name of the database user who owns the current session.
System_User	Name of the server login that owns the current session. If the user has logged on to the server using Microsoft Windows NT Authentication, this function returns the Windows NT login.
User_Name()	Name of the database user, same as Current_User.

The following stored procedure uses the System_User function to identify the user adding an order to the system:

```
create procedure dbo.ap_Order_Add
-- insert Order record
    @dtmOrderDate datetime = null,
    @dtmTargetDate datetime = null,
    @chvUserName varchar(128) = null,
    @intDestinationLocation int,
    @chvNote varchar(200),
    @intOrderid int OUTPUT

As

    declare      @intRequestedById int

    -- If user didn't specify order date
    -- default is today.
    if @dtmOrderDate = null
        Set @dtmOrderDate = GetDate()

    -- If user didn't specify target date
    -- default is 3 days after request date.
    if @dtmTargetDate = null
        Set @dtmTargetDate = DateAdd(day, 3, @dtmOrderDate)

    -- if user didn't identify himself
    -- try to identify him using login name
    if @chvUserName = null
        Set @chvUserName = System_User

    -- get Id of the user
    select @intRequestedById = ContactId
    from dbo.Contact
    where UserName = @chvUserName

    -- if you cannot identify user report an error
    If @intRequestedById = null
    begin
        Raiserror('Unable to identify user in Contact table!', 1, 2)
        return -1
    end
```

```
-- and finally create Order
Insert into [Order](OrderDate, RequestedById, TargetDate,
                    DestinationLocationId)
Values (@dtmOrderDate, @intRequestedById, @dtmTargetDate,
        @intDestinationLocation)

set @intOrderid = Scope_identity()

return
```

NOTE

Some functions such as System_User and Current_User do not require and cannot be used with pair of parentheses ().

Functions for Handling Identity Values *Identity* columns are used in SQL Server tables to automatically generate unique identifiers for each record. Numbers that are generated in this manner are based on two values—*identity seed* and *identity increment*. SQL Server starts assigning identity values from an identity seed, and every row is given a value that is greater than the previous one by the value specified in the identity increment (or less than that value if you use a negative increment value).

In Chapter 3, we covered the use of the @@identity function/global variable. It returns the last value generated by SQL Server while inserting record(s) into the table with an identity value:

```
Declare @intEqId int
Insert into Equipment(Make, Model, EqTypeId)
Values ('ACME', 'Turbo', 2)
Select @intEqId = @@identity
Select @intEqId [EqId]
```

The Scope_Identity() function returns the last identity value generated in the scope of the current process. We will discuss in detail usage of the Scope_Identity() function and the problems it solves in the "Using Identity Values" section of Chapter 15.

```
Declare @intEqId int
Insert into Equipment(Make, Model, EqTypeId)
Values ('ACME', 'Turbo', 2)
Select @intEqId = Scope_Identity()
Select @intEqId [EqId]
```

TIP

Always use Scope_Identity() instead of @@identity.

The Ident_Seed() and Ident_Incr() functions return to the user the values of the seed and the increment for the selected table or view:

```
Select IDENT_SEED('Inventory'), IDENT_INCR('Inventory')
```

The Identity() function allows a user to generate identity values while using the Select...Into command. Let me remind you that this command selects records and immediately inserts them into a new table. Without it, you would be forced to create a new table with an identity column and then insert the selected records into the table. With it, everything can be achieved in one step:

```
SELECT    Identity(int, 1,1) AS ID,
          Property.Property,
          InventoryProperty.Value,
          Property.Unit
INTO #InventoryProperty
FROM dbo.InventoryProperty InventoryProperty
   INNER JOIN dbo.Property Property
   ON InventoryProperty.PropertyId = Property.PropertyId
WHERE (InventoryProperty.InventoryId = 12)
```

Ident_Current() returns the last identity value set for a specified table (in any scope of any process). To use it, just supply the table name as a parameter:

```
Select Ident_Current('Equipment')
```

Date and Time Functions
The following set of functions is designed to process data and time values and expressions.

Get (Current) Date   GetDate() is the function that you will probably use more often than any other date and time function. It will return the system time in `datetime` format. We have already demonstrated the use of this function in the first section of this chapter, "Using Functions."

GetUtcDate() is the function that returns the date and time for the Greenwich time zone, also known as Universal Time Coordinate (UTC).

Extracting Parts of Date and Time   From time to time, you will need to extract just one component of the date and time value. The basic functionality necessary to achieve this end is implemented in the following three functions:

```
DAY(date)
MONTH(date)
YEAR(date)
```

These functions require expressions of the datetime or smalldatetime data type, and they all return the corresponding integer value.

The DatePart() and DateName() functions provide similar functionality, but they are more flexible:

```
DatePart(datepart, date)
DateName(datepart, date)
```

The user can specify which component of the date to obtain by supplying a *datepart* constant from Table 4-2 (you can use either the full name or the abbreviation).

DatePart() then returns the value of the *datepart,* and DateName() returns the string that contains the appropriate name. Naturally, DateName() is not meaningful in some cases (for example, year, second) and SQL Server will return the same value as it would for DatePart(). The following Select statement shows how you can use date functions:

```
SELECT    GetDate()'Date',
          DateName(month, GetDate()) AS 'Month Name',
          DatePart(yyyy, GetDate()) AS 'Year'
```

Notice that the first parameter is not a character parameter. You cannot fill it using an expression or variable. SQL Server will return the following:

```
Date                       Month Name       Year
-------------------------  ---------------  -----------
2003-02-20 00:45:40.867    February         2003
```

Datepart—Full	Datepart—Abbreviation
Millisecond	ms
Second	Ss, s
Minute	Mi, n
Hour	Hh
Weekday	Dw
Week	wk, ww
Dayofyear	Dy, y
Day	Dd, d
Month	mm, m
Quarter	qq, q
Year	yy, yyyy

Table 4-2 *Dateparts and Abbreviations Recognized by SQL Server*

Date and Time Calculations   Transact-SQL contains two functions for performing calculations on date and time expressions:

```
DateAdd(datepart, number, date)
DateDiff(datepart, startdate, enddate)
```

DateAdd() is used to add a *number* of *datepart* intervals to the specified *date* value. DateDiff() returns the number of *datepart* intervals between a *startdate* and an *enddate.* Both of these functions use a value from Table 4-2 to specify *datepart.* The following stored procedure uses these functions to list the due dates for leases:

```
Alter Procedure ap_Terms_List
-- return list of due days for the leasing
    @dtsStartDate smalldatetime,
    @dtsEndDate smalldatetime,
    @chvLeaseFrequency varchar(20)
As
set nocount on

declare @insDueDates smallint -- number of intervals

-- calculate number of DueDates
select @insDueDates =
    Case @chvLeaseFrequency
        When 'monthly'
            then DateDiff(month, @dtsStartDate, @dtsEndDate)
        When 'semi-monthly'
            then 2 * DateDiff(month, @dtsStartDate, @dtsEndDate)
        When 'bi-weekly'
            then DateDiff(week, @dtsStartDate, @dtsEndDate)/2
        When 'weekly'
            then DateDiff(week, @dtsStartDate, @dtsEndDate)
        When 'quarterly'
            then DateDiff(qq, @dtsStartDate, @dtsEndDate)
        When 'yearly'
            then DateDiff(y, @dtsStartDate, @dtsEndDate)
    END

-- generate list of due dates using temporary table
Create table #DueDates (ID int)

while @insDueDates >= 0
```

```
begin
    insert #DueDates (ID)
    values (@insDueDates)

    select @insDueDates = @insDueDates - 1
end

-- display list of Due dates
select ID+1, Convert(varchar,
    Case
        When @chvLeaseFrequency = 'monthly'
            then DateAdd(month,ID, @dtsStartDate)
        When @chvLeaseFrequency = 'semi-monthly'
        and ID/2 =  CAST(ID as float)/2
            then DateAdd(month, ID/2, @dtsStartDate)
        When @chvLeaseFrequency = 'semi-monthly'
        and ID/2 <> CAST(ID as float)/2
            then DateAdd(dd, 15,
                         DateAdd(month, ID/2, @dtsStartDate))
        When @chvLeaseFrequency = 'bi-weekly'
            then DateAdd(week, ID*2, @dtsStartDate)
        When @chvLeaseFrequency = 'weekly'
            then DateAdd(week, ID, @dtsStartDate)
        When @chvLeaseFrequency = 'quarterly'
            then DateAdd(qq, ID, @dtsStartDate)
        When @chvLeaseFrequency = 'yearly'
            then DateAdd(y, ID, @dtsStartDate)
    END , 105) [Due date]
from #DueDates
order by ID

-- wash the dishes
drop table #DueDates

return
```

You can see the result of the stored procedure in Figure 4-2.

String Functions

Microsoft SQL Server supports a relatively elaborate set of string functions. (Who would expect such a thing from a tool originally developed in C?)

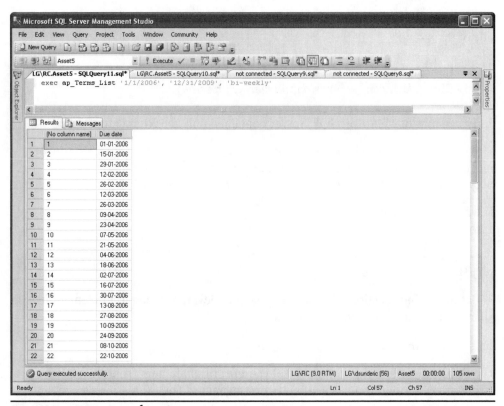

Figure 4-2 *Execution of ap_Terms_List*

Basic String Manipulation   The Len() function uses the following syntax:

```
Len(string_expression)
```

This function returns the length of a string in characters. The input parameter can be any kind of string expression. DataLength(), a similar system function, returns the number of bytes occupied by the value.

```
declare @chvEquipment varchar(30)
set @chvEquipment = 'Toshiba Portege 7020CT'
select Len(@chvEquipment)
```

The result is

```
-----------
22
```

The following two functions return the number of characters from the left or right side of the string:

Left(*character_expression, integer_expression*)
Right(*character_expression, integer_expression*)

Early versions of Microsoft SQL Server contained only the Right() function:

```
declare @chvEquipment varchar(30)
set @chvEquipment = 'Toshiba Portege 7020CT'
select Left(@chvEquipment, 7) Make, Right(@chvEquipment, 14) Model
```

The result of this batch is

```
Make      Model
-------   --------------
Toshiba   Portege 7020CT
```

Before the introduction of the Left() function, developers had to implement its functionality using the SubString() function:

```
SubString(expression, start, length)
```

The SubString() function returns a set (*length*) of characters from the string (*expression*) starting from a specified (*start*) character. The *expression* can be any character or any `text`, `image`, or `binary` data type. Because of this data type flexibility, the *length* and *start* parameters are based on the number of *bytes* when the *expression* is of the `text`, `image`, `binary`, or `varbinary` data types, rather than on the number of characters. In the case of Unicode data types, one character occupies 2 bytes. If you specify an odd number, you may get unexpected results in the form of split characters.

The following batch extracts part of a string:

```
declare @chvEquipment varchar(30)
set @chvEquipment = 'Toshiba Portege 7020CT'
select SubString(@chvEquipment, 9, 7)
```

The result set is

```
-------
Portege
```

The CharIndex() function returns the index of the first occurrence of a string (*expression1*) within a second string (*expression2*):

```
CharIndex(expression1, expression2 [, start_location])
```

There is an optional parameter that allows you to specify the start location for the search:

```
Create Procedure ap_SplitFullName
-- split full name received in format 'Sunderic, Dejan'
-- into last and first name
-- default delimiter is comma and space ', ',
-- but caller can specify other
    @chvFullName varchar(50),
    @chvDelimiter varchar(3) = ', ',
    @chvFirstName varchar(50) OUTPUT,
    @chvLastName varchar(50) OUTPUT
As
set nocount on

declare @intPosition int

Set @intPosition = CharIndex(@chvDelimiter, @chvFullName)

If @intPosition > 0
begin
    Set @chvLastName = Left(@chvFullName, @intPosition - 1)
    Set @chvFirstName = Right(@chvFullName,
        Len(@chvFullName) - @intPosition - Len(@chvDelimiter) )
end
else
    return 1

return 0
```

All of these string functions might look to you like a perfect tool for searching table columns, but there is just one problem with this application. If you apply a conversion function inside the Where clause of a Select statement, SQL Server does not use the index to query the table. Instead, it performs a table scan—even if the index exists. For example, you should not use the CharIndex() function to identify records with a particular string pattern:

```
select *
from Equipment
where CharIndex('Portege', Model) > 0
```

The Like operator with wild card characters is a much better choice if the string that you are looking for is at the beginning of the field:

```
select *
from Equipment
where Model like 'Portege%'
```

The PatIndex() function is similar to the CharIndex() function:

```
PatIndex('%pattern%', expression)
```

The major difference is that it allows the use of wild card characters in the search pattern:

```
Set @intPosition = PATINDEX('%,%', @chvFullName)
```

Again, if you use this function to search against a table column, SQL Server ignores the index and performs a table scan.

TIP

In early versions of SQL Server, PatIndex() was the only reasonable (although not very fast) way to query the contents of text columns and variables. Since version 7.0, SQL Server has had a new feature—FullText Search—that allows linguistic searches against all character data and works with words and phrases instead of with character patterns. Basically, Microsoft has included parts of a Windows Server tool called Index Server in the Workgroup, Standard, and Enterprise editions of SQL Server 2005, 2000, and 7.0.

String Conversion   The following two functions remove leading and trailing blanks from a string:

```
LTrim(character_expression)
RTrim(character_expression)
```

In the following query, we use both of them at the same time:

```
select LTrim(RTrim('   Dejan Sunderic   '))
```

The following functions convert a string to its uppercase or lowercase equivalent:

```
Upper(character_expression)
Lower(character_expression)
```

Use the Str() function to convert numeric values to strings:

```
Str(float_expression[, length[, decimal]])
```

The *length* parameter is an integer that specifies the number of characters needed for the result. This parameter includes everything: sign, digit, and decimal point. If necessary to fit the output into the specified length, SQL Server will round the value before converting it. If you do not specify a length, the default length is ten characters and the default decimal length is 0.

SQL Server provides a number of functions for representing the conversion from character types to ASCII codes and vice versa:

```
Char(integer_expression)
ASCII(character_expression)
NChar(integer_expression)
Unicode(character_expression)
```

The Char() and NChar() functions return characters with the specified integer code according to the ASCII and Unicode standards:

```
select NChar(352) + 'underi' + NChar(263)
```

Depending on fonts, operating systems, language settings, and other criteria, you may get proper or improper results from this expression (see Figure 4-3).

There is another interesting use of the Char() function. You can use it to insert control characters into output. For example, you can add tabulators Char(9) or carriage returns Char(13). In the past, this was a very important way to format output.

The ASCII() and Unicode() functions perform the opposite operation. They return the integer that corresponds to the first character of an expression (see Figure 4-4).

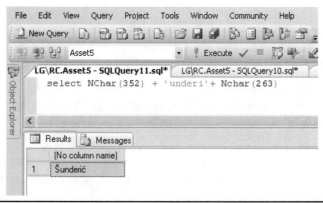

Figure 4-3   *Using Unicode characters*

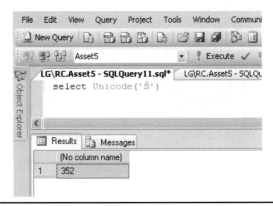

Figure 4-4 *Identifying Unicode character*

The following two functions generate a string of a specified length (*integer_expression*) and fill it with spaces or a specified character:

```
Space(integer_expression)
Replicate(character_expression, integer_expression)
```

For example:

```
select Space(4) + Replicate('*', 8)
```

This statement returns a useless result, but these functions were used at one time primarily to format output:

```
------------
     ********
```

Use the Stuff() function to stuff a string:

```
Stuff(character_expression1, start, length, character_expression2)
```

SQL Server removes a *length* of *character_expression1*, beginning at the specified *start* point, and replaces it with *character_expression2*. The specified length does not have to match that of *character_expression2*:

```
select Stuff('Sunderic, Dejan', 9, 2, Char(9))
```

This query replaces the comma and space in the target string with a tabulator:

```
------------------
Sunderic    Dejan
```

Metadata Functions

These functions are like a drill that you can use to obtain information about a database and database objects. The following table contains a partial list of metadata functions:

Function	Description
Col_Length(*table, column*)	Returns the length of the column.
Col_Name(*table_id, column_id*)	Returns the name of the column specified by table identification number and column identification number.
ColumnProperty(*id, column, property*)	Returns information about a column or stored procedure parameter.
DatabaseProperty(*database, property*)	Returns the value of the named database property for a given database and property name.
DatabasePropertyEx(*database, property*)	Returns the value of the named database property for a given database and property name. The returned value is of the `sql_variant` data type.
Db_Id(*database*)	Returns the database identification number for the given database.
Db_Name(*database_id*)	Returns the database name for a given database identification number.
Index_Col(*table, index_id, key_id*)	Returns the indexed column name.
IndexProperty(*table_id, index, property*)	Returns the value of the given property for a given table identification number and index name.
Object_Id(*object*)	Returns the identification number of the given object.
Object_Name(*object_id*)	Returns the database object name for the given object identification number.
ObjectProperty(*id, property*)	Returns information about the specified property for a given object's identification number.
@@ProcID	Returns the identification number of the current stored procedure.
Sql_Variant_Property(*expression, property*)	Returns the value of the given property for a given expression.
TypeProperty(*type, property*)	Returns information about the data type.

The Sql_Variant_Property() function retrieves information about the `sql_variant` data type. It returns specified *property* information about data stored in or obtained from the *expression* parameter. You can specify one of the following properties to be returned:

Property	Output
BaseType	The SQL Server data type
Precision	Number of digits of the base type
Scale	Number of digits behind decimal point
TotalBytes	Number of bytes required to store data and metadata
Collation	Collation of the data
MaxLength	Maximum length in bytes

The Sql_Variant_Property() function uses the following syntax:

```
SQL_Variant_Property(expression, property)
```

The *property* parameter must be specified in the form of a string:

```
SELECT   SQL_Variant_Property(Lookup,'BaseType'),
         SQL_Variant_Property(Lookup,'Precision'),
         SQL_Variant_Property(Lookup,'Scale')
FROM     Lookup
WHERE    LookupGroupId = 16
AND      LookupId = 4
```

Aggregate Functions

Aggregate functions perform an operation on a set of records and return a single value. They can be used in the following situations:

▶ The selection list of the Select statement

▶ A Having clause

▶ A Compute clause

The following table contains a list of aggregate functions:

Function	Description
Avg([All | Distinct] *expression*)	Returns the average value in the group.
Count([All | Distinct] *expression* |*)	Counts the number of items in the group.

Function	Description
Count_Big([All | Distinct] *expression* |*)	Counts the number of items in the group. The result is returned in the form of a `bigint` number.
Grouping(*Column_Name*)	Creates an additional column with a value of 1 when a row is added by the CUBE or ROLLUP operator, or 0 if it is not the result of a CUBE or ROLLUP operator.
Max(*expression*)	Returns the maximum value in the expression.
Min(*expression*)	Returns the minimum value in the expression.
Sum(*expression*)	Returns the sum of the expression's values.
StDev(*expression*)	Returns the statistical standard deviation for the values in the expression.
StDevP(*expression*)	Returns the statistical standard deviation for the population for the values in the expression.
Var(*expression*)	Returns the statistical variance of the values in the expression.
VarP(*expression*)	Returns the statistical variance for the population for the values in the expression.

Except for the Count() function, all aggregate functions ignore records that have null in the specified field from the set:

```
select Avg(Rent) [Average Rent] from Inventory
```

As you can see, SQL Server will even print a warning about nulls:

```
Average Rent
------------
200.0000

(1 row(s) affected)

Warning: Null value eliminated from aggregate.
```

You apply Count() on a specific field:

```
select Count(Rent) [Rentals] from Inventory
```

SQL Server will count only records that do not have null in the Rent field:

```
Rentals
------------
241
```

```
(1 row(s) affected)

Warning: Null value eliminated from aggregate.
```

You can apply Count() on all fields:

```
select Count(*) [Assets] from Inventory
```

SQL Server counts all records in the table:

```
Assets
------------
7298

(1 row(s) affected)
```

Ranking Functions

SQL Server 2005 introduced a set of functions for determining a rank of records in the result set. The simplest of them is the function Row_Number(). It returns the record's position in the result set and it is easiest to explain it in an example. The following query returns the equipment count from the Inventory table per location:

```
select locationId, count(*) InvCount
from Inventory
group by LocationId
order by InvCount
```

Its result would be something like this:

```
locationId  InvCount
----------- -----------
2           10
17          39
9           43
7           43
21          44
8           44
3           46
13          46
5           47
11          47
16          48
6           48

. . .
```

I will make this query a derived table called InvCount in the From clause of a new query. I will repeat columns of the derived table in the Select clause of the outer query. Then I will add a new column with the Row_Number() function. The function call contains an Over clause that must contain an Order By clause. The Order By clause specifies the field that the row numbering (and ordering) will be based on:

```
select LocationId, InvCount,
row_number()  over (order by InvCount) row_number
from (select locationId, count(*) InvCount from Inventory
group by LocationId) InvCount
```

The result is

```
LocationId  InvCount    row_number
----------- ----------- --------------------
2           10          1
17          39          2
9           43          3
7           43          4
21          44          5
8           44          6
3           46          7
13          46          8
5           47          9
11          47          10
...
```

Row numbering is perfect for some uses, but sometimes it must be recognized that that some locations (records) have the same inventory count (rank in the result set). The question is just how to declare those numbers. For example, we can easily agree that locations 9 and 7 should share third place, but what about locations 21 and 8? Should they share fourth or fifth place? Some projects will rank them one way and some another way. Fortunately, we have functions for both:

```
select
    LocationId,
    InvCount,
    row_number()  over (order by InvCount) row_number,
    Rank() over (order by InvCount) Rank,
    Dense_Rank()  over (order by InvCount) Dense_Rank
from (select locationId, count(*) InvCount
    from Inventory
    group by LocationId) InvCount
```

The result of the query is

```
LocationId   InvCount    row_number    Rank     Dense_Rank
-----------  ----------- ------------- -------- ----------
2            10          1             1        1
17           39          2             2        2
9            43          3             3        3
7            43          4             3        3
21           44          5             5        4
8            44          6             5        4
3            46          7             7        5
13           46          8             7        5
5            47          9             9        6
11           47          10            9        6
. . .
```

Rowset Functions

Functions of this type are distinguished from other functions in that they return a complete recordset to the caller. They cannot be used (as is the case of scalar functions) in any place where an expression is acceptable. They can be used in Transact-SQL statements only in situations where the server expects a table reference. An example of such a situation is the From clause of the Select statement.

Pass-through Functions

The OpenQuery() function is designed to return a recordset from a linked server. It can be used as a part of Select, Update, Insert, and Delete Transact-SQL statements. The Query parameter must contain a valid SQL query in the dialect of the linked server, since the query will be executed (as-is—as a pass-through query) on the linked server. This function uses the following syntax:

```
OpenQuery(linked_server, 'query')
```

NOTE

Linked servers are OLE DB data sources that are registered on the local SQL server. After registration, the local server knows how to access data on the remote server. All that is needed in your code is a reference to the name of the linked server.

You can register a linked server to be associated with the Northwind.mdb sample database either from Management Studio or using the following code:

```
EXEC sp_addlinkedserver
    @server = 'employees_Access',
    @provider = 'Microsoft.Jet.OLEDB.4.0',
    @srvproduct = 'OLE DB Provider for Jet',
    @datasrc = 'C:\20051009\mydoc\employees.mdb'
Go
```

Then, you can use the OpenQuery() function to return records from the linked server:

```
SELECT *
FROM OpenQuery(employees_Access, 'SELECT * FROM employees')
```

It is much simpler to create a linked server connection toward SQL Server and use it:

```
EXEC sp_addlinkedserver
    'SS2K_Asset2000',
    N'SQL Server'
GO

select * from SS2K_Asset2000.Asset2000.dbo.Inventory
```

OpenRowset() is very similar to the OpenQuery() function:

```
OpenRowset(
'provider_name',
{'datasource';'user_id';'password' | 'provider_string' },
{ [catalog.][schema.]object | 'query'}
)
```

It is designed for connecting to a server that is not registered as a linked server. Therefore, you must supply both the connection parameters and the query in order to use it. There are several options for defining the connection, such as OLE DB, ODBC, and OLE DB for ODBC, along with two options for specifying a result set: a pass-through query or a valid name for a database object.

The following query joins one table from the remote SQL Server with two tables on the local SQL Server:

```
SELECT a.au_lname, a.au_fname, titles.title
FROM OPENROWSET('SQLNCLI', 'Server=LG\ss2k;Trusted_Connection=yes;',
    'SELECT * FROM pubs.dbo.authors') AS a
INNER JOIN titleauthor
ON a.au_id = titleauthor.au_id
    INNER JOIN titles
    ON titleauthor.title_id = titles.title_id
```

TIP

Although OpenRowset() will work fine, if you plan repetitive use of some data source, you should consider registering a linked server and using OpenQuery(). The execution of OpenQuery() will be considerably faster.

Microsoft has delivered several new OLE DB data providers that can be used with the OpenRowset() function. The "Binary Data Types" section of Chapter 3 contains an interesting example of the usage of the new BULK provide that returns content of the file as a rowset. You can also use it to load fields from a text file into SQL Server.

OpenXML Function

OpenXML() provides access to an in-memory rowset that T-SQL developers can use to parse, access, and return the content of an XML document.

Before an XML document can be accessed using OpenXML(), the document must be loaded into memory using sp_xml_preparedocument. The stored procedure reads the XML document provided in *xmltext,* parses the document using the MSXML parser, and places the document into an in-memory structure. It is a tree that contains assorted nodes such as elements, attributes, comments, and text. The stored procedure returns a handle for the XML document *hdoc* that OpenXML() can use to access the information, and that sp_xml_removedocument uses to remove the document from memory. In the following example, an XML document is loaded in memory and its handle is recorded in the @intDoc variable:

```
DECLARE @intDoc int
DECLARE @chvXMLDoc varchar(max)
-- sample XML document
SET @chvXMLDoc ='
<root>
  <Equipment EquipmentID="1" Make="Toshiba" Model="Portege 7020CT">
   <Inventory InventoryID="5" StatusID="1" EquipmentID="1"/>
   <Inventory InventoryID="12" StatusID="1" EquipmentID="1"/>
  </Equipment>
</root>'
--Load the XML document into memory.
EXEC sp_xml_preparedocument @intDoc OUTPUT, @chvXMLDoc
```

OpenXML() has the following syntax:

```
OpenXML(hdoc, rowpattern, flags)
[With (SchemaDeclaration | TableVariable)]
```

hdoc is a handle that points to the tree containing the XML data. *rowpattern* is the XPath string used to identify nodes that need to be processed. *flags* is an optional parameter that controls the way that data from the XML document is mapped to the rowset and how data is to be copied to the overflow property (I will explain this a little further on in this section).

SchemaDeclaration is a declaration of the structure in which data will be returned. Alternatively, it is possible to use the name of a table variable (*TableVariable*) instead. The rowset will be formed using the structure of the table variable. The *SchemaDeclaration* can be composed using the following syntax:

```
ColName ColType [ColPattern | MetaProperty]
[, ColName ColType [ColPattern | MetaProperty]...]
```

ColName is the name and *ColType* is the data type of the column. This structure is very similar to the table structure of the Create Table statement. *ColPattern* is an optional parameter that defines how a column is to be mapped to the XML node. A *MetaProperty* is specified to extract metadata such as data types, node types, and namespace information.

Finally, take a look at an example that uses all these constructs:

```
DECLARE @intDoc int
DECLARE @chvXMLDoc varchar(max)
-- sample XML document
SET @chvXMLDoc =
'<root>
  <Equipment EquipmentID="1" Make="Toshiba" Model="Portege 7020CT">
   <Inventory InventoryID="5" StatusID="1" EquipmentID="1"/>
   <Inventory InventoryID="12" StatusID="1" EquipmentID="1"/>
  </Equipment>
  <Equipment EquipmentID="2" Make="Sony" Model="Trinitron 17XE"/>
  <Equipment EquipmentID="4" Make="HP" Model="LaserJet 4"/>
  <Equipment EquipmentID="5" Make="Bang &amp; Olafson" Model="V4000">
   <Inventory InventoryID="8" StatusID="1" EquipmentID="5"/>
  </Equipment>
  <Equipment EquipmentID="6" Make="NEC" Model="V90">
   <Inventory InventoryID="6" StatusID="2" EquipmentID="6"/>
  </Equipment>
</root>'
--Load the XML document into memory.
EXEC sp_xml_preparedocument @intDoc OUTPUT, @chvXMLDoc

-- SELECT statement using OPENXML rowset provider
```

```
SELECT *
FROM    OPENXML (@intDoc, '/root/Equipment/Inventory', 8)
        WITH    (InventoryID int '@InventoryID',
                 StatusID int '@StatusID',
                 Make varchar(25) '../@Make',
                 Model varchar(25) '../@Model',
                 Comment ntext '@mp:xmltext')
-- remove the XML document from memory
EXEC sp_xml_removedocument @intDoc
```

The result is shown in Figure 4-5.

As soon as it is no longer used, the document should be removed from memory using sp_xml_removedocument.

NOTE

The memory is not released until sp_xml_removedocument is called, and hence it should be called as soon as possible.

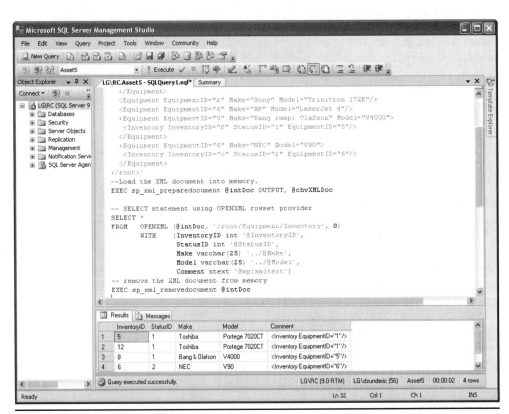

Figure 4-5   *Using OpenXML()*

In the preceding example, the OpenXML() rowset provider is used in a Select statement:

```
SELECT    *
From Openxml (@intDoc, '/root/Equipment/Inventory', 8)
    WITH     (InventoryID int '@InventoryID',
             StatusID int '@StatusID',
             Make varchar(25) '../@Make',
             Model varchar(25) '../@Model',
             Comment ntext '@mp:xmltext')
```

The *rowpattern* parameter specifies that information will be extracted (mostly) from Inventory nodes ('/root/Equipment/Inventory').

The InventoryID and StatusID columns in the rowset are filled from the attribute data. In the XPath language (unfortunately beyond the scope of this book), the @ character is used as an abbreviation that points to attribute nodes.

The Make and Model columns are not in the same group of nodes as InventoryID and StatusID. Since they are attributes of the `Equipment` node, *ColPattern* has to refer to the parent node ('../@Model') first.

The third parameter of the OpenXML() clause sets the way that the function interprets the XML and handles the overflow (data that does not get transferred into other record columns). You have to set it to 1 or 0 (default value) if the XML document is attribute-centric or to 2 if the document is element-centric. The value 8 in the preceding example specifies that the last column (Comment) should be filled with content of XML nodes that are not included in other columns.

Table 4-3 shows a list of possible values of the *flags* parameter.

XML_NOCOPY could be combined (logical OR) with XML_ATTRIBUTES (1 + 8 = 9) or XML_ELEMENTS (2 + 8 = 10). This flag can be used to generate either a string with the overflow information or a string with a complete branch

Mnemonic	Value	Description
XML_ATTRIBUTES	1	Attribute-centric mapping.
XML_ELEMENTS	2	Element-centric mapping.
XML_DEFAULT	0	Default — equivalent to XML_ATTRIBUTES (1).
XML_NOCOPY	8	Overflow metaproperty of the document (@mp:xmltext) should contain only nodes that were not extracted using the OpenXML() rowset provider.

Table 4-3   *Values of flags Parameter in OpenXML()*

of the XML document. The following example extracts the branch of the XML document/tree that describes a node with EquipmentID set to 1:

```
Select *
From Openxml (@intDoc, '/root/Equipment', 2)
      With    (EquipmentID int '@EquipmentID',
                Branch ntext '@mp:xmltext')
Where EquipmentId = 1
```

SQL Server returns the following:

```
EquipmentID Branch
----------- ------------------------------------------------------------
1                <Equipment EquipmentID="1" Make="Toshiba"
Model="Portege 7020CT">
   <Inventory InventoryID="5" StatusID="1" EquipmentID="1"/>
   <Inventory InventoryID="12" StatusID="1" EquipmentID="1"/>
</Equipment>
(1 row(s) affected)
```

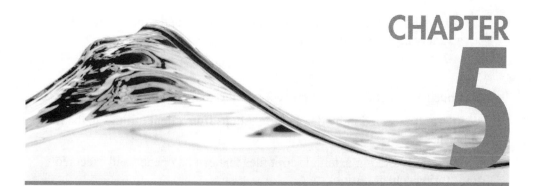

CHAPTER 5

Composite Transact-SQL Constructs: Batches, Scripts, and Transactions

IN THIS CHAPTER

Batches

Scripts

Transactions

Transact-SQL (T-SQL) statements can be grouped and executed together in a variety of ways. They can be

► Compiled as a part of a stored procedure, user-defined function, or trigger
► Written and executed individually or in groups from client utilities in the form of batches
► Grouped and stored in external script files that can be opened and executed from various client utilities
► Grouped in transactions that succeed completely or fail completely

This chapter discusses batches, scripts, and transactions.

It is not necessary to run examples from the text against the Asset5 database, but if you do, you must first make sure that the database contains the following table by executing the following script against the Asset5 database:

```
Create Table Part(PartId int identity,
                  Make varchar(50),
                  Model varchar(50),
                  Type varchar(50))
```

This table is used to illustrate the concepts discussed in this chapter. Some of the changes are destructive, so existing tables such as Equipment will not be used, which may be needed for other purposes later.

Batches

A *batch* is a set of Transact-SQL statements that are sent to and executed by SQL Server as a single unit. The most important characteristic of a batch is that it is parsed and executed on the server as an undivided entity. In some cases, batches are created implicitly. For example, if you execute a set of Transact-SQL statements from Query Analyzer, the program will treat that set as one batch and do so invisibly:

```
Insert Into Part (Make, Model, Type)
Values ('Toshiba', 'Portege 7010CT', 'notebook')
```

```
Insert Into Part (Make, Model, Type)
Values ('Toshiba', 'Portege 7020CT', 'notebook')

Insert Into Part (Make, Model, Type)
Values ('Toshiba', 'Portege 7030CT', 'notebook')
```

Some tools, such as the Query window in Management Studio and SQLCMD in SQL Server 2005, and Query Analyzer, osql, and isql in earlier versions of SQL Server, use the Go command to divide Transact-SQL code into explicitly set batches. In the following example, the code for dropping a stored procedure is in one batch and the code for creating a new stored procedure is in another. The batch is explicitly created using the Go command.

```
If Exists (Select * From sysobjects
          Where id = object_id(N'[dbo].[prPartList]')
          And OBJECTPROPERTY(id, N'IsProcedure') = 1)
    Drop Procedure [dbo].[prPartList]
Go

Create Procedure prPartList
As
     Select * from Part
Return 0
Go
```

In a Query window of Management Studio, you can highlight part of the code and execute it. Management Studio treats the selected piece of code as a batch and sends it to the server and ignores the rest of the code (see Figure 5-1).

In other utilities and development environments, batches may be divided in some other manner. In ADO, OLE DB, ODBC, and DB-Library, each command string prepared for execution (in the respective object or function) is treated as one batch.

NOTE

In SQLCMD (and command line tools in earlier version of SQL Server), the Go command has a different function. It is also a signal to the tool to start executing the code entered so far.

Using Batches

Batches reduce the time and processing associated with transferring statements from client to server, as well as that associated with parsing, compiling, and executing T-SQL statements. If you need to execute a set of 100 Insert commands against

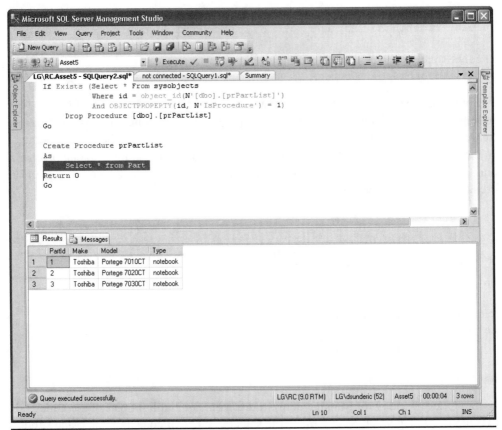

Figure 5-1   *Executing selected code in the Query window*

a database, it is preferable to group them in one batch rather than send them to the server as 100 separate statements. The overhead involved in sending 100 separate statements and receiving 100 separate results is very high. Network traffic will be increased unnecessarily, and the whole operation will be slower for the user.

Batches and Errors

The fact that the batch is compiled as an undivided entity has interesting implications for statements that contain syntax errors. Results will vary according to whether the syntax error occurs in a statement or in the name of a database object. If you create a batch that includes a statement containing a syntax error, the whole batch will fail to execute.

Consider the following batch:

```
Insert into Part (Make, Model, Type)
Values ('Toshiba', 'Portege 7020CT', 'Notebook')
Selec * from Part
```

It consists of two commands, the second of which contains a syntax error—a missing letter in the Select keyword. If you execute this batch, SQL Server will not compile or execute it but will return the following error:

```
Server: Msg 170, Level 15, State 1, Line 3
Line 3: Incorrect syntax near 'Selec'
```

If you make a typo in the name of the database object (for instance, in a table or column name), the situation is very different. Note that the name of the table in the following Insert statement is incorrect:

```
Insert into art (Make, Model, Type)
Values ('Toshiba', 'Portege 7020CT', 'Notebook')
Select * from Part
```

In this example, the application will notice an error and stop execution as soon as it encounters it:

```
Server: Msg 208, Level 16, State 1, Line 1
Invalid object name 'art'.
```

SQL Server executes the batch in three steps: it parses, compiles, and then executes. In the first phase, SQL Server verifies batch syntax. It focuses on the sequence of keywords, operators, and identifiers. The first batch used a statement with an error in a keyword. SQL Server picked up the error during the parsing phase.

The error in the second batch (an invalid object name) was picked up during execution. To further demonstrate this fact, let's investigate the following example, where the error is in the second statement:

```
Insert into Part (Make, Model, Type)
Values ('Toshiba', 'Portege 7020CT', 'Notebook')
Select * from art
```

In this case, the application behaves differently:

```
(1 row(s) affected)

Server: Msg 208, Level 16, State 1, Line 1
Invalid object name 'art'.
```

Both commands are parsed and compiled, then the first command is executed, and finally the second command is canceled. Users with experience of early versions of Microsoft SQL Server remember that such a scenario would produce very different results in those early versions.

Microsoft SQL Server 2005 supports deferred name resolution (actually introduced in SQL Server 7.0). *Deferred name resolution* allows the server to compile Transact-SQL statements even when dependent objects do not yet exist in the database. This feature can prove to be very useful when you are creating or transferring objects from one database or server to another. You do not have to worry about dependencies and the order in which objects are created. Unfortunately, the introduction of this feature also has some strange secondary effects. In the case of the last example,

▶ The server has successfully compiled a batch, since the name resolution is not part of the compilation;

▶ The first command was executed without a problem; and

▶ When a problem was encountered in the second command, the server canceled all further processing and returned a runtime error.

Keep this problem in mind when writing batches. Developers in modern programming languages like Visual Basic or Visual C++ usually employ sophisticated error-handling strategies to avoid situations like this. Transact-SQL also contains programming constructs for error handling. We will explore them in the Chapter 6.

The situation could be worse. Particular runtime errors (for example, constraint violations) do not stop execution of the batch. The following case attempts to use an Insert statement to insert a value in the identity column:

```
Select PartId, Make + ' ' + Model Part from Part
Insert into Part (PartId, Make, Model, Type)
Values (1, 'IBM', 'Thinkpad 390D', 'Notebook')
Select PartId, Make + ' ' + Model Part from Part
Go
```

The result is a "partial failure":

```
PartId      Part
----------- --------------------------------------------------
1           Toshiba Portege 7020CT

(1 row(s) affected)
```

```
Server: Msg 544, Level 16, State 1, Line 1
Cannot insert explicit value for identity column in table
'Part' when IDENTITY_INSERT is set to OFF.
PartId      Part
----------- -----------------------------------
1           Toshiba Portege 7020CT
```

```
(1 row(s) affected)
```

In some cases, "partial success" may be tolerable, but in the real world it is generally not acceptable.

Let's investigate a case in which several batches are written, divided by a Go statement, and executed together. Although the user has issued a single command to execute them, the client application will divide the code into batches and send them to the server separately. If an error occurs in any batch, the server will cancel its execution. However, this does not mean that execution of the other batches is canceled. The server will try to execute the next batch automatically.

In some cases, this may be useful, but in most cases, it may not be what the user expects to happen. In the following example, one column needs to be deleted from the Part table. One way to perform this action (very popular until we were spoiled;) with fancy tools like Enterprise Manager, Management Studio, or the Alter Table… Drop Column statement) would be to do the following:

1. Create a provisional table to preserve the information that is currently in the Part table.
2. Copy information from the Part table to the provisional table.
3. Drop the existing Part table.
4. Create a Part table without the column you want to delete.
5. Copy the preserved information back to the Part table.
6. Drop the table.

The code necessary to implement this functionality could be created in a set of five batches:

```
Create Table TmpPart (PartId int,
                      Make varchar(50),
                      Model varchar(50))
GO
```

```
Insert into TmpPart (PartId, Make, Model)
Select PartId, Make, Model from Part
GO

Drop Table Part
GO

Create Table Part (PartId int,
                   Make varchar(50),
                   Model varchar(50))
GO

Insert into Part (PartId, Make, Model)
Select PartId, Make, Model from TmpPart
GO

Drop Table TmpPart
GO
```

In theory, this set of batches would work perfectly. However, there is just one problem—it doesn't take errors into account. For example, if a syntax error occurs in the first batch, the temporary table will not be created. Part information will not be preserved in it, and when the code drops the table, the information will be lost. To observe a method that you can use to handle errors, read the next chapter.

DDL Batches

Data Definition Language (DDL) is that part of Transact-SQL dedicated to the creation and modification of database objects. Some DDL statements must stand alone in the batch, including the following statements:

Create Procedure	Create Trigger	Create Default
Create Rule	Create View	Create Function
Set Showplan_Text	Set Showplan_All	Set Showplan_XML

If any of these statements is combined with other statements in a batch, the batch will fail. Create statements must stand alone because every other statement that follows them will be interpreted as a part of the Create statement. Set Showplan_Text, Set Showplan_All, and Set Showplan_XML must stand alone in the batch because they are setting how SQL Server 2005 processes following batches and shows execution plans.

Self-sufficient Content

During compilation, the batch is converted into a single execution plan. For this reason, the batch must be self-sufficient. In the real world, this concept has vast implications for the scope of database objects, variables, and comments.

Scope of Objects

Some DDL statements can be inside batches together with other commands, but keep in mind that the resulting object will not be accessible until the batch is completed. For example, it is not possible to add new columns to the table and to access those new columns in the same batch. Therefore, the following batch will fail:

```
Alter Table dbo.Part ADD Cost money NULL
select PartId, Cost from dbo.Part
Go
```

The Select statement is not able to access the Cost column, and the whole batch will fail:

```
Server: Msg 207, Level 16, State 3, Line 1
Invalid column name 'Cost'.
```

Therefore, the batch has to be divided in two:

```
Alter Table Part ADD Cost money NULL
Go
Select PartId, Cost from Part
Go
```

NOTE

Some DDL statements can be combined with DML statements that reference them. For example, it is possible to create a table and insert records into it in the same batch. This is very important when you are working with temporary tables.

Scope of Variables

All variables referenced in a batch must also be declared in that batch. The following code will result in the failure of the second batch:

```
Declare @Name as varchar (50)
Go
Select @Name = 'Dejan'
Go
```

Scripts

A *script* is usually defined as a collection of Transact-SQL statements (in one or more batches) in the form of an external file. Client tools, such as Management Studio and SQLCMD, usually have support for managing script files.

Scripts are usually stored in plain text files with a .sql extension. This makes them manageable from any text editor as well as from many sophisticated tools, such as the Microsoft application for code control, Visual SourceSafe.

Management Studio has the basic script management features as any text editor, such as File | Open, Save, and some advanced features to generate scripts of database objects or to manage scripts as a part of project and solution files. SQLCMD is a command line utility that allows the user to specify script files with code to be executed against the server.

Database Scripting

One of the most exciting features in Management Studio is the ability to perform reverse engineering on the database without the need for external tools. The result of this process is a script that contains DDL statements, which can be used to re-create the database objects included in the script. This script can be used to

▶ Explore user and system database objects

▶ Back up source code

▶ Establish a source control process

▶ Transfer the complete database (or just some objects) to another server (and/or another database)

The process of database scripting is very simple:

1. Open a context-sensitive menu of a database in Management Studio.
2. Select Tasks | Generate Scripts and the program will open the Generate SQL Server Scripts Wizard (see Figure 5-2).
3. On the next screen the wizard will prompt you to select the database that you want to script.
4. If you select Script All Objects in the Selected Database checkbox, you will be able to click Finish and complete the process.
5. If you leave the checkbox unmarked, the wizard will prompt you to choose script options (see Figure 5-3).

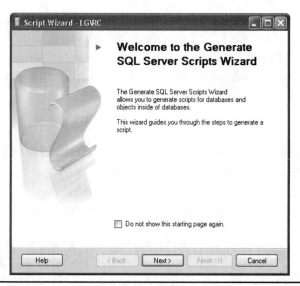

Figure 5-2 *Generate SQL Server Scripts Wizard*

6. Carefully browse the values in this dialog box. It is likely that you want to change some defaults. For example, you probably want to include indexes and object-level permissions.

7. The wizard then prompts you to choose the major object types that you want to script.

Figure 5-3 *Script options*

8. If you choose, for example, tables, the stored procedures program will prompt you to select which tables and stored procedures you want to script.

9. In the Output Option window you have to choose whether scripts will be sent to a file (using Unicode or the ANSI character set), the Clipboard, or a Query window.

TIP

If you want to be able to open a script file from regular editors (that do not support Unicode) such as Notepad, you should select ANSI as your file format.

10. You can now click Finish to start the process (or Next to see a summary of specified options).

11. The wizard will display progress in the Generate Script Progress window (see Figure 5-4). After it's done, you can click the Filter and Report buttons to manipulate the status of individual actions.

TIP

Use database scripting to explore the sample database associated with this book and the sample and system databases published with SQL Server. Exploration of other styles and methods in coding will help you to gain knowledge and build experience.

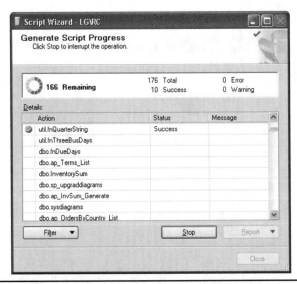

Figure 5-4 *Generate Script Progress window*

Transactions

Even from the very name of the Transact-SQL language, you can conclude that *transactions* play a major role in SQL Server. They are an important mechanism for enforcing the consistency and integrity of the database.

A transaction is the smallest unit of work in SQL Server. To qualify a unit of work as a transaction, it must satisfy the following four criteria, often referred to as the ACID test:

- ▶ **Atomicity**   All data changes must be completed successfully, or none of them will be written permanently to the database.

- ▶ **Consistency**   After a transaction, the database must be left in a consistent state. All rules must be applied during processing to ensure data integrity. All constraints must be satisfied. All internal data structures must be left in an acceptable state.

- ▶ **Isolation**   Changes to the database made by a transaction must not be visible to other transactions until the transaction is complete. Before the transaction is committed, other transactions should see the data only in the state it was in before the transaction.

- ▶ **Durability**   Once a transaction is completed, changes must not revert even in the case of a system failure.

Autocommit Transactions

In fact, every Transact-SQL statement is a transaction. When it is executed, it either finishes successfully or is completely abandoned. To illustrate this, let's try to delete all records from the EqType table. Take a look at the following diagram:

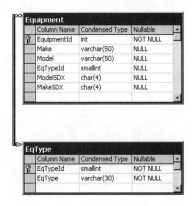

A foreign key relationship exists between the EqType and Equipment tables. The foreign key prevents the deletion of records in the EqType table that are referenced by records in the Equipment table.

Let's try to delete them anyway. You can see the result of such an attempt in Figure 5-5.

Two Select statements that will count the number of records in EqType are placed around the Delete statement. As expected, the Delete statement is aborted because of the foreign key. The count of records before and after the Delete statement is the same, which confirms that all changes made by the Delete statement were canceled. So the database remains in the state that it was in before the change was initiated.

If there were no errors, SQL Server would automatically commit the transaction (that is, it would record all changes) to the database. This kind of behavior is called *autocommit*.

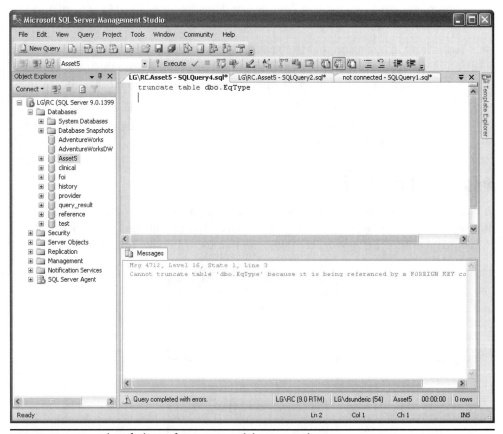

Figure 5-5 *Complete failure of attempt to delete records*

In this case, SQL Server deleted records one after the other from the EqType table until it encountered a record that could not be deleted because of the foreign key relationship, at which point the operation was canceled.

Explicit Transactions

The most popular and obvious way to use transactions is to give explicit commands to start or finish the transaction. Transactions started in this way are called *explicit transactions.* You can group Transact-SQL statements into a single transaction using the following statements:

- ▶ Begin Transaction
- ▶ Rollback Transaction
- ▶ Commit Transaction

If anything goes wrong with any of the grouped statements, all changes need to be aborted. The process of reversing changes is called *rollback* in SQL Server terminology. If everything is in order with all statements within a single transaction, all changes are recorded together in the database. In SQL Server terminology, these changes are *committed* to the database.

I will demonstrate the use of these processes on the ap_LeaseSchedule_Clear stored procedure. Its main purpose is to set monthly lease amounts to zero for each asset associated with an expired lease schedule. It also sets the total of the lease amounts to zero. These two operations must be performed simultaneously to preserve the integrity of the database.

```
Create Procedure ap_LeaseShedule_Clear
-- Set value of Lease of all equipment
-- associated with expired Lease Schedule to 0.
-- Set total amount of Lease Schedule to 0.

    @intLeaseScheduleId int
As

Begin Transaction

-- Set value of Lease of all equipment
-- associated with expired Lease Schedule to 0
Update dbo.Inventory
Set Lease = 0
Where LeaseScheduleId = @intLeaseScheduleId
```

```
If @@Error <> 0 goto PROBLEM

-- Set total amount of Lease Schedule to 0
Update dbo.LeaseSchedule
Set PeriodicTotalAmount = 0
Where ScheduleId = @intLeaseScheduleId
If @@Error <> 0 goto PROBLEM

Commit Transaction
Return 0

PROBLEM:
Print ' Unable to eliminate lease amounts from the database!'
Rollback Transaction
Return 1
```

Before the real processing starts, the Begin Transaction statement notifies SQL Server to treat all of the following actions as a single transaction. It is followed by two Update statements. If no errors occur during the updates, all changes are committed to the database when SQL Server processes the Commit Transaction statement, and finally the stored procedure finishes. If an error occurs during the updates, it is detected by If statements and execution is continued from the PROBLEM label. After displaying a message to the user, SQL Server rolls back any changes that occurred during processing.

We will review more complex transactions (including nested transactions) and ways to process errors in the next chapter.

Implicit Transactions

The third transaction mode is called the *implicit transaction*. To use this mode, you must set the Set Implicit_Transactions On statement for the connection. Any of the following statements will serve as an implicit start to a transaction:

Alter Table	Create	Delete	Drop
Fetch	Grant	Insert	Open
Revoke	Select	Truncate Table	Update

To finish the transaction, you must use the Commit Transaction or Rollback Transaction statement. After that, any of the preceding commands will start a new implicit transaction.

Transaction Processing Architecture

An explanation of how transactions are implemented in Microsoft SQL Server will give you some insight into many processes.

Every change to the database is recorded in a transaction log before it is written to the appropriate tables. Transaction logs are implemented in separate files (or sets of files) with the extension .ldf. All modifications are written to this file chronologically. The records in this transaction log can later be used to roll back the transaction (thus providing atomicity) or to commit the changes to the database (thus providing durability). Two types of records can be stored in transaction logs:

▶ Logical operations performed (for instance, Insert, Update, Delete, and start of transaction)

▶ Before and after images of the changed data (that is, copies of data before and after the change is made)

NOTE
The transaction log does not record queries that are executed against the database (since they do not modify its content).

The transaction log mechanism helps to resolve data integrity issues such as:

▶ If a client application loses its connection before a transaction is finished, SQL Server will detect a problem and roll back changes to ensure consistency.

▶ If the machine loses power during processing, SQL Server will recover the database when services are restored. All transactions that were recorded in the transaction log in an undivided manner (that is, as part of a complete transaction set) are rolled forward (written to data tables) as if nothing unusual has happened. All transactions that were not completed before the problem occurred are rolled back (deleted) from the database.

NOTE

The transaction log also plays an important role in the implementation of backups in SQL Server. When a user starts a full backup, SQL Server records a complete snapshot of the data tables in backup files. At that point, SQL Server marks the current position in the transaction log and continues to record all changes to the database in the transaction log. Transactions logged during the process are also recorded as part of the full backup. When the backup is complete, SQL Server makes another mark in the transaction log. At the time of the next backup, a transaction log backup will suffice. To restore the database, an administrator first uses the full backup and then one or more transaction log backups that have been run since the full backup. SQL Server runs through the transaction log and applies changes to the data tables.

Nested Transactions

SQL Server allows you to nest transactions. Basically, this feature means that a new transaction can start even though the previous one is not complete:

```
Begin transaction
...
    Begin transaction
    ...
    Commit transaction
...
Commit transaction
```

Usually this situation occurs when one stored procedure containing a transaction calls another stored procedure that also contains a transaction. In the following example, ap_Order_Complete_1 completes an order by setting its completion date and changing the status of the order, and then looping through associated order items and calling ap_OrderItem_Complete_1 to complete each of them. ap_OrderItem_Complete_1 sets the completion date of an order item to the last ChargeLog date associated with that OrderItem. Both of these procedures contain a transaction.

```
Create Procedure ap_Order_Complete_1
-- Complete all orderItems and then complete order
    @intOrderId int,
    @dtsCompletionDate smalldatetime
As
set nocount on

Declare @intErrorCode int,
        @i int,
        @intCountOrderItems int,
        @intOrderItemId int
```

```sql
Select @intErrorCode = @@Error

If @intErrorCode = 0
    Begin Transaction

-- complete order
If @intErrorCode = 0
Begin
    Update dbo.[Order]
    Set CompletionDate = @dtsCompletionDate,
        OrderStatusId = 4 -- completed
    Where OrderId = @intOrderId

    Select @intErrorCode = @@Error
End

-- loop through OrderItems and complete them
If @intErrorCode = 0
Begin
    Create Table #OrderItems(
        id int identity(1,1),
        OrderItemId int)

    Select @intErrorCode = @@Error
End

-- collect orderItemIds
If @intErrorCode = 0
Begin
    Insert Into #OrderItems(OrderItemId)
        Select ItemId
        From dbo.OrderItem
        Where OrderId = @intOrderId
        Select @intErrorCode = @@Error
End

If @intErrorCode = 0
Begin
    Select @intCountOrderItems = Max(Id),
        @i = 1
    From #OrderItems

    Select @intErrorCode = @@Error
End
```

```
while @intErrorCode = 0 and @i <= @intCountOrderItems
Begin
     If @intErrorCode = 0
     Begin
          Select @intOrderItemId = OrderItemId
          From #OrderItems
          Where id = @i
          Select @intErrorCode = @@Error
     End

     If @intErrorCode = 0
          Exec @intErrorCode = dbo.ap_OrderItem_Complete_1 @intOrderItemId

     If @intErrorCode = 0
          Set @i = @i + 1
End

If @intErrorCode = 0 and @@trancount > 0
     Commit Transaction
Else
     Rollback Transaction
return @intErrorCode
Go

create Procedure dbo.ap_OrderItem_Complete_1
-- Set CompletionDate of OrderItem to date
-- of last ChargeLog record associated with OrderItem.
     @intOrderItemId int
As
set nocount on
Declare @intErrorCode int
Select @intErrorCode = @@Error

If @intErrorCode = 0
     Begin Transaction

-- Set CompletionDate of OrderItem to date
-- of last ChargeLog record associated with OrderItem.
If @intErrorCode = 0
Begin
     update dbo.OrderItem
     Set CompletionDate = (Select Max(ChargeDate)
                           from dbo.ChargeLog
                           where ItemId = @intOrderItemId)
```

```
        Where ItemId = @intOrderItemId

        Select @intErrorCode = @@Error
End

If @intErrorCode = 0
Begin
        exec @intErrorCode = dbo.ap_NotifyAccounting @intOrderItemId
End

If @intErrorCode = 0 and @@trancount > 0
        Commit Transaction
Else
        Rollback Transaction
Return @intErrorCode
```

In the case of nested transactions, no Commit statements except the outer one will save changes to the database. Only after the last transaction is committed will all changes to the database become permanent. Up to that point, it is still possible to roll back all changes.

The interesting question is how SQL Server knows which transaction is the last one. It keeps the number of opened transactions in the @@trancount global variable for each user connection. When SQL Server encounters a Begin Transaction statement, it increments the value of the @@trancount, and when SQL Server encounters a Commit Transaction statement, it decrements the value of the @@trancount. Therefore, the only effect of a nested (internal) Commit Transaction statement is a change to the @@trancount value. Only the outer Commit Transaction statement (when @@trancount = 1) stores changes in data tables rather than in the transaction log.

The following is a purely academic example that does not perform any real processing, but it demonstrates the effect of nested transactions on the @@trancount global variable:

```
print 'Trancount = ' + Convert(varchar(4), @@trancount)
BEGIN TRANSACTION
    print 'Trancount = ' + Convert(varchar(4), @@trancount)
    BEGIN TRANSACTION
    print 'Trancount = ' + Convert(varchar(4), @@trancount)
    COMMIT TRANSACTION
    print 'Trancount = ' + Convert(varchar(4), @@trancount)
COMMIT TRANSACTION
print 'Trancount = ' + Convert(varchar(4), @@trancount)
```

Each transactional statement will increment and decrement the @@trancount:

```
Trancount = 0
Trancount = 1
Trancount = 2
Trancount = 1
Trancount = 0
```

An interesting inconsistency to observe is in the behavior of the Rollback Transaction statement. No matter how many transaction levels deep execution extends, the Rollback Transaction statement will cancel all changes caused by all transactions (and bring the @@trancount value down to zero). In fact, if you execute an additional Rollback Transaction statement after the first one, SQL Server will report an error.

```
print 'Trancount = ' + Convert(varchar(4), @@trancount)
BEGIN TRANSACTION
    print 'Trancount = ' + Convert(varchar(4), @@trancount)
    BEGIN TRANSACTION
    print 'Trancount = ' + Convert(varchar(4), @@trancount)
    ROLLBACK TRANSACTION
    print 'Trancount = ' + Convert(varchar(4), @@trancount)
ROLLBACK TRANSACTION
print 'Trancount = ' + Convert(varchar(4), @@trancount)
```

The following is the result of this example:

```
Trancount = 0
Trancount = 1
Trancount = 2
Trancount = 0
Server: Msg 3903, Level 16, State 1, Line 8
The ROLLBACK TRANSACTION request has no corresponding BEGIN TRANSACTION.
Trancount = 0
```

TIP

I have to admit that I had many problems with this issue at one time. Be careful.

To prevent this error, you need to test for the value of the @@trancount variable before you execute the Rollback Transaction statement. A simple way to test for this value works something like this:

```
if @@trancount > 0
    Rollback Transaction
```

You will find a much better solution in Chapter 6.

Named Transactions

Transaction statements can be named. The name must be a valid SQL Server identifier (that is, no more than 128 characters), but SQL Server will read only the first 32 characters:

```
Begin Tran[saction] [transaction_name|@transaction_name_variable]
Commit Tran[saction] [transaction_name|@transaction_name_variable]
Rollback [Tran[saction] [transaction_name|@transaction_name_variable]]
```

I know that this sounds like a perfect tool for resolving some issues with nested transactions. Unfortunately, in nested transactions, only the names of outer transactions are recorded by SQL Server. If you try to roll back any of the inner transactions, errors occur. The following listing is an academic demonstration of such an attempt:

```
BEGIN TRANSACTION t1
    BEGIN TRANSACTION t2
    ROLLBACK TRANSACTION t2
ROLLBACK TRANSACTION t1
```

SQL Server will return an error:

```
Server: Msg 6401, Level 16, State 1, Line 3
Cannot roll back t2. No transaction or savepoint of that name was found.
```

TIP

You can see that you need to know the name of the outer transaction that has called all other stored procedures/transactions. This is not a practical requirement, especially when your stored procedure will be called from more than one stored procedure. Therefore, I recommend that you do not use transaction names.

Savepoints

SQL Server contains a mechanism for rolling back only part of a transaction. This statement may seem to contradict the basic idea of a SQL Server transaction as I have explained it, but it can be justified in some cases. Microsoft recommends *savepoints* be used if it is more expensive to check whether the change will be valid in advance (for example, because of a slow connection) and when the operation has a high probability of success. For example, assume that you are trying to reserve a set of plane tickets (or to get a set of some other resources) using different companies (distributed database system).

Each leg of a journey has to be booked separately. If the reservation fails, you will roll back just that leg of the journey, not all the reservations that you already successfully made. Only in the case that it is impossible to find any alternative for the remaining part of the journey will you roll back the complete transaction.

To mark a savepoint in a transaction, use the following statement:

```
Save Tran[saction] {savepoint_name|@savepoint_variable}
```

The savepoint's name is also a SQL Server identifier, but SQL Server reads only the first 32 characters.

To roll back part of the transaction, you must use the savepoint name or variable:

```
Rollback Tran[saction] {savepoint_name|@savepoint_variable}
```

NOTE

Rollback Transaction statements without a savepoint will roll back the complete transaction.

Savepoints do not save anything to the database. They just mark the point to which you can roll back a transaction. Resources (like locks) also stay in place after a Save Transaction statement. They are released only when a transaction has been completed or canceled.

The following procedures are designed to store an order and a set of order items in a database. The ap_ScrapOrderItem_Save stored procedure uses savepoints to roll back the insertion of a particular item.

```
Create Procedure dbo.ap_ScrapOrder_Save
-- save order information.

     @dtsOrderDate smalldatetime,
     @intRequestedById int,
     @dtsTargetDate smalldatetime,
     @chvNote varchar(200),
     @insOrderTypeId smallint,
     @inyOrderStatusId tinyint
As
     Set nocount on

     Insert dbo.[Order](OrderDate,   RequestedById,
                        TargetDate,  Note,
                        OrderTypeId, OrderStatusId)
```

```
        Values (@dtsOrderDate,        @intRequestedById,
                @dtsTargetDate,        @chvNote,
                @insOrderTypeId,       @inyOrderStatusId)

Return @@identity
Go


Create Procedure dbo.ap_ScrapOrderItem_Save
-- Saves order item.
-- If error occurs, this item will be rolled back,
-- but other items will be saved.

-- demonstration of use of Save Transaction
-- must be called from sp or batch that initiates transaction
        @intOrderId int,
        @intInventoryId int,
        @intOrderItemId int OUTPUT
As
        Set nocount on
        Declare   @intErrorCode int,
                  @chvInventoryId varchar(10)

        -- name the transaction savepoint
        Set @chvInventoryId = Convert(varchar, @intInventoryId)

        Save Transaction @chvInventoryId

        -- Set value of Lease of all equipment associated
        -- with expired Lease Schedule to 0
        Insert dbo.OrderItem (OrderId, InventoryId)
        Values (@intOrderId, @intInventoryId)

        Select @intOrderItemId = @@identity,
               @intErrorCode = @@Error

        If @intErrorCode <> 0
        Begin
                Rollback Transaction @chvInventoryId
                Return @intErrorCode
        End

Return 0
Go
```

Let's assume that the caller is some external application that is trying to fulfill an order by adding line item by line item. If one line item fails, the application will detect an error, roll back to the last savepoint, and try to add some other line item.

The stored procedures are designed in such a manner that a transaction must be initiated by the caller. You can test the stored procedures by using the following batch:

```
Declare    @intOrderId int,
           @intOrderItemId int


Begin Tran
Exec @intOrderId = dbo.ap_ScrapOrder_Save
        @dtsOrderDate = '1/10/2003',
        @intRequestedById = 1,
        @dtsTargetDate = '1/1/2004',
        @chvNote = NULL,
        @insOrderTypeId = 3, -- scrap
        @inyOrderStatusId = 1 -- ordered
Exec dbo.ap_ScrapOrderItem_Save
        @intOrderId,
        5,
        @intOrderItemId OUTPUT
Exec dbo.ap_ScrapOrderItem_Save
        @intOrderId,
        6,
        @intOrderItemId OUTPUT
Exec dbo.ap_ScrapOrderItem_Save
        @intOrderId,
        8,
        @intOrderItemId OUTPUT
Commit Tran
```

In nested transaction statements, transaction names are ignored or can cause errors. If you are using transactions in stored procedures, which could be called from within other transactions, do not use transaction names. In the previous example, although stored procedures with transaction names are called from a batch (it could have been implemented as a stored procedure), the transaction itself was not nested.

Locking

Let me remind you of the requirements represented by the so-called ACID test. The isolation requirement means that changes to the database made by a transaction are not visible to other transactions that are themselves in an intermediate state at the time of that transaction's completion, and that before the transaction is committed, other transactions can see data only in the state it was in before the transaction.

To satisfy the isolation requirement, SQL Server uses locks. A *lock* is a restriction placed on the use of a resource in a multi-user environment. It prevents other users (that is, processes) from accessing or modifying data in the resource. SQL Server automatically acquires and releases locks on resources in accordance with the actions a user performs. For example, while the user is updating a table, nobody else can modify (and in some cases, even see) records that are already updated. As soon as all updates connected to the user action are completed, the locks are released and the records become accessible.

There is just one problem with this process. Other users have to wait for the resource to become available again—they are *blocked.* Such blocking can lead to performance problems or even cause a process to fail. The use of locking is a trade-off between data integrity and performance. SQL Server is intelligent enough to handle most problems, and it does a great job of preventing problems. It is also possible to control locking using *transaction isolation levels* and *optimizer (lock) hints,* both of which are described in the next section. Locks can have different levels of *granularity.* They can be acquired on

- ▶ Rows
- ▶ Pages
- ▶ Keys
- ▶ Ranges of keys
- ▶ Indexes
- ▶ Tables
- ▶ Databases

SQL Server automatically acquires a lock of the appropriate granularity on a resource. If SQL Server determines during execution that a lock is no longer adequate, it dynamically changes the lock's granularity.

Locks are acquired by connection. Even if two connections are initiated from the same application, one can block the other.

The type of lock acquired by SQL Server depends on the effect that the change statement will have on the resource. For example, different locks are applied for the Select statement and the Update statement. There are five lock types:

▶ **Shared (read) locks**   Usually acquired for operations that do not modify data (that is, read operations). Another transaction can also acquire a nonexclusive lock on the same record, and thus the lock is shared. The shared lock is released when the transaction moves on to read another record.

▶ **Exclusive (write) locks**   Acquired for statements that modify data (such as Insert, Update, and Delete). Only one exclusive lock on a resource can be held at a time. An exclusive lock can be acquired only after other locks on the resource (including shared locks) are released.

▶ **Update locks**   Resemble shared locks more than they do exclusive locks. They are used to notify SQL Server that a transaction will later modify a resource. They prevent other transactions from acquiring exclusive locks. Update locks can coexist with shared locks. Just before the resource is modified, SQL Server promotes the update lock to an exclusive lock.

▶ **Intent locks**   Set on an object of higher granularity to notify SQL Server that a process has placed a lock of lower granularity inside the object. For example, if a transaction places a lock on a page in a table, it will also place an intent lock on the table. The intent lock means that SQL Server does not have to scan the whole table to find out if a process has placed a lock on some page or record inside, in order to place a table lock for another transaction. In fact, there are three different types of intent locks: IS (intent share), IX (intent exclusive), and SIX (shared with intent exclusive).

▶ **Schema locks**   Prevent the dropping or modifying of a table or index while it is in use. There are two types of schema locks. Sch-S (schema stability) locks prevent table or index drops. Sch-M (schema modification) locks ensure that other transactions cannot access the resource while it is being modified.

Transaction Isolation Levels and Hints

You can change the default behavior of SQL Server using transaction isolation levels or lock hints. Transaction isolation levels set locking at the connection level, and lock hints set locking at the statement level. SQL Server can work on five different transaction isolation levels:

▶ **Serializable**   The highest level in which transactions are completely isolated. The system behaves as though the transactions are occurring one after another. SQL Server will hold locks on both data and key records until the end of the transaction. This may lead to some performance issues.

▶ **Repeatable Read**   Forces SQL Server to place shared locks on data records and hold them until the transaction is completed. Unfortunately, it allows *phantoms,* which occur when a transaction reads a range of records. There is no guarantee that some other concurrent transaction will not add records that fall in the range or modify keys of records so that they fall out of the range. If the uncommitted transaction repeats the read, the result will be inconsistent.

▶ **Read Committed**   The default level in SQL Server. SQL Server places shared locks while reading. It allows phantoms and *nonrepeatable reads.* There is no guarantee that the value of the record that a transaction reads multiple times during execution will stay consistent. Some other transaction could change it.

▶ **Read Uncommitted**   The lowest level of isolation in SQL Server. It ensures that physically corrupt data is not read. SQL Server will not place shared locks, and it will ignore exclusive locks. You will have the fewest performance issues when using this level, but you will also likely have many data integrity problems. It allows phantoms, nonrepeatable reads, and *dirty reads* (everybody can see the content of the changed record, even if a transaction is not yet committed and could potentially be rolled back).

▶ **Snapshot**   A new level of isolation introduced in SQL Server 2005. It is designed to support databases that use row versioning to reduce blocking of readers and writers. The engine stores versions of rows before they were modified in *tempdb* and serves them to readers until the transaction is completed. This reduces blocking time but increases the need for processing power and memory. It could lead to concurrency conflicts. Readers do not issue shared locks.

NOTE

There is one database setting that changes the behavior of SQL Server by using the same row versioning mechanism as Snapshot isolation level. It is also introduced in SQL Server 2005. In some ways it is like Snapshot and in some ways like Read Committed isolation level. Like Snapshot, it is based on row versioning. Since this is a database setting, it will preserve earlier versions of all rows changed in the database (not just rows that are changed in a session set to Snapshot isolation level). Like with Read Committed, SQL Server can return to readers consistent versions of rows (before the transaction). But since SQL Server can return to readers earlier versions of all rows that are still being changed or locked in transactions, readers do not have to wait for transactions to be completed and therefore do not have to issue read locks.

The isolation level is specified in the Set Transaction Isolation Level statement. For example:

```
Set Transaction Isolation Level Repeatable Read
```

Locking hints change the behavior of the locking manager as it processes a single Transact-SQL statement. They overwrite behavior set by the transaction isolation level. The following table describes hints that can be used to control locking:

Hints	Description
Holdlock or Serializable	Holds a shared lock until a transaction is completed. The lock will not be released when the resource is no longer needed, but rather when the transaction is completed.
Nolock	This hint applies only to Select statements. SQL Server will not place shared locks and it will ignore exclusive locks.
Updlock	Uses update instead of shared locks while reading a table.
Rowlock	Specifies the granularity of locks at the row level.
Paglock	Specifies the granularity of locks at the page level.
Tablock	Specifies the granularity of locks at the table level.
Tablockx	Specifies the granularity of locks at the table level and the type of lock to be exclusive.
Readcommitted	Equivalent to the default isolation level (Read Committed).
Readpast	This hint is applicable only in Select statements working under the Read Committed isolation level. Result sets created with this hint will not contain records locked by other transactions.
Readuncommitted	Equivalent to the Read Uncommitted isolation level.
Repeatableread	Equivalent to the Repeatable Read isolation level.

Locking hints can be used in Select, Insert, Update, or Delete statements. They are set after the table reference in SQL statements (for example, in the From clause of a Select statement or in the Insert clause of an Insert statement). Their scope is just the table that they are used for. For example, the following command will hold a lock until the transaction is completed:

```
Select *
From Inventory With (HOLDLOCK)
Where InventoryId = @intInventoryId
```

Nobody will be able to change data records that were read and keys that match the criteria of this table until the transaction is completed. Therefore, this table cannot have phantoms, nonrepeatable reads, or dirty reads.

The next example demonstrates the use of hints in an Update statement and the use of more than one hint in a statement:

```
Update Inventory With (TABLOCKX, HOLDLOCK)
Set StatusId = 4
Where StatusId = @intStatusId
```

The complete table will be locked for the duration of the transaction.

Distributed Transactions

Microsoft Distributed Transaction Coordinator (MSDTC) is a component that allows you to span transactions over two or more servers while maintaining transactional integrity.

Servers in this scenario are called *resource managers,* and MSDTC performs the function of transaction manager. In fact, all those resource managers do not even have to be Microsoft servers; they just have to be compatible with MSDTC. For example, it is possible to execute a single transaction against databases on Microsoft SQL Server and Oracle.

When transactions are distributed over different resource managers, different mechanisms have to be applied by the transaction coordinator to compensate for problems that might occur in such an environment. A typical problem is network failure. For example, everything might be executed properly by each individual resource manager, but if the transaction coordinator is not informed due to a network failure, the result is the same as if one of the resource managers had failed, and the transaction will be rolled back.

The mechanism for dealing with such problems is called the *two-phase commit (2PC).* As the name implies, it consists of two phases:

▶ **Prepare phase**   Starts when a transaction manager receives a request to execute a transaction. It notifies the resource managers and informs them of the work that needs to be done. The resource managers perform all changes and even write everything from the transaction login memory to the disk. When everything is completed, each resource manager sends a status message indicating success or failure to the transaction manager.

▶ **Commit phase**   Starts when the transaction manager receives messages from resource managers. If the resource managers successfully complete the preparation phase, the transaction manager sends a Commit command to the resource managers. Each of them makes the changes permanently to the database and reports the success of the operation to the transaction manager. If any of the resource managers reports failure during the preparation phase, the transaction manager will send a Rollback command to all resource managers.

From a developer's point of view, distributed transactions are very similar to regular transactions. The major difference is that you need to use the following statement to start the transaction:

```
Begin Distributed Tran[saction]   [transaction_name]
```

Distributed transactions can also be started implicitly, by executing a query or stored procedure that will be run against distributed servers.

Transactions are completed with regular Commit or Rollback statements. The following stored procedure updates two tables in a local database and then updates information in a remote database using a remote stored procedure:

```
Alter Procedure ap_LeaseShedule_Clear_distributed
-- Set value of Lease of all equipment associated to 0
-- Set total amount of Lease Schedule to 0.
-- notify lease company that lease schedule is completed
    @intLeaseScheduleId int
As
    Declare @chvLeaseNumber varchar(50),
            @intError int

    -- Verify that lease has expired
    If GetDate() <  (Select EndDate
                     From dbo.LeaseSchedule
                     Where ScheduleId = @intLeaseScheduleId)
        Raiserror ('Specified lease schedule has not expired yet!', 16,1)

    If @@Error <> 0
    Begin
        Print 'Unable to eliminate lease amounts from the database!'
        Return 50000
    End

    -- get lease number
    Select @chvLeaseNumber = Lease.LeaseNumber
    From dbo.Lease Lease
    Inner Join dbo.LeaseSchedule  LeaseSchedule
    On Lease.LeaseId = LeaseSchedule.LeaseId
    Where (LeaseSchedule.ScheduleId = @intLeaseScheduleId)

    Begin Distributed Transaction
```

```
    -- Set value of Lease of all equipment associated to 0
    Update dbo.Inventory
    Set Lease = 0
    Where LeaseScheduleId = @intLeaseScheduleId
    If @@Error <> 0 Goto PROBLEM

    -- Set total amount of Lease Schedule to 0
    Update LeaseSchedule
    Set PeriodicTotalAmount = 0
    Where ScheduleId = @intLeaseScheduleId
    If @@Error <> 0 Goto PROBLEM

    -- notify lease vendor
Exec @intError = lease_srvr.LeaseShedules..prLeaseScheduleComplete
                    @chvLeaseNumber, @intLeaseScheduleId

    If @intError <> 0 GoTo PROBLEM

    Commit Transaction
    Return 0

PROBLEM:
    print 'Unable to complete lease schedule!'
    Rollback Transaction
Return 50000
```

Apart from a reference to the remote stored procedure, the only thing that needed to be done was to use the Distributed keyword to start the transaction. Everything else was managed by MSDTC.

Typical Transaction-related Problems

Transactions are a powerful weapon in the hands of a programmer, but improper use can cause substantial damage. I will try to forewarn you of some typical problems.

A Never-ending Story

The worst thing that you can do is to explicitly open a transaction and then forget to close it. All changes sent to the database through that connection will become part of that transaction; resources normally released at the end of a transaction are held indefinitely; other users cannot access resources; and eventually, your server chokes.

Spanning a Transaction over Batches

A transaction can span batches. SQL Server counts transactions over the connection, so it is "legal" to issue two batches like this over one connection:

```
Begin Transaction
update dbo.Inventory
set Lease = 0
where LeaseScheduleId = 141
Go

update dbo.LeaseSchedule
Set PeriodicTotalAmount = 0
where ScheduleId = 141
Commit Transaction
Go
```

However, I cannot think of any justification for doing so, and you significantly increase the probability of error. For example, you could easily forget to finish the transaction.

TIP

There are some cases in which it is justified for a transaction to span batches; for example, when a DDL statement must be in a separate batch.

Rollback Before Begin

Sometimes you might set your error handling so that all errors that occur in a stored procedure are treated in the same way. Naturally, you will include a statement to roll back the transaction. If an error occurs before the transaction starts, the stored procedure will jump to the error handling code and another error will occur:

```
Create Procedure dbo.ap_LeaseShedule_Clear_1
-- Set value of Lease of all equipment associated
-- with expired Lease Schedule to 0
-- Set total amount of Lease Schedule to 0.

    @intLeaseScheduleId int
As

    -- Verify that lease has expired
    If GetDate() < (select EndDate
                    from dbo.LeaseSchedule
                    where ScheduleId = @intLeaseScheduleId)
        Raiserror ('Specified lease schedule has not expired yet!', 16,1)
```

```
-- If error occurs here,
-- server will execute Rollback before transaction is started!
if @@Error <> 0 goto PROBLEM

Begin Transaction

-- Set value of Lease of all equipment associated
-- with expired Lease Schedule to 0
update dbo.Inventory
set Lease = 0
where LeaseScheduleId = @intLeaseScheduleId
if @@Error <> 0 goto PROBLEM

-- Set total amount of Lease Schedule to 0
update dbo.LeaseSchedule
Set PeriodicTotalAmount = 0
where ScheduleId = @intLeaseScheduleId
if @@Error <> 0 goto PROBLEM

commit transaction
return 0
```

```
PROBLEM:

print 'Unable to eliminate lease amounts from the database!'
    rollback transaction
return 1
```

Multiple Rollbacks

Unlike Commit statements, only one Rollback statement is required to close a set of nested transactions. In fact, if more than one Rollback statement is executed, SQL Server will raise another error.

Long Transactions

SQL Server places locks on data that has been modified by a transaction, to prevent other users from further changing the data until the transaction is committed. This feature can lead to problems if a transaction takes "too long" to complete.

NOTE

There is no exact definition of "too long." The longer a transaction works, the greater the likelihood that problems will occur.

Some of the problems that might occur if a long transaction is present in the database include the following:

- Other users are blocked. They will not be able to access and modify data.

- The transaction log fills up. (SQL Server 2000 and SQL Server 7.0 can be configured to automatically increase the size of the transaction log, but you could fill your disk as well.)

- Most of the time, transaction log work is performed in memory. If all available memory is used before the transaction is complete, SQL Server will start saving changes to disk, thus reducing the overall performance of the server.

TIP

You should be particularly aware of concurrency problems because they are the problems most likely to happen. While you are developing applications, you will probably work alone (or in a small group) on the server, but the situation will change drastically when you place 50, 250, or 5000 concurrent users on the production server.

CHAPTER 6

Error Handling

A developer's effective use of error handling procedures is often an excellent indicator of his or her experience in that particular programming language. Those of us who deal with a C# or Visual Basic environment are accustomed to a whole set of feature-rich error handling objects, procedures, and functions. Compared with those, Transact-SQL seems rather inadequate. However, the situation has improved a little since earlier versions. Remember, as a professional, you cannot let the apparent limitations of this tool set justify sloppy solutions.

This section starts by investigating how errors can be returned to a caller. It then discusses the basic concept and statements from the classic @@Error function, through the new Try - Catch block, to an unorthodox solution based on the Set Xact_ Abort On statement. The chapter also includes three sections with three coherent error handling architectures/methodologies that you can use on your projects.

Raiserror()

An important tool for implementing error handling is the Raiserror statement. Its main purpose is to return a user-defined or system-defined message to the caller. Open a Query window and execute the following statement:

```
Raiserror ('An error occurred!', 0, 1)
```

The second and third parameters indicate the severity and state of the error. Management Studio will display an error message in the Results pane (see Figure 6-1).

Severity provides a rough indication of the type of problem that SQL Server has encountered. Acceptable values are 0 to 25; however, ordinary users and applications can specify only 0 to 18. Only members of the sysadmin role or users with Alter Trace permissions are allowed to set errors above 18. Severity levels 20 to 25 are considered catastrophic. SQL Server will stop executing Transact-SQL code if such an error is encountered. You should typically use severity levels 11 to 16. Severity level 10 indicates issues with values entered by the caller. Severity level 10 and below are considered warnings. If such an error is raised, the engine will display the error message as ordinary text and continue as if nothing has happened. You will see later that it will not even be caught by the Try - Catch statement. Severity levels between 11 and 16 are also used for errors that can be corrected by the user. If they occur, Management Studio will display the error as red text. Errors with a severity of 17 or higher are not considered application errors and should be reported to an administrator.

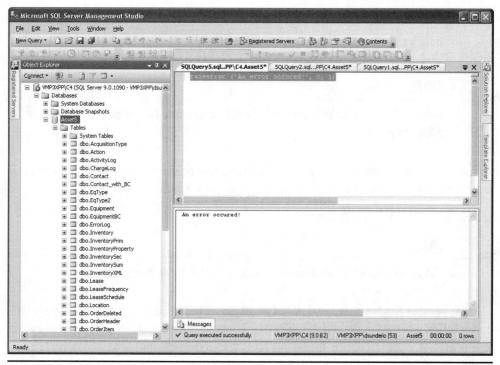

Figure 6-1   *Using Raiserror*

The *state* of the error is used when the same error is raised from multiple positions in the code. By specifying the state of the error, you will be able to distinguish between these multiple instances.

After the error is raised, the caller will be able to detect it. If the caller is written in Transact-SQL, it can, for example, investigate the value of the @@Error function. If the Raiserror statement does not specify an error number (as was the case in the preceding example), SQL Server assigns the default value of 50000 to the error.

You can also display errors that are predefined in SQL Server if you reference them by their numbers, and you can define your own errors using the sp_addmessage system stored procedure:

```
Exec sp_addmessage 50001,
                16,
                'Unable to update Total of LeaseSchedule'
```

Then you can display this message using the following statement:

```
Raiserror (50001, 16, 1)
```

The server will return the following:

```
Server: Msg 50001, Level 16, State 1, Line 1
Unable to update Total of LeaseSchedule
```

NOTE

Error numbers below 50000 are reserved for SQL Server errors. You can use any integer above 50000 for your errors.

You can set the state and severity of the error, record the error in the SQL Server Error Log, and even record the error in the Windows NT Error Log:

```
Raiserror (50001, 16, 1) WITH LOG
```

NOTE

SQL Server requires that all errors with a severity of 19 or higher be logged.

Management Studio contains a tool for displaying and editing error messages. To start it, click a server node and then choose Tools | Manage SQL Server Messages.

It is also possible to define messages (using sp_addmessage) that will accept additional arguments at runtime (using Raiserror):

```
Exec sp_addmessage 50002,
                   16,
                   'Unable to update %s.'
```

%s is a placeholder for string arguments and %d is one for integers. The syntax is inspired by the printf statement in C. You can find more information on this topic in SQL Server Books OnLine, but you will typically use just these two placeholders.

The Raiserror command can accept up to 20 arguments (values or local variables) at the end of the parameter list.

```
Raiserror (50002, 16, 1, 'LeaseSchedule table')
```

SQL Server will combine the message and arguments:

```
Msg 50002, Level 16, State 1, Line 1
Unable to update LeaseSchedule table.
```

Using Error Handling

Since Transact-SQL is so laconic (critics may say feature-poor), development DBAs commonly express themselves in a very concise manner. DBAs frequently write ad hoc scripts for one-time use or manual execution, and they thus neglect the need for consistent error handling.

Logic that is fine in standard languages like Visual Basic or C frequently does not work in Transact-SQL. For example, an error may occur in Transact-SQL, but if Transact-SQL does not consider it fatal, processing will continue. Also, if the error is fatal, all processing will stop. The process does not react—it is just killed.

Why Bother?

For many, the question is, Why be concerned with implementing error handling at all? Let us review this question through the following example:

```
Create Procedure dbo.ap_LeasedAsset_Insert1
-- Insert leased asset and update total in LeaseSchedule.
-- (demonstration of imperfect solution)
(
          @intEqId int,
          @intLocationId int,
          @intStatusId int,
          @intLeaseId int,
          @intLeaseScheduleId int,
          @intOwnerId int,
          @mnyLease money,
          @intAcquisitionTypeID int
)
As
set nocount on

begin transaction

-- insert asset
insert dbo.Inventory(EqId,           LocationId,
                     StatusId,       LeaseId,
                     LeaseScheduleId, OwnerId,
                     Lease,          AcquisitionTypeID)
```

```
values (@intEqId,        @intLocationId,
        @intStatusId,        @intLeaseId,
        @intLeaseScheduleId, @intOwnerId,
        @mnyLease,           @intAcquisitionTypeID)
-- update total
update dbo.LeaseSchedule
Set PeriodicTotalAmount = PeriodicTotalAmount + @mnyLease
where LeaseId = @intLeaseId

commit transaction

return
```

This may seem like a trivial example, and it is true that in all probability nothing would go wrong, but imagine that an error occurs on the Update statement. The error could be for any reason—overflow, violation of a constraint, or inadequate security privileges, for example. As explained earlier, transactions do not automatically roll back when an error occurs. Instead, SQL Server simply commits everything that was changed when it encounters the Commit Transaction statement as if nothing unusual had happened. Unfortunately, from that moment on, the total of the lease schedule will have the wrong value.

Error Handling Based on @@Error

In earlier versions of SQL Server, the only way to detect an error in Transact-SQL code was to test the @@Error function. The basic idea was to place error handling in critical positions in the code. The result would be something like the following:

```
Create Procedure prInsertLeasedAsset_2
-- Insert leased asset and update total in LeaseSchedule.
-- (demonstration of not exactly perfect solution)
    (
        @intEqId int,
        @intLocationId int,
        @intStatusId int,
        @intLeaseId int,
        @intLeaseScheduleId int,
        @intOwnerId int,
        @mnyLease money,
        @intAcquisitionTypeID int
    )
```

```
As
set nocount on

begin transaction

-- insert asset
insert Inventory(EqId,              LocationId,
                 StatusId,           LeaseId,
                 LeaseScheduleId,    OwnerId,
                 Lease,              AcquisitionTypeID)
values (         @intEqId,          @intLocationId,
                 @intStatusId,       @intLeaseId,
                 @intLeaseScheduleId, @intOwnerId,
                 @mnyLease,          @intAcquisitionTypeID)
If @@error <> 0
Begin
    Print 'Unexpected error occurred!'
    Rollback transaction
    Return 1
End

-- update total
update LeaseSchedule
Set PeriodicTotalAmount = PeriodicTotalAmount + @mnyLease
where LeaseId = @intLeaseId

If @@error <> 0
Begin
    Print 'Unexpected error occurred!'
    Rollback transaction
    Return 1
End

commit transaction

return 0
```

One serious limitation of the @@Error function is that it changes its value after each Transact-SQL statement. In the preceding stored procedure, if an error occurred in the Insert statement, the If statement that tests the value of the @@Error function will trap it. Unfortunately, the value of @@Error will immediately be reset to zero because the second If statement executes successfully.

Error Handling Architecture: Based on @@Error

There are ways to use @@Error more consistently. I have described them in a previous edition of this book and in an article in SQL Server Professional, "Error Handling in T-SQL: From Casual to Religious." You can find it on MSDN:

http://msdn.microsoft.com/library/default.asp?url=/library/en-us/dnsqlpro2k/html/sql00f15.asp

You should definitely read the article (and the previous edition of this book) if you are planning to work on SQL Server 2000 or earlier versions, but they are also useful if you want to go deeper into error handling techniques in the current version of SQL Server.

Try - Catch Statement

A new feature in SQL Server is the Try - Catch statement. It consists of a single Try block and a single Catch block that must be placed one after the other. You can enclose a group of other Transact-SQL statements in the Try block. If an error occurs in the Try block, control is transferred to the group of statements in the Catch block. Naturally, when an error is trapped and handled (by executing statements in the Catch block), it will not be reported to the caller. When execution of the Catch block is completed, the engine will return control to the first statement after the Catch block. (There are some exceptions. We will explore them in the upcoming "Try - Catch Statement Nesting" section.) If execution of a statement in the Try block is completed without problems, the statements in the Catch block will be skipped and the engine will start executing the statement after the Catch block.

```
Create Procedure dbo.ap_ChargeLog_Insert
    @ItemId int,
    @ActionId smallint,
    @Cost money,
    @Note varchar(max),
    @Activity varchar(1000)
as

BEGIN TRY
    INSERT [dbo].[ChargeLog]([ItemId],[ActionId],[ChargeDate],
                            [Cost],[Note])
    VALUES (@ItemId, @ActionId, GetDate(), @Cost, @Note)
```

```
    INSERT INTO [dbo].[ActivityLog]([Activity],[LogDate],
                                    [UserName],[Note])
    VALUES(@Activity, GetDate(), system_user, @Note)
END TRY
BEGIN CATCH
    INSERT INTO [dbo].[ErrorLog]([ErrorNum],[ErrorType],
                                 [ErrorMsg],[ErrorSource])
    VALUES (50000,'E', 'Unable to record transaction in ChargeLog.',
            'ap_ChargeLog_Insert')
END CATCH
```

```
Return
```

The stored procedure opens a transaction and then tries to execute two Insert statements. If either of the statements fails, the transaction will be rolled back and the record will be logged in a special table.

What Errors Are Trapped

SQL Server 2005 is better than its predecessor at trapping a wider variety of errors. I'll now discuss which types of errors can be trapped and which cannot.

The Try - Catch statement does not catch warnings:

```
BEGIN TRY
    Print 'Begin try'
    INSERT [dbo].[ChargeLog]([ItemId],[ActionId],[ChargeDate],[Cost],[Note])
    VALUES (30, 15, GetDate(), $150, null)

    raiserror ('Some Error!', 10, 1)

    INSERT INTO [dbo].[ActivityLog]([Activity],[LogDate],[UserName],[Note])
    VALUES    ('Repair',GetDate(),system_user,null)
    Print 'End try'
END TRY
BEGIN CATCH
    print 'Catch'
    INSERT INTO [dbo].[ErrorLog]([ErrorNum],[ErrorType],[ErrorMsg],[ErrorSource])
    VALUES (50000,'E', 'Unable to record transaction in
ChargeLog.','ap_ChargeLog_Insert')
END CATCH

Print 'Finished!'
```

If you execute the preceding example, you will see that the Try block ignores the warning and continues as though nothing happened:

```
Begin try

(1 row(s) affected)
Some Error!

(1 row(s) affected)
End try
Finished!
```

One big problem in previous versions was that fatal errors automatically led to discontinuation of processing. This version of SQL Server is much better at trapping and resolving fatal errors (with a severity level equal to or higher than 17). If the connection is not lost, the SQL Server engine will attempt to handle the error and continue.

In the following example, I'll raise a fatal error.

```
BEGIN TRY
    print 'Begin try'
    raiserror ('Some Error!', 23, 1)
    print 'End try'
END TRY
BEGIN CATCH
    print 'Catch'
END CATCH

Print 'Finished!'
```

SQL Server 2005 will trap this error and continue with the code in the Catch block:

```
Begin try
Catch
Finished!
```

Now, let's try the equivalent code in SQL Server 2000:

```
print 'start'
Raiserror('Some error!', 23, 1) With LOG
if @@error <> 0
    print 'Error detected!'
```

In this case, SQL Server 2000 will automatically break the connection:

```
start
Server: Msg 50000, Level 23, State 1, Line 2
Some error!
```

```
Connection Broken
```

Earlier versions of SQL Server failed to process some errors of severity levels even lower than 17. In the following example, I'll try to assign a date to an integer variable:

```
declare @i int
print 'start'
set @i = '2/2/2005'
if @@error <> 0
    print 'error occurred'
print 'finished'
```

Unfortunately, SQL Server 2000 abruptly stops execution of the stored procedure or batch:

```
start
Server: Msg 245, Level 16, State 1, Line 4
Syntax error converting the varchar value '2/2/2005' to a column of data type int.
```

Let's try the equivalent code in SQL Server 2005:

```
BEGIN TRY
    print 'Begin try'
    declare @i int
    set @i = '2/2/2'
    print 'End try'
END TRY
BEGIN CATCH
    print 'Catch'
END CATCH
print 'Finished'
```

As expected, the engine traps the error:

```
Begin try
Catch
Finished
```

Functions of the Catch Block

There is a set of special error handling functions that works only inside of the Catch block:

Function	Purpose
Error_Message()	Returns the error message that would normally be returned to the caller application
Error_Number()	Returns the identifier of the error
Error_Severity()	Returns the severity
Error_State()	Returns the state
Error_Procedure()	Returns the name of the procedure (or other programmatic database object) in which the error has occurred
Error_Line()	Returns the line number of the procedure in which the error has occurred

An important new feature of these functions (as compared to @@Error) is that they keep their values in the Catch block. You can reference them multiple times. These functions are important for investigating the error and also for notifying the caller if there are problems. For example, the following procedure uses them to assemble a custom error message that will be stored in the error log, and then raises the error to notify the caller application:

```
Alter Procedure dbo.ap_ChargeLog_Insert2
    @ItemId int,
    @ActionId smallint,
    @Cost money,
    @Note varchar(max),
    @Activity varchar(1000)
as

BEGIN TRY
    INSERT [dbo].[ChargeLog]([ItemId],[ActionId],[ChargeDate],
                             [Cost],[Note])
    VALUES (@ItemId, @ActionId, GetDate(),
            @Cost, @Note)

    INSERT INTO [dbo].[ActivityLog]([Activity],[LogDate],
                                    [UserName],[Note])
    VALUES(@Activity, GetDate(),
           system_user, @Note)
END TRY
BEGIN CATCH
    declare @severity int
    set @severity = Error_Severity()
```

```
    declare @msg varchar(255)
    set @msg = 'Unable to record transaction in ChargeLog.'
            + 'Error(' + ERROR_NUMBER() + '):' + ERROR_MESSAGE()
            + ' Severity  = ' + ERROR_SEVERITY()
            + ' State     = ' + ERROR_STATE()
            + ' Procedure = ' + ERROR_PROCEDURE()
            + ' Line num. = ' + ERROR_LINE()

    INSERT INTO [dbo].[ErrorLog]([ErrorNum],[ErrorType],[ErrorMsg],[ErrorSource])
    VALUES (ERROR_NUMBER(), 'E', @msg, ERROR_PROCEDURE())

    RAISERROR (@msg, @severity, 2)
END CATCH

Return
```

The last statement in the Catch block is re-throwing the error to the caller. Note that I could not use the Error_Severity() function in Raiserror(). Only values and variables are allowed in Raiserror().

Try - Catch Statement with Explicit Transactions

The first thing that you should note regarding Try - Catch statements and transactions is that there is nothing magical—you have to roll back the transaction in the Catch block manually.

```
Alter Procedure dbo.ap_ChargeLog_Insert_wTran
    @ItemId int,
    @ActionId smallint,
    @Cost money,
    @Note varchar(max),
    @Activity varchar(1000)
as

BEGIN TRY
    BEGIN TRAN
    INSERT [dbo].[ChargeLog]([ItemId],[ActionId],[ChargeDate],
                            [Cost],[Note])
    VALUES (@ItemId, @ActionId, GetDate(), @Cost, @Note)

    INSERT INTO dbo.ActivityLog(Activity,LogDate,UserName,Note)
    VALUES   (@Activity,GetDate(),system_user,@Note)
    COMMIT TRAN
END TRY
```

```
BEGIN CATCH
    ROLLBACK TRAN
    INSERT dbo.ErrorLog(ErrorNum,[ErrorType],[ErrorMsg],[ErrorSource])
    VALUES (50000,'E', 'Unable to record transaction in ChargeLog.',
            ERROR_PROCEDURE())
END CATCH
return
```

Theoretically, it is possible when an error occurs to investigate the state of a transaction further. The new SQL Server 2005 function Xact_State() can test the state of the transaction. The function returns 0 if no transaction is open. It returns 1 if a transaction is open and can be committed or rolled back. When it returns −1, the opened transaction is *uncommittable*. In this state, no modifications are possible. This typically occurs when something dramatic happens on the server (e.g., when the transaction log becomes full). Data can be read and all locks are preserved in place (so you can investigate everything), but in order to continue modifications, you must issue a rollback.

It is debatable how logical or justified the following stored procedure may be, but it illustrates the use of the Xact_State() function. The transaction is relatively complex, consisting of several Insert and Select statements. Therefore, the Catch block is also more complex. It first handles the two simpler cases in which a transaction is uncommittable or not open. In these cases, error handling is straightforward—the transaction should be rolled back or ignored. Most interesting is the case in which a transaction is committable. You have to perform additional checks before deciding whether to commit or roll back:

```
Alter Procedure dbo.ap_ChargeLog_Insert_wTranState
    @ItemId int,
    @ActionId smallint,
    @Cost money,
    @Note varchar(max),
    @Activity varchar(1000)
as
declare @Today smalldatetime
declare @User sysname
declare @ErrorCode int
declare @EqId int
declare @Price money

BEGIN TRY
    select @Today = GetDate()
    set @User = system_user

    BEGIN TRAN
    INSERT [dbo].[ChargeLog]([ItemId],[ActionId],[ChargeDate],
                            [Cost],[Note])
```

```
    VALUES (@ItemId, @ActionId, @Today, @Cost, @Note)

    select @EqId = EqId from dbo.OrderItem
    where ItemId = @ItemId

    select @EqId = EqId from dbo.OrderItem
    where ItemId = @ItemId

    select @Price = Price
    from dbo.PriceList
    where EqId = @EqId

    INSERT INTO dbo.Sales(EqId, [UnitPrice], [Qty], [ExtPrice] ,[SalesDate])
     VALUES (@EqId, @Price, 1, @Price, @today)

    INSERT INTO dbo.ActivityLog(Activity,LogDate,UserName,Note)
    VALUES   (@Activity, @Today , @User, @Note)

    COMMIT TRAN
END TRY
BEGIN CATCH
    set @ErrorCode = Error_Number()
    if xact_state() = -1
    begin
       -- transaction is uncommittable
       ROLLBACK TRAN
       INSERT dbo.ErrorLog(ErrorNum,ErrorType,ErrorMsg,ErrorSource, ErrorState)
       VALUES (@ErrorCode, 'E', 'Unable to record transaction in ChargeLog.',
           ERROR_PROCEDURE(), -1)
    end
    else if xact_state() = 0
    begin
       --error occurred before tran started
       INSERT dbo.ErrorLog(ErrorNum,ErrorType,ErrorMsg,ErrorSource, ErrorState)
       VALUES (@ErrorCode,'E', 'Unable to pre-process ChargeLog transaction.',
           ERROR_PROCEDURE(), 0)
    end
    else if xact_state() = 1
    begin
       --error could be committed or rolled back
       commit tran
       if exists(select * from dbo.ActivityLog
               where Activity = @Activity
               and LogDate = @Today
                   and UserName = @User)
       begin
          INSERT dbo.ErrorLog(ErrorNum,ErrorType,ErrorMsg,ErrorSource, ErrorState)
          VALUES (@ErrorCode,'E', 'Unable to record transaction in ActivityLog.',
              ERROR_PROCEDURE(), 1)
       end
```

```
        if exists(select * from dbo.Sales
                where EqId = @Activity
                and [SalesDate] = @Today)
        begin
           INSERT dbo.ErrorLog(ErrorNum,ErrorType,ErrorMsg,ErrorSource, ErrorState)
           VALUES (@ErrorCode,'E', 'Unable to record transaction in Sales.',
                ERROR_PROCEDURE(), 1)
        end
    end
END CATCH

return @ErrorCode
```

NOTE

I do not think that the design of this procedure is justifiable. Instead of performing additional checks to do error handling when the transaction is still committable, I should have split the Try block into multiple Try blocks and handled each case in a separate Catch block. Or, if all steps need not be completed to commit the transaction, then the transaction should be split into two or more transactions.

Deadlock Retries

One consequence of the wider set of errors that a Try - Catch block can trap in SQL Server 2005 is that you can create a Transact-SQL script to handle a deadlock.

Deadlocks

A *deadlock* is a situation that occurs in SQL Server when two connections are competing for resources at the same time and blocking each other's completion. There are several types of deadlocks, but the textbook example occurs when:

▶ Connection 1 locks resource (table) A and changes it.

▶ Connection 2 locks resource (table) B and changes it.

▶ Connection 1 tries to acquire a lock on table B, but it has to wait until connection 2 completes its transaction.

▶ Connection 2 tries to acquire a lock on table A, but it has to wait until connection 1 completes its transaction.

▶ SQL Server detects the deadlock and decides to kill one of the connections. Error 1502 is raised.

▶ The other connection completes the transaction.

First, let's try to simulate a deadlock. I have created two stored procedures each of which contains two modification statements and one WaitFor statement between them. The purpose of the WaitFor statement is to give me 10 seconds to operate Management Studio to execute the stored procedures so that their executions overlap. Note that the stored procedures access the same tables but in reverse order:

```
Alter Procedure [dbo].[ap_SalesByDate_IncreasePrice]
    @Factor real,
    @Date smalldatetime
as
set xact_abort on

begin tran
update dbo.Sales
set UnitPrice = UnitPrice * @Factor,
    ExtPrice = ExtPrice * @Factor
where  SalesDate = @Date

waitfor delay '0:00:10'

update dbo.PriceList
set Price = Price * @Factor

commit tran
return
GO

ALTER procedure [dbo].[ap_PriceByEqId_Set]
    @EqId int,
    @Price money
as
set xact_abort on
begin tran
update dbo.PriceList
set Price = @Price
where EqId = @EqId

waitfor delay '0:00:10'

update dbo.Sales
set UnitPrice = @Price,
    ExtPrice = @Price * Qty
where EqId = @EqId

commit tran
return
```

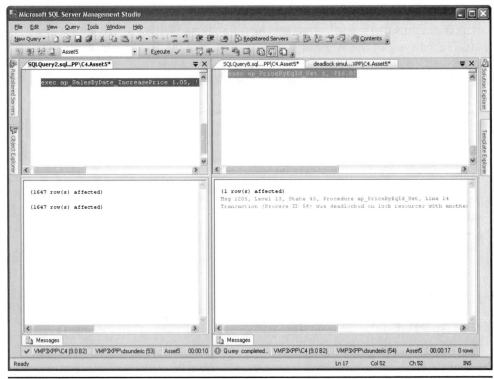

Figure 6-2   *Two connections after deadlock*

If you execute the procedures from two Query windows in Management Studio at approximately the same time (you have 10 seconds to start the second after the first), after some time SQL Server will detect a deadlock and kill one of the connections so that the other can continue (see Figure 6-2).

Deadlock errors in earlier versions of SQL Server resulted in a broken connection. In SQL Server 2005, they can be detected like any other error. Let's change one procedure to detect the error and retry execution after a delay in the loop:

```
ALTER procedure [dbo].[ap_PriceByEqId_Set_wRetry]
    @EqId int,
    @Price money
as
-- exec ap_PriceByEqId_Set_wRetry 1, $16.82
declare @i int
set @i = 1
while @i <= 10
```

```
begin
   begin try
      set xact_abort on
      begin tran

      update dbo.PriceList
      set Price = @Price
      where EqId = @EqId

      waitfor delay '0:00:10'

      update dbo.Sales
      set UnitPrice = @Price,
          ExtPrice = @Price * Qty
      where EqId = @EqId

      commit tran
      ------------
      print 'completed'
      break
   end try
   begin catch
      if ERROR_NUMBER() = 1205
      begin
         rollback tran
         set @i = @i + 1
         print 'retry'
         INSERT INTO [dbo].[ErrorLog]([ErrorNum],[ErrorType],[ErrorMsg]
           ,[ErrorSource],[CreatedBy],[CreateDT],[ErrorState])
         VALUES(Error_Number(), 'E', Error_Message(),
           Error_Procedure(), suser_sname(), GetDate(), Error_State())
         waitfor delay '0:00:03'
      end
   end catch
end
print 'Completed'
return
```

When you execute this stored procedure, it recovers from the error and succeeds the second time (see Figure 6-3).

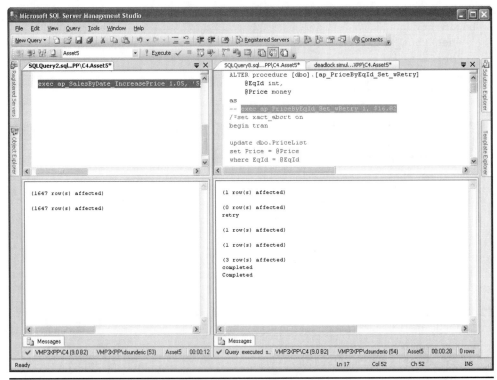

Figure 6-3 *Execution of stored procedures with loop for handling deadlock error*

NOTE

This type of deadlock error is called a cycle deadlock. The best way to handle cycle deadlocks is to change the order in which tables are modified. Changing the order would prevent a deadlock from occurring. Retry is the last resort for handling deadlocks and should be used only if they cannot be prevented (as in the case of key deadlocks).

Try - Catch Statement Nesting

It is possible to nest Try - Catch statements. For example, it is possible to have a Try - Catch statement inside a Try block. It is also possible to call a stored procedure that has a Try - Catch block from an Exec statement inside a Try block. When the error occurs, the engine will start the executing statements in the last (inner) Catch block.

There is one behavior that I want to highlight: from where will SQL Server continue execution when the error is trapped and processed in the Catch block? As I explained earlier, if the batch has a single Try - Catch block, then execution will be continued from the first statement after the Catch block. In the case of a nested stored procedure that does not have a Try - Catch block, the execution will be continued from the statement after the (caller) Catch block that has processed the error. But if the nested procedure has a Try - Catch block as well, its Catch block will process the error, but process will continue from the first statement after the Exec statement that launched the nested stored procedure (not the first statement after the nested Catch).

Error Handling Architecture: With Try - Catch Statements

We have explored different features of error handling, but the important question is what should you use for standards or guidelines on your next project.

The Try - Catch statement is very powerful and it can detect many more problems than was possible (with @@Error) in previous versions. You have two options. First, you can decide to wrap everything in every stored procedure in Try - Catch statements and use some generic error handling to pick up all errors, handle those that it recognizes, and re-throw others to the caller. This requires you to add a large amount of code and to make many agreements with client development teams about the meaning of custom errors, but in the end, the benefits are debatable. However, this option may be effective in some cases—for example, if you are required to log all errors in a table for audit purposes.

The other option is to use the Try - Catch statement only in places where you can implement some meaningful (i.e., useful) error handling. Basically, it should be used to cover real exceptions and not as a blanket to cover all possible errors. In such an architecture, all unexpected errors should be handled by the client application (or middleware components). A generic error handler must be created on the client side anyway because SQL Server cannot detect all errors. I prefer this option.

Xact_Abort

SQL Server has an equivalent to the On Error Go To command used by Visual Basic (before .NET). The Set Xact_Abort On statement forces SQL Server to roll back the complete transaction and stop further processing on the occurrence of any error. For example, execute the following script that attempts to insert one integer and one date into the integer column:

```
create table test (i int)
GO
set xact_abort on
```

```
begin tran
print 'Begin'
insert test(i) values(1)
insert test(i) values('5/5/5')
commit tran
print 'End'
GO

select * from test
```

SQL Server will detect the problem and automatically roll back the transaction:

```
Begin

(1 row(s) affected)
Msg 245, Level 16, State 1, Line 6
Syntax error converting the varchar value '5/5/5' to a column
of data type int.
i
-----------

(0 row(s) affected)
```

Unfortunately, this solution could present a potential problem. This statement will also completely stop execution of the current batch. The error can still be detected and handled from the client application, but inside the Transact-SQL code, SQL Server will treat it as a fatal error. Note that the second batch in the preceding example (the Select statement) was started and executed as though nothing had happened.

However, the Try - Catch statement can prevent batches from being terminated. In the following example, I wrapped the two Insert statements in an error handler:

```
set xact_abort on
Begin try
      begin tran
      print 'Begin try'
   insert test(i) values(1)
   insert test(i) values('5/5/5')
   commit tran
   print 'End try'
End try
```

```
Begin Catch
   rollback tran
   print 'Catch'
End Catch
select * from test
```

Note that I added the Rollback statement to the Catch block. You will get the
following text in the Results pane:

```
 Begin try

(1 row(s) affected)
Catch
i
-----------

(0 row(s)  affected)
```

Error Handling Architecture: Based on Set Xact_Abort On

You can take advantage of the fact that Set Xact_Abort On without a Try - Catch
statement stops further execution. You can decide to write all of your stored procedures
based on this behavior:

```
create Procedure dbo.ap_LeasedAsset_Insert7
-- Insert leased asset and update total in LeaseSchedule.
-- (demonstration of SET XACT_ABORT ON solution)
        (
        @intEqId int,
        @intLocationId int,
        @intStatusId int,
        @intLeaseId int,
        @intLeaseScheduleId int,
        @intOwnerId int,
        @mnyLease money,
        @intAcquisitionTypeID int
        )
As
set nocount on
SET XACT_ABORT ON
begin transaction
```

```
-- insert asset
insert Inventory(EqId,                   LocationId,
                 StatusId,               LeaseId,
                 LeaseScheduleId,        OwnerId,
                 Lease,                  AcquisitionTypeID)
values (         @intEqId,               @intLocationId,
                 @intStatusId,           @intLeaseId,
                 @intLeaseScheduleId,    @intOwnerId,
                 @mnyLease,              @intAcquisitionTypeID)


-- update total
update dbo.LeaseSchedule
Set PeriodicTotalAmount = PeriodicTotalAmount + @mnyLease
where LeaseId = @intLeaseId

commit transaction
return (0)
```

The burden of error handling for such procedures would be transferred to the developers
of client applications.

Another problem is that the Set Xact_Abort statement does not detect "compilation"
errors. According to SQL Server Books OnLine: "Compile errors, such as syntax errors,
are not affected by Set Xact_Abort." Unfortunately, because of deferred name resolution,
compilation errors can occur at runtime as well. By editing the stored procedure from the
preceding example, the Update statement references a nonexistent table:

```
-- update total
update dbo.LeaseSchedule_NON_EXISTING_TABLE
Set PeriodicTotalAmount = PeriodicTotalAmount + @mnyLease
where LeaseId = @intLeaseId
```

Next, run the stored procedure:

```
Exec dbo.ap_LeasedAsset_Insert8
         @intEqId = 100,
         @intLocationId = 1,
         @intStatusId = 1,
         @intLeaseId = 1,
         @intLeaseScheduleId = 1,
         @intOwnerId = 1,
         @mnyLease = 5000,
         @intAcquisitionTypeID = 1
```

```
-- test transaction
select *
from Inventory
where EqId = 100
and LocationId = 1
```

SQL Server simply stops the execution of the stored procedure without a rollback:

```
Server: Msg 208, Level 16, State 1, Procedure prInsertLeasedAsset_8, Line 30
Invalid object name 'LeaseSchedule_NON_EXISTING_TABLE'.
Server: Msg 266, Level 16, State 1, Procedure prInsertLeasedAsset_8, Line 36
Transaction count after EXECUTE indicates that a COMMIT or ROLLBACK
TRANSACTION statement is missing. Previous count = 0, current count = 1.
EqId        LocationId  StatusId Lease
----------- ----------- -------- ------------
100         1           1        5000.0000
```

This is a potentially significant problem. The official response concerning my support question on this matter was that SQL Server is behaving as specified in SQL Server Books OnLine. Developers have different expectations—in the case of an error, the transaction should be rolled back. This explanation makes it sound like the Set Xact_Abort statement is useless. Fortunately, the stored procedure will be promoted to production only after detailed unit testing, and therefore it should not reference nonexistent tables.

However, there is an additional problem: only the stored procedure with the syntax error is aborted. Assume that the stored procedure is executed as a nested stored procedure and that the compilation error occurs in the inner stored procedure. The earlier procedure is split into two procedures to demonstrate this scenario:

```
Create Procedure prUpdateLeaseSchedule
    @intLeaseId int,
    @mnyLease int
as
update LeaseSchedule_NON_EXISTING_TABLE
set PeriodicTotalAmount = PeriodicTotalAmount + @mnyLease
where LeaseId = @intLeaseId

return (0)
GO


create Procedure prInsertLeasedAsset_9
-- Insert leased asset and update total in LeaseSchedule.
```

```
-- (demonstration of compilation error in nested stored procedure)
        (
        @intEqId int,
        @intLocationId int,
        @intStatusId int,
        @intLeaseId int,
        @intLeaseScheduleId int,
        @intOwnerId int,
        @mnyLease money,
        @intAcquisitionTypeID int
        )
As
set nocount on
SET XACT_ABORT ON
begin transaction

-- insert asset
insert Inventory(EqId,           LocationId,
                 StatusId,       LeaseId,
                 LeaseScheduleId, OwnerId,
                 Lease,          AcquisitionTypeID)
values (         @intEqId,       @intLocationId,
                 @intStatusId,   @intLeaseId,
                 @intLeaseScheduleId, @intOwnerId,
                 @mnyLease,      @intAcquisitionTypeID)

-- update total
exec prUpdateLeaseSchedule @intLeaseId, @mnyLease

commit transaction

return (0)
GO
```

Now run them:

```
Exec prInsertLeasedAsset_9
        @intEqId = 200,
        @intLocationId = 1,
        @intStatusId = 1,
        @intLeaseId = 1,
        @intLeaseScheduleId = 1,
        @intOwnerId = 1,
        @mnyLease = 5000,
        @intAcquisitionTypeID = 1
```

```
-- test transaction
select EqId, LocationId, StatusId, Lease
from Inventory
where EqId = 200
and LocationId = 1
```

SQL Server simply stops the execution of the inner stored procedure, but the outer stored procedure continues as though nothing has happened (and even commits the transaction):

```
Server: Msg 208, Level 16, State 1, Procedure prUpdateLeaseSchedule, Line 5
Invalid object name 'LeaseSchedule_NON_EXISTING_TABLE'.
EqId        LocationId  StatusId Lease
----------- ----------- -------- ------------
200         1           1        5000.0000
```

At the time, my expectation was that the Set Xact_Abort statement would abort further execution of everything, as it does in the case of runtime errors. Unfortunately, it does not behave in that way. This is potentially very dangerous, but as I said before, problems such as this should be caught during the QA phase.

Error Handling Architecture: Xact_Abort + No Transaction Nesting

On a recent .NET project I was involved with, there were many errors when we mixed different types of transactions—COM+, DTC, ADO, and Transact-SQL. Therefore, we decided not to mix them. We went even further and decided not to nest any transactions. If the caller initiates a transaction, the nested procedure skips its own initiation of the transaction. Furthermore, the transaction should be closed only from within the procedure that initiated it. We also decided, as a rule, not to handle errors in stored procedures. The rationale was that SQL Server cannot trap all errors and that we need to write error handling in the client application (actually the middleware components) anyway.

The following procedure records the number of opened transactions on entry. The Begin Tran statement is preceded by the If statement that initiates the transaction only if the procedure is not already processing a transaction:

```
create procedure dbo.ap_Equipment_Insert
-- insert equipment (and if necessary equipment type)
-- (demonstration of alternative method for error handling and transaction
processing)
        @chvMake varchar(50),
        @chvModel varchar(50),
        @chvEqType varchar(50),
        @intEqId int OUTPUT
```

```
AS
set xact_abort on
set nocount on

declare @intTrancountOnEntry int,
        @intEqTypeId int

set @intTrancountOnEntry = @@tranCount

-- does such EqType already exist in the database
If  not exists (Select EqTypeId From dbo.EqType
                  Where EqType = @chvEqType)
--if it does not exist
Begin
    if @@tranCount = 0
        BEGIN TRAN

    -- insert new EqType in the database
    Insert dbo.EqType (EqType)
    Values (@chvEqType)

    -- get id of record that you've just inserted
    Select @intEqTypeId = @@identity
End
else
begin
    -- read Id of EqType
    Select @intEqTypeId
    From dbo.EqType
    Where EqType = @chvEqType
end

--insert equipment
Insert dbo.Equipment (Make, Model, EqTypeId)
Values (@chvMake, @chvModel, @intEqTypeId)

Select @intEqId = @@identity

if @@tranCount > @intTrancountOnEntry
    COMMIT TRAN

return 0
```

The Commit Tran statement will similarly be executed only if the transaction is initiated in the current procedure.

The following procedure demonstrates the way to return logic errors to the caller. Notice that I am using both Raiserror and Return statements. It is very important to use the Return statement to communicate an error to the caller because the caller might not be able to detect the effect of the Raiserror statement.

```
ALTER Procedure dbo.ap_Inventory_InsertXA
-- insert inventory record , update inventory count and return Id
-- (demonstration of alternative method for error handling
-- and transaction processing)

    @intEqId int,
    @intLocationId int,
    @inyStatusId tinyint,
    @intLeaseId int,
    @intLeaseScheduleId int,
    @intOwnerId int,
    @mnsRent smallmoney,
    @mnsLease smallmoney,
    @mnsCost smallmoney,
    @inyAcquisitionTypeID int,
    @intInventoryId int output

As
declare @intTrancountOnEntry int
set nocount on
set xact_abort on
set @intTrancountOnEntry = @@tranCount

if @@tranCount = 0
    begin tran

Insert into dbo.Inventory (EqId, LocationId, StatusId,
        LeaseId, LeaseScheduleId, OwnerId,
        Rent, Lease, Cost,
        AcquisitionTypeID)
values (@intEqId, @intLocationId, @inyStatusId,
        @intLeaseId, @intLeaseScheduleId, @intOwnerId,
        @mnsRent, @mnsLease, @mnsCost,
        @inyAcquisitionTypeID)
```

```
select @intInventoryId = Scope_Identity()

update dbo.InventoryCount
Set InvCount = InvCount + 1
where LocationId = @intLocationId

if @@rowcount <> 1
begin
    -- business error
    Raiserror(50133, 16, 1)
    if @@tranCount > @intTrancountOnEntry
       rollback tran
    return 50133
end

if @@tranCount > @intTrancountOnEntry
   commit tran

return 0
```

The following procedure demonstrates the detection of logic errors from the nested stored procedure:

```
create procedure dbo.ap_InventoryEquipment_Insert_XA
-- insert new inventory and new equipment
-- (demonstration of alternative method for error handling
-- and transaction processing)
    @chvMake varchar(50),
    @chvModel varchar(50),
    @chvEqType varchar(30),
    @intLocationId int,
    @inyStatusId tinyint,
    @intLeaseId int,
    @intLeaseScheduleId int,
    @intOwnerId int,
    @mnsRent smallmoney,
    @mnsLease smallmoney,
    @mnsCost smallmoney,
    @inyAcquisitionTypeID int,
    @intInventoryId int output,
    @intEqId int output
as
```

```
Set nocount on
set xact_abort on

declare @intError int,
        @intTrancountOnEntry int

set @intError = 0
set @intTrancountOnEntry = @@tranCount

if @@tranCount = 0
    begin tran

-- is equipment already in the database
if not exists(select EqId
              from Equipment
              where Make = @chvMake
              and Model = @chvModel)
EXEC @intError = dbo.ap_Equipment_Insert @chvMake, @chvModel,    @chvEqType,
                                    @intEqId OUTPUT

if @intError > 0
begin
    if @@tranCount > @intTrancountOnEntry
        rollback tran
    return @intError
end

exec @intError = dbo.ap_Inventory_InsertXA
        @intEqId,             @intLocationId,      @inyStatusId,
        @intLeaseId,          @intLeaseScheduleId, @intOwnerId,
        @mnsRent,             @mnsLease,           @mnsCost,
        @inyAcquisitionTypeID, @intInventoryId output

if @intError > 0
begin
    if @@tranCount > @intTrancountOnEntry
        ROLLBACK TRAN
    return @intError
end

if @@tranCount > @intTrancountOnEntry
    COMMIT TRAN

return 0
```

If an error has been returned, the current stored procedure will roll back the transaction (using Rollback Transaction) if a transaction has been initiated in it. The caller stored procedure can also be designed so that it knows about all (or some) error codes that can be returned from a nested stored procedure. Then it is possible to write code that will handle the errors.

To test it, run the following:

```
declare @intError int,
        @intInvId int,
        @intEqId int
begin tran

exec @intError = ap_InventoryEquipment_Insert_XA
    @chvMake = 'Compaq',
    @chvModel = 'IPaq 3835',
    @chvEqType = 'PDA',
    @intLocationId = 12,
    @inyStatusId = 1,
    @intLeaseId = null,
    @intLeaseScheduleId = 1,
    @intOwnerId = 411,
    @mnsRent = null,
    @mnsLease = null,
    @mnsCost = $650,
    @inyAcquisitionTypeID = 1,
    @intInventoryId = @intInvId output,
    @intEqId = @intEqId output
if @intError = 0
   commit tran
else
   rollback tran
select @intError Err
select * from Inventory where InventoryId = @intInvId
select * from Equipment where EqId = @intEqId
```

In the case of an error, SQL Server returns the error message and rolls back the transaction:

```
Server: Msg 50133, Level 16, State 1, Procedure ap_Inventory_InsertXA, Line 48
Unable to update inventory count.
```

```
Err
-----------
50133
(1 row(s) affected)


Inventoryid EqId          LocationId  StatusId LeaseId LeaseScheduleId
----------- -----------   ----------- -------- ------- ---------------

(0 row(s) affected)

EqId        Make                                                 Model
----------- ---------------------------------------------------- -------

(0 row(s) affected)
```

Special Types of Stored Procedures

There are seven types of Transact-SQL stored procedures:

- ► User-defined
- ► System
- ► CLR (.NET)
- ► Extended
- ► Temporary
- ► Global temporary
- ► Remote

User-defined Stored Procedures

As you may infer from the name, *user-defined stored procedures* are simply groups of Transact-SQL statements assembled by administrators or developers and compiled into a single execution plan. The design of this type of stored procedure is the primary focus of this book.

System Stored Procedures

Microsoft delivers a vast set of stored procedures as a part of SQL Server. They are designed to cover all aspects of system administration. Before Microsoft SQL Server 6.0, you had to use scripts from ISQL (a command line utility like SQLCMD) to control the server and the databases. Although administrators today customarily use Management Studio, system stored procedures are still very important, since Management Studio uses the same system stored procedures, through SQL-SMO, behind the scenes.

NOTE

SQL-SMO stands for SQL Server Management Objects. It is a collection of objects designed to manage the SQL Server environment. You can use it to create your own applications for managing SQL Server or to automate repetitive tasks.

System stored procedures are stored in the system databases (*master* and sometimes *msdb*) and they have the prefix sp_. This prefix is more than just a convention. It signals to the server that the stored procedure is located in the *master* database and that it should be accessible from all databases without the user needing to insert the database name as a prefix to fully qualify the name of the procedure:

```
Exec sp_who      -- instead of exec master.sys.sp_who
```

It also signals to the server that the stored procedure should be executed in the context of the current database. For example, the script shown in Figure 7-1 will return information about the current database, and not the *master*.

NOTE

There is a small behavioral inconsistency between stored procedures in the master database and the msdb database. Stored procedures in the msdb database are delivered with SQL Server, but they must be referenced with the database name (for example, msdb.dbo.sp_update_job), and they do not work in the context of the current database. In this respect, you can understand them as "system-supplied stored procedures" rather than as "system stored procedures" as we have defined them.

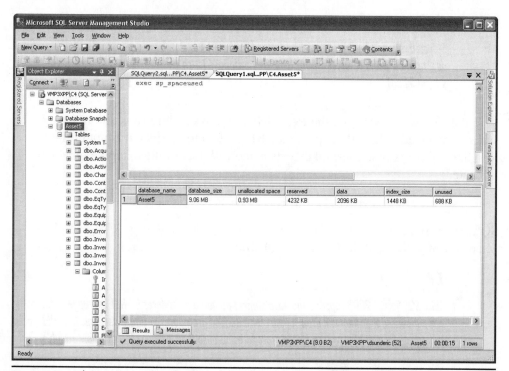

Figure 7-1   *The system procedure works in the context of the current database.*

CLR Stored Procedures

In SQL Server 2005 it is possible to create stored procedures in any (.NET) programming language that supports Common Language Runtime (CLR). Usage of such procedures is similar to usage of Transact-SQL user-defined stored procedures. They can return tabular results, integer return value, and output parameters, modify data and some database objects. We will explore them in details in Chapters 11 and 13.

Extended Stored Procedures

It was impossible to implement certain SQL Server features through Transact-SQL statements. The designers of earlier versions of SQL Server have developed a way to use the functionality encapsulated in special DLL libraries written in languages such as C or C++. Extended stored procedures are actually these C functions encapsulated in DLL files. They have a wrapper stored in the *master* database that uses the prefix xp_. Using this wrapper, you can access them just as you would any other stored procedure.

NOTE
Selected extended stored procedures stored in the master database are named with the prefix sp_ to allow users to access them from any database (such as sp_execute, sp_executesql, and sp_sdidebug).

In the following example, the extended stored procedure runs an operating system command to list all scripts in the BINN directory. Since it is not declared with the sp_ prefix, you must qualify its name with that of the database in which it is located:

```
Exec master.dbo.xp_cmdshell 'dir c:\mssql\binn\*.sql'
```

SQL Server stores DLL files of its own stored procedures in the C:\Program Files\ Microsoft SQL Server\MSSQL.x\MSSQL\Binn folder.

TIP
Since SQL Server 2005 supports the development of stored procedures in .NET languages, Microsoft has announced that they will drop support for extended procedures in future versions. Use .NET stored procedures instead of extended stored procedures because they will be safer and more scalable.

Design of Extended Stored Procedures

It is not possible to create an extended stored procedure from just any DLL file. The file must be prepared in a special way.

The development of extended stored procedures is based on the use of the Open Data Services API (ODS API). In the past, it was a tedious job and the developer had to perform all tasks manually. Nowadays, the process is automated in the Enterprise Edition of Visual C++ through the Extended Stored Proc Wizard. I will quickly demonstrate its use.

With the proper initialization code, the Extended Stored Proc Wizard generates Win32 DLL projects that contain an exported function. You should change the content of the exported function to perform the job of the future extended stored procedure. The wizard includes the header file (srv.h) and a library (opends60.lib) needed for using ODS in the code.

To create an extended stored procedure:

1. In Visual C++ Enterprise Edition, select File | New. The New dialog box should appear with the Projects tab opened. You need to set the name of the project. You could and should also use the name of the extended stored procedure as the name of the project. Extended stored procedure names commonly begin with the xp_ prefix.

2. Select Extended Stored Proc Wizard from the list of project types:

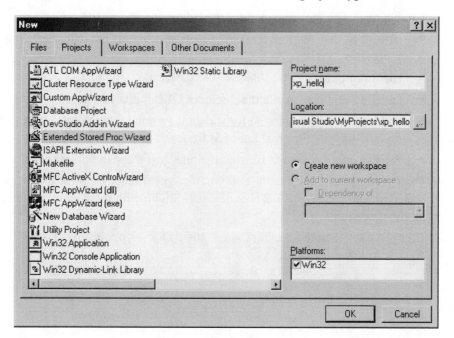

3. When you click OK, the program will launch the Extended Stored Proc Wizard. It prompts you to name your extended stored procedure:

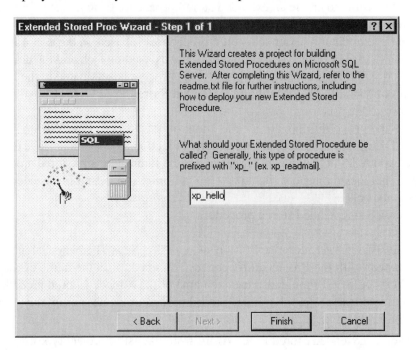

4. Click Finish. The wizard generates the following project files:

   ▶ **proc.cpp**   The exported Win32 function, which is the extended stored procedure

   ▶ **[projname].dsp**   The Visual C++ project file

   ▶ **[projname].cpp**   A file that includes DLL initialization code

   ▶ **StdAfx.h**   An include file for standard system include files, or project-specific include files that are used frequently

   ▶ **StdAfx.cpp**   A source file that includes just the standard includes

5. Open proc.cpp and change the code to implement features of the extended stored procedure. Figure 7-2 shows Visual Studio with the code of the extended stored procedure.

6. Compile the generated project to generate a DLL—**[projname].DLL**.

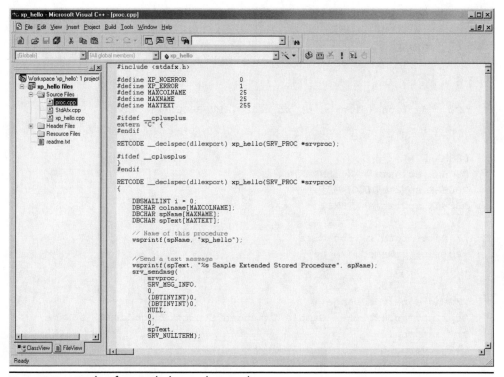

Figure 7-2   *Code of extended stored procedure*

The following code listing shows the contents of proc.cpp. It contains the exported Win32 function xp_hello. The function was generated by the wizard and it returns a simple message and a recordset that contains three records.

```cpp
#include <stdafx.h>
#define XP_NOERROR          0
#define XP_ERROR            1
#define MAXCOLNAME          25
#define MAXNAME             25
#define MAXTEXT             255

#ifdef __cplusplus
extern "C" {
#endif
```

```
RETCODE __declspec(dllexport) xp_hello(SRV_PROC *srvproc);

#ifdef __cplusplus
}
#endif

RETCODE __declspec(dllexport) xp_hello(SRV_PROC *srvproc)
{
    DBSMALLINT i = 0;
    DBCHAR colname[MAXCOLNAME];
    DBCHAR spName[MAXNAME];
    DBCHAR spText[MAXTEXT];

    // Name of this procedure
    wsprintf(spName, "xp_hello");


    //Send a text message
    wsprintf(spText, "%s Sample Extended Stored Procedure", spName);
    srv_sendmsg(
        srvproc,
        SRV_MSG_INFO,
        0,
        (DBTINYINT)0,
        (DBTINYINT)0,
        NULL,
        0,
        0,
        spText,
        SRV_NULLTERM);


    //Set up the column names
    wsprintf(colname, "ID");
    srv_describe(srvproc, 1, colname, SRV_NULLTERM, SRVINT2,
                 sizeof(DBSMALLINT), SRVINT2, sizeof(DBSMALLINT), 0);

    wsprintf(colname, "spName");
    srv_describe(srvproc, 2, colname, SRV_NULLTERM, SRVCHAR, MAXNAME,
                 SRVCHAR, 0, NULL);
```

```
wsprintf(colname, "Text");
srv_describe(srvproc, 3, colname, SRV_NULLTERM, SRVCHAR, MAXTEXT,
             SRVCHAR, 0, NULL);


// Update field 2 "spName", same value for all rows
srv_setcoldata(srvproc, 2, spName);
srv_setcollen(srvproc, 2, strlen(spName));


// Send multiple rows of data
for (i = 0; i < 3; i++) {

    // Update field 1 "ID"
    srv_setcoldata(srvproc, 1, &i);

    // Update field 3 "Text"
    wsprintf(spText,
"%d) Sample rowset generated by the %s extended stored procedure", i,
spName);

    srv_setcoldata(srvproc, 3, spText);
    srv_setcollen(srvproc, 3, strlen(spText));

    // Send the entire row
    srv_sendrow(srvproc);
}


// Now return the number of rows processed
srv_senddone(srvproc, SRV_DONE_MORE | SRV_DONE_COUNT,
             (DBUSMALLINT)0, (DBINT)i);

return XP_NOERROR ;
}
```

TIP

If you are fluent enough in the techniques required to create extended stored procedures, you should not be spending your time creating business applications. You should be working on more fundamental stuff like operating systems or RDBMSs and devoting your time to hacking. Let the rest of us collect the easy money.

Registering the Extended Stored Procedure

Once the DLL is compiled, the extended stored procedure has to be registered on the server before it can be used:

1. Copy the xp_hello.dll file to the SQL Server …\Binn folder.
2. Register the new extended stored procedure by using the SQL Server Enterprise Manager or by executing the following SQL command:

```
sp_addextendedproc 'xp_hello', 'XP_HELLO.DLL'
```

Once the extended stored procedure is registered, you can test it by using Management Studio. See Figure 7-3.

You should carefully test the new extended stored procedure. If you find out that it is not working as expected or that you need to make some modification, you need to unregister (drop) the extended stored procedure by using the following SQL command:

```
sp_dropextendedproc 'xp_hello'
```

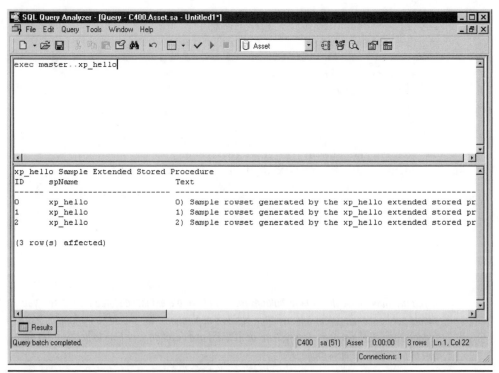

Figure 7-3   *Using the extended stored procedure*

When the extended stored procedure is executed in SQL Server, it is loaded into memory. It stays there until SQL Server is shut down or until you issue a command to remove it from memory:

```
DBCC xp_hello(FREE)
```

To register an extended stored procedure from Management Studio, right-click the Extended Stored Procedures node in the *master* database (Databases | System Databases | master | Programmability | Extended Stored Procedures) and select New Extended Stored Procedure. Management Studio prompts you for the name of the extended stored procedure and the location of the DLL file:

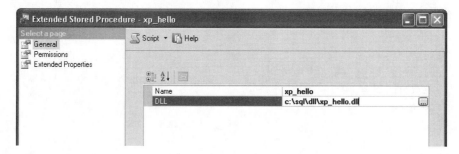

It is also simple to remove an extended stored procedure using Enterprise Manager. You merely right-click it and select Delete from the pop-up menu.

NOTE

The trouble with extended stored procedures is that they work in the address space of SQL Server. Therefore, an extended stored procedure that doesn't behave properly could crash SQL Server. Such a problem is not likely to occur because SQL Server monitors the behavior of extended stored procedures. If an extended stored procedure attempts to reference memory outside of its address space, SQL Server will terminate it. Commonsense programming practices (using error checking, doing exception handling, and thoroughly testing final code) will further reduce the possibility of errors.

Temporary Stored Procedures

Temporary stored procedures are related to stored procedures as temporary tables are related to tables. You use them when you expect to reuse the execution plan of a stored procedure within a limited time frame. Although you can achieve the same functionality with a standard user-defined stored procedure, temporary stored procedures are a better solution because you do not have to worry about maintenance issues (such as dropping the stored procedure).

Temporary stored procedures reside in the *tempdb* database and must be named with the prefix #. You create them in the same way you create user-defined stored procedures. The only change is the use of a # as a name prefix. This prefix signals the server to create the procedure as a temporary stored procedure. This kind of stored procedure can only be used from the session in which it was created. When the session is closed, it will be dropped automatically. This behavior indicates why this type of stored procedure is often also referred to as a *private temporary stored procedure.*

The following code example creates a private temporary stored procedure:

```
Create Procedure #dbo.ap_EqId_List
     @Make varchar(50),
     @Model varchar(50)
as
     Select EqId
     from dbo.Equipment
     where Make = @Make
     and Model = @Model
return
```

NOTE

Sometimes, all user-defined stored procedures in tempdb are referred to as temporary stored procedures. This is incorrect because there are major differences between the two. For example, user-defined stored procedures stored in the tempdb database are accessible to all authorized users and are not limited to the session in which they were created. These stored procedures stay in tempdb until the server is shut down, at which time the complete content of tempdb is flushed.

Global Temporary Stored Procedures

Global temporary stored procedures are related to temporary stored procedures as global temporary tables are related to private temporary tables. They also reside in the *tempdb* database, but they use the prefix ##. You create them in the same way you create temporary stored procedures. The only difference is that they are visible and usable from all sessions. In fact, permissions are not required and the owner cannot even deny other users access to them.

When the session that has created the procedure is closed, no new sessions will be able to execute the stored procedure. After all instances of the stored procedure already running are finished, the procedure is dropped automatically.

The following code example creates a global temporary stored procedure:

```
Create Procedure ##apEquipment_Insert
    @Make varchar(50),
    @Model varchar(50),
    @EqType varchar(50)
as
    declare @EqTypeId smallint
    select @EqTypeId = EqTypeId    -- This is OK in a perfect world,
    from dbo.EqType                -- but it is based on the
    Where EqType = @EqType         -- unreasonable assumption that
                                   -- you can identify the key using
                                   -- the description.
    Insert dbo.Equipment (Make, Model, EqTypeId)
    Values (@Make, @Model, @EqTypeId)
```

Remote Stored Procedures

This type is actually a user-defined stored procedure that resides on a remote server. The only challenge implicit in this type of stored procedure is that the local server has to be set to allow the remote use of stored procedures.

Run the following code on the local server:

```
EXEC sp_addlinkedserver LocalServer, N'SQL Server'
EXEC sp_addlinkedserver RemoteServer
EXEC sp_configure 'remote access', 1
RECONFIGURE
```

Stop and restart the local server.

To set up access for a login "sa" from the local server to remote server, run the following code on the remote server. It is critical that you log in using SQL Server Authentication and it is assumed that the logins on different servers have the same password.

```
EXEC sp_addlinkedserver RemoteServer, local
EXEC sp_addlinkedserver LocalServer
EXEC sp_configure 'remote access', 1
RECONFIGURE
GO
EXEC sp_addremotelogin LocalServer, sa, sa
GO
```

Stop and restart the remote server.

Using the "sa" login, you can now execute a stored procedure on the remote server from the local server.

TIP

Microsoft, in fact, considers this mechanism as a legacy of older versions of SQL Server. Heterogeneous queries are the recommended way to execute stored procedures or access tables on other servers.

8

Views

IN THIS CHAPTER

V iews are database objects that behave like stored queries or virtual tables. There are several types of views, and they differ in internal design and purpose:

▶ Standard SQL

▶ Dynamic

▶ Temporary (CTEs—Common table expressions)

▶ INFORMATION_SCHEMA

▶ Indexed

▶ Partitioned

Design of Standard SQL Views

In their basic form, views are designed simply as queries enclosed inside a Create View statement:

```
CREATE VIEW dbo.vInventory
AS
SELECT dbo.Inventory.Inventoryid, dbo.Equipment.Make, dbo.Equipment.Model,
dbo.Location.Location, dbo.Status.Status, dbo.Contact.FirstName,
dbo.Contact.LastName, dbo.Inventory.Cost, dbo.AcquisitionType.AcquisitionType,
dbo.Location.Address, dbo.Location.City, dbo.Location.ProvinceId,
dbo.Location.Country, dbo.EqType.EqType, dbo.Contact.Phone,
dbo.Contact.Fax, dbo.Contact.Email, dbo.Contact.UserName,
dbo.Inventory.Rent, dbo.Inventory.EqId, dbo.Inventory.LocationId,
dbo.Inventory.StatusId, dbo.Inventory.OwnerId, dbo.Inventory.AcquisitionTypeID,
dbo.Contact.OrgUnitId
FROM dbo.EqType
RIGHT OUTER JOIN dbo.Equipment
ON dbo.EqType.EqTypeId = dbo.Equipment.EqTypeId
    RIGHT OUTER JOIN dbo.Inventory
      INNER JOIN dbo.Status
      ON dbo.Inventory.StatusId = dbo.Status.StatusId
        LEFT OUTER JOIN dbo.AcquisitionType
        ON dbo.Inventory.AcquisitionTypeID =
          dbo.AcquisitionType.AcquisitionTypeId
    ON dbo.Equipment.EqId = dbo.Inventory.EqId
          LEFT OUTER JOIN dbo.Location
          ON dbo.Inventory.LocationId = dbo.Location.LocationId
            LEFT OUTER JOIN dbo.Contact
            ON dbo.Inventory.OwnerId = dbo.Contact.ContactId
```

After a view is created, it can be used in the same way as any other table:

```
SELECT dbo.vInventory.EqId, dbo.vInventory.Make,
dbo.vInventory.Model, dbo.vInventory.Status
FROM dbo.vInventory
WHERE LocationId = 2
```

Although data is accessible through a view, it is not stored in the database inside a view. When the view is referenced in a query, SQL Server simply processes the Select statement behind the view and combines the data with the rest of the query:

```
EquipmentId Make                Model             Status
-------------------------------------------------------------
1           Toshiba             Portege 7020CT    Active
6           NEC                 V90               Ordered
5           Bang & Olafson      V4000             Active
1           Toshiba             Portege 7020CT    Active
34          Toshiba             Portege 7030CT    Active
(5 row(s) affected)
```

A view is often created on a query that joins many tables and contains aggregate functions:

```
Create View dbo.vInventoryCost
WITH SCHEMABINDING
as
select ET.EqType, e.Make, e.Model, Sum(Cost) TotalCost, Count(*) [Count]
from dbo.Inventory I
inner join dbo.Equipment e
on i.EqId = e.EqId
    inner join dbo.EqType ET
    on e.EqTypeId = ET.EqTypeId
where Cost is not null
group by ET.EqType, e.Make, e.Model
```

Syntax

Views can be created and edited by simply executing Create View and Alter View statements:

```
{CREATE}|{ALTER} VIEW view_name [ ( column [ ,...n ] ) ]
[ WITH < view_option > [ ,...n ] ]
AS
select_statement
[ WITH CHECK OPTION ]
```

It is not necessary to specify column names in the header of the view. The view just transfers column names from the Select statement if they are uniquely identified. You just need to make sure that column names are not repeated and that all computed columns also have names assigned (for example, you can add aliases to computed columns).

As with stored procedures and functions, views can be encrypted so that nobody can see their source code. You just need to create or alter it using the With Encryption view option.

The With Schemabinding option allows you to *schema-bind* a view to database objects (such as tables, views, and user-defined functions) that it references. Once the function is schema-bound, it is not possible to make schema changes on the underlying objects. All attempts to drop the objects and alter underlying objects (which would change the object schema) will fail. When this option is used, all objects inside the view must be referenced using two-part names (owner.dbobject).

The View_Metadata option specifies that SQL Server will return information about the view's columns (not base table columns) to client-side APIs. This feature might be useful for making views with triggers that are updateable.

Design View in Enterprise Manager

When a query is complicated, it is sometimes easier to create it in the Query window of Management Studio (see Figure 8-1). Books OnLine sometimes also refer to it as the View Assisted Editor. You can launch it from the context-sensitive menu of the View node in the Object Browser. Before it displays the Query window, Management Studio prompts you for the tables, synonyms, views, and (table) functions that you want to include in your view. It consists of four components: the Diagram pane (for managing tables visually), the Criteria pane (for managing columns and filter criteria), the SQL pane (for editing SQL statements), and the Results pane (for displaying and editing data). This window is used in a manner similar to the Query Design window in Microsoft Access or Visual Studio, so I will not spend more time describing it here. Since a view is only a stored query, after you are done with query design, you can choose Save from the application menu and the Object Browser will prompt you to name the view.

Security

Typically, a user does not need permissions on underlying base tables and views when the user has permission to access a view. There are two exceptions—SQL Server checks permissions if all underlying tables and views do not belong to the same database, and when base objects belong to different schemas.

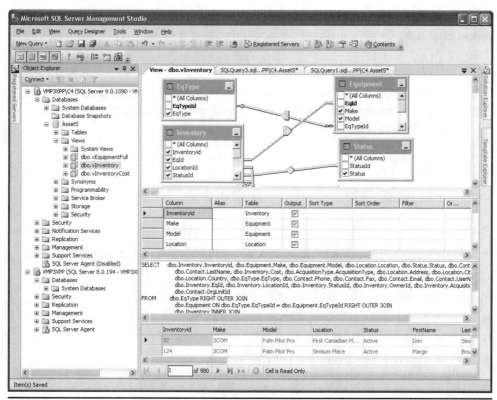

Figure 8-1   *View design in the Query window of Management Studio*

Standard SQL Views in Execution Plans

It is a common misconception that SQL Server creates, stores, and reuses an execution plan of a view. The idea behind this wishful thinking is that SQL Server would optimize the execution plan of the view, so when it is referenced from a stored procedure or a query, SQL Server would just include it in the execution plan of the caller. Although this might sound like a good idea (time would be saved since recompilation would not be necessary and since the "optimal" plan will be used), SQL Server has a better solution.

There is another common misconception about view execution. Although I used the phrase "virtual table" to describe views, SQL Server does not execute the view, create a result set in memory, and then process the rest of the query.

When a SQL view is referenced with other tables in a query, SQL Server compiles everything again and creates a new optimal execution plan. Other elements of the query (joins with other tables, additional criteria, and the list of required columns) typically change the nature of the query significantly so that a new execution plan works better than simply reusing the execution plan of a view.

NOTE

Execution plans of other types of views are constructed differently, and I will discuss them in the upcoming "Indexed Views in Execution Plans" and "Execution Plans of Distributed Partitioned Views" sections of this chapter.

Limitations of Views

Keep in mind that views have the following limitations:

▶ A view can contain up to 1,024 columns.

▶ A view can be based on tables and other views but not on temporary tables or table variables.

▶ It is possible to have only 32 levels of nested views.

▶ The Select statement in a view cannot have an Into clause (it cannot create a new table as a side effect).

▶ A view cannot have Compute and Compute By clauses.

▶ Only Instead-of triggers can be created on a view (not After triggers).

▶ An Order By clause can be used in the view only together with a Top clause.

The last statement points to a very cool workaround if you need to order the results in a view—the attempt to create a view using just the Order By clause will result in a syntax error:

```
Server: Msg 1033, Level 15, State 1, Procedure vInventory_Ordered, Line 25
The ORDER BY clause is invalid in views, inline functions, derived tables,
and subqueries, unless TOP is also specified.
```

To solve this problem and avoid the error, add Top 100 Percent to it:

```
Create VIEW dbo.vInventory_Ordered
AS
SELECT TOP 100 PERCENT
dbo.Inventory.Inventoryid, dbo.Equipment.Make, dbo.Equipment.Model
FROM dbo.Equipment
    RIGHT OUTER JOIN dbo.Inventory
    ON dbo.Equipment.EqId = dbo.Inventory.EqId
order by dbo.Equipment.Make, dbo.Equipment.Model
```

Editing Data Using Views

It is possible to modify data in base tables through a view:

```
Update dbo.vInventory
Set Cost = 2000
Where InventoryId = 1234
```

SQL Server has to be able to identify rows and fields that clearly need to be modified. The view cannot contain derived columns (columns based on calculated values such as aggregate functions or expressions).

If a view is created using With Check Option, SQL Server does not accept changes on records that will fall out of scope of the view after modification. For example, a manager who can see Inventory for his own location cannot assign it to some other location:

```
CREATE VIEW vInventoryTrigonTower
AS
SELECT *
FROM dbo.vInventory
WHERE LocationId = 2
WITH CHECK OPTION
GO

update dbo.vInventoryTrigonTower
set LocationId = 10
where InventoryId = 6
```

SQL Server will generate an error:

```
Server: Msg 550, Level 16, State 1, Line 1
The attempted insert or update failed because the target view
either specifies WITH CHECK OPTION or spans a view that specifies
WITH CHECK OPTION and one or more rows resulting from the operation
did not qualify under the CHECK OPTION constraint.
The statement has been terminated.
```

With standard SQL views, it is not possible to modify data in more than a single base table. However, when an Instead-of trigger is placed on a view, the trigger can issue separate statements that modify individual base tables. See "Triggers on Views" in Chapter 9 for a detailed example and discussion of this method. It is very interesting and useful.

Dynamic Views

Compared with stored procedures, views have one serious limitation—they do not support parameters. Fortunately, you can use a table-valued user-defined function as a *dynamic view,* which does support parameters (you can also call them *parameterized views*):

```
Create Function dbo.fnInventoryByLocationId(
        @LocationId int)
Returns Table
AS
Return (SELECT *
        FROM dbo.vInventory
        WHERE LocationId = @LocationId)
```

They can be referenced in the From clause of a Select statement, which makes them work like a view:

```
select *
from dbo.fnInventoryByLocationId (2)
```

We will discuss table-valued user-defined functions in Chapter 10.

Temporary Views—Common Table Expressions

If there are temporary stored procedures and temporary tables, are there also temporary views? Well, yes and no. Yes, there are objects that behave like views and that are temporary, but no, Microsoft has decided to call them Common table expressions (CTEs), rather than *temporary views.*

You can use CTEs to simplify your queries and wrap part of a complicated query in a CTE and reference it by name.

A CTE is defined using a With clause that is placed just before a SQL statement (Select, Insert, Update, and Delete). The scope of the CTE is limited to the SQL statement and consists of two parts. The With clause defines the name of the CTE and the names of the columns in its result set. It contains one or more query definitions in brackets:

```
WITH CompOrg(ParentID, CompOrgCount) AS
(
    SELECT ParentOrgUnitID, COUNT(*)
    FROM dbo.OrgUnit
```

```
    WHERE ParentOrgUnitID IS NOT NULL
    GROUP BY ParentOrgUnitID
)
SELECT OrgUnit.OrgUnit, CompOrgCount
FROM CompOrg p
inner join dbo.OrgUnit OrgUnit
on p.ParentId = OrgUnit.OrgUnitId
ORDER BY OrgUnit.OrgUnit
```

The CompOrg CTE returns a list of composite organizations (organizations that have children) and the count of their children. The CTE is referenced by a following query.

NOTE

The With clause of the CTE must be placed after the semicolon (;) that marks the end of the previous Transact-SQL statement (except when the previous statement is Create View). In earlier versions of SQL Server, semicolons were allowed but they were not a required way to delimit individual Transact-SQL statements. It was enough to put white space between statements. This is the first structure in SQL Server that requires a semicolon.

Limitations of Nonrecursive CTEs

Naturally, CTEs have some limitations:

▶ Query definitions in a CTE cannot contain these clauses: Compute, Compute By, Into, For Xml, For Browse, or an Option clause with query hints.

▶ Query definitions in a CTE can contain an Order By clause only if it contains a Top clause.

▶ Query definitions in a CTE cannot contain query hints that will contradict hints in the query.

▶ If there are multiple query definitions in a CTE, they must be linked using one of the following set operators: Union All, Union, Intersect, or Except.

▶ You can define multiple CTEs one after the other (by putting With clauses one after the other), but you cannot nest With clauses (that is, a query definition cannot contain a With clause).

▶ A CTE can reference only itself or a previously defined CTE, not CTEs that are defined later.

Recursive CTEs

One very cool feature is that a CTE can call itself recursively. This method allows you to manage hierarchies easily. A recursive CTE must contain at least two types of query definitions. The first type of query definition is called the *anchor member* and it can contain only reference(s) to base table(s). The second type is called the *recursive member* and it must contain a reference to the CTE itself. Anchor and recursive members must be linked together using the Union All set operator.

```
WITH SubOrg(ParentOrgUnitID, OrgUnitID, OrgLevel) AS
(
    -- anchor member (for first iteration)
    SELECT ParentOrgUnitID, OrgUnitID, 0 AS OrgLevel
    FROM dbo.OrgUnit
    WHERE ParentOrgUnitID IS NULL
    UNION ALL
    -- recursive member (for later iterations)
    SELECT o.ParentOrgUnitID, o.OrgUnitID, p.OrgLevel + 1
    FROM dbo.OrgUnit o
        INNER JOIN SubOrg p
        ON o.ParentOrgUnitID = p.OrgUnitID
)
SELECT s.OrgUnitID, o.OrgUnit, s.ParentOrgUnitID, s.OrgLevel
FROM SubOrg s
INNER JOIN dbo.OrgUnit o
ON o.OrgUnitId = s.OrgUnitId
ORDER BY s.OrgLevel
```

A mistake during the design of the CTE could lead to an infinite loop. Such a mistake typically occurs when the recursive member returns the same values for both parent and child columns. By default, the SQL Server engine will stop processing the CTE after 100 iterations:

```
Msg 530, Level 16, State 1, Line 1
The statement terminated. The maximum recursion 100 has been exhausted before
statement completion.
```

You can limit the number of iterations using the MaxRecursion option:

```
WITH SubOrg(ParentOrgUnitID, OrgUnitID, OrgLevel) AS
(
    SELECT ParentOrgUnitID, OrgUnitID, 0 AS OrgLevel
    FROM dbo.OrgUnit
    WHERE ParentOrgUnitID IS NULL
    UNION ALL
    SELECT o.ParentOrgUnitID, o.OrgUnitID, p.OrgLevel + 1
```

```
      FROM dbo.OrgUnit o
          INNER JOIN SubOrg p
          ON o.ParentOrgUnitID = p.OrgUnitID
)
SELECT s.OrgUnitID, o.OrgUnit, s.ParentOrgUnitID, s.OrgLevel
FROM SubOrg s
inner join dbo.OrgUnit o
on o.OrgUnitId = s.OrgUnitId
order by s.OrgLevel
OPTION (MAXRECURSION 10);
```

If you do not want to limit the number of iterations, set the MaxRecursion option to 0.

Limitations of Recursive CTEs

Recursive CTEs have a different set of rules from nonrecursive CTEs:

▶ There can be more than one anchor member and there can be more than one recursive member.

▶ All anchor members must be positioned before recursive members.

▶ You can link anchor members using the Union All, Union, Intersect, or Except set operators.

▶ The recursive members must be linked using the Union All operator.

▶ A set of anchor members must be linked with a set of recursive members using the Union All operator.

▶ The number and data type of the columns in all query definition members must match.

▶ A recursive member must have one (and only one) reference to its CTE.

▶ Recursive members cannot contain Select Distinct, Group By, Having, scalar aggregations, Top, subqueries, or hints on CTE references.

▶ Only Inner Join is allowed to link tables and CTEs inside a recursive member.

INFORMATION_SCHEMA Views

SQL Server 2005 contains a group of system views that are used to obtain metadata. Their names consist of three parts. The first part is the database name (optional), the second part is always INFORMATION_SCHEMA (as opposed to being the database owner, which is why these views are so named), and the third part references the type of metadata that the view contains.

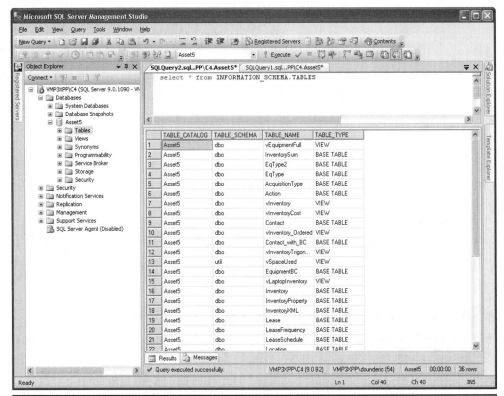

Figure 8-2 *Using INFORMATION_SCHEMA views*

In Figure 8-2, you can see the usage of an INFORMATION_SCHEMA.TABLES view. It returns the names of all tables (and views—virtual tables) that the current user has permission to see in the current database. INFORMATION_SCHEMA views work like system stored procedures—they are defined in the *master* database, but they return information in the context of the current database (or the database that is referenced in the first part of the name).

NOTE

INFORMATION_SCHEMA views are designed to be compatible with SQL-92 naming standards. Therefore, instead of database-, owner-, object-, and user-defined data types, INFORMATION_SCHEMA views are named with catalog, schema, object, and domain as a third part of the name, respectively.

Microsoft recommends that you reference these views (as well as system stored procedures) instead of directly referencing system tables in your procedures.

Indexed Views

It is possible to *materialize* a view—to create a table in the database that will contain all the data that is referenced by a view. This technique can significantly improve the performance of a Select statement when SQL Server has to join many tables, and can return or aggregate a large number of records.

When you create a *unique clustered index* on a view, SQL Server materializes the view. Records are saved in the database in the same manner that clustered indexes on regular tables are stored:

```
Create View vLaptopInventory
WITH SCHEMABINDING
as
select i.Inventoryid, i.EqId, i.StatusId, e.Make, e.Model
from dbo.Inventory I
inner join dbo.Equipment e
on i.EqId = e.EqId
where EqTypeId = 1
GO


CREATE UNIQUE CLUSTERED INDEX idxvLaptopInventory
ON vLaptopInventory (InventoryID)
```

Although the index references only a subset of columns, the index (indexed view) contains all columns in the leaf-level nodes (as does every clustered index).

Indexed View Limitations

There are many limitations with which a view must comply to be converted to an indexed view:

► The view must be created using the With Schemabinding option.

► The view must reference only tables—not other views, derived tables, rowset functions, or subqueries.

► All base tables must have the same owner as the view.

► The view cannot join tables from more than one database.

► The view cannot contain an outer- or self-join.

► The view cannot have a Union, Top, or Order By clause, or a Distinct keyword.

▶ Some aggregate functions are not allowed: Count(*) [use Count_Big(*) instead], Avg(), Max(), Min(), Stdev(), Stdevp(), Var(), or Varp(). But all of these aggregate functions can be re-engineered using valid functions [such as Sum() and Count_Big(*)].

▶ If a query contains a Group By clause, it must contain Count_Big(*) in the Select list.

▶ The view and all base tables must be created with Set Ansi_Nulls On.

▶ All tables and user-defined functions in the view must be referenced using two-part names (owner.dbobject).

▶ All columns must be explicitly specified—Select * is not allowed.

▶ The view cannot contain `text`, `ntext`, or `image` columns.

▶ Having, Rollup, Cube, Compute, and Compute By clauses are not allowed.

▶ The same table column must not be converted to more than a single view column.

▶ You can only create indexed views in the Enterprise and Developer editions of SQL Server.

▶ The Create Index statement and all subsequent Insert, Update, and Delete statements must be executed with the following option settings (explicitly or implicitly):

```
Set ANSI_NULLS ON
Set ANSI_PADDING ON
Set ANSI_WARNINGS ON
Set ARITHABORT ON
Set CONCAT_NULL_YIELDS_NULL ON
Set QUOTED_IDENTIFIERS ON
Set NUMERIC_ROUNDABORT OFF
```

Indexed Views in Execution Plans

Optimizer treats indexed views as tables. SQL Server simply joins them with other tables. There is one exception—Optimizer can use an indexed view even when the view is not explicitly referenced in the query (when the query is referencing only some of the base tables). SQL Server compares the cost of the execution plan with base tables and the execution plan with the indexed view and chooses the cheapest one.

You can force SQL Server to ignore the indexed view using the Expand View hint. Conversely, you can also force SQL Server to use the indexed view using the Noexpand hint.

Nonclustered Indexes on Views

Once a clustered index is added to a view, you can add more nonclustered indexes:

```
CREATE INDEX idxvLaptopInventory_MakeModel
ON dbo.vLaptopInventory (Make, Model)
```

Performance Implications

Indexed views typically improve the performance of data warehouse systems and other systems that predominantly have queries that read data. On the other hand, indexed views can reduce the performance of OLTP systems. Updates to an indexed view become part of transactions that modify the base tables. This fact may increase the cost of OLTP transactions and offset the savings achieved on read operations.

Partitioned Views

Views can be a very useful tool for managing very large databases (VLDBs). Typically, data warehouse systems contain huge volumes of uniform data. A textbook example is a retailer that collects information about sales over years. Some analyses would process many years of data, but others would focus on only a few months or the current year. If everything were in a single table, queries and management of data would become increasingly difficult. In such a scenario, the retailer's sales information would be split into several horizontally partitioned tables such as OrderItem2005, OrderItem2006, and OrderItem2007. For analyses (queries) that span all tables, you can create a view that puts them all together:

```
Create View dbo.vOrderItem
as
select * from dbo.OrderItem2005
UNION ALL
select * from dbo.OrderItem2006
UNION ALL
select * from dbo.OrderItem2007
```

Horizontal and Vertical Partitioning

Views based on multiple instances of the same table are called *partitioned views*. A *horizontal partitioning* occurs when different subsets of records are stored in different table instances (as in the preceding example).

It is also possible to do *vertical partitioning*—to put columns in separate tables based on the frequency with which they are needed. On "wide" tables, each record occupies a substantial amount of space. Since each data page is limited to 8KB, a smaller number of records can fit onto a single data page. As a result, the number of IO operations needed to access a large number of records is much higher. To reduce it, we can put frequently used fields in one table and other fields in a second table. The tables will have a one-to-one relationship. In the following example, the InventorySum table has been split into InventoryPrim and InventorySec tables:

```
CREATE TABLE [dbo].[InventoryPrim] (
    [Inventoryid]   [int]         NOT NULL ,
    [Make]          [varchar] (50) NULL ,
    [Model]         [varchar] (50) NULL ,
    [Location]      [varchar] (50) NULL ,
    [FirstName]     [varchar] (30) NULL ,
    [LastName]      [varchar] (30) NULL ,
    [UserName]      [varchar] (50) NULL ,
    [EqType]        [varchar] (50) NULL ,
    CONSTRAINT [PK_InventoryPrim] PRIMARY KEY  CLUSTERED
    (
        [Inventoryid]
    )  ON [PRIMARY]
) ON [PRIMARY]
GO


CREATE TABLE [dbo].[InventorySec] (
    [Inventoryid]      [int]         NOT NULL ,
    [AcquisitionType] [varchar] (12) NULL ,
    [Address]         [varchar] (50) NULL ,
    [City]            [varchar] (50) NULL ,
    [ProvinceId]      [char]    (3)  NULL ,
    [Country]         [varchar] (50) NULL ,
    [EqType]          [varchar] (50) NULL ,
    [Phone]           [typPhone]     NULL ,
    [Fax]             [typPhone]     NULL ,
    [Email]           [typEmail]     NULL ,
    CONSTRAINT [PK_InventorySec] PRIMARY KEY  CLUSTERED
    (
        [Inventoryid]
    )  ON [PRIMARY]
) ON [PRIMARY]
GO
```

The following creates a view that joins them:

```
create view dbo.vInventoryVertSplit
as
select IP.Inventoryid, IP.Make,       IP.Model,
       IP.Location,    IP.FirstName, IP.LastName,
       IP.UserName,    IP.EqType,    ISec.AcquisitionType,
       ISec.Address,   ISec.City,    ISec.ProvinceId,
       ISec.Country,   ISec.Phone,   ISec.Fax,
       ISec.Email
from dbo.InventoryPrim IP
full join dbo.InventorySec ISec
on IP.Inventoryid = ISec.Inventoryid
```

The following creates a query that references only fields from one table:

```
SET STATISTICS PROFILE ON
SELECT Make, Model, Location, UserName
FROM dbo.vInventoryVertSplit
where Inventoryid = 1041
```

In this case, SQL Server realizes that there is no need to access both tables:

```
Make       Model                             Location       UserName
---------  ------------------------------    ------------   ----------
Compaq     18.2GB 10K RPM Ultra2 Disk Dr Royal Hotel  PMisiaszek

(1 row(s) affected)

Rows Executes StmtText
---- -------- -----------------------------------------------------------
1    1        SELECT [Make]=[Make],[Model]=[Model],[Location]=[Locatio
1    1         |--Clustered Index Seek(OBJ:(Asset5.dbo.InventoryPrim.P
(2 row(s) affected)
```

Unfortunately, this is not always the case. If we remove criteria from the previous Select statement, SQL Server accesses both tables (although the columns selected are in only one table):

```
Rows Executes StmtText
---- -------- -----------------------------------------------------------
980  1        SELECT [Make]=[Make],[Model]=[Model],[Location]=[Locatio
980  1         |--Merge Join(Full Outer Join, MERGE:(InventorySec.Inve
980  1          |--Clustered Index Scan(OBJ:(Asset5.dbo.InventorySec.
980  1          |--Clustered Index Scan(OBJ:(Asset5.dbo.InventoryPrim
```

NOTE

You can always force SQL Server to use just one table if you reference the table and not the view.

Distributed Partitioned Views

If all base tables of a view are stored on a single server, it is called a *local partitioned view*. If the underlying tables of a view are stored on separate servers, it is called a *distributed partitioned view*. Distributed partitioned views are always created on tables that are horizontally partitioned. In the following example, the vSales view on server Alpha references tables on servers Beta and Gamma:

```
Create view dbo.vSales
as
select * from Sales.dbo.OrderItem2007
UNION ALL
select * from Beta.Sales.dbo.OrderItem2006
UNION ALL
select * from Gamma.Sales.dbo.OrderItem2005
```

That's the basic idea, but it is not that simple. I will discuss all the details and then show a complete example.

Servers that host horizontally partitioned tables and that work together are called *federated servers*. This technology was one of the major new features of SQL Server 2000 and it has allowed Microsoft to beat the competition consistently on TPC-C benchmarks since it became available in the Beta version of SQL Server 2000.

The strategy of splitting the transaction and query load among a set of distributed servers is often called *scaling-out* (as opposed to *scaling-up,* which refers to the brute-force method of simply applying bigger and faster hardware instead).

Partitioned tables are split based on a *partitioning key*—a column that determines which of the partitioned tables/federated servers the record will fall into. In the previous example, the partitioning key is a year. A partitioning key should be selected to ensure that the majority of queries are served from a single table/server. The success of a federated server project depends largely on the selection of an appropriate partitioning key.

NOTE

You do not have to have multiple physical servers to test federated servers. You can install several instances of SQL Server on the same machine to develop and test the solution. Naturally, it would be pointless to implement federated servers that way in a production environment.

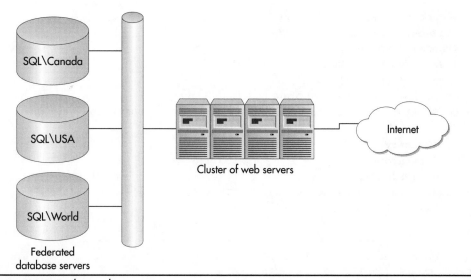

Figure 8-3   *Federated servers*

By way of example, assume that your Asset database is serving a Canadian company and that it is functionally divided into three divisions—one serves the Canadian market, the second the U.S. market, while the third serves the international market (see Figure 8-3). This schema is very good when reporting is typically done per division.

You will partition the table using the Country column as a partitioning key. To assist the resolution of the distributed partitioned view, make Country the first field of the primary key and create Check constraints to prevent entry of records from an incorrect geographic location. It is very important that data ranges do not overlap and that a single record can end up only on a single server. The following Create Table statements should be executed on the respective servers:

```
-- on Canada server
CREATE TABLE [dbo].[InventoryCanada] (
    [Inventoryid] [int] NOT NULL ,
    [Make] [varchar] (50) NULL ,
    [Model] [varchar] (50) NULL ,
    [Location] [varchar] (50) NULL ,
    [FirstName] [varchar] (30) NULL ,
    [LastName] [varchar] (30) NULL ,
    [AcquisitionType] [varchar] (12) NULL ,
    [Address] [varchar] (50) NULL ,
    [City] [varchar] (50) NULL ,
    [ProvinceId] [char] (3) NULL ,
```

```
    [Country] [varchar] (50) NOT NULL ,
    [EqType] [varchar] (50) NULL ,
    [Phone] [typPhone] NULL ,
    [Fax] [typPhone] NULL ,
    [Email] [typEmail] NULL ,
    [UserName] [varchar] (50) NULL ,
    CONSTRAINT [PK_InventoryCanada] PRIMARY KEY  CLUSTERED
     (
        [Country],
        [Inventoryid]
     )  ON [PRIMARY] ,
    CONSTRAINT [chkInventoryCanada] CHECK ([Country] = 'Canada')
) ON [PRIMARY]
GO
----------------------------------------------------------------
-- on US server
CREATE TABLE [dbo].[InventoryUSA] (
    [Inventoryid] [int] NOT NULL ,
    [Make] [varchar] (50) NULL ,
    [Model] [varchar] (50) NULL ,
    [Location] [varchar] (50) NULL ,
    [FirstName] [varchar] (30) NULL ,
    [LastName] [varchar] (30) NULL ,
    [AcquisitionType] [varchar] (12) NULL ,
    [Address] [varchar] (50) NULL ,
    [City] [varchar] (50) NULL ,
    [ProvinceId] [char] (3) NULL ,
    [Country] [varchar] (50) NOT NULL ,
    [EqType] [varchar] (50) NULL ,
    [Phone] [typPhone] NULL ,
    [Fax] [typPhone] NULL ,
    [Email] [typEmail] NULL ,
    [UserName] [varchar] (50) NULL ,
    CONSTRAINT [PK_InventoryUS] PRIMARY KEY  CLUSTERED
    (
        [Country],
        [Inventoryid]
    )  ON [PRIMARY] ,
    CONSTRAINT [chkInventoryUSA] CHECK ([Country] = 'USA')
) ON [PRIMARY]
GO
----------------------------------------------------------------
-- on World server
```

```
CREATE TABLE [dbo].[InventoryWorld] (
    [Inventoryid] [int] NOT NULL ,
    [Make] [varchar] (50) NULL ,
    [Model] [varchar] (50) NULL ,
    [Location] [varchar] (50) NULL ,
    [FirstName] [varchar] (30) NULL ,
    [LastName] [varchar] (30) NULL ,
    [AcquisitionType] [varchar] (12) NULL ,
    [Address] [varchar] (50) NULL ,
    [City] [varchar] (50) NULL ,
    [ProvinceId] [char] (3) NULL ,
    [Country] [varchar] (50) NOT NULL ,
    [EqType] [varchar] (50) NULL ,
    [Phone] [typPhone] NULL ,
    [Fax] [typPhone] NULL ,
    [Email] [typEmail] NULL ,
    [UserName] [varchar] (50) NULL ,
    CONSTRAINT [PK_InventoryWorld] PRIMARY KEY  CLUSTERED
    (
        [Country],
        [Inventoryid]
    )  ON [PRIMARY] ,
    CONSTRAINT [chkInventoryWorld] CHECK ([Country] in ('UK',
            'Ireland', 'Australia'))
) ON [PRIMARY]
GO
```

Create linked servers that reference all other servers that will participate in the distributed partitioned view on each server. In the current example, on server Canada, you need to create linked servers that reference the USA and World servers; on server USA, create linked servers that reference the Canada and World servers; and on the World server, create linked servers that reference the Canada and USA servers.

```
exec sp_addlinkedserver N'(local)\USA', N'SQL Server'
GO
exec sp_addlinkedserver N'(local)\WORLD', N'SQL Server'
GO
```

NOTE

As you can see, I am running these statements against three instances of SQL Server running on the same physical machine.

To achieve better performance, it is necessary to set each linked server with the Lazy Schema Validation option. In the current example, on server Canada, you should execute

```
USE master
EXEC sp_serveroption '(local)\USA', 'lazy schema validation', 'true'
EXEC sp_serveroption '(local)\World', 'lazy schema validation', 'true'
```

Other servers should be set with the option for their linked servers. After that, the partitioned view will request metadata that describes the underlying table only if it is really needed.

Create distributed partitioned views that reference the local table and two tables on remote servers. On server Canada, you should execute

```
use Asset5
GO
Create view dbo.vInventoryDist
as
select * from Asset5.dbo.InventoryCanada
UNION ALL
select * from [(local)\USA].Asset5.dbo.InventoryUSA
UNION ALL
select * from [(local)\World].Asset5.dbo.InventoryWorld
GO
```

Now, you can test the distributed partitioned view. Figure 8-4 shows the query that calls all three servers. The highlighted part of the result shows that the view is redirecting parts of the query to other servers. Figure 8-5 shows execution of the same query against database objects.

NOTE

Complete code for the creation and linking of all three databases on all three servers used in this example can be downloaded from the Trigon Blue web site: www.trigonblue.com.

Execution Plans of Distributed Partitioned Views

If the query contains a criterion based on the partitioning key, SQL Server evaluates which servers contain matching data and executes the query against them only:

```
set statistics Profile ON
select * from dbo.vInventoryDist
where Country = 'UK'
```

```
Rows Executes StmtText
---- -------- -----------------------------------------------------------
154      1 SELECT * FROM [dbo].[vInventoryDist] WHERE [Country]=@1
154      1  |--Compute Scalar(DEFINE:([InventoryWorld].[Inventoryid
154      1  |--Clustered Idx Seek(OBJ:(([Asset5].[dbo].[InventoryWo
```

The profile shows that the query was executed on the local server. In a case in which the data resides on another server, the profile would look like this:

```
set statistics Profile ON
select * from vInventoryDist
where Country = 'CANADA'
```

```
Rows Executes StmtText
---- -------- -----------------------------------------------------------
872      1 SELECT * FROM [dbo]. [vInventoryDist] WHERE [Country]=@1
872      1  |--Compute Scalar(DEFINE:([(local)\CANADA].[Asset5].[d
872      1    |--Remote Query(SOURCE:((local)\CANADA), QUERY:(SE
```

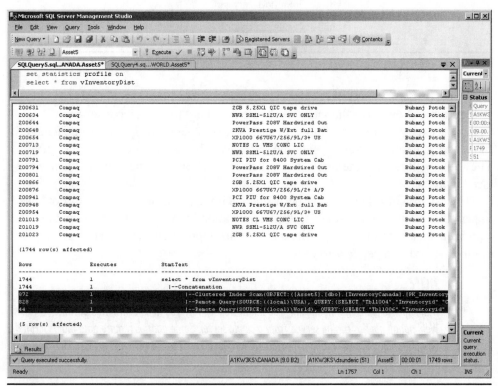

Figure 8-4   *Usage of distributed partitioned view*

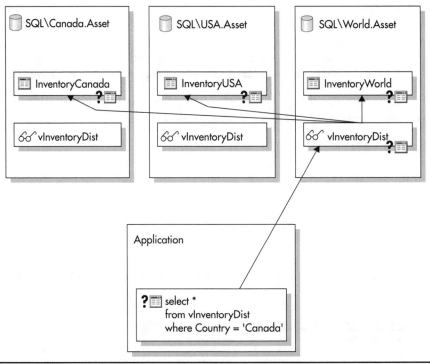

Figure 8-5 *Distributed partitioned view connects to tables on all member servers.*

Figure 8-6 shows how the view will route the query to the remote server.

It is necessary to create partitioned views on two other servers with identical names. In that way, an application can get the data through the view on any of the servers. The views will reroute the query to the server that contains the data that is needed (see Figure 8-7).

The system will achieve better performance if the partitioned view does not have to perform query routing—that is, if the application knows which server contains the data needed and therefore sends the query to the appropriate server. This technique is often called *data-dependent routing*.

NOTE

If the application is that intelligent, you might wonder why you need distributed partitioned views. Well, not all queries can be served from a single server. Some queries require data that is located on more than one server, and a distributed partitioned view would give you access to it.

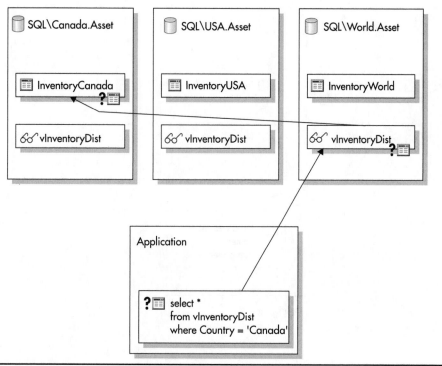

Figure 8-6 *Distributed partitioned view routes the query to the remote server.*

The selection of a partitioning key and implementation of a Check constraint have a critical impact on the performance of the system. You would have seen this fact demonstrated had you implemented the partitioning key using the nonoptimizable argument (an argument that leads the optimizer to create an execution plan that will ignore indexes):

```
. . .
 CONSTRAINT [chkInventoryWorld] CHECK ([Country] <>'USA'
                                   and [Country] <>'Canada'))
) ON [PRIMARY]
```

In such a case, SQL Server cannot determine where data is located and the query will always be routed to the World server as well:

```
Rows Executes StmtText
---- -------- --------------------------------------------------------------
872          1 SELECT * [dbo].FROM [vInventoryDist] WHERE [Country]=@1
872          1  |--Concatenation
```

Figure 8-7   *Data-dependent routing*

```
872          1    |--Remote Query(SOURCE:((local)\CANADA), QUERY:(SELECT
0            1    |--Clustered Idx Seek(OBJ:(Asset.dbo.InventoryWorld.P
```

As you can see, the query was executed unnecessarily on one of the servers—no records were returned. SQL Server compares Check constraints with the partition key ranges specified in the Where clause and builds the execution plan accordingly.

You might think that SQL Server won't do such a good job when stored procedures are used against distributed partitioned views. It is true that SQL Server does not know which parameter will be specified in the stored procedure, and therefore it creates an execution plan that runs the query against all servers. However, the plan will have dynamic filters that serve as conditional logic and execute only the queries that are needed. To demonstrate, I will create a stored procedure that references the view:

```
CREATE PROCEDURE dbo.ap_Inventory_ListDist
    @chvCountry varchar(50)
AS

SELECT *
FROM dbo.vInventoryDist
WHERE Country = @chvCountry
```

I will now execute it so that you can review the profile:

```
set statistics Profile ON
exec dbo.ap_Inventory_ListDist 'CANADA'
```

The execution plan will contain queries against all tables:

```
Rows Executes StmtText
---- -------- -------------------------------------------------------
872        1 select * from vInventoryDist where Country = @chvCoun
872        1 |--Concatenation
872        1 |   |--Clustered Index Seek(OBJECT:([Asset].[dbo].[
0          1 |--Filter(WHERE:(STARTUP EXPR([@chvCountry]='USA')))
0          0 |   |--Remote Query(SOURCE:(.\USA), QUERY:(SELECT C
0          1 |--Filter(WHERE:(STARTUP EXPR([@chvCountry]='Ireland
0          0     |--Remote Query(SOURCE:(.\World), QUERY:(SELECT
```

But two of these queries are not executed (as you can see in the Executes column).

Updateable Distributed Partitioned Views

Data can be modified through a distributed partitioned view:

```
set xact_abort on
update vInventoryDist
set UserName = 'unknown'
where UserName is null
and Country = 'Canada'
```

I needed to set the Xact_Abort option because each such statement is treated as a distributed transaction. Therefore, Distributed Transaction Coordinator must be running on each server. The result will look like this:

```
(2 row(s) affected)

Rows Executes StmtText
```

```
---- -------- -------------------------------------------------------
0            1 update vInventoryDist set UserName = 'unknown' where Use
0            1 |--Sequence
0            1    |--Remote Query(SOURCE:((local)\CANADA), QUERY:(UPDAT
0            1       |--Filter(WHERE:(STARTUP EXPR(0)))
0            0       |  |--Remote Query(SOURCE:((local)\USA), QUERY:(UP
0            1       |--Clustered Index Update(OBJECT:(Asset.dbo.Invent
0            1          |--Filter(WHERE:(STARTUP EXPR(0)))
0            0             |--Clustered Index Seek(OBJECT:(Asset.dbo.Inv
```

Note that SQL Server has again created dynamic filters, and only the appropriate queries will be executed, although they are all incorporated in the execution plan.

Unfortunately, views and modification statements have to satisfy additional requirements to allow modifications in that manner. I will mention only the most interesting and most restrictive ones:

▶ Member tables on other servers must be referenced using four-part names, the OpenRowset function, or the OpenDataSource function. These functions must not use pass-through queries.

▶ Member tables must not have triggers and cascading deletes or updates defined.

▶ All columns of a member table must be included in the distributed partitioned view. The order of the columns must be identical.

▶ The column definitions in all base tables must match (data type, scale, precision, and collation).

▶ Ranges of partition key values in member tables must not overlap.

▶ There can be only one Check constraint on the partitioning column and it may use only these operators: BETWEEN, AND, OR, <, <=, >, >=, =.

▶ Tables cannot have identity values (otherwise, Insert statements will fail).

▶ Partitioning keys cannot have defaults, allow nulls, be computed columns, or be timestamp values.

▶ smallmoney and smalldatetime columns on remote tables are automatically converted to money and datetime columns. Since all data types must match, the local table must use money and datetime. To avoid confusion, it is best not to use smallmoney and smalldatetime.

It is sometimes possible to work around some of these rules—you can create an Instead-of trigger to modify the member tables directly. Unfortunately, in that case, query Optimizer might not be able to create an execution plan as good as the one that would be created for a view that follows all the rules.

Scalability and Performance of Distributed Systems

Federated servers and distributed partitioned views are not a magic bullet that will solve all your problems. Note that distributed partitioned views are primarily designed to improve scalability of the system, not its performance. Although these two parameters might seem similar to you, there is a significant difference. Performance refers to the speed of execution of the system (or of individual transactions), while scalability refers to the ability to increase transactional load or the number of concurrent users without significant performance degradation. For example, if a metric describing system performance is 100 percent on a single server, adding another server might cause performance to fall to, for example, 50 percent. In this case, end users would notice improvements only after a third server is added (3×50 percent). But the advantage is that we now have a system with nearly *linear scalability*—every additional server would increase performance by another 50 percent.

Federated servers (like other distributed database systems) are also more difficult to manage. Even "simple" operations such as backups and restores become very complicated. Promotion of hot fixes or new code in a production environment requires significant manual intervention or development of specialized tools.

It is very important to evaluate the pros and cons of this design before you start. A rule of thumb is that all other options should be explored and exhausted first, and only then should scaling-out be attempted. The game plan should be something like this:

1. Optimize the database and the application.
2. Scale up the server.
3. Scale out the system.

A Poor Man's Federated Server

It is possible to create a distributed system without the use of distributed partitioned views. For example, if you are in a business that has only a few, large customers (with a heavy transactional load), you could create a single database per customer instead of storing all transactions in the same database. Then, you could divide databases between several servers or install each one on a separate dedicated server. An application can be designed to direct each query or transaction to the appropriate server—to perform data-dependent routing.

A similar design would be applicable for an organization that can easily be partitioned into its suborganizations, based, for example, on geographic locations.

The key requirement is that there be no (or very little) need to aggregate data on the complete system—that is, to run queries (or transactions) that span multiple servers.

Using SQL Views

SQL views can have different roles in your database system. Their basic role is to customize table data, but there are more complex roles. You can use standard SQL views to implement security and to ease export and import of data, or you can use the other types of views to achieve performance improvement.

Export and Import

Because they can transform and join data from one or more tables, standard SQL views are useful for exporting data out of your database system. Standard SQL views alone are not convenient for importing data, since you can insert data only in one base table at the time. Fortunately, you can add an Instead-of trigger to the view and then you will be able to modify multiple base tables (see "Triggers on Views" in Chapter 9).

Security Implementation

Standard SQL views are the preferred means of setting security when users are accessing the database through generic tools for accessing and editing database information (such as Access or Excel). Different users could have permissions to use different views with different filters on tables:

```
CREATE VIEW dbo.vInventoryTrigonTower
AS
SELECT *
FROM dbo.vInventory
WHERE LocationId = 2
```

Using this technique, the developer can also "filter" which columns are accessible by certain users. For example, you could allow only users from the accounting or human resources departments to view and edit salary data in a table containing employee information.

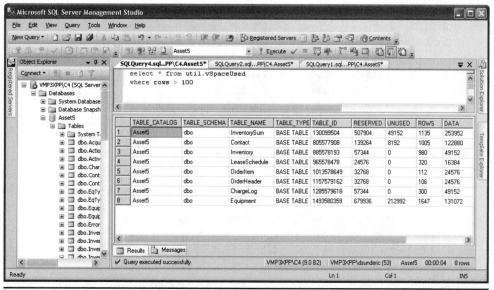

Figure 8-8   *Using util.vSpaceUsed*

Reduce Complexity

Views are a very nice way to simplify queries. As shown in Figure 8-8, I've created a util.vSpaceUsed view, which lists all database tables and their sizes. Its results are very similar to the results of sp_spaceused. In the past, I used this procedure to get the size of tables. As you may remember, Microsoft recommends that developers use system procedures, instead of querying system tables directly, since the structure of tables might change between SQL Server versions. Unfortunately, sp_spaceused returns data about a single object only, and I often need a recordset that contains all tables. So, instead of calling sp_spaceused in a loop to collect data in the temporary table, I created a view that returns all data that I might be interested in:

```
create view util.vSpaceUsed
as
select  distinct TOP 100 PERCENT
      db_name()           as TABLE_CATALOG
    , user_name(obj.uid)  as TABLE_SCHEMA
    , obj.name            as TABLE_NAME
    , case obj.xtype
        when 'U' then 'BASE TABLE'
        when 'V' then 'VIEW'
```

```
end                     as TABLE_TYPE
, obj.ID                as TABLE_ID
, Coalesce((select sum(reserved)
          from sysindexes i1
          where i1.id = obj.id
          and i1.indid in (0, 1, 255))
      *    (select d.low from master.dbo.spt_values d
          where d.number = 1 and d.type = 'E')
    , 0)            as RESERVED
, Coalesce((select Sum (reserved) - sum(used)
          from sysindexes i2
          where i2.indid in (0, 1, 255)
          and id = obj.id)
        * (select d.low from master.dbo.spt_values d
          where d.number = 1    and d.type = 'E')
    , 0)            as UNUSED
, case obj.xtype
    when 'U' then Coalesce((select i3.rows
                          from sysindexes i3
                          where i3.indid < 2
                          and i3.id = obj.id), 0)
    when 'V' then NULL
    end             as [ROWS]
  ,   Coalesce
  (     (   (select sum(dpages)    from sysindexes
              where indid < 2 and id = obj.id
          ) + (select isnull(sum(used), 0) from sysindexes
              where indid = 255 and id = obj.id
              )
      ) * (select d.low from master.dbo.spt_values d
              where d.number = 1 and d.type = 'E'
          ), 0)        as [DATA]
, Coalesce(
      ((select sum(reserved)
      from sysindexes i1
      where i1.id = obj.id
      and i1.indid in (0, 1, 255)
      ) - ( (select sum(dpages) from sysindexes
                where indid < 2 and id = obj.id
            ) + (select isnull(sum(used), 0) from sysindexes
                where indid = 255 and id = obj.id)
      ) )
```

```
    *  (select d.low from master.dbo.spt_values d
        where d.number = 1 and d.type = 'E')
        , 0)                    as [INDEX]
from sysobjects obj
where obj.xtype in ('U', 'V')
and    permissions(obj.id) != 0
order by db_name(), user_name(obj.uid), obj.name
```

The view has a very complex structure, but its use is very simple. You just need to reference it in a SQL statement (see Figure 8-8).

Performance Improvement

Views are often used as a mechanism for improving system performance. When an index is added to the view, SQL Server typically does not have to query and join underlying tables—the request will be satisfied using data from the indexed view. Unfortunately, this feature can also degrade overall performance if the system is mostly modifying underlying tables.

Distributed partitioned views can divide the execution of workload among servers and provide an exciting new way to linearly scale out the performance of the system. Unfortunately, this is not a magic bullet, either—if typical queries need data from multiple servers, performance may be degraded.

CHAPTER 9

Triggers

*T*riggers are a unique type of procedure. They are very similar to events—a type of procedure in certain programming languages such as Visual Basic. Events in Visual Basic are initiated by the system when certain actions occur (for instance, a form is loaded, a text box receives focus, or a key is pressed). Triggers are associated with SQL Server objects (such as tables) and executed by SQL Server when a specific change occurs.

In the following sections, we'll first examine conceptually different types of triggers: the classic (After) triggers, the Instead-of triggers, and finally DDL triggers. In the remaining sections, we'll discuss methods for managing triggers from Transact-SQL code and in Management Studio, and then finally discuss trigger design recommendations.

DML Triggers

SQL Server 7.0 and earlier versions recognized only one type of trigger. In SQL Server 2000 and SQL Server 2005, this type is called an *After trigger.* SQL Server 2000 introduced a new type—the *Instead-of trigger.* Both types are fired on the same types of modification statements:

▶ Insert

▶ Update

▶ Delete

Since these statements are considered Data Modification Language (DML), After triggers and Instead-of triggers are jointly called *DML triggers.*

Physical Design of After Triggers

The following is the simplified syntax for implementing the core functionality of After triggers:

```
Create Trigger trigger_name
On table
{After { [Delete] [,] [Insert] [,] [Update] }
   As
     sql_statement [...n]
```

As a stored procedure, a trigger logically consists of

► A *header,* which is a Transact-SQL statement for creating a trigger. It consists of three components:

  ► The name of the trigger

  ► The name of the table with which the trigger will be associated

  ► A modification statement (that is, an event) that will initiate the trigger

► A *body,* which contains Transact-SQL statement(s) to be executed at runtime.

The following example first creates a new table called MyEquipment, then populates it with Make and Model information from the Equipment table, and finally creates a trigger. The trigger is named trMyEquipment_D and is associated with the MyEquipment table. It is fired after a Delete statement is executed against the table. Its function is very simple—it notifies the user regarding actions and the number of records that have been deleted.

```
Create Table dbo.MyEquipment
     (Id int identity,
     Description varchar(500))
GO


-- populate table
Insert dbo.MyEquipment(Description)
     Select top 5 Make + ' ' + Model from dbo.Equipment
GO


Create Trigger dbo.trMyEquipment_D
On dbo.MyEquipment
After Delete   -- For Delete
As
     Print 'You have just deleted '
          + Cast(@@rowcount as varchar)
          + ' record(s)!'
Go
```

To execute the trigger, you need to execute the Delete statement:

```
Delete dbo.MyEquipment
Where Id = 2
```

SQL Server returns the following:

```
You have just deleted 1 record(s)!
```

```
(1 row(s) affected)
```

You can also execute the Delete statement to delete multiple records:

```
Delete dbo.MyEquipment
```

Even in this case, the trigger will *not* be fired once for each record. You will receive just one message:

```
You have just deleted 4 record(s)!
```

```
(4 row(s) affected)
```

For this reason, it is important to design your trigger to handle actions against multiple records. You will see more reasons in following paragraphs.

Inserted and Deleted Virtual Tables

SQL Server maintains two temporary virtual tables during the execution of a trigger: *Deleted* and *Inserted*. These tables contain all the records inserted or deleted during the operation that fired the trigger. You can use this feature to perform additional verification or additional activities on affected records.

You are probably wondering if there is an Updated table. No. Because an Update can be performed as a combination of the Delete and Insert statements, records that were updated will appear in both the Deleted and Inserted tables.

SQL Server does not create both tables in all cases. For example, in a trigger fired during a Delete statement, only a Deleted virtual table is accessible. A reference to an Inserted virtual table will cause an error.

The following table summarizes the presence of virtual tables in the relevant Transact-SQL statements:

Modification Statement	Deleted	Inserted
Insert	N/A	New records
Update	Old version of updated records	New version of updated records
Delete	Deleted records	N/A

The following modifies the trigger from the previous section to display which records are deleted:

```
Alter Trigger trMyEquipment_D
On dbo.MyEquipment
After Delete      -- For Delete
As
     Select 'You have just deleted following '
          + Cast(@@rowcount as varchar)
          + ' record(s)!'

     Select * from deleted
go
```

When you delete all records from the MyEquipment table, SQL Server returns the following:

```
--------------------------------------------------------------
You have just deleted following 5 record(s)!

(1 row(s) affected)

Id          Description
----------- --------------------------------------------------
1           Toshiba Portege 7020CT
2           Sony Trinitron 17XE
3           NEC V90
4           HP LaserJet 4
5           HP LaserJet 4

(5 row(s) affected)
```

You can use values from these tables, but you cannot modify them directly. If you need to perform some operation on records that were inserted, for example, you should not try to change them in the Inserted table. The proper method would be to issue a regular Transact-SQL statement against the original table. In the Where or From clause, you can reference the virtual table (Inserted) and in that way limit the subset of the original table that you are targeting.

In the following example, the trigger calculates a SOUNDEX code for the Make and Model of the Equipment records affected by the Insert or Update statement that has fired the trigger:

```
Alter Trigger trEquipment_IU
On dbo.Equipment
```

```
After Insert, Update     -- For Insert, Update
As
     -- precalculate ModelSDX and MakeSDX field
     -- to speed up use of SOUNDEX function
     update dbo.Equipment
     Set ModelSDX = SOUNDEX(Model),
         MakeSDX = SOUNDEX(Make)
     where EqId IN (Select EqId from Inserted)
```

What Triggers a Trigger?

A DML trigger is executed *once for each modification statement* (Insert, Update, or
Delete). An After trigger is fired *after* the modification statement finishes *successfully*.
If a statement fails for another reason (for example, foreign key or Check constraints),
the trigger is not invoked. For example, the Equipment table has the following Delete
trigger:

```
Alter Trigger Equipment_DeleteTrigger
On dbo.Equipment
After Delete      -- For Delete
As
Print 'One or more rows are deleted in Equipment table!'
```

If you attempt to delete all records from the table:

```
delete dbo.Equipment
```

SQL Server aborts the execution because there is a foreign key relationship with the
Inventory table. The execution is aborted before the trigger is invoked:

```
Msg 547, Level 16, State 0, Line 2
The DELETE statement conflicted with the
REFERENCE constraint "FK_Inventory_EqId".
The conflict occurred in database "Asset5",
table "Inventory", column 'EqId'.
The statement has been terminated.
```

A trigger and developer might have different definitions of what is a successfully
finished modification to a table. The trigger will fire even when a modification
statement affected zero records. The following example is based on the assumption
that the record with EqId set to 77777 does not exist in the database:

```
Delete dbo.Equipment
Where EqId = 77777
```

SQL Server nonchalantly prints from the trigger:

```
One or more rows are deleted in Equipment table!
```

Full Syntax of After Triggers

The After trigger was the only type of trigger before SQL Server 2000. After triggers in SQL Server 2000 have the same syntax as before except that the keyword For is (optionally) replaced with After:

```
Create Trigger trigger_name
On table
[With Encryption]
{
    {After | For { [Delete] [,] [Insert] [,] [Update] }
        [With Append]
         [Not For Replication]
        As
            sql_statement [...n]
    }
    |
    {After | For { [Insert] [,] [Update] }
        [With Append]
        [Not For Replication]
        As
        {    If Update (Column)
            [{And | Or} Update (Column)]
                [...n]
            | If (Columns_Updated()
                            {bitwise_operator}
                            updated_bitmask)
                { comparison_operator} column_bitmask [...n]
        }
            sql_statement [ ...n]
    }
}
```

If a trigger is defined with the With Encryption clause, SQL Server encrypts it so that its code remains concealed. Keep in mind that you need to preserve the source code in a script outside SQL Server if you plan to modify it later.

The Not For Replication clause indicates that SQL Server should not fire a trigger during replication of the table.

The With Append clause is used only when the compatibility mode of SQL Server is set to a value less than 70. For more details, refer to SQL Server Books OnLine.

It is possible to determine which columns were updated during the Update operation. Transact-SQL includes two functions that you can use within the trigger—Update() and Columns_Updated():

```
If Update (column)
sql_statement [ ...n]


If (Columns_Updated() {bitwise_operator} updated_bitmask)
                     {comparison_operator} column_bitmask [...n]
    sql_statement [ ...n]
```

You can now modify your previously used trigger to update only the fields that were changed:

```
Alter Trigger trEquipment_IU
On dbo.Equipment
After Insert, Update    -- For Insert, Update
As
     -- precalculate ModelSDX and MakeSDX field
     -- to speed up use of SOUNDEX function
     if Update(Model)
         update dbo.Equipment
         Set ModelSDX = SOUNDEX(Model)
         where EqId IN (Select EqId from Inserted)

     if Update(Make)
         update dbo.Equipment
         Set MakeSDX = SOUNDEX(Make)
         where EqId IN (Select EqId from Inserted)
     go
```

The Update() function might not perform exactly as you expect. In fact, it returns True for columns that were *referenced* during the Transact-SQL statement rather than for columns that were actually *changed*. For example, if you issue the following Update statement, SQL Server references the Make column of all records, and the trigger recalculates the SOUNDEX code in all records:

```
Update dbo.Equipment
Set Make = Make
```

TIP

This behavior might cause some problems for you if you forget about it. However, in some cases, you can use it to your advantage. For example, to speed up the upload of information to the table, you can temporarily disable triggers (see the "Disabling DDL Triggers" and "Disabling DML Triggers" sections near the end of this chapter). Later, when you want to execute the triggers (for example, to verify their validity and/or perform additional activities), you can use this feature to initiate triggers for records that are present in the table.

Too often, developers forget that the presence of a Default constraint in a column causes the Update() function to return True for that column during the execution of the Insert statement. This will occur even if the Insert statement did not reference the column itself.

The Columns_Updated() function operates with a bitmap that is related to the positions of columns. You can investigate its contents if you use an integer bitmask. To test whether the third column in a table was updated, you can use the following:

```
if Columns_Updated() & 3 = 3
      print 'Column 3 was updated!'
```

The ampersand (&) is a *binary and* operator, with which you can test the value of the flag.

Naturally, hard-coding the order of columns does not make much sense. The real value of this function is as a means of looping through all the columns that were updated and performing specified actions.

The following trigger loops through columns and displays which ones were updated:

```
Create Trigger trEquipmentN_IU_2
-- list all columns that were changed
On dbo.EquipmentN
after Insert, Update
As

    Set Nocount Off
    declare @intCountColumn int,
          @intColumn int

    -- count columns in the table
    Select @intCountColumn = Count(Ordinal_position)
    From Information_Schema.Columns
    Where Table_Name = 'EquipmentN'
```

```
    Select Columns_Updated() "COLUMNS UPDATED"
    Select @intColumn = 1

    -- loop through columns
    while @intColumn <= @intCountColumn
    begin
        if Columns_Updated() & @intColumn = @intColumn
            Print 'Column ('
                + Cast(@intColumn as varchar)
                + ') '
                + Col_Name(Object_ID('EquipmentN'), @intColumn)
                + ' has been changed!'
        set @intColumn = @intColumn + 1
    End
```

Use the following statement to test this trigger:

```
Insert EquipmentN(Make, Model, EqTypeID)
Values('Acme', '9000', 1)
```

You will notice that unlike an Update statement, an Insert statement will make changes to all columns.

Handling Changes on Multiple Records

The following example is a trigger designed to record the name of the user that changed the status of an order in the ActivityLog table, along with some additional information:

```
Create Trigger dbo.trOrderStatus_U_1
On dbo.OrderHeader
After Update     -- For Update
As
    declare @intOldOrderStatusId int,
            @intNewOrderStatusId int

    If Update (OrderStatusId)
    Begin

        select @intOldOrderStatusId = OrderStatusId from deleted
        select @intNewOrderStatusId = OrderStatusId from inserted
        Insert into dbo.ActivityLog( Activity,
                                     LogDate,
                                     UserName,
                                     Note)
```

```
values ( 'OrderHeader.OrderStatusId',
            GetDate(),
            User_Name(),
            'Value changed from '
            + Cast( @intOldOrderStatusId as varchar)
            + ' to '
            + Cast((@intNewOrderStatusId) as varchar)
          )
    End
```

This method is far from perfect. Can you detect the problem? It records the user who has changed the status of an order only when the user changes no more than a single order:

```
select @intOldOrderStatusId = OrderStatusId from deleted
```

Let me remind you that if the Select statement returns more than one record, the variable(s) will be filled with values from the last record. This is sometimes all that is required. If you have restricted access to the table and the only way to change the status is through a stored procedure (which allows only one record to be modified at a time), then this is sufficient.

Unfortunately, there is always a way to work around any restriction and possibly issue an Update statement that will change the status of all tables. The following is the proper solution:

```
Alter Trigger dbo.trOrderStatus_U
On dbo.OrderHeader
After Update -- For Update
As
    If Update (OrderStatusId)
    begin

        Insert into ActivityLog( Activity,
                                 LogDate,
                                 UserName,
                                 Note)
        Select   'OrderHeader.OrderStatusId',
                 GetDate(),
                 User_Name(),
                 'Value changed from '
                 + Cast( d.OrderStatusId as varchar)
                 + ' to '
                 + Cast( i.OrderStatusId as varchar)
```

```
                    from deleted d inner join inserted i
                    on d.OrderId = i.OrderId
        end
```

In this case, a set operation is used and one or more records from the Deleted and Inserted virtual tables will be recorded in ActivityLog.

Nested and Recursive Triggers

A trigger can fire other triggers on the same or other tables when it inserts, updates, or deletes records in them. This technique is called *nesting triggers*.

If a trigger changes records in its own table, it can fire another instance of itself. Such an invocation is called *direct invocation of recursive triggers*.

There is another scenario in which invocation of recursive triggers might occur. The trigger on one table might fire a trigger on a second table. The trigger on the second table might change the first table again, and the first trigger will fire again. This scenario is called *indirect invocation of recursive triggers*.

All these scenarios might be ideal for implementing referential integrity and business rules, but they might also be too complicated to design, understand, and manage. If you are not careful, the first trigger might call the second, then the second might call the first, then the first the second, and so on.

Very often, the SQL Server environment is configured to prevent this kind of behavior. To disable nested triggers and recursive triggers, you need to use the stored procedure sp_configure to set the Nested Triggers server option, and then use the Alter Table statement to set the Recursive_Triggers option to Off mode. Keep in mind that recursive triggers will be disabled automatically if you disable nested triggers.

After Trigger Restrictions

The following are the trigger restrictions, none of which usually causes any difficulties:

- ▶ The trigger must be created with the first statement in a batch.

- ▶ The name of the trigger is its Transact-SQL identifier, and therefore must be no more than 128 characters long.

- ▶ The trigger's name must be unique in the database.

- ▶ A trigger can only be associated with one table, but one table can have many triggers. In the past, only one trigger could be associated with one modification statement on one table. Now, each required function can be implemented in a separate trigger. By implementing these features in separate triggers, you assure that the triggers will be easier to understand and manage.

▶ Triggers cannot be nested to more than 32 levels, nor can they be invoked recursively more than 32 times. Attempting to do so causes SQL Server to return an error.

▶ A trigger must not contain any of the following Transact-SQL statements:

Alter Database	Drop Database
Alter Procedure	Drop Default
Alter Table	Drop Index
Alter Trigger	Drop Procedure
Alter View	Drop Rule
Create Database	Drop Table
Create Default	Drop Trigger
Create Index	Drop View
Create Procedure	Grant
Create Rule	Load Database
Create Schema	Load Log
Create Table	Reconfigure
Create Trigger	Restore Database
Create View	Restore Log
Deny	Revoke
Disk Init	Truncate Table
Disk Resize	Update Statistics

▶ You cannot reference `text`, `Ntext`, or `image` columns in triggers, but there are no problems with referencing `varchar(max)`, `Nvarchar(max)`, and `varbinary(max)` columns:

```
CREATE TRIGGER dbo.trOrderHeader_D
ON dbo.OrderHeader
AFTER DELETE
AS
```

```
BEGIN
SET NOCOUNT ON

-- collect OrderItems and Orders in OrderDeleted
INSERT INTO [dbo].[OrderDeleted]
    ([OrderId],[OrderDate],[RequestedById]
    ,[TargetDate],[CompletionDate],[DestinationLocationId]
    ,[Note],[OrderTypeId],[OrderStatusid]
    ,[UserName],[ChangeDT])
SELECT [OrderId],[OrderDate],[RequestedById]
    ,[TargetDate],[CompletionDate],[DestinationLocationId]
    ,[Note],[OrderTypeId],[OrderStatusid]
    , SUSER_SNAME(), GETDATE()
FROM deleted

END
```

Instead-of Triggers

Instead-of triggers are executed instead of the modification statement that has initiated them. The following trigger is executed when an attempt is made to delete records from the MyEquipment table. It will report an error instead of allowing the deletion:

```
Create Trigger dbo.itrMyEquipment_D
On dbo.MyEquipment
instead of Delete
As
    -- deletion in this table is not allowed
    raiserror('Deletion of records in MyEquipment
table is not allowed', 16, 1)
GO
```

Instead-of triggers are executed after changes to base tables occur in Inserted and Deleted virtual tables, but before any change to the base tables is executed. Therefore, the trigger can use information in the Inserted and Deleted tables. In the following example, a trigger tests whether some of the records that would have been deleted are in use in the Equipment table:

```
Create Trigger itrEqType_D
On dbo.EqType
instead of Delete
As
```

```
If exists(select *
    from Equipment
    where EqTypeId in (select EqTypeId
                          from deleted)
    )
    raiserror('Some recs in EqType are in use in Equipment table!',
              16, 1)
else
    delete EqType
    where EqTypeId in (select EqTypeId from deleted)
GO
```

Instead-of triggers are initiated before any constraints. This behavior is very different from that of After triggers. Therefore, the code for an Instead-of trigger must perform all checking and processing that would normally be performed by constraints.

Usually, an Instead-of trigger executes the modification statement (Insert, Update, or Delete) that initiates it. The modification statement does not initiate the trigger again. If some After triggers and/or constraints are defined on the table or view, they will be executed as though the Instead-of trigger does not exist.

A table or a view can have only one Instead-of trigger (and more than one After trigger) per modification type.

Triggers on Views

Instead-of triggers can be defined on views also. In the following example, a trigger is created on a view that displays fields from two tables:

```
Create View dbo.vEquipment
AS
Select Equipment.EqId,
       Equipment.Make,
       Equipment.Model,
       EqType.EqType
From dbo.Equipment Equipment
Inner Join dbo.EqType EqType
On Equipment.EqTypeId = EqType.EqTypeId
Go

Create Trigger itr_vEquipment_I
On dbo.vEquipment
instead of Insert
As
```

```
-- If the EqType is new, insert it
If exists(select EqType
          from inserted
          where EqType not in (select EqType
                                      from EqType))
    -- we need to insert the new ones
    insert into EqType(EqType)
        select EqType
        from inserted
        where EqType not in (select EqType
                                    from EqType)


-- now you can insert new equipment
Insert into Equipment(Make, Model, EqTypeId)
Select inserted.Make, inserted.Model, EqType.EqTypeId
From inserted Inner Join EqType
On inserted.EqType = EqType.EqType


GO


Insert Into vEquipment(EqId, Make, Model, EqType)
Values (-777, 'Microsoft', 'Natural Keyboard', 'keyboard')
```

The trigger first examines whether the Inserted table contains EqType values that do not exist in EqTable. If they exist, they will be inserted in the EqType table. At the end, values from the Inserted table are added to the Equipment table.

The previous example illustrates one unusual feature in the use of Instead-of triggers on views. Since EqId is referenced by the view, it can (and must) be specified by the modification statement (Insert statement). The trigger can (and will) ignore the specified value since it is inserted automatically (EqId is an identity field in the base table). The reason for this behavior is that the Inserted and Deleted tables have different structures from the base tables on which the view is based. They have the same structure as the Select statement inside the view.

Columns in the view can be nullable or not nullable. The column is nullable if its expression in the Select list of the view satisfies one of the following criteria:

▶ The view column references a base table column that is nullable.

▶ The view column expression uses arithmetic operators or functions.

If the column does not allow nulls, an Insert statement must provide a value for it. This is the reason a value for the EqId column was needed in the previous example.

An Update statement must provide values for all non-nullable columns referenced by the Set clause in a view with an Instead-of update trigger.

NOTE

You must specify values even for view columns that are mapped to `timestamp`, *Identity, or computed-base table columns.*

You can use the AllowNull property of the ColumnProperty() function (table function) to examine which fields are nullable from code.

NOTE

The previous code example is much more important than you might think. It allows you to insert a whole set of records at one time into the view (actually to the set of base tables behind the view). Before Instead-of triggers, you had to do this record by record with a stored procedure. This capability is very useful for loading information into a SQL Server database. For example, you can load information from a denormalized source (such as a flat file) and store it in a set of normalized, linked tables.

Another unusual feature of Instead-of triggers is the fact that they support `text`, `ntext`, and `image` columns in Inserted and Deleted tables. After triggers cannot handle these data types. In base tables, `text`, `ntext`, and `image` columns actually contain pointers to the pages holding data. In Inserted and Deleted tables, `text`, `ntext`, and `image` columns are stored as continuous strings within each row. No pointers are stored in these tables, and therefore the use of the Textptr() and Textvalid() functions and the Readtext, Updatetext, and Writetext statements is not permitted. All other uses are valid, such as references in the Select list or Where clause, or the use of Charindex(), Patindex(), or Substring() functions.

However, you can always use new varchar(max), Nvarchar(max), and varbinary(max) instead of old BLOB fields:

```
CREATE TRIGGER itrOrder_D ON dbo.OrderHeader
INSTEAD OF DELETE
AS
BEGIN

SET NOCOUNT ON

-- collect deleted Orders in OrderDeleted
INSERT INTO [dbo].[OrderDeleted]
```

```
       ([OrderId],[OrderDate],[RequestedById]
       ,[TargetDate],[CompletionDate],[DestinationLocationId]
       ,[Note],[OrderTypeId],[OrderStatusid]
       ,[UserName],[ChangeDT])
SELECT [OrderId],[OrderDate],[RequestedById]
    ,[TargetDate],[CompletionDate],[DestinationLocationId]
    ,[Note],[OrderTypeId],[OrderStatusid]
    , SUSER_SNAME(), GETDATE()
FROM deleted

delete dbo.[OrderHeader]
where OrderId in (select OrderId from deleted)

END
GO
```

DML Trigger Order of Execution

SQL Server 7.0 introduced the idea that more than one trigger could be created per modification statement. However, the execution order of such triggers could not be controlled. In SQL Server 2000 and SQL Server 2005, it is possible to define which DML After trigger to execute first and which to execute last against a table. For example, the following statement will set trInventory_I to be the first trigger to be executed in the case of an Insert modification statement:

```
Exec sp_settriggerorder @triggername = 'trInventory_I',
                        @order = 'first',
                        @stmttype = 'INSERT'
```

The @order parameter must have one of these values: 'first', 'last', or 'none'. The value 'none' is used to reset the order of the execution of the trigger after it has been specified. The @stmttype parameter must have one of these values: 'INSERT', 'UPDATE', or 'DELETE'.

Since only one Instead-of trigger can be associated with a table, and since it is executed before any other trigger (or constraint), it is not possible to set its order.

NOTE

Alter trigger statements reset the order of the trigger. After altering the trigger, you must execute the sp_SetTriggerOrder statement to set it again.

DDL Triggers

DDL triggers are new in SQL Server 2005. They can be fired after the engine invokes Data Definition Language (DDL) statements such as:

- ▶ Create Table
- ▶ Drop Table
- ▶ Alter Procedure
- ▶ Drop Schema
- ▶ Create Login

DDL triggers are typically used to audit or control changes in database and server objects. In the following example, the trigger will prevent changes to any table in the current database:

```
CREATE TRIGGER trdPreventTableChanges
ON DATABASE
FOR DROP_TABLE, ALTER_TABLE, CREATE_TABLE
AS

RAISERROR('This database contains sensitive data. Changes to the
tables are typically not allowed and are rolled back by a trigger.
If you do have a permission to change tables,
temporarily disable the trigger by using:

DISABLE TRIGGER trdPreventTableChanges ON DATABASE
<your batch with table changes>
ENABLE TRIGGER trdPreventTableChanges ON DATABASE;

', 16, 1)
ROLLBACK;
GO
```

DDL triggers are After triggers, which means that:

- ▶ You can replace the For keyword with After (as in the third line of the preceding example).
- ▶ You have to explicitly invoke Rollback statements to cancel the changes made by DDL statements.

Since it is not an Instead-of trigger, you do not have to actually execute changes in the code yourself. A DDL trigger will not fire if there is another reason to prevent completion of a DDL modification statement. For example, if a table that you are trying to drop does not exist, SQL Server will not invoke a DDL trigger to log the identity of a user who issues a Drop Table statement.

Scope and Events of DDL Triggers

DDL triggers can be set to react on database or server objects. In the following example, the trigger will prevent the creation of new logins (server objects stored in the database):

```
CREATE TRIGGER trdPreventLoginCreation
ON ALL SERVER FOR CREATE_LOGIN
AS

RAISERROR('It is not allowed to add logins to this server
without permission. Call DBA Security Group.', 16, 1)

INSERT INTO [dbo].[ActivityLog]([Activity],[LogDate],[UserName])
VALUES ('LOGIN CHANGE', GetDate(),SYSTEM_USER)

ROLLBACK
GO
```

If you want to prevent any change on any login, instead of referencing all login events (CREATE_LOGIN, DROP_LOGIN, ALTER_LOGIN), you can reference the event group—DDL_LOGIN_EVENTS:

```
CREATE TRIGGER trdPreventLoginChanges
ON SERVER FOR DDL_LOGIN_EVENTS
AS
RAISERROR('It is not allowed to add logins to this server
without permission. Call DBA Security Group.', 16, 1)
ROLLBACK
GO
```

Similarly, to reference all table modification statements you can use the DDL_TABLE_EVENTS group, and if you decide to fire a trigger after all table, view, index, and statistics modification events, you can use the DDL_TABLE_VIEW_EVENTS group. To see a complete list of events and their groups, search "Event Groups for Use with DDL Triggers" in Books OnLine.

EventData()

Since DDL triggers are not tied to table modifications, as in the case of DML triggers, they do not have Inserted and Deleted virtual tables. Instead, you can get information about the DDL modification statement that has fired the trigger using a special EventData() function. In the following example, changes to the table are allowed, but they are recorded for audit purposes in the special table:

```
CREATE TRIGGER trdAuditTableChanges
ON DATABASE
FOR DDL_TABLE_EVENTS
AS
    declare @event varchar(max)
    set @event = Convert(nvarchar(max), EVENTDATA())

    INSERT INTO [dbo].[ActivityLog]([Activity],[LogDate],[UserName],[Note])
    VALUES ('TABLE CHANGE', GetDate(),SYSTEM_USER, @event)

GO
```

When the statement that modifies a table is issued, EventData() will return data in the form of an XML document:

```
<EVENT_INSTANCE>
  <EventType>CREATE_TABLE</EventType>
  <PostTime>2004-09-08T21:56:37.727</PostTime>
  <SPID>52</SPID>
  <ServerName>V505\C4</ServerName>
  <LoginName>V505\dsunderic</LoginName>
  <UserName>V505\dsunderic</UserName>
  <DatabaseName>Asset5</DatabaseName>
  <SchemaName>dbo</SchemaName>
```

```
<ObjectName>test</ObjectName>
<ObjectType>TABLE</ObjectType>
<TSQLCommand>
    <SetOptions ANSI_NULLS="ON" ANSI_NULL_DEFAULT="ON"
    ANSI_PADDING="ON" QUOTED_IDENTIFIER="ON" ENCRYPTED="FALSE" />
    <CommandText>create table test(id int)</CommandText>
</TSQLCommand>
</EVENT_INSTANCE>
```

You can use XQuery methods to parse the content of an event document. In the following example, the Activity, UserName, and Note columns of the ActivityLog table were extracted from the EventType, LoginName, and TSQLCommand nodes of the event document:

```
CREATE TRIGGER trdAuditTableChanges
ON DATABASE
AFTER DDL_TABLE_EVENTS
AS

declare @event xml
set @event = EVENTDATA()

INSERT INTO [dbo].[ActivityLog]([Activity],[LogDate],[UserName],[Note])
VALUES
(@event.value('(/EVENT_INSTANCE/EventType)[1]', 'nvarchar(100)'),
 GETDATE(),
 @event.value('(/EVENT_INSTANCE/LoginName)[1]', 'nvarchar(100)'),
 @event.value('(/EVENT_INSTANCE/TSQLCommand)[1]', 'nvarchar(2000)') );
GO
```

The preceding XQuery value() methods simply access the values of the specified nodes. The value() method is better suited for use in Transact-SQL than the alternative query() method, since it returns data with carriage return and linefeed (CR/LF) characters invisible. The query() method returns CR and LF in an ampersand-escaped sequence of characters. For more information on how to use XQuery, search "XQuery Against the XML Data Type" in Books OnLine.

NOTE

EventData() can be used only inside the DDL trigger. It is not guaranteed to return a meaningful result after a change is rolled back or committed.

The function uses different schemas to return data when it is invoked by database and server modification statements. The schema also depends on the actual modification statement, since not all nodes are applicable for all events.

Syntax of DDL Triggers

DDL triggers are designed using the following syntax:

```
CREATE TRIGGER trigger_name
ON { ALL SERVER | DATABASE }
[ WITH [ ENCRYPTION ] | [ EXECUTE AS CALLER | SELF | 'user_name' ]
{ FOR | AFTER } { event_type | event_group } [ ,...n ]
AS { sql_statement  [ ; ] [ ...n ]}
```

The On clause controls the scope of the trigger—it is tied to database or server events. Like stored procedure triggers, DDL triggers can be encrypted and executed alternatively by caller, schema owner, or specific database user.

Managing Triggers

You can manage triggers using GUI tools such as SQL Server Management Studio or Visual Studio, or by using Transact-SQL statements.

Managing DML Triggers in Management Studio

You can access triggers from Management Studio:

1. Expand the node of the table with which the trigger is associated.
2. Expand the trigger's node.
3. Right-click the trigger and choose Modify from the pop-up menu.

SQL Server displays a form for editing trigger properties (see Figure 9-1). This editor is very similar to the editor you use to edit stored procedures.

To create a new trigger on the table, right-click the trigger's subnode of the table and choose New Trigger from the pop-up menu. SQL Server initially fills the form with a template for creating a new trigger.

Once you have created or modified the trigger, you can choose Assisted Editor | Check Syntax to verify it, and then File | Save to attach it to the table.

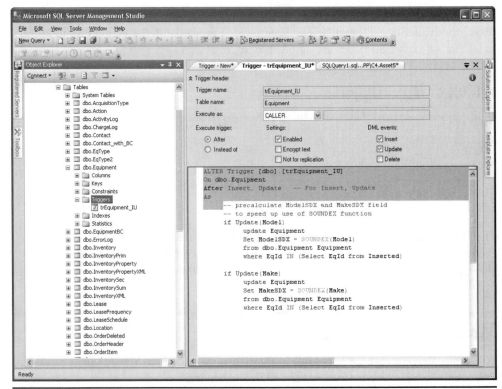

Figure 9-1   *Managing triggers in Management Studio*

You can delete a trigger by right-clicking the trigger and choosing Delete from the pop-up menu.

Managing DDL Triggers from Management Studio

Database-level DDL triggers are managed from *server* | Databases | *database* | Programmability | Database Triggers (see Figure 9-2). Server-level DDL triggers are managed from *server* | Programmability | Server Triggers.

Managing Triggers Using Transact-SQL Statements

SQL Server has a rich palette of system stored procedures, functions, and views for managing triggers from Transact-SQL.

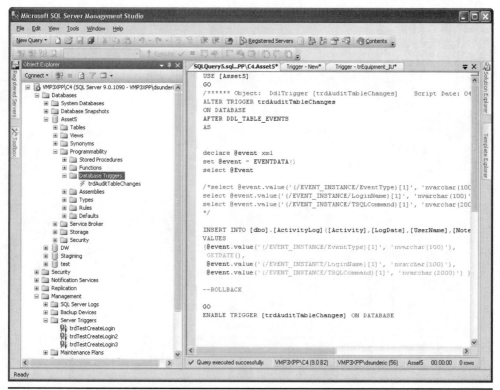

Figure 9-2   *Managing database-level DDL triggers*

Listing Triggers

To list triggers associated with a table, use the system stored procedure sp_helptrigger:

```
Exec sp_helptrigger 'dbo.OrderHeader'
```

The server returns the list of triggers associated with the specified table and displays the type of trigger found in the isupdate, isdelete, isinsert, isafter, and isinteadof columns (see Figure 9-3).

Viewing Triggers

You can obtain the code for a trigger using the system stored procedure sp_helptext:

```
Exec sp_helptext 'dbo.trOrderStatus_U'
```

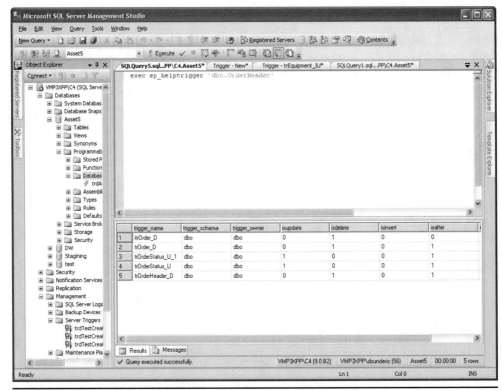

Figure 9-3 *Trigger information from sp_helptrigger*

The server returns the code for the specified trigger:

```
Text
--------------------------------------------------------------------
CREATE Trigger trOrderStatus_U
On dbo.[OrderHeader]
After Update      -- For Update
As
     If Update (OrderStatusId)
     Begin

          Insert into ActivityLog( Activity,
                                   LogDate,
                                   UserName,
                                   Note)
```

```
    Select          'OrderHeader.OrderStatusId',
                    GetDate(),
                    USER_NAME(),
                    'Value changed from '
                    + Cast( d.OrderStatusId as varchar)
                    + ' to '
                    + Cast( i.OrderStatusId as varchar)
    From deleted d inner join inserted i
    On d.OrderId = i.OrderId
  End
```

Deleting DML Triggers

A trigger can be deleted, as can all other database objects, using the appropriate Drop statement:

```
if  exists (select * from sys.objects
          where object_id = object_id(N'[dbo].[trEquipment_IU]')
          and type in (N'TA', N'TR'))
DROP TRIGGER [dbo].[trEquipment_IU]
```

Deleting DDL Triggers

The statement for dropping DDL triggers contains a reference to the scope (level) of the trigger:

```
if  exists (select * from master.sys.server_triggers
          where name = N'trdTestCreateLogin2' and parent_class=100)
DROP TRIGGER [trdTestCreateLogin2] ON ALL SERVER
GO

if  exists (select * from sys.triggers
          where name = N'trdAuditTableChanges' and parent_class=0)
DROP TRIGGER [trdAuditTableChanges] ON DATABASE
```

NOTE

You should check the presence of server-level triggers in the master.sys.server_triggers view and the presence of database-level triggers in the sys.triggers view.

Modifying Triggers

Earlier in this chapter, you saw details of the syntax of a Transact-SQL statement for creating triggers. Triggers can be modified using the Alter Trigger statement. Since the features of the Alter Trigger and Create Trigger statements are identical, we will not explore the syntax a second time.

It is much better to use the Alter Trigger statement to modify a trigger than to drop and then re-create the trigger. During the period between dropping and creating a trigger, a user might make a change to the table, the consequence of which is that the rules that are usually enforced by the trigger will not be enforced.

NOTE

Keep in mind that the order of execution is lost when the trigger is altered — you must reset it using sp_SetTriggerOrder.

Renaming Triggers

Triggers are often renamed using Transact-SQL statements designed for the creation and modification of triggers, such as Alter Trigger. As with all other database objects, a trigger can be forced to change its name using the following system stored procedure:

```
Exec sp_rename 'Orders_Trigger1', 'trOrders_IU'
```

The first parameter is the current name of the database object, and the second parameter is the new name of the object.

Disabling DML Triggers

It is possible to temporarily disable and enable triggers without dropping them:

```
Alter Table [OrderHeader] Disable Trigger trOrders_IU
```

After the execution of this statement, the specified trigger will not fire, but it will still be associated with the table. This technique is often used to load large amounts of data into a table without initiating the business logic encapsulated in a trigger.

An alternative statement has been added to SQL Server 2005 (to make it compatible with statements for DDL triggers):

```
DISABLE TRIGGER dbo. trOrderHeader_IU ON dbo.OrderHeader
```

Disabling DDL Triggers

Disable Trigger statements for DDL triggers contain a reference to trigger scope (Database or All Server):

```
DISABLE TRIGGER trdAuditLoginCreation ON All Server
```

Trigger Design Recommendations

Since triggers are relatively complex database objects, it is easy to create design, performance, or maintainability problems inside your database. Therefore, I will spend some time pointing out a proper way to use them.

Go Out ASAP

Triggers take time to execute. If your server is very busy and/or other users are locking resources in the database, execution might take much more time than expected. On the other hand, locks that you (or rather SQL Server) have placed in the database while the trigger is executing will not be released until the trigger is finished. Thus, your trigger may increase competition for resources and affect other users and their sessions.

For these reasons, you should always try to exit a trigger as soon as possible. For example, you could start (almost) every DML trigger with the following test:

```
If @@rowcount = 0
    Return
```

It will abort further execution of the trigger if no records were changed.

Keep in mind that this If clause must occur at the very beginning of the trigger. If you put it after any other statement, @@rowcount will return the number of records affected by that statement. For example, if you put a simple Print statement at the beginning of the trigger and then this test, the remainder of the trigger will not be executed:

```
Alter Trigger trOrderStatus_U
On dbo.[OrderHeader]
After Update    -- For Update
As

Print 'Start of trOrderStatus_U'
If @@Rowcount = 0   -- This is always true
                    -- and the rest will NEVER be executed.
    Return

    If Update (OrderStatusId)
    Begin

        Insert into ActivityLog( Activity,
                                 LogDate,
                                 UserName,
                                 Note)
```

```
        Select      'OrderHeader.OrderStatusId',
                    GetDate(),
                    USER_NAME(),
                    'Value changed from '
                    + Cast( d.OrderStatusId as varchar)
                    + ' to '
                    + Cast( i.OrderStatusId as varchar)


        From deleted d inner join inserted i
        On d.OrderId = i.OrderId
    End
```

Make It Simple

It is true that DML triggers are suitable for implementing complex business rules, particularly if those business rules are too complex to be handled by simpler database objects such as constraints. However, just because you are using them to handle complex business rules, you do not have to make your code so complex that it is difficult to understand and follow. It is challenging enough to work with DML triggers; keep them as simple as possible.

Divide and Conquer

In early versions of Microsoft SQL Server, only one After trigger per modification statement could be associated with a table. This physical restriction led developers to produce poor (very complex) code. Features that were not related had to be piled up in a single After trigger. However, this restriction no longer applies. There is no reason to couple the code for multiple After triggers. Each distinct piece of functionality can be implemented in a separate trigger (except in the case of Instead-of triggers).

Do Not Use Select and Print Inside a Trigger

The Print and Select commands are very useful in triggers during the debugging process. However, they can be very dangerous if left in a trigger after it has been introduced into production. These statements generate additional result sets, which might cause the client application to fail if it is not able to handle them or does not expect them.

Do Not Use Triggers at All

If you can implement the required functionality using constraints, do not use triggers! If you can implement the required functionality using stored procedures, and if you can prevent users from accessing your tables directly, do not use triggers!

Triggers are more difficult to implement, debug, and manage. You will save both time and money for your company or your client if you can find simpler ways to implement the required functionality.

Transaction Management in Triggers

A trigger is always part of the transaction that initiates it. That transaction can be explicit (when SQL Server has executed Begin Transaction). It can also be implicit—basically, SQL Server treats each Transact-SQL statement as a separate transaction that will either succeed completely or fail completely.

It is possible to abort the entire transaction from inside the trigger by using Rollback Transaction. This command, shown in action next, is valid for both implicit and explicit transactions:

```
Alter Trigger trOrderStatus_U
On dbo.[Order]
After Update      --For Update
As

    If @@Rowcount = 0
        Return

    If Update (OrderStatusId)
    Begin

        Insert into ActivityLog( Activity,
                                 LogDate,
                                 UserName,
                                 Note)
        Select    'Order.OrderStatusId',
                  GetDate(),
                  USER_NAME(),
                  'Value changed from '
                  + Cast( d.OrderStatusId as varchar)
                  + ' to '
                  + Cast( i.OrderStatusId as varchar)
```

```
        From deleted d inner join inserted i
        On d.OrderId = i.OrderId

        If @@Error <> 0
        Begin
            RAISERROR ("Error in trOrderStatus_U", 16, 1)
            Rollback Transaction
        End
End
```

In this trigger, SQL Server investigates the presence of the error and rolls back the complete operation if it is unable to log changes to the ActivityLog table.

The processing of Rollback Transaction inside a trigger differs from its processing inside a stored procedure. It also differs in different versions of Microsoft SQL Server.

When a Rollback statement is encountered in a stored procedure, changes made since the last Begin Transaction are rolled back, but the processing continues.

In Microsoft SQL Server 2005, when a Rollback statement is executed within a trigger, a complete batch is aborted and all changes are rolled back. SQL Server continues to process from the beginning of the next batch (or stops if the next batch does not exist).

Microsoft SQL Server 2000, 4.2, and 7.0, and all versions of Sybase SQL Server behaved in this manner. In Microsoft SQL Server 6.0, execution was continued through the trigger, but the batch was canceled. Version 6.5 went to an opposite extreme; execution of both the trigger and the batch was continued. It was the responsibility of the developer to detect an error and stop further processing.

NOTE

Statements in the trigger after the Rollback statement will be executed normally. Any modifications done after the rollback point will not be rolled back. However, nested triggers will not be fired as a result of modifications after the rollback point.

Using Triggers

In SQL Server, DML triggers may have the following roles:

▶   To enforce data integrity, including referential integrity and cascading deletes

▶   To enforce business rules too complex for Default and Check constraints

- ▶ To log data changes and send notification to administrators via e-mail

- ▶ To maintain derived information (computed columns, running totals, aggregates, and so on)

Triggers can be implemented to replace all other constraints on a table. A typical example is the use of a trigger to replace the functionality enforced by a foreign key constraint.

It is possible to implement *cascading deletes* using triggers. For example, if you do not have a foreign key between the Inventory and InventoryProperty tables, you might implement a trigger to monitor the deletion of Inventory records and to delete all associated InventoryProperty records.

Check and Default constraints are limited in that they can base their decision only on the context of current records in the current tables. You can implement a trigger that functions in a manner similar to Check constraints and that verifies the contents of multiple records or even the contents of other tables.

Triggers can be set to create an audit trail of activities performed on a table. For example, you might be interested in obtaining information on who changed the contents of, or specific columns in, the Lease table, and when that user made the changes.

It is possible to create a trigger to notify you when a specific event occurs in the database. For example, in a technical support system, you might send e-mail to the person responsible for dispatching technical staff, to inform that person that a request for technical support has been received. In an inventory system, you might automatically generate a purchase order if the quantity of an inventory item falls below the specified level.

Triggers are suitable for computing and storing calculated columns, running totals, and other aggregates in the database. For example, to speed up reporting, you might decide to keep a total of ordered items in an order table.

DDL triggers are presenting us with completely new area of opportunities. They could be used:

- ▶ To establish a traceable record of schema changes to database objects for auditing purposes

- ▶ To log security changes on a server

- ▶ To prevent certain types of schema changes

- ▶ To ensure that a set of database objects is identical across a group of databases or servers

Cascading Deletes

Usually, referential integrity between two tables is implemented with a foreign key, such as in the following illustration:

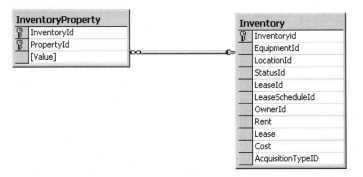

In such cases, a foreign key prevents the user from deleting records from a parent table (Inventory) if a record is referenced in a linked table (InventoryProperty). The only way to delete the record would be to use the following code:

```
Delete dbo.InventoryProperty
Where InventoryId = 222

Delete dbo.Inventory
Where InventoryId = 222
```

In some cases, the system design requirements might call for *cascading deletes,* which automatically delete records from the linked table when the record in the parent table is deleted. In this case, only one command is required to delete any instance of an asset with an InventoryId value of 222:

```
Delete dbo.Inventory
Where InventoryId = 222
```

SQL Server 2000 introduced cascading referential integrity constraints that can implement this behavior. In SQL Server 7.0 and earlier versions, you had to use triggers to implement cascading operations. It is now recommended to use cascading referential integrity constraints, but since that is not possible in some cases (for example, when tables are in different databases), you should know how to do it with triggers.

The following example creates two new tables (without a foreign key), populates them with a few records, and creates a trigger that will implement a cascading delete:

```
Create Table dbo.MyInventory
    (
    Inventoryid int Not Null Identity (1, 1),
    EqId int Null,
    LocationId int Null,
    StatusId tinyint Null,
    LeaseId int Null,
    LeaseScheduleId int Null,
    OwnerId int Null,
    Rent smallmoney Null,
    Lease smallmoney Null,
    Cost smallmoney Null,
    AcquisitionTypeID tinyint Null
    )
Go


Alter Table dbo.MyInventory Add Constraint
    PK_Inventory Primary Key Nonclustered
    (
    Inventoryid
    )
Go


Create Table dbo.MyInventoryProperty
    (
    InventoryId int Not Null,
    PropertyId smallint Not Null,
    Value varchar(50) Null
    )
Go
Alter Table dbo.MyInventoryProperty Add Constraint
    PK_InventoryProperty Primary Key Nonclustered
    (
    InventoryId,
    PropertyId
    )
Go
```

```
Create Trigger dbo.trMyInventory_CascadingDelete_D
On dbo.MyInventory
After Delete      --For delete
As

If @@Rowcount = 0
     Return
Delete dbo.MyInventoryProperty
where InventoryId In (Select InventoryID from deleted)
Go

Insert into dbo.MyInventory(EqId) Values (1)
Insert into dbo.MyInventory(EqId) Values (2)
Insert into dbo.myInventory(EqId) Values (3)
Insert into dbo.myInventory(EqId) Values (4)
Insert into dbo.myInventory(EqId) Values (5)

Insert into MyInventoryProperty(InventoryId, PropertyId, Value)
Values (1, 1, 'ACME')
Insert into MyInventoryProperty(InventoryId, PropertyId, Value)
Values (1, 2, 'Turbo')
Insert into MyInventoryProperty(InventoryId, PropertyId, Value)
Values (1, 3, '311')
Insert into MyInventoryProperty(InventoryId, PropertyId, Value)
Values (2, 1, 'ACME')
Insert into MyInventoryProperty(InventoryId, PropertyId, Value)
Values (2, 2, 'TurboPro')
Insert into MyInventoryProperty(InventoryId, PropertyId, Value)
Values (2, 3, '312')
Go

Delete MyInventory
Where InventoryId = 1

Select * from MyInventory
Select * from MyInventoryProperty
```

Aggregates

Imagine that users of an Asset5 database are often clogging the Inventory table. One
operation that they perform frequently is the execution of reports that prepare the sum
of all monthly lease payments per lease schedule. If the sum were prepared in advance,
the report would be available in an instant, the table would be less clogged, and the
user would experience fewer locking and deadlocking problems.

To provide this functionality, you could create one or more triggers to maintain the PeriodicTotalAmount field in the LeaseSchedule table. The field will contain the sum of lease payments for assets in the Inventory table that are associated with a lease schedule.

It is possible to implement diverse solutions for this task. This solution is based on separate triggers for different modification statements.

The Insert trigger is based on a relatively complex Update statement with a subquery based on the contents of the Inserted table. Each new record increments the total in the related lease schedule.

The Coalesce statement is used to replace nulls with zeros in the calculation. The trigger evaluates the number of records affected by the modification statement at the beginning and, if no records are affected, aborts further execution.

This solution executes properly even when multiple records are inserted with one statement:

```
Create Trigger dbo.trInventory_Lease_I
On dbo.Inventory
after Insert        -- For Insert
As


If @@Rowcount = 0
     return


-- add inserted leases to total amount
Update LeaseSchedule
Set LeaseSchedule.PeriodicTotalAmount =
     LeaseSchedule.PeriodicTotalAmount
     + Coalesce(i.Lease, 0)
from dbo.LeaseSchedule LeaseSchedule
   inner join inserted i
   on LeaseSchedule.ScheduleId = i.LeaseScheduleId
Go
```

The Delete trigger is very similar to the previous trigger. The main difference is that the values from the Deleted table are subtracted from the total, as shown here:

```
Create Trigger dbo.trInventory_Lease_D
On dbo.Inventory
After Delete     -- For delete
As


If @@Rowcount = 0
     Return
```

```
-- subtract deleted leases from total amount
Update LeaseSchedule
Set LeaseSchedule.PeriodicTotalAmount =
    LeaseSchedule.PeriodicTotalAmount
    - Coalesce(d.Lease, 0)
from dbo.LeaseSchedule LeaseSchedule
   inner join deleted d
   on LeaseSchedule.ScheduleId = d.LeaseScheduleId
Go
```

The Update trigger is the most complicated. The calculation of a total is performed only if the Lease and LeaseScheduleId fields are referenced by the Update statement. The trigger then subtracts the Lease amounts from the deleted records and adds the Lease amounts from the inserted records to the related totals:

```
Create Trigger dbo.trInventory_Lease_U
On dbo.Inventory
After Update  -- For Update
As

if @@Rowcount = 0
    return

If Update (Lease) or Update(LeaseScheduleId)
begin
    -- subtract deleted leases from total amount
    Update LeaseSchedule
    Set LeaseSchedule.PeriodicTotalAmount =
            LeaseSchedule.PeriodicTotalAmount
            - Coalesce(d.Lease, 0)
    From dbo.LeaseSchedule LeaseSchedule
       inner join deleted d
       On LeaseSchedule.ScheduleId = d.LeaseScheduleId

    -- add inserted leases to total amount
    Update LeaseSchedule
    Set LeaseSchedule.PeriodicTotalAmount =
            LeaseSchedule.PeriodicTotalAmount
            + Coalesce(i.Lease, 0)
    From dbo.LeaseSchedule LeaseSchedule
    inner join inserted i
    On LeaseSchedule.ScheduleId = i.LeaseScheduleId

End
Go
```

Enforce Schema Integrity Among Objects on Different Servers or Databases

I showed you earlier how DDL triggers can be used to audit and prevent changes on database objects. They could also be used to maintain a database schema. In the following example, a large table is horizontally partitioned into quarterly tables (to make management easier). Each table should store sales information about sales in one quarter. Therefore, there are four tables that should be maintained identically:

```
Create database Quarterly
Go
Use Quarterly
Go
Create table Sales1(
    PartId int,
    CustomerId int,
    SalesDate smallint,
    Sales float)
Go
Create table Sales2(
    PartId int,
    CustomerId int,
    SalesDate smallint,
    Sales float)
Go
Create table Sales3(
    PartId int,
    CustomerId int,
    SalesDate smallint,
    Sales float)
Go
Create table Sales4(
    PartId int,
    CustomerId int,
    SalesDate smallint,
    Sales float)
Go
```

After the set of tables is created, we could create a DDL trigger to capture database changes on the Sales1 table and propagate it to other tables. The trigger is based on the Transact-SQL command captured using EventData():

```
CREATE TRIGGER trdReplicateSalesTableChanges
ON DATABASE
AFTER DDL_TABLE_EVENTS
AS
Print 'trdReplicateSalesTableChanges started.'
declare @event xml
declare @Object sysname,
        @ObjectType sysname,
        @TSQLCommand nvarchar(max),
        @TSQLCommand2 nvarchar(max),
        @i int

set @event = EVENTDATA()
set @Object = @event.value('(/EVENT_INSTANCE/ObjectName)[1]',
'nvarchar(100)')
1234567890123456789012345678901234567890123456789012345678901234567890
set @ObjectType = @event.value('(/EVENT_INSTANCE/ObjectType)[1]',
'nvarchar(100)')
set @TSQLCommand = @event.value('(/EVENT_INSTANCE/TSQLCommand)[1]',
'nvarchar(max)')

if (@ObjectType = 'TABLE')
begin
   if (@Object = 'Sales1')
   begin
      -- replace Sales1 string with 2-4
      Set @i = 2
      While @i <= 4
      Begin
         Set @TSQLCommand2 = REPLACE(@TSQLCommand,'Sales1',
                                     'Sales' + Cast(@i as varchar))
         --execute
         print @TSQLCommand2
         Exec Sp_executeSql @TSQLCommand2
         set @i = @i + 1
      end
   end
end
GO
```

To test the trigger, we will add a column to the table:

```
alter table Sales1
   add StoreId int null
```

The trigger will replicate the change to other tables and print the debug information:

```
trdReplicateSalesTableChanges started.
alter table Sales2
   add StoreId int null
alter table Sales3
   add StoreId int null
alter table Sales4
   add StoreId int null
```

It is justified to leave the print statement in this trigger, since the trigger is designed to be used only during the administrative tasks on table schemas.

NOTE

There may be changes that are too complex and that cannot be propagated correctly this way. You should test results in development and test environment before you use this method in production.

You can apply similar triggers in a scenario when data is split among databases or even servers.

User-defined Functions

T he ability to design user-defined Transact-SQL functions (UDF) was introduced in SQL Server 2000. In earlier versions, you were only able to use built-in functions. Apart from the ability to create them in .NET programming languages (that we will cover later), there were not many changes to UDFs in SQL Server 2005. This chapter will focus on the design of UDFs in Transact-SQL.

Design of Scalar User-defined Functions

User-defined functions can be created using the Create Function statement, changed using Alter Function, and deleted using Drop Function. You can use sp_help and sp_stored_procedures to get information about a function, and sp_helptext to obtain its source code. From Management Studio, you can use the same technique to manage user-defined functions that you used to create and manage stored procedures.

Functions can accept zero, one, or more input parameters, and must return a single return value. The returned value can be scalar or it can be a table. Input parameters can be values of any data type except `timestamp`, `cursor`, and `table`. Return values can be of any data type except `timestamp`, `cursor`, `text`, `ntext`, and `image`.

The Create Function statement has the following syntax:

```
Create Function [schema_name.]function_name
(
     [ {@parameter_name scalar_data_type [= default]} [,...n] ]
)
returns scalar_data_type
        |Table
        |return_variable Table({column_def|table_constraint}[,…n])
[With {Encryption|Schemabinding}[,…n] ]
[As]
{Begin function_body End}
| Return [(] {value|select-stmt} [)]
```

The following example produces a function that will return the quarter for a specified date:

```
Create Function util.fnQuarterString
-- returns quarter in form of '3Q2000'.
    (
    @dtmDate datetime
    )
```

```
Returns char(6) -- quarter like 3Q2000
As
Begin
    Return (DateName(q, @dtmDate) + 'Q' + DateName(yyyy, @dtmDate))
End
```

To reference a function, you must specify both the schema and the object identifier. It is not possible to fall back on default schema:

```
Select util.fnQuarterString(GetDate())
```

The function in the previous example had just one Return statement in the body of the function. In fact, a function can be designed with flow control and other Transact-SQL statements. A function can even contain more than one Return statement. Under different conditions, they can serve as exit points from the function. The only requirement is that the last statement in the function body be an unconditional Return statement. The following function illustrates this principle in returning a date three business days after the specified date:

```
Create Function util.fnThreeBusDays
-- returns date 3 business days after the specified date
    (@dtmDate datetime)
Returns datetime
As
Begin
Declare @inyDayOfWeek tinyint
Set @inyDayOfWeek = DatePart(dw, @dtmDate)
Set @dtmDate = Convert(datetime, Convert(varchar, @dtmDate, 101))

If @inyDayOfWeek = 1 -- Sunday
    Return DateAdd(d, 3, @dtmDate )
If @inyDayOfWeek = 7 -- Saturday
    Return DateAdd(d, 4, @dtmDate )
If @inyDayOfWeek = 6 -- Friday
    Return DateAdd(d, 5, @dtmDate )
If @inyDayOfWeek = 5 -- Thursday
    Return DateAdd(d, 5, @dtmDate )
If @inyDayOfWeek = 4 -- Wednesday
    Return DateAdd(d, 5, @dtmDate )

Return DateAdd(d, 3, @dtmDate )
End
```

Side Effects

User-defined functions have one serious limitation—they cannot have side effects.
A *function side effect* is any permanent change to resources (such as tables) that have
a scope outside of the function (such as a nontemporary table that is not declared in
the function). Basically, this requirement means that a function should return a value
while changing nothing in the database.

TIP

*In some development environments like C or Visual Basic, a developer can write a function that
can perform some additional activities or changes, but it is a matter of good design and discipline
not to abuse that opportunity.*

SQL Server prevents you from creating side effects by limiting which Transact-SQL
statements can be used inside a function:

▶ Assignment statements (Set or Select) referencing objects local to the function
  (such as local variables and a return value)

▶ Flow control statements

▶ Update, Insert, and Delete statements that update local table variables

▶ Declare statements that define local variables or cursors

▶ Statements that declare, open, close, fetch, and deallocate local cursors (the only
  Fetch statements allowed are ones that retrieve information from a cursor into
  local variables)

Use of Built-in Functions

User-defined functions cannot call built-in functions that return different data on each
call, such as these:

@@CONNECTIONS	@@TOTAL_ERRORS
@@CPU_BUSY	@@TOTAL_READ
@@IDLE	@@TOTAL_WRITE
@@IO_BUSY	GetDate()
@@MAX_CONNECTIONS	GetUTCDate()
@@PACK_RECEIVED	NewId()
@@PACK_SENT	Rand()
@@PACKET_ERRORS	TextPtr()
@@TIMETICKS	

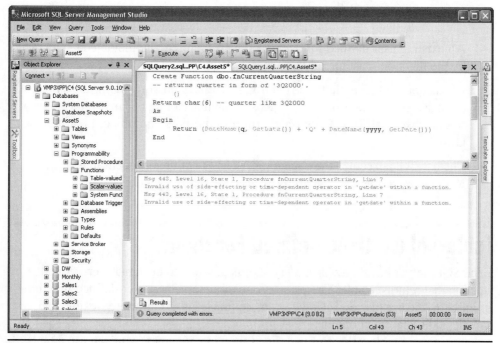

Figure 10-1   *Limitation on use of built-in functions in user-defined functions*

Notice that GetDate() is among the forbidden functions. If you try to use it inside a user-defined function, SQL Server will report an error, as shown in Figure 10-1.

Encryption

As is the case with stored procedures, functions can be encrypted so that nobody can see their source code. You just need to create or alter the function using the With Encryption option.

Schema-binding

A new option, With Schemabinding, allows developers to *schema-bind* a user-defined function to database objects (such as tables, views, and other user-defined functions) that it references. Once the function is schema-bound, it is not possible to make schema changes on underlying objects. All attempts to drop the objects and all attempts to alter underlying objects (which would change the object schema) will fail.

A function can be schema-bound only if all of the following criteria are satisfied:

▶ All existing user-defined functions and views referencing the objects referenced by the function must already be schema-bound.

▶ All database objects that the function references must reside in the same database as the function. References to database objects cannot have server or database qualifiers. Only object owner qualifiers and object identifiers are allowed.

▶ The user who executes the Create (or Alter) Function statement must have References permissions on all referenced database objects.

Table-valued User-defined Functions

Since SQL Server has a `table` data type, it is possible to design a user-defined function that returns a table. The primary use of table-valued user-defined functions is similar to the use of views. However, these functions are far more flexible and provide additional functionality.

You can use a table-valued user-defined function anywhere you can use a table (or view). In this respect, table-valued user-defined functions implement the functionality of views, but functions can have parameters, and therefore are dynamic. Views are also limited to a single Select statement. Functions can have one or more Transact-SQL statements inside, enabling them to implement more complex functionality. That is why functions of this type are often referred to as *multistatement table-valued user-defined functions.* Stored procedures can also return a result set, but the use of such result sets is somewhat limited. For example, only a result set returned by a function (and not a stored procedure) can be referenced in the From clause of a Select statement.

To demonstrate this functionality, the following Select statement references the user-defined function fnDueDays(), which returns a list of lease payment due dates. The statement returns a list of remaining payments and due dates.

```
select DD.TermId, DD.DueDate, Inventory.Lease
from dbo.fnDueDays('12/1/2005','12/1/2009','monthly') DD, Inventory
where InventoryId = 8
and DD.DueDate > GetDate()
```

The result looks like this:

```
TermId      DueDate                   Lease
----------- ------------------------- ----------
1           2006-01-01 00:00:00       87.75
2           2006-02-01 00:00:00       87.75
3           2006-03-01 00:00:00       87.75
4           2006-04-01 00:00:00       87.75
5           2006-05-01 00:00:00       87.75
6           2006-06-01 00:00:00       87.75
7           2006-07-01 00:00:00       87.75
...
```

The stored procedure ap_Terms_List has functionality similar to the functionality of the fnDueDates() function. But to perform additional filtering of the result set returned by the stored procedure, you would first need to load the result set into a temporary table:

```
Create Table #tbl(TermId int, DueDate smalldatetime)

Insert Into #Tbl(TermId, DueDate)
    Exec dbo.ap_Terms_List '12/1/2005','12/1/2009','monthly'

Select #tbl.TermId, #tbl.DueDate, Inventory.Lease
From #tbl, Inventory
Where InventoryId = 8
And #tbl.DueDate > GetDate()


Drop Table #tbl
```

This is much more complicated than using the comparable function.

Let's investigate the internals of the fnDueDates() function:

```
Create Function dbo.fnDueDays
-- return list of due days for the leasing
(
    @dtsStartDate smalldatetime,
    @dtsEndDate smalldatetime,
    @chvLeaseFrequency varchar(20)
)
Returns @tblTerms table
    (
    TermID int,
    DueDate smalldatetime
    )
```

```
As
Begin

Declare @insTermsCount smallint -- number of intervals
Declare @insTerms smallint -- number of intervals

-- calculate number of terms
Select @insTermsCount =
  Case @chvLeaseFrequency
    When 'monthly'
            then DateDIFF(month, @dtsStartDate, @dtsEndDate)
    When 'semi-monthly'
            then 2 * DateDIFF(month, @dtsStartDate, @dtsEndDate)
    When 'bi-weekly'
            then DateDIFF(week, @dtsStartDate, @dtsEndDate)/2
    When 'weekly'
            then DateDIFF(week, @dtsStartDate, @dtsEndDate)
    When 'quarterly'
            then DateDIFF(qq, @dtsStartDate, @dtsEndDate)
    When 'yearly'
            then DateDIFF(y, @dtsStartDate, @dtsEndDate)
  End

-- generate list of due dates
Set @insTerms = 1
While @insTerms <= @insTermsCount
Begin
  Insert @tblTerms (TermID, DueDate)
  Values (@insTerms, Convert(smalldatetime, CASE
        When @chvLeaseFrequency = 'monthly'
            then DateADD(month,@insTerms, @dtsStartDate)
        When @chvLeaseFrequency = 'semi-monthly'
        and @insTerms/2 =  Cast(@insTerms as float)/2
            then DateADD(month, @insTerms/2, @dtsStartDate)
        When @chvLeaseFrequency = 'semi-monthly'
        and @insTerms/2 <> Cast(@insTerms as float)/2
            then DateADD(dd, 15,
                        DateADD(month, @insTerms/2, @dtsStartDate))
        When @chvLeaseFrequency = 'bi-weekly'
            then DateADD(week, @insTerms*2, @dtsStartDate)
        When @chvLeaseFrequency = 'weekly'
            then DateADD(week, @insTerms, @dtsStartDate)
```

```
      When @chvLeaseFrequency = 'quarterly'
            then DateADD(qq, @insTerms, @dtsStartDate)
      When @chvLeaseFrequency = 'yearly'
            then DateADD(y, @insTerms, @dtsStartDate)
      End , 105))


    Select @insTerms = @insTerms + 1
End


Return
End
```

Let me point out to you a few differences between these functions and scalar functions. User-defined functions that return a table have a table variable definition in the Returns clause:

```
...
Returns @tblTerms table
    (
    TermID int,
    DueDate smalldatetime
    )
...
```

In the body of the function, there are statements that fill the contents of the table variable:

```
    Insert @tblTerms (TermID, DueDate)
    Values (@insTerms, Convert(smalldatetime, CASE
                        When @chvLeaseFrequency = 'monthly'
```

The Return statement at the end of the function does not specify a value. As soon as it is reached, SQL Server returns the contents of the table variable to the caller:

```
Return
End
```

Inline Table-valued User-defined Functions

An *inline table-valued user-defined function* is a special type of table-valued user-defined function. Its purpose is to implement parameterized views.

The syntax of an inline table-valued user-defined function is a bit different from the syntax of other functions:

```
Create Function [schema_name.]function_name
(
     [ {@parameter_name scalar_data_type [= default]} [,...n] ]
)
Returns Table
         [With {Encryption|Schemabinding}[,...n] ]
[As]
| Return (select-stmt)
```

You do not have to define the format of the return value. It is enough to specify just the Table keyword. An inline table-valued function does not have the body of a function. A result set is created by a single Select statement in the Returns clause. It is best to demonstrate this feature with an example. The following function returns only a segment of a table based on a role the user belongs to. The idea is that a manager or any other employee can see only equipment from his own department:

```
Create Function dbo.fn_DepartmentEquipment
     ( @chvUserName sysname )
Returns table
As
Return (
     Select InventoryId, Make + ' ' + model Model, Location
     From dbo.Inventory Inventory inner join dbo.Contact C
     On Inventory.OwnerId = C.ContactId
          Inner Join dbo.Contact Manager
          On C.OrgUnitId = Manager.OrgUnitId
               Inner Join dbo.Equipment Equipment
               On Inventory.EqId = Equipment.EqId
                    Inner Join dbo.Location Location
                    On Inventory.LocationId = Location.LocationId
     Where Manager.UserName = @chvUserName
     )
Go
```

You can use this function in any place where a view or table is allowed, such as in a Select statement:

```
Select *
From fn_DepartmentEquipment ('dejans')
Go
```

The result of such a statement will be

```
InventoryId Model                                Location
----------- ------------------------------------ --------------------
32          3COM Palm Pilot Pro                  First Canadian Place
32          3COM Palm Pilot Pro                  First Canadian Place
8           Bang & Olafson V4000                 Trigon Tower
8           Bang & Olafson V4000                 Trigon Tower
31          Brother PL-1700                      First Canadian Place
31          Brother PL-1700                      First Canadian Place
...
```

Managing User-defined Functions in Management Studio

You can access user-defined functions from Management Studio, as shown in Figure 10-2.

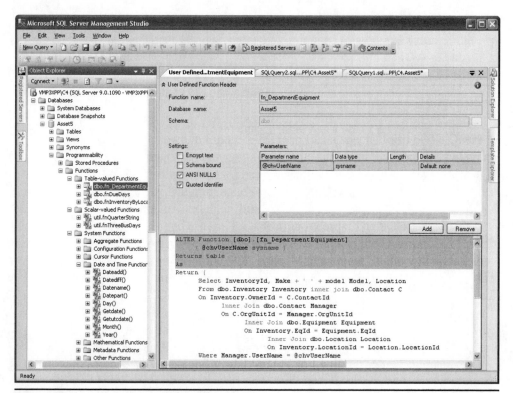

Figure 10-2   *Editing user-defined functions*

When you right-click a function and choose Modify from the context menu, SQL Server displays a form for editing its properties, parameters, and code. This editor is identical to the editor you use to edit stored procedures. When you right-click the Functions node, you can select New | User Table-valued Function or New | Scalar-valued Function, or SQL Server opens a form with a template for creating a new function. Once you have written or changed the function, you can simply save the function and Management Studio will deploy it on the server.

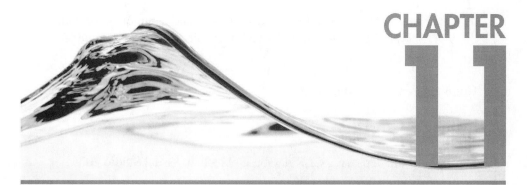

CHAPTER
11

Fundamentals of .NET Programming in SQL Server 2005

IN THIS CHAPTER

Unmanaged vs. Managed Code

Common Language Runtime (CLR)

CLR Integration in SQL Server 2005

Development, Deployment, and Usage of CLR Database Objects in Visual Studio 2005

Development and Deployment of CLR Database Objects Without Visual Studio 2005

Cataloging Assemblies and CLR Database Objects

T his chapter introduces architecture, concepts, and techniques for coding SQL Server 2005 programmatic database objects in .NET languages. Topics include

▶ Common Language Runtime (CLR)

▶ Assemblies

▶ Just-in-time compilation

▶ Developing and deploying CLR database objects in Visual Studio 2005

▶ Developing and deploying CLR database objects without (!) Visual Studio 2005

▶ Cataloging assemblies and CLR database objects in a database

Unmanaged vs. Managed Code

Unmanaged executable files are binary images of x86 code loaded into memory. The role of the operating system in this case is to load the application into memory and let it run. Although there are some protections regarding memory management and I/O ports, the operating system does not have any idea what the application is doing.

By contrast, *managed* code is under full control of the operating system. At any point in time, the operating system can stop running the CPU and investigate the runtime state. It can also insert exception handling, array bounds and indexes, traps, garbage collection hooks, and other things. In this way, it mitigates a whole class of security concerns and typical programming errors. All programming languages that support the .NET Framework produce managed code. There are currently over 30 such languages. Several are provided by Microsoft (C#, Visual Basic .NET, managed C++, J#, JScript .NET), while others are developed by third parties (everything from COBOL to Pascal).

Common Language Runtime (CLR)

Common Language Runtime (CLR) is the engine behind the .NET Framework that handles the execution of all managed application code.

Compiled .NET application code is organized into units called, in .NET terminology, *.NET assemblies*. These assemblies consist of two major parts:

▶ **Intermediate Language (IL) code** Assembly code in a form that will be converted to executable code at runtime by the CLR engine. This type of process is called *Just-in-time* (JIT) compilation.

▶ **Metadata** Generated by the compiler to describe the assembly and its structure (contained classes).

The assembly process consists of the stages shown in Figure 11-1.

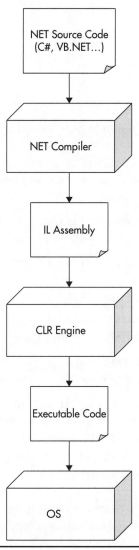

Figure 11-1 *CLR assembly process*

CLR Integration in SQL Server 2005

SQL Server 2005 leverages integration with CLR to allow the development, deployment, and execution of database programmatic objects. It supports the following object types:

- ▶ Stored procedures
- ▶ User-defined functions
- ▶ Triggers
- ▶ User-defined (data) types
- ▶ User-defined aggregates

Pros and Cons

Some advantages of CLR integration in SQL Server 2005 are listed here:

- ▶ **Rich programming model**   .NET languages are very productive since they offer constructs and features that are not available in Transact-SQL (such as arrays, classes, and collections).

- ▶ **Access to the .NET Framework library**   This library contains a vast set of classes that cover all sorts of programming challenges.

- ▶ **Cross-language integration**   You can integrate code developed in different programming languages.

- ▶ **Improved security and stability**   CLR manages various aspects of the execution of IL assemblies. As a result, the number of potential security holes is reduced, and the stability of the whole system is improved.

- ▶ **Object lifetime management**   Automatic garbage collections, destructors, and lease policies simplify management.

- ▶ **Potential for performance and scalability improvements**   Some solutions can be developed to execute faster or to scale better in .NET Framework languages, or by using the .NET Framework Library. Managed code is a better selection for CPU-intensive operations or complex tasks such as string manipulation, cryptography, and file access.

However, managed code may also degrade the system. The performance or scalability of a system can be degraded if .NET database objects are used for operations for which they are not optimal. One typical example is using .NET code to get something from a database and processing it record by record, when the same type of operation could be done using a set operation (a SQL statement).

In addition, the complexity of the system could be increased and maintainability degraded if you make uncritical use of CLR user-defined types for data that should actually be stored as separate columns in an existing or a new table.

Supported and Not Supported

In this section, I will give you an overview of the functionality that is supported or not supported when you create CLR database objects. If you are new to .NET languages, you should skip this section.

It is not possible to use all base class libraries from CLR database objects, but most System.* assemblies/namespaces are available, including:

- ▶ mscorlib.dll
- ▶ system.data.dll
- ▶ system.dll
- ▶ system.xml.dll
- ▶ system.security.dll
- ▶ Microsoft.visualbasic.dll
- ▶ system.web.services.dll

Support for functionality that is not appropriate for database server objects is eliminated:

- ▶ System.Windows.Forms
- ▶ System.Drawing
- ▶ System.Web

Even in supported assemblies, some APIs are not supported, such as the Environment.Exit() method and the Console class. The .NET Framework contains a new class of attributes—HostProtectionAttribute (HPA)—designed to declare which methods and classes are too risky to be loaded into an unmanaged host such as SQL Server.

Potentially unreliable constructs are also disabled:

- ▶ No thread creation
- ▶ No listening on sockets in server
- ▶ No finalizers
- ▶ No shared state or synchronization

As a final approval step, SQL Server checks assemblies through a verification process when the assembly is being attached to a database object (in the Create statement).

Minimally Required Namespaces

To be able to create CLR database objects, you need to add references to the following namespaces in your modules:

```
Using System.Data;
Using System.Data.Sql;
Using System.Data.SqlTypes;
Using Microsoft.SqlServer.Server;
```

These namespaces are all part of the system.data.dll assembly, which is a part of the .NET Framework. You do not have to reference it either in Visual Studio or in the command line because it is referenced automatically.

Naturally, in Visual Basic .NET you would insert something like this:

```
Imports System.Data
Imports System.Data.Sql
Imports System.Data.SqlTypes
Imports Microsoft.SqlServer.Server
```

It is also possible to register .NET Framework assemblies and namespaces that are not by default available for development of CLR database objects. I will demonstrate this in Chapter 13.

Development, Deployment, and Usage of CLR Database Objects in Visual Studio 2005

I will demonstrate the development and deployment of database objects in Visual Studio 2005 first (upon creation of a stored procedure), and then in the next section I will show you how to do it without Visual Studio. Follow these steps:

1. Launch Visual Studio 2005.

2. Select File | New | Project.

3. In the New Project window's Project Types pane, expand Visual C# or Visual Basic, then Database, and select the SQL Server Project template. Set Name (for example, CShrpSqlServerSp or VbSqlServerSp), Location, and Solution Name of the project (see Figure 11-2).

4. Click OK.

5. The program will prompt you to add a new database reference (connection) or to select an existing one. Create a reference to the Asset5 database.

6. The program will prompt you to enable debugging for SQLCLR for this connection. Choose Yes.

7. In the Solution Explorer pane (View | Solution Explorer), open the context-sensitive menu for the solution (top node). Choose Add | Stored Procedure. (Alternatively, you can execute Project | Add Stored procedure from the main menu.)

8. The program will prompt you to select a template. Select Stored Procedure and change the name from the default name to ap_First (see Figure 11-3).

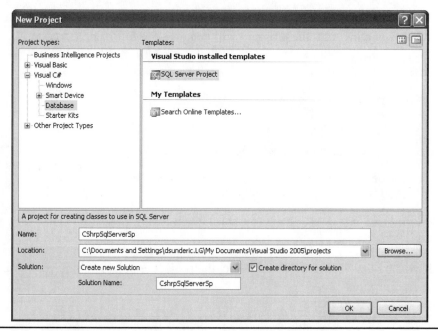

Figure 11-2 *Creating a new database project in Visual Studio 2005*

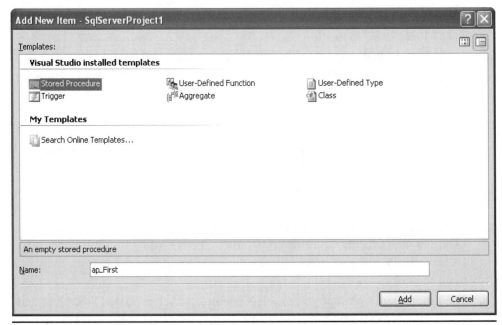

Figure 11-3 *Templates of database objects*

9. When you click Add, the program will generate the following C# code:

```
using System;
using System.Data;
using System.Data.SqlClient;
using System.Data.SqlTypes;
using Microsoft.SqlServer.Server;


public partial class StoredProcedures
{
    [Microsoft.SqlServer.Server.SqlProcedure]
    public static void ap_First()
    {
        // Put your code here
    }
};
```

If you are developing in Visual Basic, the project template will be very similar:

```
Imports System
Imports System.Data
Imports System.Data.SqlClient
```

```
Imports System.Data.SqlTypes
Imports Microsoft.SqlServer.Server


Partial Public Class StoredProcedures
    <Microsoft.SqlServer.Server.SqlProcedure()> _
    Public Shared Sub  ap_First ()
        ' Add your code here
    End Sub
End Class
```

The templates consist of references to namespaces that are required and to definitions of the class. The class contains a single static method that will become a CLR stored procedure.

The class is defined as *public* to denote that other classes can instantiate objects of this type (and use them).

In .NET Framework 2.0, the CLR class does not have to be defined in a single file. The idea is that the source code of each database object should be in a separate file (to be easier to manage). Therefore, Visual Studio names the file and the method using the same name. You just need to declare it as *partial* (as in *public partial class* in C# or as *Partial Public Class* in Visual Basic).

The method is preceded by the [Microsoft.SqlServer.Server.SqlProcedure] attribute in C# (or <Microsoft.SqlServer.Server.SqlProcedure()> in Visual Basic) that notifies Visual Studio and the compiler how to treat the method and prepare it for deployment in SQL Server.

Methods that will become database objects must be declared as *public static* in C#, or *Public Shared* in Visual Basic. The keyword *public* means that they are accessible from outside and *static* (or *Shared*) means that they behave like procedures (not like methods of objects that have state). The keyword *void* is in the position that declares an output value for the method (that is, for the stored procedure) and declares that the method does not return anything. If you want it to return 4-byte integers, you should declare it as int. In Visual Basic, subroutines (Sub) do not return values, while functions (Func) do.

10. Add the following line (where it says "Add your code here"):

```
SqlContext.Pipe.Send("Hello world!\n");
```

If you are using C#, the semicolon (;) at the end of the row denotes the end of the statement (but if you are using Visual Basic, you must omit it, since Visual Basic syntax does not require row delimiters).

11. We will now create an assembly. Verify that the Solution Configurations combo box on the toolbar is set to Debug (and not Release). Choose Build | Build CShrpSqlServerSp from the menu. Visual Studio has created a CShrpSqlServerSp.dll file in the bin\debug subfolder of the project folder.

NOTE

If there were errors during compilation, you can see them in the Error List pane (View | Error List).

12. Deploy to stored procedures by choosing Build | Deploy *project_name* from the menu.

NOTE

If there were errors during compilation, you can see them in the Output pane (View | Output).

13. Open the Query window in Management Studio and execute against the Asset5 database:

```
Exec ap_First
Go
```

And that's all. You have to admit that it was not too difficult.

TIP

If you want, you can put multiple static methods (future stored procedures, user-defined functions and procedures) in a single class and build and deploy them together (in a single operation) in Visual Studio.

As an alternative to Management Studio, you can execute scripts in the Test Scripts node of Solution Explorer. Scripts in this node are also entry points into the debugger. You can find more information about using them in Chapter 16.

Development and Deployment of CLR Database Objects Without Visual Studio 2005

You can develop and deploy CLR database objects "manually" without Visual Studio. All you need is .NET Framework 2.0, which contains a compiler that you can use.

The process is done in several basic steps:

1. Develop code in any ASCII editor.
2. Compile the .dll.
3. Load to SQL Server 2005; record assembly metadata using the Create Assembly statement.
4. Bind to the entry point; execute the Create (Procedure or other appropriate) statement.
5. Test and use the new CLR database object.

Develop Code

Create a simple program that consists of a single static method in a public class:

```
using System;
using System.Data;
using System.Data.SqlClient;
using System.Data.SqlTypes;
using Microsoft.SqlServer.Server;


public partial class StoredProcedures
{
    [Microsoft.SqlServer.Server.SqlProcedure]
    public static void ap_MyFirst()
    {
        SqlContext.Pipe.Send("Calculation completed!\n");
    }
};
```

If you are developing in the Visual Basic program, the template should be something like this:

```
Imports System
Imports System.Data
Imports System.Data.SqlClient
Imports System.Data.SqlTypes
Imports Microsoft.SqlServer.Server


Partial Public Class StoredProcedures
    <Microsoft.SqlServer.Server.SqlProcedure()> _
```

```
      Public Shared Sub  ap_MyFirst ()
          SqlContext.Pipe.Send("Calculation completed!\n")
      End Sub
End Class
```

Save the file in ap_myfirst.cs or ap_myfirst.vb.

Compile Program

.NET Framework is delivered with the C# (csc.exe) and the Visual Basic .NET (vbc.exe) command line compilers. The compilers are typically installed in the folder with the remainder of the .NET Framework. The folder name is the number of the .NET Framework version (see Figure 11-4).

You should first find out the latest version that is installed on your computer. Go to C:\WINDOWS\Microsoft.NET\Framework and investigate your options. SQL Server 2005 installs .NET Framework v2.0. You will need one of its minor versions. The computer in Figure 11-4 has only one v2.0 folder.

TIP

This folder is not in the Path environment variable, so you will have to include the path in every statement that references compilers. If you plan to use this program often, it makes more sense to include the path in the Path variable.

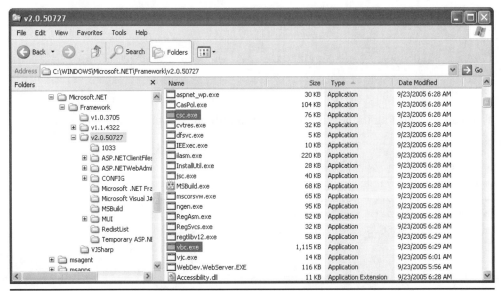

Figure 11-4   *.NET Framework folder*

To compile the C# program, you should use a command such as:

```
csc /target:library ap_MyFirst.cs
```

This command assumes that csc.exe is in the path.

For the Visual Basic program you should use a command such as:

```
vbc /target:library ap_myFirst.vb
```

Setting the /target switch (or alternatively /t) to *library* notifies the compiler to create a .dll file. Other possible options are console application (*exe*), Windows application (*winexe*), and a module that can be added to another module (*module*). However, for producing assemblies that will be attached to SQL Server database objects, you have to use the /t:library option.

The result of the compilation is a .dll file in the same folder in which the source code was produced (see Figure 11-5). It makes sense to have a dedicated folder on the server to store all assembly files, such as c:\sqlclr\.

By default, the name of the .dll file is the same as the name of the source code file. However, you can change it if you wish, using the /out switch in the compiler command (for example, /out:c:\sqlclr\MyFirstUdp.dll).

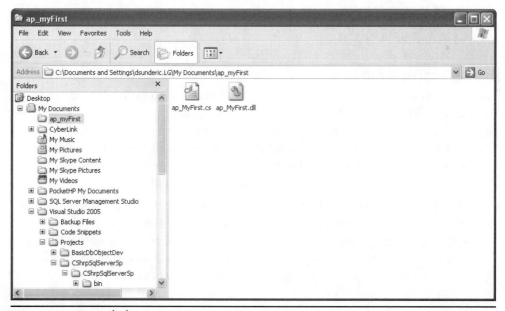

Figure 11-5 *Compiled DLL*

Load Assembly to SQL Server Database

Before you can use the assembly, you must register it in a database. This is done using the Create Assembly statement:

```
CREATE ASSEMBLY MyFirst
FROM 'c:\sqlclr\ap_MyFirst.dll'
WITH PERMISSION_SET = SAFE;
```

You must assign it a name that is unique in the current database. SQL Server does not allow registration of more than one version of an assembly with the same name. Exceptions are assemblies designed to work on different languages (*cultures,* in .NET Framework terminology) and assemblies that have different public keys. Therefore, you must drop the old version of the assembly before you can attach a new one:

```
DROP ASSEMBLY MyFirst;
CREATE ASSEMBLY MyFirst
FROM 'c:\sqlclr\ap_MyFirst.dll'
WITH PERMISSION_SET = SAFE;
```

Alternatively, you can refresh (replace) the old version with the new version of the assembly using:

```
ALTER ASSEMBLY MyFirst
FROM 'c:\sqlclr\ap_MyFirst.dll'
WITH PERMISSION_SET = SAFE;
```

Assembly External Access

The With Permission_Set clause controls the type of access to external resources from the assembly. There are three options for Permission_Set:

▶ **SAFE** will prevent code in the assembly from accessing external resources. This is the default option. It should be used for assemblies that perform only local operations such as data management or calculations.

▶ **EXTERNAL_RESOUCES** will allow assembly code to access some external resources—*files, environment variables, registry,* and *network*. By default, assemblies run under a SQL Server service account. This is a potential security problem. Keep that in mind when allowing users access to the assemblies or setting database objects to run in the security context of the current user.

►   **UNSAFE** will allow code access to any resource both on the server and outside the server. This option is required to make calls to unmanaged libraries. It can potentially compromise SQL Server security and, therefore, you should only use it on assemblies that you are certain that you can trust.

To be able to add CLR objects that require the External_Resources or Unsafe permission setting to the Asset5 database, or any other database, you will need to set the database to Trustworthy On and to grant the database owner External Access Assembly permission:

```
Grant EXTERNAL ACCESS ASSEMBLY to [LG\dsunderic]
GO
Alter Database Asset5
set TRUSTWORTHY ON
```

By default, the database Trustworthy option is set to Off. This is one of those options that makes SQL Server "secure by default." The idea is that a DBA has to make a conscious decision to accept this risk.

TIP

Your assembly can reference system assemblies other than those specified in the earlier "Supported and Not Supported" section. However, in such a case, you need to register those other assemblies in your database as well.

Create SQLCLR Database Objects

Now that the assembly is registered in the database, I can create a database object based on it:

```
CREATE PROCEDURE dbo.ap_MyFirst
AS
EXTERNAL NAME MyFirst.StoredProcedures.ap_MyFirst
```

The External Name clause contains a reference to the individual assembly, class, and static method in the format *assembly_name.class_name.method_name*.

After the database object is created you can use it regardless of the way it was designed.

Cataloging Assemblies and CLR Database Objects

An important part of the management of assemblies and CLR database objects is to be able to find out what is installed on the database—and what is not.

Cataloging Assemblies

The place to start is the sys.assemblies catalog view that contains information about the assembly names, identifiers, permissions, and visibility.

```
SELECT * FROM sys.assemblies
```

The result of the query will be something like Table 11-1.

There is a system stored procedure that provides access to this and other related tables. The sys.sp_assemblies_rowset procedure returns information about the assembly along with its binary. Figure 11-6 shows the result. The result may contain multiple rows for each file that is larger than 8,000 bytes.

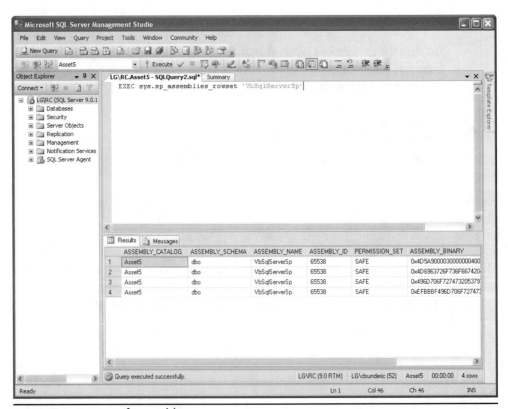

Figure 11-6 *Rowset of assemblies*

Name	principal_id	assembly_id	clr_name	permission_set	permission_set_desc	is_visible	create_date	modify_date
VbSqlServerSp	1	65538	vbsqlserversp, version=0.0.0.0, culture=neutral, publickeytoken=null, processorarchitecture=msil	1	SAFE_ACCESS	1	2005-10-30 22:04:33.297	2005-10-30 22:04:33.513
CShrpSqlServerSp	1	65540	cshrpsqlserversp, version=0.0.0.0, culture=neutral, publickeytoken=null, processorarchitecture=msil	1	SAFE_ACCESS	1	2005-10-30 22:11:44.107	2005-10-30 22:11:44.357

Table 11-1   *Assemblies in a Database*

Cataloging Procedures

You have probably noticed that I sometimes use the word *procedure* in a broader context—to reference all types of programmable database objects (such as stored procedures, functions, and triggers). Some parts of BOL refer to them as *modules*. I think that both BOL and I should have chosen different terms. In the software development books that I learned from, modules were larger sets of programmable objects (such as C# classes as sets of methods and properties, C libraries as sets of functions, and Visual Basic 6 modules as files that contain subroutines and functions). On the other hand, the distinction between procedure and stored procedure is too subtle.

In SQL Server 2005, you can query for modules (programmable database objects) and assembly modules (CLR database objects):

```
SELECT * FROM sys.assembly_modules
```

An example of a result is shown in Table 11-2.

To read metadata that is collected in a database about a database object, such as a stored procedure, you can use the following query:

```
SELECT schema_name(sp.schema_id) + '.' + sp.[name] AS [Name]
    , sp.create_date
    , sp.modify_date
    , sa.permission_set_desc AS [Access]
    , sp.is_auto_executed
FROM sys.procedures AS sp
    INNER JOIN sys.module_assembly_usages AS sau
        ON sp.object_id = sau.object_id
    INNER JOIN sys.assemblies AS sa
        ON sau.assembly_id = sa.assembly_id
WHERE sp.type_desc = N'CLR_STORED_PROCEDURE'
```

Version of .NET Framework

You can find out which version of CLR is loaded in SQL Server by querying the version of the Microsoft .NET Runtime Execution Engine module:

```
SELECT mdl.product_version
FROM sys.dm_os_loaded_modules AS mdl
WHERE mdl.[name] LIKE N'%\MSCOREE.DLL'
```

object_id	assembly_id	assembly_class	assembly_method	null_on_null_input	execute_as_principal_id
1086626914	65538	VbSqlServerSp.StoredProcedures	ap_FirstVB	0	NULL
1118627028	65540	StoredProcedures	ap_First	0	NULL

Table 11-2 *Assembly Modules*

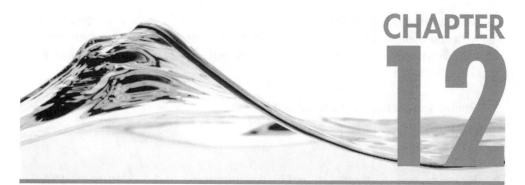

Fundamentals of CLR Stored Procedure Development

In the previous chapter, I showed you how to create a CLR database object both with and without Visual Studio 2005. In this section, I am going to focus on stored procedure development in managed code. By the end of this chapter you should be able to:

▶ Return a value from a stored procedure

▶ Declare and use output parameters

▶ Return a result

▶ Reuse the connection that is used by the current stored procedure to execute additional queries and batches

▶ Manage LOB parameters

Structure of a CLR Stored Procedure

The CLR database objects that were created and deployed in the previous chapter were stored procedures:

```
using System;
using System.Data;
using System.Data.SqlClient;
using System.Data.SqlTypes;
using Microsoft.SqlServer.Server;


public partial class StoredProcedures
{
    [SqlProcedure]
    public static void ap_First()
    {
        SqlContext.Pipe.Send("Hello world!\n");
    }
};
```

Or in Visual Basic:

```
Imports System
Imports System.Data
Imports System.Data.SqlClient
Imports System.Data.SqlTypes
Imports Microsoft.SqlServer.Server
```

```
Partial Public Class StoredProcedures
    <SqlProcedure()> _
    Public Shared Sub  ap_First ()
        SqlContext.Pipe.Send("Hello world!\n")

    End Sub
End Class
```

The first part of the file is a set of references to namespaces that will be used later in the code. The second part is a class (or actually a part of a class) that contains a method that will be promoted to a database object.

The class is defined as *public* to denote that other classes can instantiate objects of this type (and use them).

In .NET Framework 2.0, the CLR class does not have to be defined in a single file. The idea is that the source code for every database object should be in a separate file (to be easier to manage). Therefore, Visual Studio names the file and method using the same name. You just need to declare it as *partial* (as in *public partial class* in C# or as *Partial Public Class* in Visual Basic).

The method is preceded by the [Microsoft.SqlServer.Server.SqlProcedure] attribute in C# (or <Microsoft.SqlServer.Server.SqlProcedure()> in Visual Basic) that notifies Visual Studio and the compiler how to treat the method and prepare it for deployment in SQL Server. Since the Microsoft.SqlServer.Server namespace is referenced in the *using* (or Imports in Visual Basic) statement, it is sufficient to put only [SqlProcedure] as an attribute of the method.

Methods that will become database objects must be declared as *public static* in C# or *Public Shared* in Visual Basic. The keyword *public* means that they are accessible from outside and *static* (or *Shared*) means that they behave like procedures (not like methods of objects that have state). The keyword *void* is in the position that declares an output value of the method (stored procedure). The keyword *void* declares that the method does not return anything. If you want it to return 4-byte integers, you should declare it as int. In Visual Basic, subroutines (Sub) do not return values, while functions (Func) do.

Database Access from CLR Procedures

.NET Framework 2.0 has a set of classes that are specifically designed to accommodate access to database objects from CLR procedures. They are extensions of ADO.NET designed for in-process use and are based on the .NET Framework Data Provider for SQL Server, also known as SqlClient. This provider is also used from regular managed applications and components. Therefore, if you are familiar with SqlClient and

ADO.NET, you will be able to leverage this knowledge during development of CLR procedures. CLR procedures do not support the full functionality of ADO.NET, so we will focus on restrictions as well as in-process extensions in SQLCLR.

To start on a positive note, let's briefly review the main in-process ADO.NET extensions. The SqlContext class is used to provide access to the context of the caller from the CLR code running on the server. Its most important use is to provide access to the SqlPipe member (another extension of ADO.NET) that is used to send messages and results to the caller.

SqlPipe also contains the SqlTriggerContext member (another extension) that provides access to the trigger's virtual tables, a map of updated fields, and information about the operation that has fired the trigger.

SqlContext also provides access to the Windows identity of the caller that initiated the process. This is needed to implement impersonation—to execute operations in the context of the caller, instead of the context of a service account.

TIP

You can find more information about the SqlContext class in Microsoft Visual Studio 2005 documentation than you can in Books OnLine.

CLR Data Types Mapping

The System.Data.SqlTypes namespace is especially designed for CLR in SQL Server. BOL contains a table with SQL Server data types, their equivalents in the System.Data .SqlTypes namespace, and the native CLR equivalents in .NET Framework. You can find it in Books OnLine under "SQL Server Data Types and Their .NET Framework Equivalents."

I will point to a couple of interesting details. Non-Unicode strings (char, varchar, and varchar(max)) are not supported. You must use Unicode strings (Nchar, Nvarchar, and Nvarchar(max)) or actually their CLR for SQL Server equivalents (SqlChars and SqlString) or .NET equivalents (string or char[]). There is a difference between SqlChars and SqlString. SqlChars is a stream-based type that will perform better in stream operations, such as data access and data transfer, while SQLString is tailored for String manipulations.

Old BLOB data types (text, Ntext, and image) are not supported. You must use the new LOB data types (Nvarchar(max) and varbinary(max)). The equivalents for the smalldatetime and datetime data types are SqlDateTime and DateTime. Instead of the numeric and decimal data types, you should use SqlDecimal or Decimal. Exotic Transact-SQL data types such as table, cursor, sql_variant, and timestamp do not have equivalents.

Basic Operations with Stored Procedures

In this section we will focus on support for traditional stored procedure features such as:

- ▶ Returning a result set
- ▶ Returning the value
- ▶ Using input and output parameters

Returning Value

Transact-SQL stored procedures can return int values to the caller. CLR stored procedures can be declared to return no value (void) or to return 2-byte (SQLInt16 or System.Int16) or 4-byte integers (SQLInt32 or System.Int32):

```
using System;
using System.Data;
using System.Data.SqlClient;
using System.Data.SqlTypes;
using Microsoft.SqlServer.Server;


public partial class StoredProcedures
{
    [SqlProcedure]
    public static System.Int32 ap_MyFirst()
    {
        SqlContext.Pipe.Send("Hello world!\n");
        return 0;
    }
};
```

In C#, you must return a value using a return statement. If you are developing a stored procedure in Visual Basic .NET, then to return a value you must use a function, not Sub(routine):

```
Imports System
Imports System.Data
Imports System.Data.SqlClient
Imports System.Data.SqlTypes
Imports Microsoft.SqlServer.Server
```

```
Partial Public Class StoredProcedures
    <SqlProcedure()> _
    Public Shared Function  ap_MyFirst () As System.Int32
        SqlContext.Pipe.Send("Hello world!\n")
        ap_MyFirst = 0
    End Function
End Class
```

TIP

You can also use int as a CLR alias for a 4-byte integer.

Connection Context

It is possible to create a new connection inside of a CLR procedure using System
.Data.SqlClient.SqlConnection. A developer would just need to specify connection
parameters (such as login info) and open a connection:

```
SqlConnection con = new SqlConnection()
con.ConnectionString = "Data Source=SQL2005;
  Initial Catalog=Asset5; Integrated Security=True; ";
con.Open();
// Operations that use the connection
```

Unfortunately, such a connection would not be part of the caller transaction; it
would not have access to temporary tables created on the caller, it would have different
Set options, and it would be slower because commands and results would have to go
through several additional layers and other similar issues.

This problem is solved by opening a connection that invokes a Transact-SQL
statement that starts the CLR procedure. This is called a *context connection*. You
can open such a connection if you specify "Context Connection=true" instead of the
regular connection string:

```
SqlConnection conn = new SqlConnection();
conn.ConnectionString = "Context Connection=true";
conn.Open();
```

It's even better if you combine the first two lines into a single Using construct with
a block:

```
using(SqlConnection con = new SqlConnection("context connection=true"))
{
    con.Open();
    // Operations that use the connection

}
```

However, there are some restrictions on context connections, such as:

► You can have only one such connection open.

► It's not possible to use Multi Active Result Sets (MARS).

► It's not possible to set other connection attributes (once it contains "Context Connection=true").

► It's not possible to cancel requests using SqlCommand.Cancel. The engine will simply ignore them.

Returning a Result

SqlPipe is the class that contains the Send method that is designed to return a result to the caller. There are three overloaded methods with that name that take as their parameter a string, a record object, or a reader object. You have seen in earlier sections how to return a string. In the following examples, I will focus on returning a tabular result.

I will start by demonstrating the creation of a result based on a reader object. SqlDataReader and SqlCommand classes are part of the core ADO.NET (as well as SqlConnection). The following stored procedure creates a connection and then a command object based on it. The command object will execute the specified batch when the connection is opened. The reader object is created when the ExecuteReader method is invoked on the SqlCommand object. Finally, rows from the reader are returned through SqlPipe using the Send method:

```
using System;
using System.Data;
using System.Data.SqlClient;
using System.Data.SqlTypes;
using Microsoft.SqlServer.Server;


public partial class StoredProcedures
{
    [Microsoft.SqlServer.Server.SqlProcedure]
    public static void cp_EqTypeList()
    {
        using (SqlConnection conn = new SqlConnection("Context Connection=true"))
        {
            SqlCommand cmd = new SqlCommand();
            cmd.Connection = conn;
```

```
                cmd.CommandText = "select * from dbo.EqType";
                cmd.CommandType = CommandType.Text;

                conn.Open();

                SqlDataReader rdr = cmd.ExecuteReader();
                SqlContext.Pipe.Send(rdr);

                rdr.Close();
            }
        }
};
```

In Visual Basic .NET, this would be something like the following:

```
Imports System
Imports System.Data
Imports System.Data.SqlClient
Imports System.Data.SqlTypes
Imports Microsoft.SqlServer.Server

Partial Public Class StoredProcedures
 <Microsoft.SqlServer.Server.SqlProcedure()> _
    Public Shared Sub cp_EqTypeListVB()
        ' Add your code here
        SqlContext.Pipe.Send("Hello world!\n")
        Using conn As New SqlConnection("Context Connection=true")
            Dim cmd As New SqlCommand()
            cmd.Connection = conn
            cmd.CommandText = "select * from dbo.EqType"
            cmd.CommandType = CommandType.Text

            conn.Open()

            Dim rdr As SqlDataReader
            rdr = cmd.ExecuteReader()
            SqlContext.Pipe.Send(rdr)

            rdr.Close()
        End Using
    End Sub
End Class
```

You can run a stored procedure this way as well. One way is to simply create a batch that contains an Exec statement and the name of a stored procedure. However, the preferred way is to specify that the type of command that you are running is CommandType.StoredProcedure:

```
cmd.CommandText = "ap_Eq_List";
cmd.CommandType = CommandType.StoredProcedure;
```

In this case you should *not* put the Exec command in front of the stored procedure name.

You can do the same without connection and reader objects. The pipe contains the ExecuteAndSend method that can consume a SqlCommand object and send the result through the pipe.

```
[Microsoft.SqlServer.Server.SqlProcedure]
public static void cp_EqType_List2()
{
    using (SqlCommand cmd = new SqlCommand())
    {
        //cmd.Connection = conn;
        cmd.CommandText = @"SELECT * FROM dbo.EqType";

        SqlContext.Pipe.ExecuteAndSend(cmd);
    }
}
```

It is also possible to assemble a table "manually" with results and return it to the caller. I will show you this feature in the next section.

Returning Custom Records

Many of the examples I have shown so far have been artificial/academic because I was obtaining data from Transact-SQL statements and passing them (even with minimal or no transformation) to the caller from CLR. They were meant to demonstrate the usage of one class or the other, not to serve as architecture prototypes. You will often need to do the opposite—to return a custom recordset of values obtained during processing in a CLR procedure to the caller. You can create your records using the SqlDataRecord class and then send them through SqlPipe. Before you create an instance of SqlDataRecord, you need to define its structure as an array of objects of the SqlMetaData class:

```
SqlMetaData[] fields = new SqlMetaData[3];
fields [0] = new SqlMetaData("LeaseId", SqlDbType.Int);
fields [1] = new SqlMetaData("LeaseVendor", SqlDbType.NVarChar, 50);
fields [2] = new SqlMetaData("LeaseNumber", SqlDbType.NVarChar, 50);
fields [3] = new SqlMetaData("ContactDate", SqlDbType.DateTime);
fields [4] = new SqlMetaData("TotalAmount", SqlDbType.Money);
```

When the schema is finished, you will create an instance of SqlDataRecord and populate it with data:

```
SqlDataRecord record = new SqlDataRecord(fields);
record.SetInt32(0, 1001);
record.SetString(1, "LeaseLeaseLease Inc.");
record.SetString(2, "123-456-7890");
record.SetDateTime(3, DateTime.Now);
record.SetSqlMoney(4, 2000);
```

As the last step, you will send the record through the pipe to the caller:

```
SqlContext.Pipe.Send(record);
```

SQL Server will allow you to repopulate the record with different values and send it again through the pipe. However, the result of that action would be two recordsets with one record each (see Figure 12-1).

It is possible to get one recordset with two records instead, but you will have to use the SendResultsStart, SendResultsRow, and SendResultsEnd methods of the SqlPipe class:

```
// set record
SqlDataRecord record = new SqlDataRecord(fields);

// start record set
SqlContext.Pipe.SendResultsStart(record);

//assemble first record
record.SetInt32(0, 1001);
record.SetString(1, "LeaseLeaseLease Inc.");
record.SetString(2, "123-456-7890");
record.SetDateTime(3, DateTime.Now);
record.SetSqlMoney(4, 2000);
```

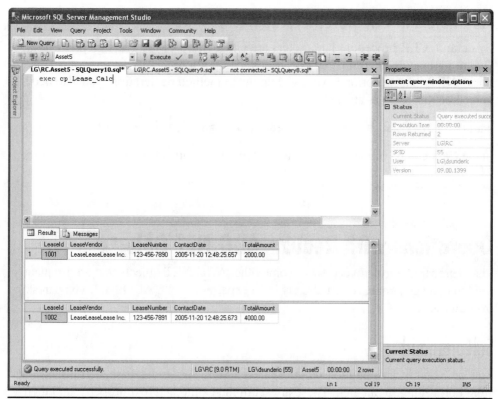

Figure 12-1 *Stored procedure with two custom recordsets*

```
// send record
SqlContext.Pipe.SendResultsRow(record);


// assemble second record
record.SetInt32(0, 1002);
record.SetString(1, "LeaseLeaseLease Inc.");
record.SetString(2, "123-456-7891");
record.SetDateTime(3, DateTime.Now);
record.SetSqlMoney(4, 4000);

// send record
SqlContext.Pipe.SendResultsRow(record);

// send record set
SqlContext.Pipe.SendResultsEnd();
```

Parameters in CLR Stored Procedures

By default, CLR procedure parameters are returned by value. The exceptions are Output parameters that must be declared to be by reference. In the case of Visual Basic .NET, this exception is very visible in the method declaration. You also need to include the <Out()> attribute:

```
Public Shared Sub ExtPriceSum( <Out()> ByRef value As SqlMoney)
```

In the C# method, you simply need to precede the parameter with the *out* keyword.

```
public static void ExtPriceSum(out SqlMoney value)
```

Operations with Regular ADO.NET Objects

I have prepared a little overview of some other ADO.NET objects that are frequently used in managed code. If you already have experience with ADO.NET, you can skip over this section.

SqlCommand

SqlCommand is designed to execute against a SQL Server database, a Transact-SQL stored procedure, or a batch. These are set in the CommandText property, and then the SqlCommand can be executed using one of many methods.

Which methods you should use depends primarily on the type of result that you expect. ExecuteReader is used for stored procedures and batches that return a result. The result is in the form of a SqlDataReader object. ExecuteXmlReader is identical with the exception that it returns an XmlReader object. ExecuteScalar is designed for commands that return a result with a single value. ExecuteNonQuery is used for stored procedures and batches that do not return a result but only modify a database. There is an equivalent set of BeginExecute… and EndExecute… methods that is designed for asynchronous execution, but I do not think you will use them in CLR stored procedures.

It is possible to set the CommandText property to another value, once you finish working with the previous command instance.

If an error occurs during execution of a command, a SqlException is generated. If the error has a severity 20 or higher, SqlConnection will typically be closed. The user has to reopen the connection to continue.

SqlCommand and Parameters

The following example demonstrates how to call a stored procedure that has input and output parameters and a return value. To set these values you must utilize the SqlParameter class and add them to the Parameters collection of a SqlCommand object:

```
[SqlProcedure]
public int ap_Eq_Insert(string Make, string Model, string EqType)
{
    using (SqlConnection conn = new SqlConnection("Context Connection=true"))
    {
        // ALTER procedure [dbo].[ap_Equipment_Insert]
        //        @chvMake varchar(50),
        //        @chvModel varchar(50),
        //        @chvEqType varchar(50),
        //        @intEqId int OUTPUT

        conn.Open();
        SqlCommand cmd = new SqlCommand("dbo.ap_Equipment_Insert", conn);
        cmd.CommandType = CommandType.StoredProcedure;

        cmd.Parameters.AddWithValue("@chvMake", Make);
        cmd.Parameters["@chvMake"].Direction = ParameterDirection.Input;

        cmd.Parameters.AddWithValue("@chvModel", Model);
        cmd.Parameters["@chvModel"].Direction = ParameterDirection.Input;

        cmd.Parameters.AddWithValue("@chvEqType", EqType);
        cmd.Parameters["@chvEqType"].Direction = ParameterDirection.Input;

        SqlParameter paramEqId = cmd.Parameters.Add("@intEqId", SqlDbType.Int);
        paramEqId.Direction = ParameterDirection.Output;


        SqlParameter paramRC = cmd.Parameters.Add("@return", SqlDbType.Int);
        paramRC.Direction = ParameterDirection.ReturnValue;

        //execute command
        cmd.ExecuteNonQuery();

        //return id
        int returnValue = (int)paramRC.Value;
        int EqId = (int)paramEqId.Value;
        return EqId;
    }
}
```

I have added all input parameters to the Parameters collection using the AddWithValue method. The next line sets the direction of the parameter:

```
cmd.Parameters.AddWithValue("@chvMake", Make);
cmd.Parameters["@chvMake"].Direction = ParameterDirection.Input;
```

NOTE

Before .NET Framework 2.0, you could set the value of a parameter using the Add method. You may find some older ADO.NET examples on the Internet that are still doing this.

To add the output and return values, I will declare objects of the SqlParameter class:

```
SqlParameter paramEqId = cmd.Parameters.Add("@intEqId", SqlDbType.Int);
paramEqId.Direction = ParameterDirection.Output;
SqlParameter paramRC = cmd.Parameters.Add("@return", SqlDbType.Int);
paramRC.Direction = ParameterDirection.ReturnValue;
```

References to these objects are needed after the stored procedure is executed to read the output and return values:

```
int returnValue = (int)paramRC.Value;
int EqId = (int)paramEqId.Value;
```

SqlDataReader

SqlDataReader is designed to provide a forward-only stream of rows (cursor) from a SQL Server database. It cannot be created directly using only a constructor. It must be created using the ExecuteReader method of the SqlCommand class.

The fact that the class provides a forward-only stream of rows is significant because it will prevent you from doing anything else on the SqlConnection that it is based on, until you close the SqlDataReader object. Even the RecordsAffected property of SqlDataReader should be read only after executing the Close method.

The SqlDataReader class contains a Read method that reads the next row of the result. If the row is not available, the method will return False. Therefore, rows can be read one by one using, for example, a while statement:

```
[SqlProcedure]
public static void cp_EqType_GetCommaDelimList(out string EqType)
// returns comma-delimited list of EqTypes
// example of getting data from a stored procedure that returns result
// example of using reader object
```

```
{
    using (SqlConnection conn = new SqlConnection("Context Connection=true"))
    {
        EqType = "";

        // Set up the command object used to execute the stored proc
        SqlCommand cmd = new SqlCommand("dbo.ap_EqType_List", conn);
        cmd.CommandType = CommandType.StoredProcedure;

        //execute sp
        conn.Open();

        using (SqlDataReader reader = cmd.ExecuteReader())
        {
            while (reader.Read()) // Advance one row, until you can
            {
                // Return output parameters from returned data stream
                //id = reader.GetInt32(0); // do not need first column
                EqType = EqType + reader.GetString(1) + ", ";
            }
        }
    }
}
```

When a row is read, you can access the values in its columns using names or ordinal numbers. To avoid data type conversion, it is recommended that you use one of the special Get… functions (such as GetString, GetInt32, GetInt16, and GetDateTime).

Managing LOB Parameters

Before SQL Server 2005 and the introduction of LOB data types (`varbinary(max)`, `varchar(max)`, and `Nvarchar(max)`), it was very inconvenient to work with BLOBs. The only real way to operate with them was through ADO.NET. Now, with the new LOB data types, it is easier to manipulate BLOBs from Transact-SQL. However, I will show you how to work with them in a CLR procedure instead.

In the following example, a SqlDataReader object is used to get a photo, and then FileStream and BinaryWriter objects are used to save the photo in a specified file:

```
[SqlProcedure]
public static void cp_EqImage_Save(int EqID, string FileName)
{
    //save vabinary(max) returned by stored procedure to the file

    const int bufferSize = 8000;
```

```csharp
// The BLOB byte[] buffer to be filled by GetBytes.
byte[] outbyte = new byte[bufferSize];
using (SqlConnection conn =
    new SqlConnection("Context Connection=true"))
{

    conn.Open();
    SqlCommand command = conn.CreateCommand();

    // Set up the command to execute the stored procedure.
    command.CommandText = "dbo.ap_EqImage_List";
    command.CommandType = CommandType.StoredProcedure;

    // Set up the input parameter.
    SqlParameter paramID =
        new SqlParameter("@EqID", SqlDbType.Int);
    paramID.Value = EqID;
    command.Parameters.Add(paramID);

    // Execute the stored procedure.
    command.ExecuteNonQuery();

    using (SqlDataReader reader =
        command.ExecuteReader(CommandBehavior.SequentialAccess))
    {
        while (reader.Read())
        {
            //SqlContext.Pipe.Send("reader read");

            //define the file (stream)
            using (FileStream fileStream =
            new FileStream(FileName,
                        FileMode.OpenOrCreate,
                        FileAccess.Write))
            {
                //SqlContext.Pipe.Send("file stream created.");

                //Define a writer that will stream BLOB
                //to the file (FileStream).
                using (BinaryWriter binaryWriter =
                    new BinaryWriter(fileStream))
                {
                    //SqlContext.Pipe.Send("BinaryWriter created");
                    //The starting position in the BLOB output.
                    long startIndex = 0;
```

```
//Read the bytes into outbyte[] array.
//Get number of bytes that were read.
long retval = reader.GetBytes(0,
    startIndex, outbyte, 0, bufferSize);

//SqlContext.Pipe.Send("outbyte filled.");

//While number of bytes read is equal
// to size of buffer,
//continue reading
while (retval == bufferSize)
{
    //write to stream
    binaryWriter.Write(outbyte);
    //SqlContext.Pipe.Send("outbyte written.");

    //write to file
    binaryWriter.Flush();

    //SqlContext.Pipe.Send("writer flushed.");

    // Reposition the start index
    startIndex += bufferSize;
    //Read number of records again
    //and fill the buffer.
    retval = reader.GetBytes(
        0, startIndex, outbyte, 0, bufferSize);
}

//SqlContext.Pipe.Send("outbyte last time.");
// Write the remainder to the file
binaryWriter.Write(outbyte);
//write to file
binaryWriter.Flush();
//SqlContext.Pipe.Send("flushed last time.");
            }
        }
    }
}
return;
    }
}
```

Naturally, in order to compile this procedure, you must reference the System.IO namespace in the Using statement at the top of the file.

The stored procedure requires you to set Permission Set to External_Resources. The "Assembly External Access" section in Chapter 11 shows how to do it in Transact-SQL. If you are performing this operation in Visual Studio, you need to open Project | <project name> Properties, switch to the Database tab, and set Permission Level to External (see Figure 12-2).

TIP

If you have a problem with deployment, you probably didn't set the database to Trustworthy On and you didn't give External Access Assembly permission to the database owner (as described earlier).

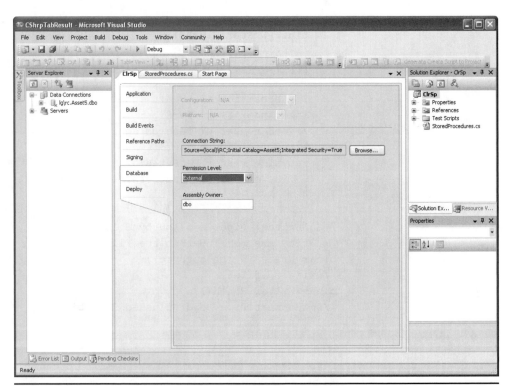

Figure 12-2 *Setting the permission level in Visual Studio 2005*

When the project is successfully deployed, you can test the stored procedure from Management Studio:

```
Use Asset5
GO
DECLARE @EqID int
DECLARE @FileName nvarchar(4000)

Select  @EqId = Min(EqId) from Eq where EqImage is not null
Set @FileName = 'c:\download\Eq' + cast(@EqId as varchar(30)) + '.jpg'

EXECUTE [Asset5].[dbo].[cp_EqImage_Save]
   @EqID
  ,@FileName
```

The opposite operation is implemented by the following CLR stored procedure. cp_EqImage_Update uses the FileStream and BinaryReader objects to read the contents of the file into an array of bytes. The array is then assigned to the value of a SqlParameter. It is used (along with the other parameter) to execute a SqlCommand object and update the specified equipment image.

```
[SqlProcedure]
public static void cp_EqImage_Update(int EqID, string FileName)
{
    //read image from the file and put it in varbinary(max)

    //define the file (stream)
    using (FileStream fileStream =
    new FileStream(FileName,
                FileMode.Open,
                FileAccess.Read))
    {
        //SqlContext.Pipe.Send("file stream created.");

        //Define a writer that will stream BLOB
        //to the file (FileStream).
        using (BinaryReader binaryReader =
           new BinaryReader(fileStream))
        {
            //SqlContext.Pipe.Send("BinaryWriter created");
            byte[] blob=binaryReader.ReadBytes((int)fileStream.Length);

            using (SqlConnection conn =
                new SqlConnection("Context Connection=true"))
```

```
        {
            conn.Open();
            SqlCommand command = conn.CreateCommand();

            // Set up the command to execute the stored procedure.
            command.CommandText = "ap_EqImage_Update";
            command.CommandType = CommandType.StoredProcedure;

            // Set up the input parameter.
            SqlParameter paramID =
                new SqlParameter("@EqID", SqlDbType.Int);
            paramID.Value = EqID;
            command.Parameters.Add(paramID);

            // Set up the output parameter to retrieve the image.
            SqlParameter paramEqImage =
                new SqlParameter("@EqImage",SqlDbType.VarBinary,-1);
            paramEqImage.Value = blob;
            command.Parameters.Add(paramEqImage);

            // Execute the stored procedure.
            command.ExecuteNonQuery();

        }

      }
    }
    return;
}
```

As in the case of the previous C3 example, you must add a reference to the System.IO namespace in the Using statement at the top of your file.

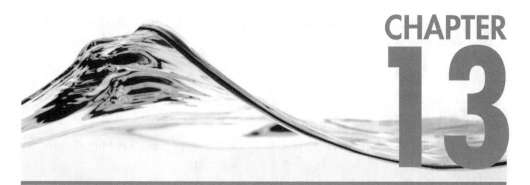

CLR Functions and Triggers

T his chapter explores the details of developing SQL Server 2005 managed functions and managed triggers.

CLR Functions

SQL Server 2005 also supports the creation of CLR user-defined functions. It is possible to create three different types of these functions:

► Scalar-valued

► Table-valued

► User-defined Aggregations

I will show you how to create scalar- and table-valued CLR functions in this chapter, and I will cover User-defined Aggregations in the next chapter.

CLR functions are created as CLR stored procedures—as static functions or methods with a SqlFunction attribute in a .NET class. The class is then deployed on SQL Server as an assembly, and finally functions are then linked with their names in a database. From that point on, the functions are accessible from Transact-SQL or managed code.

Scalar-valued CLR Functions

Functions of this type return a single value (scalar) to the caller. Like their Transact-SQL counterparts, they can be used as part of any Transact-SQL expression (for example, in Where clauses, select lists, or conditional statements). They can have input parameters or return values of any SQL Server data type except these:

► `text`

► `ntext`

► `image`

► `timestamp`

► `rowversion`

► `cursor`

► `table`

Managed code must use .NET data types that are compatible with SQL Server data types (as described earlier in the "CLR Data Types Mapping" section in Chapter 12.

In the following function, I used the .NET function for conversion of dates. It supports some predefined formats and cultures and also custom formats based on a set of format specifiers. It goes far beyond the limited set of formats available in the Transact-SQL Convert function. The CLR function is preceded by a SqlFunction attribute. The return statement is used to perform conversion and return the result to the caller.

```
[SqlFunction]
public static String cf_DateConv(DateTime dt, string format)
{
        return dt.ToString(format);
}
```

User-defined CLR functions can be deployed in Visual Studio in the same way as stored procedures. If you want to deploy them manually, the only difference is that you will use a Create Function statement, and that it will contain a Returns clause that defines the data type of the returned value:

```
CREATE ASSEMBLY MyCShrpUdf FROM 'MyCShrpUdf.dll'
GO
CREATE FUNCTION dbo.cf_DateConv()
RETURNS Varchar(30)
AS EXTERNAL NAME MyCShrpUdf.CLRModules.cf_DateConv
```

You can use statements such as the following one to test it:

```
SELECT [Asset5].[dbo].[cf_DateConv] (GetDate(),'dddd - d - MMMM')
```

The result, on a machine using U.S. English culture, will be

```
----------------------
Sunday - 4 - December
(1 row(s) affected)
```

The next function performs almost the opposite operation. It is used when you have string dates in another language (culture) and some unusual format. It uses the Parse method of the DateType class to recognize the string as a date written in a specific language (culture).

```
[SqlFunction]
public static String cf_DateConv_DtFmtCult(string dt,
                                           string format,
                                           string culture)
```

```
    {
        CultureInfo MyCultureInfo = new CultureInfo(culture);
        DateTime MyDateTime = DateTime.Parse(dt, MyCultureInfo);

        return MyDateTime.ToString(format);
    }
```

You can test it like this:

```
SELECT [dbo].cf_DateConv_DtFmtCult ('12 June 2002',
                                    'dddd - d - MMMM, yyyy',
                                    'de-DE')
```

NOTE

To use the CultureInfo class, you must include a reference to the System.Globalization namespace in your code.

The following function verifies that the string that is passed as a parameter is a valid string. It is based on the Regex.IsMatch function that is defined in the System .Text.RegularExpressions namespace.

```
[SqlFunction]
public static bool cf_IsValidEmail(string email)
{
        //Is it a valid email address:
        return Regex.IsMatch(email,
@"^([\w-]+\.)*?[\w-]+@[\w-]+\.([\w-]+\.)*?[\w]+$");
}
```

You can test it with this:

```
select dbo.cf_IsValidEmail('dejan@trigonblue.com')
select dbo.cf_IsValidEmail('dejan@trigon.blue..com')
```

The result is

```
-----
1

(1 row(s) affected)


-----
0

(1 row(s) affected)
```

SqlFunction Attribute

The primary purpose of this attribute is to notify the .NET compiler that the following managed static function will be converted to a CLR function. However, there are some additional useful properties, explained next, that you can use with the attribute.

DataAccess

The DataAccess property of the SqlFunction attribute helps the compiler to optimize the function by not using an in-process provider code if the function does not require it. The simple functions shown earlier did not use this additional property. Instead, they relied on the default behavior of CLR functions in SQL Server—that data is not accessed. This default is equivalent to declaring it using the DataAccess property:

```
[SqlFunction(DataAccess = DataAccessKind.None)]
```

The following function accesses data through the database and requires the additional property:

```
[SqlFunction(DataAccess = DataAccessKind.Read)]
public static int cf_OrderCount()
{
    using (SqlConnection sqlConn
        = new SqlConnection("context connection=true"))
    {
        sqlConn.Open();
        SqlCommand sqlCmd = new SqlCommand(
            "select count(*) AS 'Order Count' from dbo.OrderHeader",
            sqlConn);
        return (int)sqlCmd.ExecuteScalar();
    }
}
```

You can test it with this:

```
SELECT Asset5.dbo.cf_OrderCount()
```

NOTE

*SQL Server 2005 Books OnLine contains the following statement: "The SqlFunction attribute indicates whether or not the function accesses or **modifies data**...." I believe that this is a mistake in the documentation, and that the only allowed enumerators are DataAccessKind.Read and DataAccessKind.None.*

IsDeterministic

This attribute allows SQL Server 2005 to optimize indexing of the results of user-defined functions that are used in calculated columns.

```
[SqlFunction(IsDeterministic = true)]
```

IsPrecise

This attribute is also used to help SQL Server decide whether the results of the function should be indexed if used in a computed column. The idea is that floating point operations are not precise and therefore cannot be used on indexed computed columns.

```
[SqlFunction(IsDeterministic = true, IsPrecise = true)]
```

SystemDataAccess

This attribute defines whether a CLR function requires access to system virtual tables and catalogs. Possible values are SystemDataAccessKind.Read and SystemDataAccessKind .None (which is the default value).

```
[SqlFunction(SystemDataAccess = SystemDataAccessKind.Read)]
```

Name

By default, Visual Studio 2005 will name the CLR function using the name of the static method in managed code. This attribute is used to force Visual Studio 2005 to change the name of the CLR function.

```
[SqlFunction(Name = "cf_OrderCount",
                   DataAccess = DataAccessKind.Read)]
public static int OrderCount()
...
```

Table-valued CLR Functions

Table-valued CLR functions (CLR TVFs) can be used as Transact-SQL TVFs in any Transact-SQL construct in which a table can be used.

The CLR TVF interface is very strange and complex from the standpoint of object-oriented languages such as C# and Visual Basic .NET, so these functions must be declared in a very specific way and require a relatively complex and unusual structure.

Creating a Table-valued CLR Function

To define a CLR TVF, you must define two methods in managed code:

▶ **InitMethod**   A function that returns an object of the IEnumerable class (or some other class derived from IEnumerable), which is preceded by the SqlFunction attribute and which will become a CLR TVF

▶ **FillRow**   A method that returns (fills) a single result row

> **NOTE**
>
> *It is not required, but it is acceptable to actually name these two methods using these names. Personally, I like to name InitMethod after the function that it is implementing, and I typically leave the second method as FillRow. However, even if the names are changed, I will continue to refer to these methods as InitMethod and FillRow.*

The SqlFunction attribute of InitMethod uses FillRowMethodName to point to the FillRow method. This is the place where you can change the name of the FillRow method if you want:

```
[SqlFunction(FillRowMethodName = "FillRow",
```

With the attribute set in this way, the framework calls the MoveNext() method once for each row of the object (row set) to be returned. It then calls the FillRow() method each time. The procedure must have a generic parameter of the type *object* (which can be filled with anything) and a list of out parameters that correspond to the columns of the CLR TVF:

```
public static void FillRow(object obj,
                           out string fileName,
                           out long size)
{
    Object[] row = (object[])obj;

    fileName = (string)row[0];
    size = (long)row[1];
}
```

This procedure returns (as output parameters) the content of a generic (input) object (parameter).

Data for the generic object is collected in the first function. An object of the ArrayList class is filled with generic objects that contain file information. In the following function, the system loops through files and gathers full filenames (path) and sizes in bytes. At the end, the ArrayList object is returned as a return value of the function, since it implements the IEnumerable interface (that is, it is derived from the interface):

```
public static IEnumerable ClrTvfFolderList(string folder)
{
    ArrayList fileArray = new ArrayList();

    // loop through files in the folder
    foreach (string file in Directory.GetFiles(folder,
        "*.*", SearchOption.TopDirectoryOnly))
    {
        FileInfo fi = new FileInfo(file);

        object[] row = new object[2];
        row[0] = fi.FullName;
        row[1] = fi.Length;

        fileArray.Add(row);
    }

    return fileArray;
}
```

To pull everything together, I have added references to System.IO and System.Collections and wrapped everything in a public class:

```
using System;
using System.Data;
using System.Data.SqlClient;
using System.Data.SqlTypes;
using Microsoft.SqlServer.Server;

using System.IO;
using System.Collections;

public partial class UserDefinedFunctions
{
    [SqlFunction(FillRowMethodName = "FillRow",
        TableDefinition = "fileName nvarchar(max), size bigint")]

    public static IEnumerable ClrTvfFolderList(string folder)
    {
        ArrayList fileArray = new ArrayList();

        // loop through files in the folder
        foreach (string file in Directory.GetFiles(folder,
            "*.*", SearchOption.TopDirectoryOnly))
```

```
        {
            FileInfo fi = new FileInfo(file);

            object[] row = new object[2];
            row[0] = fi.FullName;
            row[1] = fi.Length;

            fileArray.Add(row);
        }

        return fileArray;
    }

    public static void FillRow(object obj, out string fileName, out long size)
    {
        Object[] row = (object[])obj;

        // get data from obj
        fileName = (string)row[0];
        size = (long)row[1];
    }
};
```

To deploy the function using Visual Studio 2005, I set Permission Level to External and made the function part of the dbo schema. It is also critical to add a TableDefinition attribute in the SqlFunction identifier. It should contain a list of column definitions (result set) for the CLR TVF. Only then will Visual Studio 2005 know how to populate the Table clause of the Create Function statement. However, if you are deploying the function manually, you do not need to have this attribute.

To deploy the procedure manually, you should use a script that creates the assembly and creates the function:

```
CREATE ASSEMBLY ClrTvfFolderList
FROM' C:\Projects\ClrTvfFolder\bin\Debug\ClrTvfFolderList.dll'
WITH PERMISSION_SET = External_Resources
GO
CREATE FUNCTION ClrTvfFolderList(string folder)
RETURNS TABLE (fileName nvarchar(max), size bigint)
AS
EXTERNAL NAME ClrTvfFolderList.UserDefinedFunctions.ClrTvfFolderList
GO
```

The Create Function statement can be used to set the name of the function. It could be different from, or the same as, the name of the method it references in the External Name clause. The format of External Name is *Assembly.Class.Method*.

The following table-valued function parses a delimited string and returns it as a recordset. The function can be used to accept arrays as input values for stored procedures:

```csharp
using System;
using System.Data;
using System.Data.Sql;
using System.Data.SqlTypes;
using System.Data.SqlClient;
using Microsoft.SqlServer.Server;
using System.Text.RegularExpressions;
using System.Text;
using System.Collections;

namespace Samples.SqlServer
{
    public class stringsplits
    {

        [SqlFunction(
            FillRowMethodName = "FillRow",
            TableDefinition = "segment nvarchar(max)")]
        public static IEnumerable clrtvf_Split(SqlString str, string splitChar)
        {

            string[] m_strlist;
            if (!str.IsNull)
            {
                m_strlist = str.Value.Split(splitChar.ToCharArray());
                return m_strlist;
            }
            else
                return "";
        }

        public static void FillRow(Object obj, out string segment)
        {
            segment = (string)obj;
        }
    }
};
```

Most of the work is performed using the .NET Framework Split() function, which parses the string and splits it into an array.

To test this function, use something like this:

```
select *
from clrtvf_Split('Memory,CPU,Resolution,Size,Weight,
Color,HDD-count,HDD-capacity', ',')
```

You will get the following result:

```
Segment
--------------
Memory
CPU
Resolution
Size
Weight
Color
HDD-count
HDD-capacity


(8 row(s) affected)
```

The following function is another version of the Split function. It differs slightly from the previous one in that it returns a row number (array index) in the result. It is based on the use of the SplitParts struct, designed to store pairs of string segments and indexes in the array.

```
using System;
using System.Data;
using System.Data.Sql;
using System.Data.SqlTypes;
using System.Data.SqlClient;
using Microsoft.SqlServer.Server;
using System.Text.RegularExpressions;
using System.Text;
using System.Collections;

namespace Samples.SqlServer
{
    public class stringsplit
    {

        internal struct SplitParts
        {
            // structure that will be used to store parts
            public int id;
```

```csharp
    public string result;
    public SplitParts(int splitId, string split)
    {
        id = splitId;
        this.result = split;
    }
}


[Microsoft.SqlServer.Server.SqlFunctionAttribute(
    FillRowMethodName = "FillRow",
    TableDefinition = "segment nvarchar(max),
                       i int")]
public static IEnumerable clrtvf_Split1(SqlString str,
                                        string splitChar)
{
    // split str using delimiter in splitChar
    //and return it as table valued function
    // in format: segment varchar(max), i (row_number) int

    string[] m_strlist;
    SplitParts[] a;
    if (!str.IsNull)
    {
        m_strlist = str.Value.Split(splitChar.ToCharArray());
        int count = m_strlist.GetUpperBound(0);
        a = new SplitParts[count + 1];
        for (int i = 0; i < m_strlist.GetUpperBound(0) + 1; i++)
        {
            a[i] = new SplitParts(i, m_strlist[i]); ;
        }
        return a;
    }
    else
        return "";
}

public static void FillRow(Object obj, out string segment, out int i)
{

    SplitParts ab = (SplitParts)obj;
    segment = ab.result;
    i = ab.id;
}
    }
}
```

NOTE

It is possible to do this in other ways as well. For example, you could create a static variable to serve as a counter of rows. The problem with such a solution is that the use of static variables is not permitted in Safe assemblies.

To test the function, execute the following:

```
select *
from clrtvf_Split1('Memory,CPU,Resolution,Size,Weight,'
+'Color,HDD-count,HDD-capacity', ',')
```

The result will be

```
str          ind
-----------  -----------
Memory       0
CPU          1
Resolution   2
Size         3
Weight       4
Color        5
HDD-count    6
HDD-capacity 7

(8 row(s) affected)
```

Output Values in Visual Basic

Output values for the FillRow method in C# are parameters passed by reference. Visual Basic .NET does not support output parameters, although it does support pass-by-reference parameters. You need to add a special <Out()> attribute to the ByRef declaration of the parameter:

```
Public Shared Sub FillRow (ByVal obj As Object,
                           <Out()> ByRef Segment As SqlChars,
                           <Out()> ByRef i As SqlInt32)
```

For everything to work, you also need to add a reference to the System.Runtime .InteropServices namespace in the Visual Basic .NET assemblies.

Using Nonstandard .NET Framework Assemblies

The following table-valued function returns a list of logical drives on the system, along with their types and free space values. It is based on the class library in the

System.Management namespace, which is not in the list of assemblies/namespaces that are loaded by default in SQL Server. Thus, this function not only demonstrates how to create a table-valued function and how to read free space on a drive, but also how to use nonstandard .NET Framework assemblies.

The function uses ManagementObjectSearcher to query ("SELECT * From Win32_LogicalDisk"!☺!) the system for disks registered in Windows and return it as ManagementObjectCollection. Data is then loaded to the array of the LogicalDriveList struct and finally returned as a table by the FillRow function.

```
using System;
using System.Data;
using System.Data.Sql;
using System.Data.SqlTypes;
using System.Data.SqlClient;
using Microsoft.SqlServer.Server;

using System.Management;
using System.Collections;
using System.Collections.Generic;


internal struct LogicalDriveList
{
    public int DriveId;
    public string DriveLogicalName;
    public Int64 DriveFreeSpace;
    public string DriveType;

    public LogicalDriveList(int driveId,
                            string driveLogicalName,
                            string driveType,
                            int driveFreeSpace)
    {
        DriveId = driveId;
        this.DriveLogicalName = driveLogicalName;
        this.DriveType = driveType;
        this.DriveFreeSpace = driveFreeSpace;
    }
}

public class GetDrives
```

```
{

    [Microsoft.SqlServer.Server.SqlFunctionAttribute(
        FillRowMethodName = "FillRow",
        TableDefinition = "i int,
                           DriveLogicalName nvarchar(255),
                           DriveType nvarchar(255),
                           DriveFreeSpace bigint")]
    public static IEnumerable clrtvf_GetLogicalDrives()
    {

        List<LogicalDriveList> drs = new List<LogicalDriveList>();
        ManagementObjectCollection queryCollection = getDrives();
        const int Removable = 2;
        const int LocalDisk = 3;
        const int Network = 4;
        const int CD = 5;
        int count = 0;
        string driveType = string.Empty;
        foreach (ManagementObject mo in queryCollection)
        {
            count++;
            switch (int.Parse(mo["DriveType"].ToString()))
            {
                case Removable: //removable drives
                    driveType = "Removable";
                    break;
                case LocalDisk: //Local drives
                    driveType = "LocalDisk";
                    break;
                case CD: //CD rom drives
                    driveType = "CD";
                    break;
                case Network: //Network drives
                    driveType = "Network";
                    break;
                default: //defalut to folder
                    driveType = "UnKnown";
                    break;
            }

            LogicalDriveList a = new LogicalDriveList();
            a.DriveId = count;
            a.DriveLogicalName = mo["Name"].ToString();
```

```
            a.DriveType = driveType;
            if (mo["FreeSpace"] != null)
                a.DriveFreeSpace = Int64.Parse(mo["FreeSpace"].ToString());
            else
                a.DriveFreeSpace = 0;
            drs.Add(a);
        }
        return drs;
    }


    protected static ManagementObjectCollection getDrives()
    {
        //get drive collection
        ManagementObjectSearcher query = new
            ManagementObjectSearcher("SELECT * From Win32_LogicalDisk ");
        ManagementObjectCollection queryCollection = query.Get();
        return queryCollection;
    }



    public static void FillRow(Object obj,
        out int i,
        out string DriveLogicalName,
        out string DriveType,
        out Int64 DriveFreeSpace)
    {

        LogicalDriveList ld = (LogicalDriveList)obj;
        DriveLogicalName = ld.DriveLogicalName;
        i = ld.DriveId;
        DriveType = ld.DriveType;
        DriveFreeSpace = ld.DriveFreeSpace;
    }
}
```

The System.Management namespace/assembly can be registered using the following Transact-SQL statement (just make sure that you are referencing the right folder and version of the .NET Framework):

```
CREATE ASSEMBLY Management FROM
'C:\WINDOWS\Microsoft.NET\Framework\v2.0.50727\System.Management.dll'
WITH permission_set=unsafe;
go
```

Note that it must be declared as Unsafe since it accesses resources that are outside of SQL Server. Management Studio will issue a set of warnings:

```
Warning: The Microsoft .Net frameworks assembly 'system.management,
version=2.0.0.0, culture=neutral, publickeytoken=b03f5f7f11d50a3a,
processorarchitecture=msil.' you are registering is not fully tested
in SQL Server hosted environment.
Warning: The Microsoft .Net frameworks assembly
'system.configuration.install, version=2.0.0.0, culture=neutral,
publickeytoken=b03f5f7f11d50a3a, processorarchitecture=msil.' you are
registering is not fully tested in SQL Server hosted environment.
Warning: The Microsoft .Net frameworks assembly
...
```

Now, you also need to include in your project a reference to the new component that has been registered on the SQL Server:

1. Choose Project | Add Reference from the Visual Studio 2005 menu.
2. In the Add References dialog box, select the SQL Server tab and then select Management in the list of component names (see Figure 13-1).

   Since the function references objects that are not in SQL Server, you also need to declare the project Unsafe (Project | Options | Database | Permission Level). Now you can deploy it and then test the function using:

```
select * from dbo.clrtvf_GetLogicalDrives()
```

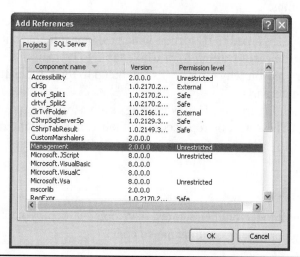

Figure 13-1   *Adding a reference to a component of a database project*

The result will look like this:

```
DriveLogicalName DriveType           i           DriveFreeSpace
A:               Removable           1           0
C:               LocalDisk           2           20331072000
D:               Network             3           140518309888
E:               CD                  4           0
F:               Network             5           140518297600
H:               Network             6           81000570880
N:               Network             7           120188755968
T:               Network             8           174118621184
W:               Network             9           120188755968
```

NOTE

All examples of CLR TVFs so far have been based on either data from external sources or data generated inside the function. If a CLR TVF needs access to SQL Server data (for example, if it executes a Transact-SQL query), you need to set the SqlFunctionAttribute attribute to DataAccess= DataAccessKind.Read.

Differences Between Transact-SQL and CLR TVFs

The most important difference is that a Transact-SQL table-valued function must materialize the whole result as an intermediate table. Since Transact-SQL TVFs are based on tables, a developer can specify some constraints such as Unique index and nullability of columns.

CLR table-valued functions are based on a streaming model. As soon as a row is materialized, it is streamed to the caller, which can consume it immediately. The caller can use rows without waiting for a whole table to be materialized or received. This is the primary reason why CLR TVFs can be up to three times faster than their Transact-SQL counterparts.

CLR TVFs cannot return non-Unicode strings such as `varchar`, `char`, `text`, or `varchar(max)`. They must be replaced with their Unicode counterparts.

CLR Triggers

In this section, I will focus on the features, development, deployment, usage, and limitations of triggers developed in managed code.

Supported Features

SQL Server 2005 supports the creation of DML and DDL triggers in managed code. Both types of DML triggers are also supported—After triggers and Instead-of triggers.

Creation of DML Triggers

I will demonstrate the creation of a DML trigger in Visual Studio 2005:

1. Open Visual Studio 2005 and select File | New Project.
2. Select Database | SQL Server Project and set its name (for example, to CSrpTrigger).
3. Select or create a new database reference.
4. On the Project menu, select Add Trigger and set the name of the file. Visual Studio will create the file with the trigger template:

```
using System;
using System.Data;
using System.Data.SqlClient;
using Microsoft.SqlServer.Server;


public partial class Triggers
{
    // Enter existing table or view for the target
    // and uncomment the attribute line
    // [Microsoft.SqlServer.Server.SqlTrigger (Name="Trigger1",
    //                                         Target="Table1",
    //                                         Event="FOR UPDATE")]
    public static void Trigger1()
    {
        // Replace with your own code
        SqlContext.Pipe.Send("Trigger FIRED");
    }
}
```

As you can see, triggers are also created as public static methods. They should not return a value (it is set to void) to the caller. To force the compiler to add everything needed for this method to become a trigger, you need to enable the Microsoft.SqlServer .Server.SqlTrigger attribute before the method declaration. It contains several properties that are important for the creation of the assembly and the CLR trigger. The Name property sets the name of the trigger. The Target property sets the table the trigger will be associated with. Event defines the type of trigger and the action that triggers it.

Possible trigger types are *Instead-of* and *After* (or you can use *For* as a synonym for *After*). Possible actions are Insert, Update, and Delete. For example, if you want to create an After trigger that will be invoked by Insert and Update statements, you should define the following attribute:

```
[SqlTrigger (Name="dbo.ctr_Contact_iu",
             Target="Contact",
             Event="AFTER UPDATE, INSERT")]
```

You can deploy the trigger in the usual manner by choosing Build | Deploy on the Visual Studio menu. To test it, you can insert a new record in the Contact table using Management Studio.

NOTE

I deliberately didn't put the schema name in front of the name of the table. It is also a problem to assign a trigger to a table that is in a nondefault schema. There is a known bug in initial versions of Visual Studio 2005 and SQL Server 2005 that prevents this. Sometimes you will get a Visual Studio error stating that it cannot find the specified table to deploy the trigger on. As a workaround, you can try closing then reopening the project before testing.

To access trigger-related features, you need to get the context of the current trigger. You will be able to get it using SqlContext:

```
SqlTriggerContext triggerContext = SqlContext.GetTriggerContext();
```

It returns some of the available information to the caller:

```
string action = triggerContext.TriggerAction.ToString();
string sObj = triggerContext.ToString();

SqlContext.Pipe.Send("Trigger " + sObj
                    + " FIRED on " + action);
```

You can also identify which columns have been changed:

```
string s = "";
int iCount = triggerContext.ColumnCount;
for (int i = 0; i < iCount; i++)
{
    if (triggerContext.IsUpdatedColumn(i) == true)
        s = s + i.ToString() + ", ";
}
SqlContext.Pipe.Send("Trigger updated columns: " + s);
```

You can execute additional Transact-SQL commands through an existing connection (using the same method as in stored procedures):

```
SqlConnection connection = new SqlConnection("context connection = true");
connection.Open();
SqlCommand command = connection.CreateCommand();
```

In this way, you can access any database object, but more importantly, you can access the content of Inserted and Deleted virtual tables:

```
if (triggerContext.TriggerAction == Sql.TriggerAction.Insert)
{
    command.CommandText = "SELECT * FROM INSERTED";
    SqlDataRecord record = command.ExecuteRow();
    string email = (string)record[5];

    if (Regex.IsMatch(email,
        @"^([\w-]+\.)*?[\w-]+@[\w-]+\.([\w-]+\.)*?[\w]+$") == false)
        SqlContext.Pipe.Send("Not a valid email!");
}
```

The only problem with the preceding method is that it does not work as expected in the case where more than one record is updated or inserted in a single statement (if you remember, this was also a typical error during the design of Transact-SQL triggers).

The solution is to load e-mails from all inserted or updated records and check them one by one. The following trigger uses the SqlDataReader class to get all records from the Inserted virtual table. The SqlDataReader.GetValue method will be used to read data from the specified column.

```
using System;
using System.Data;
using System.Data.SqlClient;
using Microsoft.SqlServer.Server;

using System.Text.RegularExpressions;


public partial class Triggers
{
    [SqlTrigger(Name = "dbo.ctr_Contact_iu_Email",
                Target = "Contact",
                Event = "AFTER UPDATE, INSERT")]
    public static void ctr_Contact_iu_Email()
```

```csharp
    {
        //get trigger context to access trigger related features
        SqlTriggerContext triggerContext = SqlContext.TriggerContext;


        //test validity of email
        using (SqlConnection con
                = new SqlConnection("context connection = true"))
        {
            con.Open();
            using (SqlCommand cmd = con.CreateCommand())
            {
                if (triggerContext.TriggerAction == TriggerAction.Insert)
                {
                    cmd.CommandText = "SELECT * FROM INSERTED";
                    using (SqlDataReader rdr = cmd.ExecuteReader())
                    {
                        while (rdr.Read())
                        {

                            string email = rdr.GetValue(5).ToString();

                            if (Regex.IsMatch(email, @"^([\w-]+\.)*?[\w-]
+@[\w-]+\.([\w-]+\.)*?[\w]+$") == false)
                            {
                                SqlContext.Pipe.Send("Not a valid email!");
                                //Transaction.Current.Rollback();
                            }
                        }
                    }
                }
            }
        }


    }
}
```

Using an additional connection (along with a SqlCommand and a SqlDataReader) object), you can return a list of columns that were updated:

```csharp
//list of updated column names
using (SqlConnection con = new SqlConnection("context connection = true"))
```

```
{
    con.Open();
    using (SqlCommand cmd = con.CreateCommand())
    {
        cmd.CommandText = "SELECT * FROM INSERTED";

        using (SqlDataReader rdr = cmd.ExecuteReader())
        {
            rdr.Read();

            if (triggerContext.TriggerAction == TriggerAction.Update)
            {
                string sCol = "Updated columns: ";
                for (int icol = 0; icol < triggerContext.ColumnCount; icol++)
                    if (triggerContext.IsUpdatedColumn(icol) == true)
                        sCol = sCol + rdr.GetName(icol) + ", ";
                SqlContext.Pipe.Send(sCol);
            }
        }
    }
}
```

In all of the trigger examples so far, I have used Pipe.Send() just to demonstrate how to create triggers. In the real world, it is not generally recommended that you return text messages from a trigger to a caller. More likely, the operation would be rolled back and/or written to the database and/or an audit file.

It is very simple to write content to file in .NET. For example, you can use the StreamWriter class to create a file and log information in it. The Boolean parameter in the constructor specifies that data will be appended to the file if the file already exists.

```
StreamWriter file = new StreamWriter("c:\\Audit.txt", true);
file.WriteLine("Delete trigger is fired!");
file.Close();
```

The following Delete Instead-of trigger will write log information in a file:

```
using System;
using System.Data;
using System.Data.SqlClient;
using Microsoft.SqlServer.Server;

using System.IO;

public partial class Triggers
```

```
{
    [SqlTrigger(Name = "citr_OrderItem_D",
                Target = "OrderItem",
                Event = "INSTEAD OF DELETE")]
    public static void TriggerDelete()
    {
        string lines;

        //create a new file or append an existing
        using (StreamWriter file =
            new StreamWriter("c:\\Audit.txt", true))
        {
            using (SqlConnection con =
                new SqlConnection("context connection = true"))
            {
                con.Open();
                using (SqlCommand cmd = con.CreateCommand())
                {
                    cmd.CommandText = "select   system_user as [user], "
                        + " GetDate() as [time], 'OrderItem' as [table]"
                        + " from deleted for xml raw";

                    using (SqlDataReader rdr = cmd.ExecuteReader())
                    {
                        // there could be multiple records
                        while (rdr.Read())
                        {
                            lines = rdr.GetValue(0).ToString();
                            //SqlContext.Pipe.Send(lines);
                            file.WriteLine(lines);
                        }
                    }
                }
            }
            file.Close();
        }
    }
}
```

TIP

The advantage of writing to file is that the data will stay in the file even when the operation is rolled back. However, you should use this technique only for operations that are very rare, so that you do not degrade the performance of the system and do not encounter issues with concurrency.

Creation of DDL Triggers

SQL Server also supports managed DDL triggers. I will first show you how to create them with Visual Studio and then without it.

Visual Studio 2005 does not have a special template for DDL triggers. In fact, BOL is definitely not detailed enough on the subject of SqlTrigger attribute requirements for DDL triggers (but that is why you need this book). The Target identifier of the SqlTrigger attribute of a DDL trigger defines the scope of the trigger, which can be Database or All Server. The trigger will be fired after one or more server or database events that are listed in the Event identifier. Naturally, you must also set the Name identifier so that Visual Studio knows how to name the trigger object in the database.

The following Visual Basic .NET trigger records event information about changes to functions and procedures in the current database to a log file on a local hard drive. It will react to DDL statements that change stored procedures and functions (which include Create, Drop, and Alter statements). It will be implemented in the current database as ctrd_DdlProcedureEvents_vb:

```vb
Imports System

Imports System.Data
Imports System.Data.SqlClient
Imports System.Data.SqlTypes
Imports Microsoft.SqlServer.Server

Imports System.IO

Partial Public Class Triggers

    <SqlTrigger(Name:="ctrd_DdlProcedureEvents_vb", _
        Target:="DATABASE", _
        Event:="AFTER DDL_PROCEDURE_EVENTS, DDL_FUNCTION_EVENTS")> _
    Public Shared Sub trigger_DDL_PROCEDURE_EVENTS()
        'get info about all procedure modifications in the database

        'get trigger context
        Dim triggerContext As SqlTriggerContext = SqlContext.TriggerContext

        'get event info
        Dim sXml As String = triggerContext.EventData.Value

        'log info
        Using file As New StreamWriter("c:\\sp_change.log", True)
```

```
          file.WriteLine(sXml)
          file.Close()
    End Using

  End Sub

End Class
```

The method uses the System.IO.StreamWriter class to create or append the file and write text to a file.

> **NOTE**
>
> *This is a somewhat academic example. Naturally, you should use a trigger to write to file only for events that you expect to occur seldom. A better place to log changes such as this would be to a database.*

To customize the behavior of the trigger, you need to get hold of trigger context in the same manner as with a DML trigger. However, the DDL trigger contains a different set of properties. The property that is available only in DDL triggers, and which you will use most often, is SqlTriggerContext.EventData.Value. It contains an XML document with information about the event that fired the trigger. For example:

```
<EVENT_INSTANCE>
   <EventType>CREATE_PROCEDURE</EventType>
   <PostTime>2005-12-17T16:07:00</PostTime>
   <SPID>54</SPID>
   <ServerName>LG\RC</ServerName>
   <LoginName>LG\dsunderic</LoginName>
   <UserName>dbo</UserName>
   <DatabaseName>Asset5</DatabaseName>
   <SchemaName>dbo</SchemaName>
   <ObjectName>ap_test</ObjectName>
   <ObjectType>PROCEDURE</ObjectType>
   <TSQLCommand>
      <SetOptions ANSI_NULLS="ON" ANSI_NULL_DEFAULT="ON"
 ANSI_PADDING="ON" QUOTED_IDENTIFIER="ON" ENCRYPTED="FALSE" />
      <CommandText>
         create proc dbo.ap_Invetory_List
         as
         select * from dbo.Inventory
      </CommandText>
   </TSQLCommand>
</EVENT_INSTANCE>
```

The following C# managed trigger will react to table DDL events (which include Create Table, Drop Table, and Alter Table statements). It will be implemented in the current database as ctrd_CreateTableDdl:

```csharp
using System;
using System.Data;
using System.Data.SqlClient;
using Microsoft.SqlServer.Server;

using System.Xml;
using System.Diagnostics;
using System.IO;

public partial class Triggers
{

[SqlTrigger(
    Name = "ctrd_TableDdl",
    Target = "DATABASE",
    Event = "AFTER DDL_TABLE_EVENTS")]
public static void ddl_table()
{
    //get trigger context to access trigger related features
    SqlTriggerContext triggerContext = SqlContext.TriggerContext;
    //read xml with info about event that fired trigger
    string sXml = triggerContext.EventData.Value;
    string login = "";
    string sql = "";

    using (StringReader srXml = new StringReader(sXml))
    {
        using (XmlReader rXml = new XmlTextReader(srXml))
        {
            //loop through nodes to the end of XML
            while (!(rXml.EOF))
            {
                rXml.MoveToContent();
                if (rXml.IsStartElement()
                    && rXml.Name.Equals("LoginName"))
                    login = rXml.ReadElementString("LoginName");
                else if (rXml.IsStartElement()
                    && rXml.Name.Equals("CommandText"))
                    sql = rXml.ReadElementString("CommandText");

                //move to the next node
                rXml.Read();
            }
        }
```

```
                    //if the source does not exist create it
                    if (!EventLog.SourceExists("Asset5"))
                        EventLog.CreateEventSource("Asset5", "Asset5 database");

                    //write event info in event log
                    EventLog EventLog1 = new
                        EventLog("Asset5 database", "LG", "Asset5");
                    string log = "Login: "+login+" executed: ["+sql+"]";
                    EventLog1.WriteEntry(log);
                }
            }
        }
    }
```

The trigger obtains the XML document and then parses it using the System.Xml .XmlTextReader class. It is a class that is designed for performing XML reading and writing without loading a complete XML document into memory. The trigger will obtain a login and the statement that fired it.

```
    using (StringReader srXml = new StringReader(sXml))
    {
        using (XmlReader rXml = new XmlTextReader(srXml))
        {
            //loop through nodes to the end of XML
            while (!(rXml.EOF))
            {
                rXml.MoveToContent();
                if (rXml.IsStartElement()
                        && rXml.Name.Equals("LoginName"))
                    login = rXml.ReadElementString("LoginName");
                else if (rXml.IsStartElement()
                        && rXml.Name.Equals("CommandText"))
                    sql = rXml.ReadElementString("CommandText");

                //move to the next node
                rXml.Read();
            }
        }
```

The collected information is eventually written in Event Log. Recording is performed using the System.Diagnostics.EventLog class:

```
                    //if the source does not exist create it
                    if (!EventLog.SourceExists("Asset5"))
                        EventLog.CreateEventSource("Asset5", "Asset5 database");
```

```
//write event info in event log
EventLog EventLog1 = new
        EventLog("Asset5 database", "LG", "Asset5");
string log = "Login: "+login+" executed: ["+sql+"]";
EventLog1.WriteEntry(log);
```

If you want to deploy DDL triggers manually, you can use a script such as the
following:

```
CREATE ASSEMBLY VbTriggers
FROM C:\Projects\VbTriggers\VbTriggers\bin\VbTriggers.dll
WITH PERMISSION_SET = EXTERNAL_ACCESS
GO

CREATE TRIGGER ctrd_TableDdl
ON DATABASE
FOR CREATE_ASSEMBLY
AS EXTERNAL NAME VbTriggers.Triggers.ddl_table
GO
```

NOTE

*You will have to manually deploy server-scoped managed DDL triggers. Unfortunately, Visual
Studio 2005 does not support their manual deployment.*

Microsoft has written an interesting and very useful DDL trigger that registers all
user-defined database objects of every assembly that is registered in the database.
It is a very useful script and will be the last script for managed database objects
that you need to write. You can also explore its internals to see how Microsoft
engineers are doing them. You can find the script at http://blogs.msdn.com/sqlclr/
articles/495428.aspx.

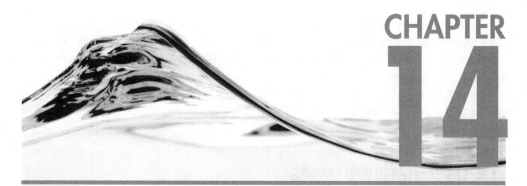

CHAPTER

14

CLR Database Objects Advanced Topics

I n this chapter I will first cover the creation and use of some managed database objects that are more complex to develop, and which you will probably seldom create or use—CLR user-defined types and CLR user-defined aggregations (or *aggregate functions*). The focus will then change to some generic aspects of managed database object development—transaction management and architectural guidelines for justified uses of managed database objects.

CLR User-defined Types

Microsoft has included the ability to create user-defined types (UDT) in managed code in SQL Server 2005. I am not sure how much you will use this feature of SQL Server. Everybody I have asked which UDT functions they would like to have in SQL Server answered the same—time and date—but nobody asked for much on top of that.

To differentiate them from old Transact-SQL user-defined data types, BOL and Management Studio refer to managed UDTs as *user-defined types* (see Figure 14-1), while those that were already available in Transact-SQL are referred to as *user-defined data types*. The distinction is too subtle for my taste.

Structure of Managed UDT

User-defined types have a more complex implementation than other CLR database objects that I have shown you so far. They are implemented as a class if they are designed as reference types, or as a structure (struct) if they are designed as value types. Structures inherit from System.ValueType, while classes inherit from System .Object. You can instantiate an object based on a class, while you can only set values of components of a structure.

Multiple methods must be defined in a class (or a structure) for a managed UDT to achieve basic behavior. For example:

▶ Parse() to set UDT values (properties) based on a string

▶ ToString() to convert a UDT instance to its string interpretation

▶ Properties to expose data components of a UDT

▶ A method and a couple of properties as an implementation of System.Data .SqlTypes.INullable interface for the UDT to support nullability

▶ Read() and Write() methods and MaxByteSize property of the IBinarySerialize interface to allow a UDT to support storing an intermediate state

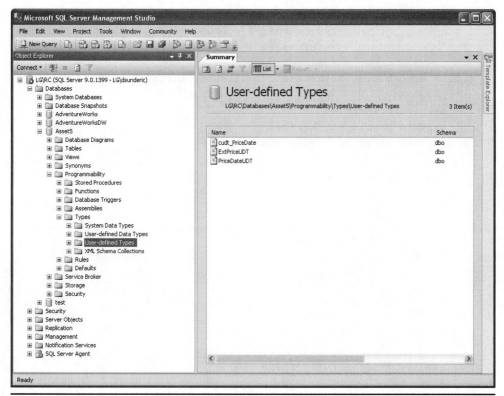

Figure 14-1 *User-defined types*

The following struct is designed to store stock price information on the specified date:

```
using System;
using System.Data.Sql;
using System.Data.SqlTypes;
using Microsoft.SqlServer.Server;

using System.IO;
using System.Runtime.InteropServices;

namespace MyUDTs
{
    [Serializable]
    [StructLayout(LayoutKind.Sequential)]
```

```csharp
[SqlUserDefinedType(Format.UserDefined,
                    IsByteOrdered = true,
                    MaxByteSize = 4096,
                    IsFixedLength = false)]
public struct cudt_PriceDate : INullable, IBinarySerialize
{
    #region Properties
    private Double stockPrice;
    private DateTime businessDay;

    public Double StockPrice
    {
        get
        {
            return this.stockPrice; ;
        }
        set
        {
            stockPrice = value;
        }
    }

    public DateTime BusinessDay
    {
        get
        {
            return this.businessDay;
        }
        set
        {
            businessDay = value;

        }
    }
    #endregion

    #region NULL
    private bool isNull;

    public bool IsNull
    {
        get
```

```csharp
        {
            return (isNull);
        }
    }

    public static cudt_PriceDate Null
    {
        get
        {
            cudt_PriceDate h = new cudt_PriceDate();
            h.isNull = true;
            return h;
        }
    }
    #endregion

    #region Default
    public static cudt_PriceDate DefaultValue()
    {
        return cudt_PriceDate.Null;
    }
    #endregion

    #region Cast
    public override string ToString()
    {
        if (this.IsNull)
            return "NULL";
        else
        {
            return stockPrice + ";" + businessDay.Date;
        }
    }

    public static cudt_PriceDate Parse(SqlString s)
    {
        if (s.IsNull || s.Value.ToLower() == "null")
            return Null;
        cudt_PriceDate st = new cudt_PriceDate();
        string[] xy = s.Value.Split(";".ToCharArray());
        st.stockPrice = Double.Parse(xy[0]);
        st.businessDay = DateTime.Parse(xy[1]);
        return st;
    }
```

```csharp
#endregion

#region Serialization
public void Read(BinaryReader r)
{
    stockPrice = r.ReadDouble();
    businessDay = DateTime.Parse(r.ReadString());
}

public void Write(BinaryWriter w)
{
    w.Write(stockPrice);
    w.Write(businessDay.ToString());
}
#endregion

#region Custom Methods
//The following calculations do not make much sense.
//They are simple demonstrations of methods in UDT.

[SqlMethod(
    OnNullCall = false,
    DataAccess = DataAccessKind.None,
    IsDeterministic = false,
    IsMutator = false,
    IsPrecise = false)]
public static SqlInt32 DiffDate(cudt_PriceDate from,
                                cudt_PriceDate to)
{
    TimeSpan delta = to.BusinessDay.Subtract(from.BusinessDay);
    return delta.Days;
}

[SqlMethod(OnNullCall = false)]
public static SqlDouble DiffPrice(cudt_PriceDate from,
                                  cudt_PriceDate to)
{
    return to.StockPrice - from.StockPrice;
}

#endregion
    }
}
```

Namespaces

A struct or class that will become a UDT must contain references to the System, System.Data.Sql, System.Data.SqlTypes, and Microsoft.SqlServer.Server namespaces. You can add additional references as needed.

```
using System;
using System.Data.Sql;
using System.Data.SqlTypes;
using Microsoft.SqlServer.Server;

using System.IO;
using System.Runtime.InteropServices;
```

Attributes

A struct that will be converted to a UDT must be preceded by several attributes.

The Serializable attribute is set to notify the compiler that the struct can be serialized and deserialized. *Serialization* is the process of converting the object into a series of bytes for storing (or transmitting to other system).

The StructLayout attribute is used to determine the way that the components of a UDT will be stored in memory.

The SqlUserDefinedType attribute notifies the compiler that the struct should be compiled as a UDT. The attribute contains a couple of properties. The Format property specifies the format of serialization. If Format.UserDefined is used, the type must implement its own serialization by implementing the IBinarySerialize.Read() and IBinarySerialize.Write() methods. IsByteOrdered specifies that SQL Server can perform binary comparisons of UDT instances, instead of comparing UDT instances in managed code. MaxByteSize defines the maximum size of a struct when it is serialized in bytes. In SQL Server 2005, the size of a serialized UDT is limited to 8000 bytes. IsFixedLength declares whether all instances of the UDT are of the same size. You can find more details about these attributes in Visual Studio 2005 documentation (but unfortunately not in BOL).

Interfaces

The declaration of a struct contains the names of the interfaces the struct is implementing:

```
public struct cudt_PriceDate : INullable, IBinarySerialize
```

These interfaces are defined in the .NET Framework and all classes and structs that inherit from them must contain implementations of specified methods and properties.

For example, for UDT to be nullable, the struct must implement the INullable interface, which means that it must contain the following methods:

```
private bool isNull;

public bool IsNull
{
    get
    {
        return (isNull);
    }
}

public static cudt_PriceDate Null
{
    get
    {
        cudt_PriceDate h = new cudt_PriceDate();
        h.isNull = true;
        return h;
    }
}
```

For a UDT to be serializable, it must contain an implementation of IBinarySerialize—the use of Read() and Write() methods:

```
public void Read(BinaryReader r)
{
    stockPrice = r.ReadDouble();
    businessDay = DateTime.Parse(r.ReadString());
}

public void Write(BinaryWriter w)
{
    w.Write(stockPrice);
    w.Write(businessDay.ToString());
}
```

Properties

The carriers of information in the struct are private fields:

```
private Double stockPrice;
private DateTime businessDay;
```

The information in these fields is accessed through property methods (and the corresponding get and set methods):

```
public Double StockPrice
{
    get
    {
return this.stockPrice;;
    }
    set
    {
stockPrice = value;
    }
}


public DateTime BusinessDay
{
    get
    {
return this.businessDay;
    }
    set
    {
businessDay = value;

    }
}
```

Conversion Methods

The ToString() and Parse() methods implement ways to convert a UDT to a string and a string to a UDT:

```
public override string ToString()
{
    if (this.IsNull)
return "NULL";
    else
    {
return stockPrice + ";" + businessDay.Date;
    }
}

public static cudt_PriceDate Parse(SqlString s)
```

```
{
    if (s.IsNull || s.Value.ToLower() == "null")
return Null;
    cudt_PriceDate st = new cudt_PriceDate();
    string[] s = s.Value.Split(";".ToCharArray());
    st.stockPrice = Double.Parse(s[0]);
    st.businessDay = DateTime.Parse(s[1]);
    return st;
}
```

The CLR engine is smart enough to use these methods whether they are referenced explicitly or implicitly through Transact-SQL Convert and Cast functions.

DefaultValue Method

To be able to set the default value of a UDT, its managed class must contain the DefaultValue() method, even if it returns only an instance set to Null:

```
public static cudt_PriceDate DefaultValue()
{
    return cudt_PriceDate.Null;
}
```

Custom Methods and SqlMethodAttribute

It is also possible to define custom methods inside of the UDT that could be called as functions from Transact-SQL. The following two methods calculate difference in price and days between two instances of the UDT:

```
[SqlMethod(
    OnNullCall = false,
    DataAccess = DataAccessKind.None,
    IsDeterministic = false,
    IsMutator = false,
    IsPrecise = false)]
public static SqlInt32 DiffDate(cudt_PriceDate from, cudt_PriceDate to)
{
    TimeSpan delta = to.BusinessDay.Subtract(from.BusinessDay);
    return delta.Days;
}

[SqlMethod(OnNullCall = false)]
public static SqlDouble DiffPrice(cudt_PriceDate from, cudt_PriceDate to)
{
    return to.StockPrice - from.StockPrice;
}
```

Such methods may be marked with the SqlMethod attribute, which may contain additional properties:

DataAccess	Specifies whether the function uses ADO.NET to access data on SQL Server, and whether the compiler should include components for database access to the assembly. Default is DataAccessKind.None.
IsDeterministic	Important if an index is created on the result of the function. It shows whether the function produces the same output values for the same input values. Default is false.
IsMutator	Signifies whether the method changes the values stored in an instance of the UDT. Default is false.
IsPrecise	Works like a hint that forces the compiler to include floating point operations in the assembly. Default is false.
Name	Used if you want to set the name of the Transact-SQL function to be different from the default (name of the method).
OnNullCall	Set to true if the method is called when null reference input arguments are specified. Default is true.

Deploying CLR UDT Without Visual Studio 2005

If you do not have Visual Studio 2005, you can create assembly and type using the following commands:

```
CREATE ASSEMBLY MyUDTs FROM
'C:\Projects\CShrpPriceDate\bin\Debug\cudt_PriceDate.dll'
WITH permission_set=Safe;

CREATE TYPE cudt_PriceDate
EXTERNAL NAME MyUDTs.MyUDTs.cudt_PriceDate;
GO
```

Using CLR User-defined Types

I will now demonstrate how to use a managed UDT. I will use a new UDT created in Visual Basic .NET. This is a structure that consists of fields for quantity and price:

```
Imports System
Imports System.Data
Imports System.Data.Sql
Imports System.Data.SqlClient
Imports System.Data.SqlTypes
Imports Microsoft.SqlServer.Server
Imports System.Runtime.InteropServices
Imports System.IO
```

```vbnet
<Serializable()> _
<StructLayout(LayoutKind.Sequential)> _
<SqlUserDefinedType(Format.UserDefined, IsByteOrdered:=True, _
                    MaxByteSize:=4096, IsFixedLength:=False, _
                    ValidationMethodName:="ValidateExtPrice")> _
Public Structure ExtPriceUDT
    Implements INullable, IBinarySerialize

#Region "Properties"
    'field members
    Private m_Qty As Decimal
    Private m_Price As Decimal

    Public Property Price() As Decimal
        Get
            Return (Me.m_Price)
        End Get

        Set(ByVal Value As Decimal)
            m_Price = Value
        End Set
    End Property

    Public Property Qty() As Decimal
        Get
            Return (Me.m_Qty)
        End Get

        Set(ByVal Value As Decimal)
            m_Qty = Value
        End Set
    End Property
#End Region

#Region "Cast"
    <SqlMethod(OnNullCall:=False)> _
    Public Shared Function Parse(ByVal s As SqlString) As ExtPriceUDT
        If s.IsNull Then
            Return Null
        End If

        Dim u As ExtPriceUDT = New ExtPriceUDT
```

```vb
        Dim x() As String = s.Value.Split("x".ToCharArray())
        u.m_Qty = Decimal.Parse(x(0))
        u.m_Price = Decimal.Parse(x(1))

        If Not u.ValidateExtPrice() Then
            Throw New ArgumentException("Invalid extended price values.")
        End If

        Return u
    End Function


    <SqlMethod(OnNullCall:=False)> _
    Public Overrides Function ToString() As String
        Return m_Qty.ToString + " x $" + m_Price.ToString
    End Function
#End Region


#Region "Null"
    ' Private member
    Private m_Null As Boolean

    Public ReadOnly Property IsNull() As Boolean _
            Implements INullable.IsNull
        Get
            Return m_Null
        End Get
    End Property

    Public Shared ReadOnly Property Null() As ExtPriceUDT
        Get
            Dim h As ExtPriceUDT = New ExtPriceUDT
            h.m_Null = True
            Return h
        End Get
    End Property
#End Region


#Region "Method"
    <SqlMethod(OnNullCall:=False)> _
    Private Function ValidateExtPrice() As Boolean
        If (m_Qty >= 0) And (m_Price >= 0) Then
            Return True
        Else
            Return False
```

```vbnet
        End If
    End Function


    ' Return extended price
    <SqlMethod(OnNullCall:=False)> _
    Public Function ExtPrice() As Decimal
        Return m_Qty * m_Price
    End Function


    <SqlMethod(OnNullCall:=False)> _
    Public Function Diff(ByVal a As ExtPriceUDT) As ExtPriceUDT
        'The following calculation does not make much mathematical sense.
        'It is a simple demonstration of method in UDT.

        Dim d As New ExtPriceUDT

        If a.ExtPrice >= Me.ExtPrice Then
            d.m_Price = a.m_Price - Me.m_Price
            d.m_Qty = a.m_Qty - Me.m_Qty
        Else
            d.m_Price = Me.m_Price - a.m_Price
            d.m_Qty = Me.m_Qty - a.m_Qty
        End If

        Return d

    End Function

    Public Shared Function DefaultValue() As ExtPriceUDT
        Return ExtPriceUDT.Parse("0 x 0")
    End Function
#End Region

#Region "Serialization"
    <SqlMethod(OnNullCall:=False)> _
    Public Sub Read(ByVal r As BinaryReader) _
            Implements IBinarySerialize.Read

        m_Qty = r.ReadDecimal()
        m_Price = r.ReadDecimal()

    End Sub
```

```
    <SqlMethod(OnNullCall:=False)> _
    Public Sub Write(ByVal w As BinaryWriter) _
            Implements IBinarySerialize.Write

        w.Write(m_Qty)
        w.Write(m_Price)

    End Sub
#End Region

End Structure
```

To deploy the UDT, choose Build | Deploy from the menu.

TIP

A user must have Execute permission on a UDT to use it. I was not emphasizing this requirement on earlier programmatic objects, such as stored procedures and functions, because this requirement is the same for CLR objects and Transact-SQL objects. A user needs a permission to use a managed UDT, unlike a Transact-SQL UDT. The reason is that a managed UDT contains methods.

UDT in Tables and Variables

The use of a managed UDT in a table is very similar to the use of native SQL Server data types:

```
create table OrderItem_wUDT
(
    OrderItemId int NOT NULL,
    OrderId int NOT NULL,
    PartId int NOT NULL,
    ExtPrice ExtPriceUDT NULL
)
GO
```

It is simple to declare variables as instances of a CLR UDT:

```
declare @ext_price ExtPriceUDT
```

Invoking Static Methods

Static methods of a UDT are called using the :: operator. Note that this concerns static methods—not methods of an object instance.

```
declare @a cudt_PriceDate
set @a = CONVERT(cudt_PriceDate, '911.799;2005-11-02')
```

```
declare @b cudt_PriceDate
set @b = Cast ('912.35;2005-11-03' as cudt_PriceDate)

select cudt_PriceDate::DiffDate (@a, @b),
       cudt_PriceDate::DiffPrice(@a, @b)
```

The following statement creates a table with a column of the type ExtPriceUDT and sets a default value for it. Default values of UDT fields can be created by referencing static methods of UDTs.

```
create table OrderItem_wUDT
(
   OrderItemId int NOT NULL,
   OrderId int NOT NULL,
   PartId int NOT NULL,
   ExtPrice ExtPriceUDT NOT NULL
       DEFAULT ExtPriceUDT::DefaultValue()
)
GO
```

Populating a Table

You can populate the OrderItem_wUDT table in almost the same way as if it were created with regular data types only. You can use a modification statement in the same way, but you have to use one of the methods that produces instances of ExtPriceUDT. In the following example, I used the Parse() method, which converts a string into an instance of ExtPriceUDT:

```
INSERT INTO [dbo].[OrderItem_wUDT]
   ([OrderItemId],[OrderId],[PartId],[ExtPrice])
values( 1, 1, 1, ExtPriceUDT::Parse('35 x 450'))
```

Accessing Values

Accessing properties or the complete UDT is very straightforward:

```
select
   ExtPrice.Qty qty,
   ExtPrice.Price price,
   ExtPrice
from OrderItem_wUDT
```

The query will return string representations of properties and binary representations of the UDT:

```
Qty Price ExtPrice
--- ----- ----------------------------------------------------------
35  45    0x230000000000000000000000000000000C201000000000000000000
```

We can go a step further and access methods that are defined in the UDT:

```
select
    ExtPrice.ExtPrice() [ExtPrice()],
    ExtPrice.ToString() [ToString()],
    ExtPrice.Diff(ExtPriceUDT::Parse('25 x 250')).ToString() [Diff()]
from OrderItem_wUDT
```

The first and second columns display calculated values—decimal and string representations of extended price. The third column is a little more complicated. I wanted to display the difference between quantities and the difference between unit prices combined into a new instance of ExtPriceUDT. (I know that this calculation does not make much sense—I just wanted to demonstrate how to invoke a method.) Therefore, I created a new instance of ExtPrice using the Parse() method and used it as an argument of the Diff() method. It returns a result in the form of an ExtPriceUDT, so I applied the ToString() method to it (at the end) to convert it to a string. The result will be something like this:

```
ExtPrice()      ToString()        Diff()
--------------  ----------------  ---------------
15750           35 x $450         10 x $200
```

Converting Values

All conversions that were performed in the previous section were based on the invocation of static methods and are relatively straightforward. But let's see some UDT magic:

```
declare @ext_price ExtPriceUDT
select @ext_price = Convert(ExtPriceUDT, '25 x 250')
select @ext_price [Convert()]
```

CLR will invoke the Parse() method although you have not implicitly invoked it. The result will be a binary representation of the UDT:

```
Convert()
----------------------------------------------------------------
0x190000000000000000000000000000000FA000000000000000000000000000000
```

The same would happen if you used Cast() instead of Convert(). You can apply additional methods to it to get useful results:

```
select Convert(ExtPriceUDT, '25 x 250').ExtPrice() ExtPrice
```

The result will be

```
ExtPrice
---------------
6250
```

You can perform conversion in the opposite direction as well. You can use the Convert()
or Cast() function to convert data to a string instead of ToString():

```
Select Cast(ExtPrice as varchar(30)) ExtPrice
From OrderItem_wUDT
```

The result will be

```
ExtPrice
----------------
35 x $450
```

Comparing Values

When a UDT is created with the IsByteOrdered of SqlUserDefinedType attribute set
to True, its instances can be compared:

```
Select *
From OrderItem_wUDT
where ExtPrice > Convert(ExtPriceUDT, '25 x 250')
```

Updating Values

It is possible to update the complete UDT field:

```
Update OrderItem_wUDT
Set ExtPrice = Convert(ExtPriceUDT, '25 x 250')
where OrderItemId = 1
```

It is also possible to update an individual property:

```
Update OrderItem_wUDT
Set ExtPrice.Qty = 25
where OrderItemId = 1
```

However, it is not possible to update more than one property of the same column in
a single Update statement:

```
Update OrderItem_wUDT
Set ExtPrice.Qty = 25,
    ExtPrice.Price = 250
where OrderItemId = 1
```

The engine will return the following error:

```
Msg 264, Level 16, State 1, Line 1
Column name 'ExtPrice' appears more than once in the result column list.
```

You can solve this problem using a method that returns an instance of the UDT, such as Parse() (see the first Update statement in this section). Alternatively (or if you need to set just a subset of properties), you can create a new method to set the values.

Cross-database CLR User-defined Types

Managed UDTs are database-level objects. To use a single UDT in multiple databases, it must be deployed in each of them. That means that you have to execute Create Assembly and Create Type statements in each database. After that, SQL Server 2005 will perform implicit conversions of values from one database to the other.

The same applies when referencing a managed UDT in a temporary table. Although temporary tables work in the context of the current database, since they are actually created in the tempdb database, they cannot reference CLR UDTs that are defined in the current database. For example, the following script will not be executed successfully:

```
Use Asset5
go
create table #tmp(pd cudt_PriceDate)
```

SQL Server will return the following error:

```
Msg 2715, Level 16, State 7, Line 1
Column, parameter, or variable #1: Cannot find data type cudt_PriceDate.
```

To UDT or Not to UDT

Managed UDTs have several significant limitations:

▶ Instance of a UDT is limited to 8KB.

▶ Database objects that contain a UDT must be schema-bound; maintenance is therefore more complex and more expensive.

▶ You cannot change a UDT once you start using it. It is technically possible to do so (by exporting data, dropping database objects, and then using Drop and Create or Alter Assembly), but changes to the UDT would invalidate all tables and indexes that reference it. One side of this problem can be solved. If you are expecting methods to change, you could write properties in one class and methods in another class. Then, when you decide to change methods, you can rewrite them and redeploy them without affecting the data stored in the first class (database).

▶ It is possible to create overloaded methods in a managed UDT, but it is not possible to call them from Transact-SQL. However, it is possible to call them from inside the UDT.

▶ It is not possible to call a UDT from Transact-SQL constructors with parameters. Constructors without parameters are automatically executed when the UDT is implemented as a class (reference type) and not invoked at all if it is implemented as a struct (value type). However, within the type it is possible to invoke any type of constructor.

▶ All data in a single UDT must be read and written in a single update operation.

TIP

Do not go overboard with types—the fact that you can implement something as a type does not mean that you should not try to implement it first as columns and tables.

User-defined Aggregate CLR Functions

All versions of SQL Server have supported built-in aggregate functions such as Count(), Sum(), and Max(). SQL Server 2005 introduces user-defined aggregate CLR functions. They are categorized by usage as (scalar) functions. However, their implementation makes them more like UDTs (and just as complex), so I am introducing them here.

Structure of Managed Aggregates

Aggregates are defined as structures (structs) or classes that must implement specific interfaces so that the compiler can convert them to aggregate functions in SQL Server 2005. Managed aggregates must contain the SqlUserDefinedAggregate attribute, an interface for aggregating values in the form of four aggregation methods, and the IBinarySerialize interface for storing intermediate states of aggregation.

Aggregation Methods

The interface that CLR will use to aggregate values consists of four methods:

▶ Init()
▶ Accumulate()

▶ Merge()

▶ Terminate()

The Init() method is used by the query processor to initialize computation of the aggregation:

```
Public Sub Init()
    arr = New Double(100) {}
    count = 0
End Sub
```

It should also perform any cleanup that is needed to start the processing of a set of values.

Accumulate() is called for each value of the set that is being aggregated. It updates the total of the aggregate instance with the value that is used as an argument. The data type of the parameter should be a managed SQL Server data type equivalent to a native SQL Server data type that will be used in the Create Aggregate statement, or it could also be a managed UDT:

```
Public Sub Accumulate(ByVal value As SqlDouble)
    arr(count) = value.Value
    count = count + 1
End Sub
```

Merge() is used by the query processor to put together another instance of aggregation (processing one subset of values) with the current instance (processing its own subset of values). This is used when the query processor divides the original set into multiple subsets for parallel processing. The data type of its parameter must be the aggregation class itself:

```
Public Sub Merge(ByVal group As MedianFloat)
    For Each mem As Double In group.arr
        arr(count) = mem
        count = count + 1
    Next mem
End Sub
```

The Terminate() function performs the final calculations and returns the result to the caller:

```
Public Function Terminate() As SqlDouble

    Array.Resize(arr, count)
    Array.Sort(arr)
```

```
    Dim n As Integer = count \ 2
    If n * 2 = count Then
        median = (arr(n + 1) + arr(n)) / 2.0
    Else
        median = arr(n + 1)
    End If

    Return median

End Function
```

IBinarySerialize Interface

The IBinarySerialize interface, with Read() and Write() methods, is used for storing intermediate states of the aggregate instance. The aggregate class must also be preceded with the Serializable attribute and the class must be marked to implement the IBinarySerialize interface:

```
<Serializable()> _
...
    Public Class MedianFloat
      Implements IBinarySerialize

...

      Public Sub Read(ByVal r As BinaryReader) _
                Implements IBinarySerialize.Read
          count = r.ReadInt32()
          arr = New Double(count) {}
          For i As Integer = 1 To count - 1
              arr(i) = r.ReadDouble()
          Next i
      End Sub

      Public Sub Write(ByVal w As BinaryWriter) _
                Implements IBinarySerialize.Write

          w.Write(count)
          For Each m As Double In arr
              w.Write(m)
          Next m

      End Sub
```

The format of a stream or a file that stores the intermediate state that I have selected is very simple. It consists of an integer that contains a count of elements in the array and then individual elements of the array.

SqlUserDefinedAggregate Attribute and Its Properties

Like all other managed database objects, a class of aggregates must be preceded by an argument that specifies its type—SqlUserDefinedAggregate. It also contains a set of properties of the attribute:

Format	Specifies how the class will be serialized. Possible values are Format.UserDefined and Format.Native.
IsNullIfEmpty	Forces the query processor to return a Null value if the aggregate is applied to an empty set.
IsInvariantToNulls	Notifies the query processor that Null values have no effect on the result of the aggregate.
IsInvariantToDuplicates	Notifies the query optimizer that duplicates should not affect the result of the aggregate.
IsInvariantToOrder	Has no effect in SQL Server 2005.
MaxByteSize	Specifies the maximum size of the attribute instance.

When you put elements from the previous sections together, the aggregate looks like this:

```
Imports System
Imports System.Data
Imports System.Data.SqlClient
Imports System.Data.SqlTypes
Imports Microsoft.SqlServer.Server

Imports System.Collections
Imports System.IO
Imports System.Text

<Serializable()> _
<SqlUserDefinedAggregate( _
    Format.UserDefined, _
    IsInvariantToDuplicates:=True, _
    IsInvariantToNulls:=True, _
    IsInvariantToOrder:=True, _
    IsNullIfEmpty:=True, _
    MaxByteSize:=8000)> _
```

```vb
Public Class MedianFloat
    Implements IBinarySerialize

    Public Sub Init()
        arr = New Double(100) {}
        count = 0
    End Sub

    Public Sub Accumulate(ByVal value As SqlDouble)
        arr(count) = value.Value
        count = count + 1
    End Sub

    Public Sub Merge(ByVal group As MedianFloat)

        For Each mem As Double In group.arr
            arr(count) = mem
            count = count + 1
        Next mem

    End Sub

    Public Function Terminate() As SqlDouble

        Array.Resize(arr, count)
        Array.Sort(arr)

        Dim n As Integer = count \ 2
        If n * 2 = count Then
            median = (arr(n + 1) + arr(n)) / 2.0
        Else
            median = arr(n + 1)
        End If

        Return median
    End Function

    Public Sub Read(ByVal r As BinaryReader) _
                Implements IBinarySerialize.Read
        count = r.ReadInt32()
        arr = New Double(count) {}
```

```
        For i As Integer = 1 To count - 1
            arr(i) = r.ReadDouble()
        Next i
    End Sub

    Public Sub Write(ByVal w As BinaryWriter) _
            Implements IBinarySerialize.Write

        w.Write(count)
        For Each m As Double In arr
            w.Write(m)
        Next m

    End Sub

    ' field members
    Private median As Double
    Public arr() As Double
    Public count As Integer

End Class
```

Or in C#, a similar aggregate function would look like this:

```
using System;
using System.Data.Sql;
using System.Data.SqlTypes;
using Microsoft.SqlServer.Server;

using System.Runtime.InteropServices;
using System.Collections;
using System.IO;
using System.Text;

namespace MyAggs
{
    [Serializable]
    [SqlUserDefinedAggregate(
        Format.UserDefined,
        IsInvariantToNulls = true,
        IsInvariantToDuplicates = false,
        MaxByteSize = 8000)
    ]
```

```csharp
public class MedianDouble : IBinarySerialize
{
    private double[] arr;
    double median;
    private int count = 0;

    public void Init()
    {
        arr = new double[100];
    }

    public void Accumulate(SqlDouble value)
    {
        arr[count] = value.Value;
        count++;
    }

    public void Merge(MedianDouble group)
    {
        foreach (double mem in group.arr)
        {
            arr[count] = mem;
            count++;
        }
    }

    public SqlDouble Terminate()
    {
        Array.Resize(ref arr, count);
        Array.Sort(arr);

        int n = count / 2;

        if (n * 2 == count)
            median = (arr[n + 1] + arr[n]) / 2;
        else
            median = arr[n + 1];

        return median;
    }

    public void Read(BinaryReader r)
```

```
        {
            count = r.ReadInt32();

            arr = new double[count];

            for (int i = 1; i < count; i++)
                arr[i] = r.ReadDouble();

        }

        public void Write(BinaryWriter w)
        {
            w.Write(count);

            foreach (double m in arr)
                w.Write(m);

        }
    }
}
```

Deploying CLR Aggregates

As with other CLR database objects, you can deploy CLR aggregates using Visual
Studio 2005 or using a custom script:

```
If exists(select * from sys.assembly_modules
          where assembly_class = 'VbAgg.MedianFloat')
    drop AGGREGATE MedianFloat
GO


IF EXISTS (select * from sys.assemblies where name = N'VbAgg')
DROP ASSEMBLY VbAgg;
GO


CREATE ASSEMBLY Aggregates
FROM 'C:\Projects\VbAgg\VbAgg\bin\debug\VbAgg.dll'
WITH permission_set=Safe;
GO

CREATE AGGREGATE MedianFloat(@input float)
RETURNS float
EXTERNAL NAME [VbAgg].[MyAggs.MedianFloat];
GO
```

Using CLR Aggregates

You can use managed aggregates on any set of data on which you can use built-in aggregates. The easiest example would be to create a table and the aggregate function on it:

```
if object_id('Data') is not null
    drop table dbo.Data

create table dbo.Data(id int identity, num real)
INSERT INTO dbo.Data (num) VALUES (-911.5);
INSERT INTO dbo.Data (num) VALUES (9.6);
INSERT INTO dbo.Data (num) VALUES (91.88);
INSERT INTO dbo.Data (num) VALUES (509.86);
INSERT INTO dbo.Data (num) VALUES (-911.5);
INSERT INTO dbo.Data (num) VALUES (90.6);
INSERT INTO dbo.Data (num) VALUES (-1.88);
INSERT INTO dbo.Data (num) VALUES (19.86);
INSERT INTO dbo.Data (num) VALUES (18888.86);


select * from Data order by num

select dbo.MedianFloat(num) MedianFloat
from Data
```

The result of last two lines is

```
id          num
----------- -------------
1           -911.5
5           -911.5
7           -1.88
2           9.6
8           19.86
6           90.6
3           91.88
4           509.86
9           18888.86

(9 row(s) affected)

MedianFloat
-----------
19.86

(1 row(s) affected)
```

The following example is based on cudt_PriceDate, which was created earlier in the chapter. It calculates the moving average price in the window of a predefined set of days.

```csharp
using System;
using System.Data.Sql;
using System.Data.SqlTypes;
using Microsoft.SqlServer.Server;

using System.IO;
using System.Text;
using MyUDTs;


namespace MyAggs
{
    [Serializable]
    [SqlUserDefinedAggregate(
        Format.UserDefined,
        IsInvariantToNulls = true,
        IsInvariantToDuplicates = false,
        IsInvariantToOrder = false,
        MaxByteSize = 8000)
        ]
    public class agg_MovingAvg : IBinarySerialize
    {
        private double sum = 0;
        private DateTime startDt;
        private DateTime endDt;
        private double ma;
        private Int32 count = 1;
        public static readonly int daysNum = 50;

        #region Aggregation Methods
        /// <summary>
        /// Initialize the internal data structures
        /// </summary>
        public void Init()
        {
            startDt = DateTime.Today;
            endDt = startDt.AddDays(-1 * daysNum);
        }
```

```csharp
/// <summary>
/// Accumulate the next value, not if the value is null
/// </summary>
/// <param name="value">Another value to be aggregated</param>
public void Accumulate(cudt_PriceDate value)
{

    if (value.IsNull)
    {
        return;
    }
    if (value.BusinessDay > endDt && value.BusinessDay < this.startDt)
    {
        sum += (double)value.StockPrice;
        count++;
    }
}


/// <summary>
/// Merge the partially computed aggregate with this aggregate
/// </summary>
/// <param name="other">Another set of data to be added</param>
public void Merge(agg_MovingAvg other)
{
    sum += other.sum;
    count += other.count;
}


/// <summary>
/// Called at the end of aggregation
/// to return the results of the aggregation.
/// </summary>
/// <returns>the aggregated value</returns>
public SqlDouble Terminate()
{
    ma = sum / count;
    return new SqlDouble(ma);
}

#endregion

#region IBinarySerialize
```

```
        public void Read(BinaryReader r)
        {
            sum = r.ReadDouble();
            count = r.ReadInt32();
        }

        public void Write(BinaryWriter w)
        {
            w.Write(sum);
            w.Write(count);
        }
        #endregion
    }


}
```

To test the new aggregation function, I will create a table based on the UDT. I will insert a couple of records in it and then perform the aggregation.

```
if object_id('dbo.Stock') is not null
    drop table dbo.Stock

create table dbo.Stock(
    id int identity,
    stock varchar(100),
    priceClose cudt_PriceDate)

INSERT INTO  dbo.Stock(stock, priceClose)
values('NT', Cast('3.05;2-Dec-05' as cudt_PriceDate))
INSERT INTO  dbo.Stock(stock, priceClose)
values('NT', Cast('3.08;1-Dec-05' as cudt_PriceDate))
INSERT INTO  dbo.Stock(stock, priceClose)
values('NT', Cast('2.90;30-Nov-05' as cudt_PriceDate))
INSERT INTO  dbo.Stock(stock, priceClose)
values('NT', Cast('2.84;29-Nov-05' as cudt_PriceDate))
INSERT INTO  dbo.Stock(stock, priceClose)
values('NT', Cast('2.92;28-Nov-05' as cudt_PriceDate))
INSERT INTO  dbo.Stock(stock, priceClose)
values('NT', Cast('3.01;25-Nov-05' as cudt_PriceDate))
INSERT INTO  dbo.Stock(stock, priceClose)
values('NT', Cast('3.06;23-Nov-05' as cudt_PriceDate))
INSERT INTO  dbo.Stock(stock, priceClose)
values('NT', Cast('3.04;22-Nov-05' as cudt_PriceDate))
```

```
INSERT INTO  dbo.Stock(stock, priceClose)
values('NT', Cast('5.10;21-Nov-05' as cudt_PriceDate))
```

```
select
   Stock,
   dbo.agg_MovingAvg(priceClose) MovingAvg
from Stock
group by stock
```

The result will be

```
Stock    MovingAvg
-------- ----------------
NT       3.22222222222222
```

Transactions in CLR Code

Managed database objects (such as stored procedures and triggers) can participate in
transactions in several ways including (but not limited to) the following:

► A managed object can be enlisted (can participate) in a transaction that is initiated
by a caller, no matter what type of caller that may be—client application,
Transact-SQL batch, stored procedure, managed database object, etc.

► A managed object can be designed to perform its operation outside of an existing
transaction that is initiated by a caller.

► A transaction can be rolled back inside the managed object (no matter where the
transaction was initiated—client, Transact-SQL, managed database object, etc.).

► A managed database object can initiate a transaction against a single database
or multiple (distributed) databases.

For example, you do not need to do anything special to the code of a CLR stored
procedure to participate in a transaction initiated by Begin Tran in a Transact-SQL
batch (or initiated in any other way). However, if you want to test some condition
and, based on it, roll back the entire transaction, your code must include a reference
to System.Transactions and a call to System.Transactions.Transaction.Current
.Rollback(). In the following C# example, a command object will be executed
against a database. If the error is trapped, the code will perform some error handling
and finally roll back the transaction (which was initiated by a caller such as Transact-
SQL batch):

```
try
{
   Cmd1.ExecuteNonQuery();
}
catch
{
   //some custom error handling
   ...
   System.Transactions.Transaction.Current.Rollback()
}
```

Using TransactionScope Class

Code written using .NET Framework 1.0 and 1.1 had to use support for transactions from System.EnterpriseServices and System.Data.IDbTransaction. Working with it is somewhat similar to doing transactions in Transact-SQL. A developer has to:

▶ Declare (create) a connection object.

▶ Instantiate (open) the connection object.

▶ Declare the transaction object.

▶ Request (begin) a transaction object from the connection.

▶ Create all command objects using the transaction.

▶ Execute commands.

▶ If there are no errors, commit the transaction.

▶ If there is an error, roll back the transaction.

▶ Close the connection.

.NET Framework 2.0 has introduced System.Transactions, which is easier to use and addresses some complexity issues.

By combining the TransactionScope class and a *using* (or Using in Visual Basic) statement, development of code that uses transactions is as simple as:

▶ Creating an instance of the transaction in a Using statement via the TransactionScope() constructor

▶ Creating an instance of the connection class in the Using statement

▶ Executing Transact-SQL commands (one or more)

▶ Completing the transaction

In Visual Basic .NET code, this would be something like the following:

```vbnet
Imports System
Imports System.Data
Imports System.Data.SqlClient
Imports System.Data.SqlTypes
Imports Microsoft.SqlServer.Server

Imports System.Transactions


Partial Public Class StoredProcedures
    <Microsoft.SqlServer.Server.SqlProcedure()> _
    Public Shared Sub cp_LeasedAsset_Insert( _
        ByVal EqId As Integer, ByVal LocId As Integer, _
        ByVal StatusId As Integer, ByVal LeaseId As Integer, _
        ByVal LeaseScheduleId As Integer, ByVal OwnerId As Integer, _
        ByVal LeaseAmount As Decimal, ByVal AcqTypeId As Integer)

        Dim Cmd1 As String = "insert Inventory(EqId, LocationId, " + _
            "StatusId,          LeaseId, " + _
            "LeaseScheduleId,   OwnerId, " + _
            "Lease,             AcquisitionTypeID)" + _
            "values (" + EqId.ToString() + ", " + LocId.ToString() + ", " + _
            StatusId.ToString() + " , " + LeaseId.ToString() + " , " + _
            LeaseScheduleId.ToString() + ", " + OwnerId.ToString() + ", " + _
            LeaseAmount.ToString() + " , " + AcqTypeId.ToString() + ")"

        Dim Cmd2 As String = "update dbo.LeaseSchedule " + _
            "Set PeriodicTotalAmount = PeriodicTotalAmount + " _
            + LeaseAmount.ToString() + _
            "where LeaseId = " + LeaseId.ToString()


        Using TxScope As TransactionScope = New TransactionScope()

            Using Con As New SqlConnection("Context Connection=true")
                Con.Open()

                Dim Cmd As SqlCommand = New SqlCommand(Cmd1, Con)
                Cmd.ExecuteNonQuery()

                'I will reuse the same connection and command object
                'for next segment of operation.
                Cmd.CommandText = Cmd2
                Cmd.ExecuteNonQuery()
```

```
          ' commit/complete transaction
          TxScope.Complete()

        End Using 'connection is implicitly closed
      End Using 'transaction is implicitly closed or rolled back

    End Sub
End Class
```

The transaction is declared in a Using statement around a code block. The statement allows you to localize usage of an object (or a variable) to a code block and deallocate it with an implicit call to the Dispose() method of the object. Inside the code block, one or more Transact-SQL commands is being executed, and if everything is successfully completed, the operation (transaction) will be completed (committed). If an exception occurs, the code execution would leave the code block and the transaction would be considered discontinued (implicitly rolled back by calling TransactionScope.Dispose behind the scene).

NOTE

To use the described features, you must add a System.Transactions reference to your project and then reference it in an Import statement in Visual Basic .NET (or a Using statement in C#).

Transaction Options

The TransactionScope() constructor has several overloaded methods. They allow you to specify different combinations of transaction parameters.

Isolation Level

Of all transaction parameters, you will most often change the isolation level. By default, the isolation level of transactions is set to Serializable. As you may remember from Chapter 5, this would preserve all locks until the completion of the transaction. It would make the system too slow and it is typically not required.

To set some other isolation level, such as ReadCommitted, you must use an object of the TransactionOptions class:

```
Dim options As TransactionOptions = New TransactionOptions()
options.IsolationLevel = Transactions.IsolationLevel.ReadCommitted
options.Timeout = TransactionManager.DefaultTimeout

Using TxScope As TransactionScope = _
    New TransactionScope(TransactionScopeOption.Required, options)
...
End Using
```

Transaction Duration

The TransactionOptions object also has a Timeout property. Its value determines when the engine will stop further execution of a transaction as too long. By default, it is set to 60 seconds.

Nested Transactions

The TransactionScope() constructor requires *scopeOption* as its first parameter. Its values are set using TransactionScopeOption enumeration. By default, the value of scopeOption is TransactionScopeOption.Required—the current scope (code block) requires a transaction. If the code block is executed inside of a transaction, the engine will not initiate a nested transaction. The engine will return the context of an outer transaction as the TransactionScope object—it will use (participate in) the existing (outer) transaction. If the code block has been executed without a transaction context (no transaction was in progress), a new transaction will be created for the code block.

Alternative values are RequiresNew and Suppress. RequiresNew forces the engine to create a new transaction whether the code block is executed inside of a transaction or not. Suppress is used to execute the current code block without an outer transaction. These options open up some interesting opportunities. For example, it is possible to log something in a table inside the code block. Then, even when the outer transaction is rolled back, the contents of the log table should be intact. It is also possible to develop something inside a code block, the success or failure of which would affect the outer transaction.

NOTE

A nested transaction can participate in an outer transaction only if they have the same isolation level; otherwise, an exception will be thrown.

Distributed Transactions

A *resource manager* (RM) is a transaction-aware component that performs some useful operation. An RM can participate (enlist) within a transaction and interact with a transaction manager. An example of a resource manager is a SqlConnection object that connects to a SQL Server 2005 database.

A *transaction manager* is a component that orchestrates the communication between various resource managers and preserves the integrity of the entire operation. Examples of transaction managers are Lightweight Transaction Manager (LTM), used for transactions on a single resource manager (SqlConnection object against SQL Server), and Microsoft Distributed Transaction Coordinator (MSDTC), which is used to communicate with multiple (distributed) resource managers (for example, different or even heterogeneous databases on different servers). MSDTC uses a two-phase commit (see Chapter 5) to maintain the integrity of the operation. Since MSDTC is very heavy for local operations (there is no need for a two-phase commit), it is better to use Lightweight Transaction Manager (LTM) for that situation.

You do not have to do anything special when your transaction is spanning more than one server. CLR will automatically promote a lightweight, local transaction into a distributed transaction involving MSDTC when you open a second connection against another server.

In the following example, the first connection is made to a local SQL Server 2005 database to execute an Insert statement against the Inventory table. The second connection is created against another database on another server. When the connection to the first database is opened, the transaction is created as a lightweight transaction. However, when the second SqlConnection is opened, the transaction is promoted to a distributed transaction:

```
<Microsoft.SqlServer.Server.SqlProcedure()> _
    Public Shared Sub cp_LeasedAsset_InsertDistributed( _
        ByVal EqId As Integer, ByVal LocId As Integer, _
        ByVal StatusId As Integer, ByVal LeaseId As Integer, _
        ByVal LeaseScheduleId As Integer, ByVal OwnerId As Integer, _
        ByVal LeaseAmount As Decimal, ByVal AcqTypeId As Integer)

    Dim sCmd1 As String = "insert Inventory(EqId, LocationId, " + _
        "StatusId,           LeaseId, " + _
        "LeaseScheduleId,    OwnerId, " + _
        "Lease,              AcquisitionTypeID)" + _
        "values (" + EqId.ToString() + ", " + LocId.ToString() + ", " + _
        StatusId.ToString() + " , " + LeaseId.ToString() + " , " + _
        LeaseScheduleId.ToString() + ", " + OwnerId.ToString() + ", " + _
        LeaseAmount.ToString() + " , " + AcqTypeId.ToString() + ")"

    Dim sCmd2 As String = "update dbo.LeaseSum " + _
        "Set PeriodicTotalAmount = PeriodicTotalAmount + " _
        + LeaseAmount.ToString() + _
        "where LeaseId = " + LeaseId.ToString()
```

```
    Dim ConString1 As String = "Context Connection=true"

    Dim ConString2 As String = _
        "Data Source=lg/DW;Initial Catalog=Asset5DW;" + _
        "Integrated Security=True"

    Using TxScope As TransactionScope = New TransactionScope()

        Using Con1 As New SqlConnection(ConString1)

            Con1.Open()

    Dim Cmd2 As SqlCommand = New SqlCommand(sCmd1, Con1)
        Cmd2.ExecuteNonQuery()

        End Using

        Using Con2 As New SqlConnection(ConString2)

            'Creation of second connection automaticaly promotes
            'the transaction to distributed.
            Con2.Open()

    Dim Cmd2 As SqlCommand = New SqlCommand(sCmd2, Con2)
        Cmd2.ExecuteNonQuery()

        End Using 'connection is implicitly closed

        'commit/complete transaction
        TxScope.Complete()

    End Using 'transaction is implicitly closed or rolled back

End Sub
```

The Complete() method of the transaction scope object will finally commit the transaction.

NOTE

Automatic promotion from a lightweight transaction to a distributed transaction can occur only when the operation is executed against SQL Server 2005.

Explicit Transactions

It is still possible to use older transactional classes such as SqlTransaction to implement transactions explicitly in SQL CLR. The following procedure executes two Transact-SQL statements wrapped in SqlConnection.BeginTransaction and SqlConnection .Commit(). In the case of an error, SqlConnection.Rollback() is called:

```vb
<Microsoft.SqlServer.Server.SqlProcedure()> _
Public Shared Sub cp_LeasedAsset_InsertDeclarative( _
    ByVal EqId As Integer, ByVal LocId As Integer, _
    ByVal StatusId As Integer, ByVal LeaseId As Integer, _
    ByVal LeaseScheduleId As Integer, ByVal OwnerId As Integer, _
    ByVal LeaseAmount As Decimal, ByVal AcqTypeId As Integer)

    Dim sCmd1 As String = "insert Inventory(EqId, LocationId, " + _
        "StatusId,           LeaseId, " + _
        "LeaseScheduleId,    OwnerId, " + _
        "Lease,              AcquisitionTypeID)" + _
        "values (" + EqId.ToString() + ", " + LocId.ToString() + ", " + _
        StatusId.ToString() + " , " + LeaseId.ToString() + " , " + _
        LeaseScheduleId.ToString() + ", " + OwnerId.ToString() + ", " + _
        LeaseAmount.ToString() + " , " + AcqTypeId.ToString() + ")"

    Dim sCmd2 As String = "update dbo.LeaseSum " + _
        "Set PeriodicTotalAmount = PeriodicTotalAmount + " _
        + LeaseAmount.ToString() + _
        "where LeaseId = " + LeaseId.ToString()


    ' declare here because try and catch have different scope
    Dim trans As SqlTransaction = Nothing
    Dim connection As SqlConnection = _
    New SqlConnection("Context Connection=true")

    connection.Open()
    Try
        trans = connection.BeginTransaction

        Dim command As SqlCommand = _
            New SqlCommand(sCmd1, connection, trans)

        command.ExecuteNonQuery()
```

```
        command.CommandText = sCmd2
        command.ExecuteNonQuery()

        trans.Commit()

    Catch ex As Exception
        trans.Rollback()

        'Todo: additional error hanndling

        're-throw exception
        Throw ex
    Finally
        'called every time
        connection.Close()
    End Try

End Sub
```

NOTE

The SqlCommand constructor has a SqlTransaction object as a parameter to enlist itself under a transaction.

Benefits of New Transaction Paradigm

It is still possible to use older transactional classes to implement transactions in SQL CLR. However, the new model has several important benefits:

▶ Application programming is decoupled from transaction managers—code that is written for the lightweight transaction manager will automatically be promoted and work without problems if the engine detects usage of another durable resource (database).

▶ It is not required to enlist resources explicitly under a transaction. The engine will automatically make resource managers work as part of the transaction.

▶ Nesting of transactions is easier to implement.

▶ Nested code blocks or procedures can be written so that they do not participate in an outer transaction.

▶ It is easier to handle exceptions and manage resources (disposal of objects is automatic).

To CLR or Not to CLR (Design and Performance Considerations)

It is important to exercise caution when you are designing CLR database objects—do not overuse them. As always, it is important to use the right tool for the job. I will go through some general rules, as well as some specific ones, for implementing code in CLR:

▶ As a rule of thumb, Transact-SQL code is better for relational operations and CLR code is better for operations that include lots of computations or that require access to classes in the .NET Framework. Transact-SQL set operations are the optimal way for implementing data access, and even if you need to perform them in managed code, you do so by issuing Transact-SQL commands through ADO.NET.

▶ Complex computations (or business rules) should not be implemented in CLR procedures. Implement them as middleware components instead. If you need to transfer large quantities of data to middleware, you may decide to break this rule and implement processing on a database server.

▶ Monitor sys.dm_clr_appdomains.cost to differentiate CPU usage of CLR components from the rest of the server in order to prevent the database server from becoming a bottleneck in the system. If CPU usage is too high, move more of the business logic or processing from the data to the middle tier.

▶ Scalar functions are typically good candidates for implementation in managed code. You should test to find out whether the overhead of switching between Transact-SQL and CLR code outweighs the disadvantages to processing in Transact-SQL alone.

▶ CLR table-valued functions are typically faster than their Transact-SQL counterparts. The reason is that a CLR TVF is implemented using a streaming model that does not require the materializing of results in an intermediate table as a Transact-SQL TVF does.

▶ Aggregations are easier to implement in CLR and they are typically an order of magnitude faster than the Transact-SQL code needed to perform the same operation. Unfortunately, they have to be implemented for a specific data type in CLR, which might be an issue.

▶ CLR code is a more reliable, more secure, and often faster alternative to documented and undocumented extended stored procedures.

▶ Queries can be parallelized (split into parts to be executed in parallel) if they are executed in Transact-SQL.

▶ If the procedure contains many DML statements, it is probably faster to implement it in Transact-SQL because it will be parsed, checked syntactically, and compiled during creation instead of at runtime.

▶ I recommend that you implement data rules (a subset of business rules that is closely tied to data) as close to the data as possible. Managed user-defined types and managed triggers should be considered (along with standard constructs such as constraints or Transact-SQL triggers) as a way to implement them.

▶ Managed UDTs are a long-term risk because they cannot be changed without invalidating the content of tables. Something will probably have to be changed in the future—data rules or the version of CLR delivered with a version of SQL Server, or some future service pack.

▶ ADO.NET has some interesting transaction-related features. If you want to create a nested stored procedure to work outside of the caller's transaction, implement it in a CLR stored procedure.

Don't Say I Didn't Warn You

Have you guessed yet that I'm not completely thrilled with CLR database procedures?

I urge you to be cautious in implementing CLR database procedures. You want to create lasting solutions, but the jury is still out on CLR. It is new and exciting and presents many opportunities for ingenious solutions, but because it is new, it is also bound to change. If you overuse them (simply because you can), you leave yourself (or the database developer who comes after you) open to a nightmare rewrite.

Transact-SQL is here to stay. It is a safer choice, and it is a better choice for data access and set operations than managed code. Even managed code reverts to Transact-SQL for data access, so there's really no point in re-inventing the wheel in these situations.

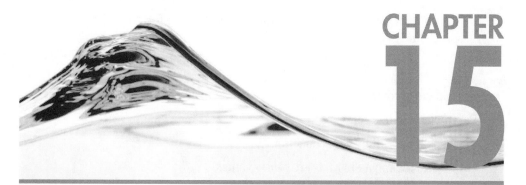

Advanced Stored Procedure Programming

Thihis chapter introduces some advanced techniques for coding stored procedures, including:

▶ Dynamically constructed queries

▶ Parameterized queries

▶ Methods for handling SQL Injection

▶ Optimistic locking using `timestamp` values

▶ Full-text searches and indexes

▶ Nested stored procedures

▶ Passing data to nested stored procedures using temporary tables and cursors

▶ Inserting the results of a stored procedure into a table

▶ Techniques for generating identity and unique identifier values and potential problems associated with their use

▶ Additional looping methods

Dynamically Constructed Queries

This section examines some ways in which you can construct queries dynamically, including:

▶ Executing a string statement

▶ Querying by form

▶ Using parameterized queries

Executing a String

Transact-SQL contains a variation of the Execute statement that you can use to run a batch recorded in the form of a character string:

```
EXEC[UTE] ({@string_variable | [N]'tsql_string'} [+...n])
```

You can supply a Transact-SQL batch in the form of a character string, a variable, or an expression:

```
Exec ('select * from Contact')
```

The Execute statement allows you to assemble a batch or a query dynamically. This might look like magic to you:

```
declare @chvTable sysname
set @chvTable = 'Contact'
Exec ('select * from ' + @chvTable)
```

The Execute statement is necessary because the following batch, which you might expect to work, will actually result in a syntax error:

```
declare @chvTable sysname
set @chvTable = 'Contact'
select * from @chvTable  -- this will cause an error
```

The error occurs because SQL Server expects a table name, and will not accept a string or a variable, in a From clause.

It is important to realize that you are dealing with two separate batches in the example with the Execute statement. You can use the variable to assemble the second batch, but you cannot reference variables from the batch that initiated the Execute statement in the string batch. For example, the following code will result in a syntax error:

```
declare @chvTable sysname
set @chvTable = 'Contact'
Exec ('select * from @chvTable')
```

The server will return

```
Server: Msg 137, Level 15, State 2, Line 1
Must declare the variable '@chvTable'.
```

NOTE

Even if you were to declare the variable in the second batch, the Select statement would fail because you cannot use a string expression or variable in the From clause.

You cannot use a database context from the other batch, either:

```
Use Asset
exec ('Use Northwind select * from Employees')
select * from Employees    -- Error
```

Query by Form

One of the simplest ways to create a search form in a client application is to list all the fields in a table as text boxes on a form. The user will fill some of them in, and they can be interpreted as search criteria.

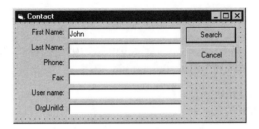

The trouble with this kind of solution is that, most of the time, the user will leave blank most of the text boxes. This does not mean that the user wants to find only those records in which the values of the blank fields are set to empty strings, but rather that those fields should not be included in the criteria. Stored procedures have a static structure, but something dynamic would be more appropriate to launch this kind of query.

The following stored procedure assembles a character-string query. The contents of the Where clause are based on the criteria that were specified (that is, fields that were not set to null). When all components are merged, the query returns a list of matching contacts:

```
Create Procedure dbo.ap_QBF_Contact_List
-- Dynamically assemble a query based on specified parameters.
-- Test: exec dbo.ap_QBF_Contact_List @chvFirstName = 'Dejan'
(
    @chvFirstName    varchar(30)   = NULL,
    @chvLastName     varchar(30)   = NULL,
    @chvPhone        typPhone      = NULL,
    @chvFax          typPhone      = NULL,
    @chvEmail        typEmail      = NULL,
    @insOrgUnitId    smallint      = NULL,
    @chvUserName     varchar(50)   = NULL,
    @debug           int           = 0
)
As
set nocount on

Declare @chvQuery nvarchar(max),
        @chvWhere nvarchar(max)
```

```
Select @chvQuery = 'SET QUOTED_IDENTIFIER OFF SELECT * FROM dbo.Contact',
       @chvWhere = ''

If @chvFirstName is not null
    Set @chvWhere = @chvWhere + ' FirstName = "'
                  + @chvFirstName + '" AND'

If @chvLastName is not null
    Set @chvWhere = @chvWhere + ' LastName = "'
                  + @chvLastName + '" AND'

If @chvPhone is not null
    set @chvWhere = @chvWhere + ' Phone = "'
                  + @chvPhone + '" AND'

If @chvFax is not null
    set @chvWhere = @chvWhere + ' Fax = "'
                  + @chvFax + '" AND'

If @chvEmail is not null
    set @chvWhere = @chvWhere + ' Email = "'
                  + @chvEmail + '" AND'

If @insOrgUnitId is not null
    set @chvWhere = @chvWhere + ' OrgUnitId = '
                  + @insOrgUnitId + ' AND'

If @chvUserName is not null
    set @chvWhere = @chvWhere + ' UserName = "'
                  + @chvUserName + '"'

if @debug <> 0
    select @chvWhere chvWhere

-- remove ' AND' from the end of string
begin try
    If Substring(@chvWhere, Len(@chvWhere) - 3, 4) = ' AND'
       set @chvWhere = Substring(@chvWhere, 1, Len(@chvWhere) - 3)
end try
begin Catch
    Raiserror ('Unable to remove last AND operator.', 16, 1)
    return
end catch
```

```
if @debug <> 0
   select @chvWhere chvWhere

begin try
   If Len(@chvWhere) > 0
      set  @chvQuery = @chvQuery + ' WHERE ' + @chvWhere

   if @debug <> 0
      select @chvQuery Query

   -- get contacts
      exec (@chvQuery)
end try
begin Catch
   declare @s varchar(max)
   set @s = 'Unable to execute new query: ' + @chvQuery
   Raiserror (@s, 16, 2)
   return
end catch

return
```

The procedure is composed of sections that test the presence of the criteria in each parameter and add them to the Where clause string. At the end, the string with the Select statement is assembled and executed. Figure 15-1 shows the result of the stored procedure (along with some debugging information).

TIP

You are right if you think that this solution can probably be implemented more easily using client application code (for example, in Visual Basic).

Data Script Generator

Database developers often need an efficient way to generate a set of Insert statements to populate a table. In some cases, data is already in the tables, but it may need to be re-created in the form of a script to be used to deploy it on another database server, such as a test server.

One solution is to assemble an Insert statement dynamically for every row in the table using a simple Select statement:

```
select 'Insert dbo.AcquisitionType values('
       + Convert(varchar, AcquisitionTypeId)
       + ', ''' + AcquisitionType
       + ''')' from dbo.AcquisitionType
```

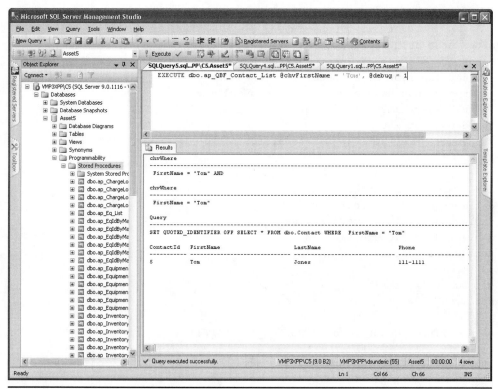

Figure 15-1   *The results of Query By Form*

When you set Query Analyzer to Result In Text and execute such a statement, you get a set of Insert statements for each row:

```
----------------------------------------------------------------
Insert dbo.AcquisitionType values(1, 'Purchase')
Insert dbo.AcquisitionType values(2, 'Lease')
Insert dbo.AcquisitionType values(3, 'Rent')
Insert dbo.AcquisitionType values(4, 'Progress Payment')
Insert dbo.AcquisitionType values(5, 'Purchase Order')

(5 row(s) affected)
```

The Insert statements can now be encapsulated inside a pair of Set Insert_Identity statements and then saved as a script file or copied (through Clipboard) to the Query pane. This process can save you a substantial amount of typing time, but you still have to be very involved in creating the original Select statement that generates the desired results.

An alternative solution is to use the util.ap_DataGenerator stored procedure:

```
alter proc util.ap_DataGenerator
-- generate a set of Insert statements
-- that can reproduce content of the table.
-- It does not handle very very long columns.
   @table sysname = 'Inventory',
   @debug int = 0
-- debug:  exec util.ap_DataGenerator @table  = 'Location', @debug = 1
as

declare @chvVal varchar(max)
declare @chvSQL varchar(max)
declare @chvColList varchar(max)
declare @intColCount smallint
declare @i smallint

set @chvColList = ''
set @chvVal = ''

select @intColCount = Max([ORDINAL_POSITION]),
       @i = 1
FROM      [INFORMATION_SCHEMA].[COLUMNS]
where     [TABLE_NAME] = @table

while @i <= @intColCount
begin
   SELECT @chvVal = @chvVal
   + '+'','''+case when ' + [COLUMN_NAME]
   + ' is null then ''null'' else '
   + case when DATA_TYPE in ('varchar', 'nvarchar', 'datetime',
                      'smalldatetime', 'char', 'nchar')
               then ''''''''''+convert(varchar(max),'
         else '+ convert(varchar(max),'
      end
   + convert(varchar(max),[COLUMN_NAME])
   + case when DATA_TYPE in ('varchar', 'nvarchar', 'datetime',
                      'smalldatetime','char', 'nchar')
               then ')+'''''''''
         else ')'
      end
   + ' end '
   FROM      [INFORMATION_SCHEMA].[COLUMNS]
```

```
    where     [TABLE_NAME] = @table
    and [ORDINAL_POSITION] = @i


--    if @debug <> 0 select @chvVal [@chvVal]

    -- get column list
    SELECT    @chvColList = @chvColList
            + ',' + convert(varchar(max),[COLUMN_NAME])
    FROM      [INFORMATION_SCHEMA].[COLUMNS]
    where     [TABLE_NAME] = @table
    and [ORDINAL_POSITION] = @i

    set @i = @i + 1
end

if @debug <> 0 select @chvColList [@chvColList]

-- remove first comma
set @chvColList = substring(@chvColList, 2, len(@chvColList))

set @chvVal = substring(@chvVal, 6, len(@chvVal))


-- assemble a command to query the table to assemble everything
set @chvSQL = 'select ''Insert dbo.' + @table
        + '(' + @chvColList +') values (''+'
        + @chvVal + ' + '')''from ' +@table

-- get result
if @debug <> 0 select @chvSQL chvSQL
exec(@chvSQL)

return
```

The procedure is based on the INFORMATION_SCHEMA.COLUMNS system view. It simply loops through columns of a specified table and collects data in two variables. The @chvColList variable collects a comma-delimited list of columns:

```
@chvColList
----------------------------------------------------------------------
,LocationId,Location,Address,City,ProvinceId,Country
(1 row(s) affected)
```

The @chvVal variable collects a set of Case statements that will be used to generate Values clauses of the Insert statements (I formatted it so that you can understand it more easily):

```
@chvVal
----------------------------------------------------------
+','+
case when LocationId is null then 'null'
     else + convert(varchar(max),LocationId)
end+','+
case when Location is null then 'null'
     else ''''+convert(varchar(max),Location)+''''
end +','+
case when Address is null then 'null'
     else ''''+convert(varchar(max),Address)+''''
end +','+
case when City is null then 'null'
     else ''''+convert(varchar(max),City)+''''
end +','+
case when ProvinceId is null then 'null'
     else ''''+convert(varchar(max),ProvinceId)+''''
end +','+
case when Country is null then 'null'
     else ''''+convert(varchar(max),Country)+''''
end

(1 row(s) affected)
```

Data for this string is gathered in a similar manner, but the code is more complex in order to handle nullability of columns and to insert different delimiters for different data types.

In the final step before execution, these strings are put together in a Select statement that will retrieve data from the table (again, I formatted the string so that you can more easily understand its structure):

```
chvSQL
-----------------------------------------------------------------
select 'Insert dbo.Location(LocationId,Location,Address,City,
ProvinceId,Country) values (
'+case when LocationId is null then 'null'
       else + convert(varchar(max),LocationId)
end +',
```

```
'+case when Location is null then 'null'
       else ''''+convert(varchar(max),Location)+''''
end +',
'+case when Address is null then 'null'
       else ''''+convert(varchar(max),Address)+''''
end +',
'+case when City is null then 'null'
else ''''+convert(varchar(max),City)+''''
end +',
'+case when ProvinceId is null then 'null'
       else ''''+convert(varchar(max),ProvinceId)+''''
end +',
'+case when Country is null then 'null'
       else ''''+convert(varchar(max),Country)+''''
end  + ')'
from Location

(1 row(s) affected)
```

The result is a set of Insert statements:

```
-------------------------------------------------------------------
Insert dbo.Location(LocationId,Location,Address,City,ProvinceId,Country)
values (2,'Trigon Tower','1 Trigon Av.','Toronto','ON ','Canada')
Insert dbo.Location(LocationId,Location,Address,City,ProvinceId,Country)
values (3,'Sirmium Place','3 Sirmium St.','Toronto','ON ','Canada')
Insert dbo.Location(LocationId,Location,Address,City,ProvinceId,Country)
values (4,'Singidunum Plaza','27 Trigon Av.','Toronto','ON ','Canada')
Insert dbo.Location(LocationId,Location,Address,City,ProvinceId,Country)
values (5,'Mediana Tower','27 Istlington St.','London','ON ','Canada')
...
```

Using the sp_executesql Stored Procedure

An important advantage stored procedures have over ad hoc queries is their capability to reuse an execution plan. SQL Server, and developers working in it, can use two methods to improve the reuse of queries and batches that are not designed as stored procedures. Autoparameterization is covered in Appendix B. This section focuses on using a system stored procedure to enforce parameterization of a query.

If you know that a query will be re-executed with different parameters and that reuse of its execution plan will improve performance, you can use the sp_executesql system stored procedure to execute it. This stored procedure has the following syntax:

```
sp_executesql [@stmt =] stmt
[
    {, [@params =] N'@parameter_name data_type [,...n]' }
    {, [@param1 =] 'value1' [,...n] }
]
```

The first parameter, @stmt, is a string containing a batch of Transact-SQL statements. If the batch requires parameters, you must also supply their definitions as the second parameter of the sp_executesql procedure. The parameter definition is followed by a list of the parameters and their values. The following script executes one batch twice, each execution using different parameters:

```
EXECUTE sp_executesql
    @Stmt = N'SELECT * FROM Asset.dbo.Contact WHERE ContactId = @Id',
    @Parms = N'@Id int',
    @Id = 11
EXECUTE sp_executesql
    @Stmt = N'SELECT * FROM Asset.dbo.Contact WHERE ContactId = @Id',
    @Parms = N'@Id int',
    @Id = 313
```

There is one unpleasant requirement to this exercise. If all database objects are not *fully qualified* (that is, hard-coded with the database name and schema name), the SQL Server engine will not reuse the execution plan.

In some cases, you may be able to ensure that all database objects are fully qualified. However, this requirement becomes a problem if you are building a database that will be deployed under a different name or even if you use more than one instance of the database in your development environment (for example, one instance for development and one for testing).

The solution is to obtain the name of a current database using the Db_Name() function. You can then incorporate it in a query:

```
Declare @chvQuery nvarchar(200)
Set @chvQuery = N'Select * From ' + DB_NAME()
                + N'.dbo.Contact Where ContactId = @Id'
EXECUTE sp_executesql @stmt = @chvQuery,
                    @Parms = N'@Id int',
                    @Id = 1
EXECUTE sp_executesql @stmt = @chvQuery,
                    @Parms = N'@Id int',
                    @Id = 313
```

Solutions based on this system stored procedure with parameters are better than solutions based on the execution of a character string using the Execute statement. The execution plan for the latter is seldom reused. It might happen that it will be reused only when parameter values supplied match those in the execution plan. Even in a situation in which you are changing the structure of a query, the number of possible combinations of query parameters is finite (and some of them are more probable than others). Therefore, reuse will be much more frequent if you force parameterization using sp_executesql.

When you use Execute, the complete batch has to be assembled in the form of a string each time. This requirement also takes time. If you are using sp_executesql, the batch will be assembled only the first time. All subsequent executions can use the same string and supply an additional set of parameters.

Parameters that are passed to sp_executesql do not have to be converted to characters. That time is wasted when you are using Execute, in which case parameter values of numeric type must be converted. By using all parameter values in their native data type with sp_executesql, you may also be able to detect errors more easily.

Security Implications

As a reminder, the following are two security concerns that are important in the case of dynamically assembled queries:

▶ Permissions on underlying tables

▶ SQL injection

Permissions on Underlying Tables

The fact that a caller has permission to execute the stored procedure that assembles the dynamic query does not mean that the caller has permission to access the underlying tables. You have to assign these permissions to the caller separately. Unfortunately, this requirement exposes your database—someone might try to exploit the fact that you are allowing more than the execution of predefined stored procedures.

SQL Injection

Dynamically assembled queries present an additional security risk. A malicious user could use a text box to type something like this:

```
Acme' DELETE INVENTORY --
```

A stored procedure (or application) can assemble this into a query, such as

```
Select *
from vInventory
Where Make = 'Acme' DELETE INVENTORY --'
```

The quote completes the parameter value and, therefore, the Select statement, and then the rest of the query is commented out with two dashes. Data from an entire table could be lost this way.

Naturally, a meticulous developer, such as you, would have permissions set to prevent this kind of abuse. Unfortunately, damage can be done even using a simple Select statement:

```
Acme' SELECT * FROM CUSTOMERS --
```

In this way, your competitor might get a list of your customers:

```
Select *
from vInventory
Where Make = 'Acme' SELECT * FROM CUSTOMERS --'
```

A hack like this is possible not just on string parameters; it might be even easier to perform on numeric parameters. A user can enter the following:

```
122121 SELECT * FROM CUSTOMERS
```

The result might be a query such as this:

```
Select *
from vInventory
Where InventoryId = 122121 SELECT * FROM CUSTOMERS
```

Fortunately, it's not too difficult to prevent this. No, you do not have to parse strings for SQL keywords; it's much simpler. The application must validate the content of text boxes. If a number or date is expected, the application must make sure that values really are of numeric or date data types. If text (such as a T-SQL keyword) is added, the application should prompt the user to supply a value of the appropriate data type.

Unfortunately, if a text box is used to specify a string, there is little that you can validate. The key is to prevent the user from adding a single quote (') to the query. There are several ways to do this. The quote is not a legal character in some types of fields (such as keys, e-mails, postal codes, and so forth) and the application should not accept it in such fields. In other types of fields (such as company names, personal names, descriptions, and so on), use of quotes may be valid. In that case, in the procedure that assembles the string, you should replace a single quote—char(39)—with two single quotes—char(39) + char(39)—and SQL Server will find a match for the string:

```
set @chvMake = Replace(@chvMake, char(39), char(39) + char(39))
```

The dynamic query will become a query that works as expected:

```
Select *
from vInventory
Where Make = 'Dejan''s Computers Inc.'
```

In the case in which someone tries to inject a SQL statement, SQL Server will just treat it as a part of the parameter string:

```
Select *
from vInventory
Where Make = 'Dejan'' SELECT * FROM CUSTOMERS --'
```

Another possibility is to replace a single quote—char(39)—with a character that looks similar onscreen but that is stored under a different code, such as (`)—char(96). Naturally, you have to make this substitution for all text boxes (on both data entry and search pages). In some organizations, this substitution might be inappropriate, since existing databases may already contain quotes.

NOTE

You are at risk not only when you are passing strings directly from a GUI into the stored procedure that is assembling a query, but also when an application is reading the field with injected SQL into a variable that will be used in a dynamic query. A user might attempt to weaken security with some administrative procedure—there is no need for direct interaction with the code by the attacker. Therefore, you should convert all string input parameters and local variables that are participating in the dynamic assembly of the query.

You also might want to prevent users from injecting special characters (such as wild cards) into strings that will be used in Like searches. The following function will make a string parameter safe for use in dynamic queries:

```
CREATE FUNCTION util.fnSafeDynamicString
-- make string parameters safe for use in dynamic strings
    (@chvInput nvarchar(max),
     @bitLikeSafe bit = 0) -- set to 1 if string will be used in LIKE
RETURNS nvarchar(max)
```

```
AS
BEGIN
    declare @chvOutput nvarchar(max)
    set @chvOutput = Replace(@chvInput, char(39), char(39) + char(39))
    if @bitLikeSafe = 1
    begin
        -- convert square bracket
        set @chvOutput = Replace(@chvOutput, '[', '[[]')
        -- convert wild cards
        set @chvOutput = Replace(@chvOutput, '%', '[%]')
        set @chvOutput = Replace(@chvOutput, '_', '[_]')
    end
    RETURN (@chvOutput)
END
```

You can test the function with the following:

```
SELECT 'select * from vInventory where Make = '''
    + util.fnSafeDynamicString ('Dejan' + char(39) + 's Computers Inc.', 0)
    + ''''
```

This test simulates a case in which a user enters the following text on the screen:

```
Dejan' s Computers Inc.
```

The result becomes

```
-----------------------------------------------------------------
select * from vInventory where Make = 'Dejan''s Computers Inc.'
(1 row(s) affected)
```

In the case of a Like query, you must prevent the user from using wild cards. The following query simulates a case in which a user enters % in the text box. It also assumes that the application or stored procedure is adding another % at the end of the query.

```
SELECT 'select * from vInventory where Make like '''
    + util.fnSafeDynamicString ('%a', 1)
    + '%'''
```

When you set the second parameter of the function to 1, the function replaces the first % character with [%], in which case it will not serve as a wild card:

```
---------------------------------------------
select * from vInventory where Make = '[%]a%'
(1 row(s) affected)
```

Optimistic Locking Using `timestamp` Values

When more than one user is working in a database, you might expect some concurrency problems to appear. The most common problem is the following: User A reads a record. User B also reads the record and then changes it. Any changes that user A now decides to commit to the database will overwrite the changes that user B made to it, without knowing that user B already changed it. Two standard solutions for this kind of problem are the following:

▶ Pessimistic locking

▶ Optimistic locking

In the *pessimistic locking* scenario, user A acquires a lock on the record so that nobody can change it until user A is finished with it. User A is a pessimist and expects that someone will attempt to change the record while user A is editing it.

NOTE

I will not go into the details of how locks are implemented. Locks are covered in detail in other SQL Server books. At this time, it is important to know that it is possible to mark a record so that nobody else can change it.

When user A changes the record, the lock is released and user B can now access the updated record and change it.

The trouble with this solution is that user A might go out for lunch—or on vacation—and, if user A didn't close the application that retrieved the record, the lock will not be released. This scenario is one of the reasons why this kind of solution is not recommended in a client/server environment.

In the *optimistic locking* scenario, user A locks the record only while he or she is actually performing the change. User A is an optimist who believes that nobody will change the record while user A is editing it. A mechanism in SQL Server will notify other users if somebody has changed the record in the meantime. The user can then decide either to abandon their changes or to overwrite the updated record.

A simple way to find out whether somebody has changed a record since the time user A read it would be to compare all fields. To run this comparison, user A must keep both an "original" and a "changed" record and needs to send them both to the server. Then, a process on the server must compare the original record with the current record in the table to make sure that it wasn't changed. Only then can the record be updated with the changed record. This process is obviously slow and increases network traffic, but there are solutions in the industry that use precisely this method.

timestamp

SQL Server has a timestamp data type. It is used for versioning records in a table. When you insert or update a record in a table with a timestamp field, SQL Server "timestamps" the change. Figure 15-2 demonstrates such behavior.

The table is created with a timestamp field. When a record is inserted, SQL Server automatically sets its value. When the record is updated, SQL Server increases the value of the timestamp.

It is important to realize that timestamp values are not actually a kind of timekeeping. They are just binary values that are increased with every change in the database and, therefore, are unique within the database. You should not make any assumptions about their values and growth. Somebody (or some process) might change something in the database concurrently, and even two changes that you executed consecutively might not have consecutive timestamp values.

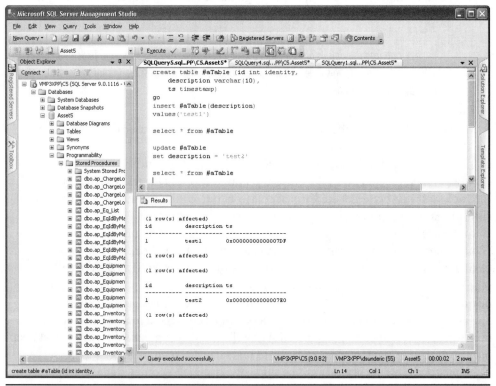

Figure 15-2 *Use of timestamp data type*

To make sure that nobody has changed a record since it was read, you should include criteria that compare original value (in variable) and current value (in column) in the Where clause:

```
update #aTable
set description = 'test3'
where id = 1
and ts = 0x00000000000007E0
```

The record will be updated only if the timestamp is unchanged.

You can wrap such update statement in a stored procedure:

```
Create Procedure dbo.ap_Contact_Update
-- update record from contact table
-- prevent user from overwriting changed record
    (
        @intContactId int,
        @chvFirstName varchar(30),
        @chvLastName varchar(30),
        @chvPhone typPhone,
        @chvFax typPhone,
        @chvEmail typEmail,
        @insOrgUnitId smallint,
        @chvUserName varchar(50),
        @tsOriginal timestamp
    )
As
Set nocount on

Update dbo.Contact
Set FirstName = @chvFirstName,
    LastName = @chvLastName,
    Phone = @chvPhone,
    Fax = @chvFax,
    Email = @chvEmail,
    OrgUnitId = @insOrgUnitId,
    UserName = @chvUserName
Where ContactId = @intContactId
and ts = @tsOriginal

return @@rowcount
```

You can execute this code from Transact-SQL:

```
Declare @intRecordCount int
Exec @intErrorCode = dbo.ap_Contact_Update1
                     1,         'Dejan',     'Sunderic',
                     '121-1111', '111-1112', 'dejans@hotmil.com',
                     1,         'dejans',    0x00000000000009C3
Select @ intRecordCount intRecordCount
```

You can determine if the record was updated by examining the returned value.

TSEqual() Function

The trouble with the previous solution is that you will not know what happens after the statement is executed. Maybe everything is okay and the record has been successfully changed. It is possible that the record was not updated because the timestamp was changed, but it is also possible that the record is not in the table anymore.

Old versions of SQL Server supported the TSEqual() function to compare timestamp values in the table and the Transact-SQL statement:

```
update #aTable
set description = 'test4'
where id = 1
and TSEQUAL(ts, 0x000000000000007A)
```

If they do not match, this function raises an error 532 and aborts the statement. Then you would know that the record has been changed in the meantime, and you could use appropriate error-handling actions properly (for example, the user can be prompted for further action). Unfortunately, on SQL Server 2005, you can use this function only against databases that are running in 80 (SQL Server 2000) or earlier compatibility mode (see sp_dbcmptlevel in BOL).

Full-text Search and Indexes

The Standard and Enterprise editions of SQL Server include SQL Server FullText Search service, a search engine that allows *full-text indexing and querying* like the search engines used to query the Web. You can search for combinations of words and phrases. It allows linguistic searches whereby the engine also matches variations of the original word (singular, plural, tenses, and so on). The result may be a simple list or a table that ranks how well the results match the search criteria. Part of the criteria may also be the proximity of words and phrases—that is, how close one word is to another.

These capabilities are different from those of standard database search engines, in which you can do the following:

► Search for an exact match of a word or phrase.

► Use wild card characters and the Like operator to search for character patterns.

► Use indexes only if a pattern matches the beginning of the field.

SQL Server FullText Search service was first introduced as a component of Internet Information Server. At that time, it was called Index Server.

I will not go into the details of SQL Server FullText Search service's architecture and administration, except to note that

► Full-text indexes are not stored in databases but in files (usually in C:\Program Files\Microsoft SQL Server\MSSQL\MSSQL.x\FTDATA).

► You have to set the full-text index search capability and create full-text catalogs on tables and columns explicitly.

► A table must have a unique index based on a single field to be indexed in this manner.

I will focus on full-text search capabilities. The two most important predicates are Contains and Freetext. They are designed to be used in the Where clause of a Select statement.

The Contains predicate returns true or false for records that contain specified keywords. Variations of this predicate accommodate linguistic searches for variations of words and for words that are in proximity to other words. For more details, see SQL Server Books OnLine.

Freetext orders the search engine to evaluate specified text and extract "important" words and phrases. It then constructs queries in the background to be executed against the table.

The following stored procedure implements different forms of full-text search on the ActivityLog.Note field:

```
Alter Procedure ap_FT_ActivityLog_Search
-- full-text search of ActivityLog.Note
-- this will only work if you enable full-text search
```

```
        (
                @chvKeywords varchar(255),
                @inySearchType tinyint
        )
As
set nocount on
--------- Constants -----------
declare     @c_Contains int,
            @c_FreeText int,
            @c_FormsOf int

Set         @c_Contains = 0
Set         @c_FreeText = 1
Set         @c_FormsOf = 2
--------- Constants -----------

if @inySearchType = @c_Contains
    exec ('select * from dbo.Activity Where Contains(Note, '
        + @chvKeywords + ')')
else if @inySearchType = @c_FreeText
    exec ('select * from dbo.Activity Where FreeText(Note, '
        + @chvKeywords + ')')
else if @inySearchType = @c_FormsOf
    exec ('select * from dbo.Activity '
        + 'Where FreeText(Note, FORMSOF(INFLECTIONAL,'
        + @chvKeywords + ')')

Return
```

NOTE

Full-text search has additional features related to the use of ContainsTable and FreeText table and the use of the Formsof, Near, and Weight keywords, but the description of these features is beyond the scope of this chapter and this book.

Nested Stored Procedures

Nested stored procedures are simply stored procedures that were called by other stored procedures. Using SQL Server 2005, it is possible to do 32 levels of nesting. You can investigate the current nesting level using the @@nestlevel function. This section explores methods for passing recordsets between a nested stored procedure and its caller.

Using Temporary Tables to Pass a Recordset to a Nested Stored Procedure

Some programming languages (such as Visual Basic and Pascal) use the concept of global and module variables. These types of variables are very useful for passing complex parameters (like arrays or recordsets) to a procedure when its parameter list supports only basic data types.

The same problem exists with stored procedures. You cannot pass a recordset through a parameter list to a stored procedure from the current batch or stored procedure, and neither recordsets nor local variables from the outer stored procedure (or batch) are visible to the inner stored procedure unless they are passed as a parameter to that procedure.

Unfortunately, SQL Server does not support "user-defined global variables." Modules, and therefore module variables, do not even exist in Transact-SQL.

One way to pass a recordset is to create and fill a temporary table and then reference that temporary table from the inner stored procedure, which will be able to see and access its contents. The following example consists of two stored procedures. The first is business-oriented and collects a list of properties associated with an inventory asset. The list is implemented as a temporary table:

```
Alter Procedure dbo.ap_InventoryProperties_Get_wTempTblOuter
/*
Return comma-delimited list of properties
that are describing asset.
i.e.: Property = Value unit;Property = Value unit;Property =
Value unit; Property = Value unit; Property = Value unit; Property =
Value unit;
--test:
exec dbo.ap_InventoryProperties_Get_wTempTblOuter 5

*/
     @intInventoryId int
As
set nocount on

declare     @chvProperties varchar(max)

Create table #List(Id int identity(1,1),
               Item varchar(255))

-- identify Properties associated with asset
```

```
insert into #List (Item)
    select Property + '=' + Value + ' ' + Coalesce(Unit, '') + '; '
    from InventoryProperty inner join Property
    on InventoryProperty.PropertyId = Property.PropertyId
    where InventoryProperty.InventoryId = @intInventoryId

-- call sp that converts records to a single varchar
exec util.ap_TempTbl2Varchar @chvProperties OUTPUT

-- display result
select @chvProperties Properties

drop table #List

return 0
go
```

The second stored procedure, the nested stored procedure, is not business-oriented—unlike the caller stored procedure, the nested stored procedure does not implement the business rule. It simply loops through the records in the temporary table (which was created in the caller stored procedure) and assembles them into a single `varchar` variable:

```
Alter Procedure util.ap_TempTbl2Varchar
-- Convert information from #List temporary table to a single varchar
    @chvResult varchar(max) output
As
set nocount on

declare   @intCountItems int,
          @intCounter int,
          @chvItem varchar(255)

-- set loop
select @intCountItems = Count(*),
       @intCounter = 1,
       @chvResult = ''
from #List

-- loop through list of items
while @intCounter <= @intCountItems
```

```
begin
    -- get one property
    select @chvItem = Item
    from #List
    where Id = @intCounter

    -- assemble list
    set @chvResult = @chvResult + @chvItem

    -- let's go another round and get another item
    set @intCounter = @intCounter + 1
end

return 0
go
```

You can execute the outer stored procedure from Management Studio:

```
exec dbo.ap_InventoryProperties_Get_TempTblOuter 5
```

SQL Server will return the result in the form of a string:

```
Properties
-----------------------------------------------------------------------
CPU=Pentium II ; RAM=64 MB; HDD=6.4 GB; Resolution=1024x768 ;
Weight=2 kg; Clock=366 MHz;
```

You may question when this kind of solution is justified and whether these stored procedures are coupled. It is true that neither of these stored procedures can function without the other. If you have other stored procedures that also use util.ap_TempTbl2Varchar, I would consider this solution justified.

Using a Cursor to Pass a Recordset to a Nested Stored Procedure

Similar solutions can be implemented using cursors. Cursors are also visible to, and accessible from, nested stored procedures.

The following example also consists of two stored procedures. The first is business-oriented and creates a cursor with properties associated with specified inventory:

```
create procedure dbo.ap_InventoryProperties_Get_wNestedCursor
/*
Return comma-delimited list of properties
that are describing asset.
i.e.: Property = Value unit;Property = Value unit;Property =
```

```
Value unit; Property = Value unit; Property = Value unit; Property =
Value unit;
--test:
declare @chvResult varchar(max)
exec dbo.ap_InventoryProperties_Get_wNestedCursor 5, @chvResult OUTPUT, 1
select @chvResult
*/
    (
        @intInventoryId int,
        @chvProperties varchar(max) OUTPUT,
        @debug int = 0
    )
As


Select @chvProperties = ''

Declare curItems Cursor For
    Select Property + '=' + [Value] + ' '
        + Coalesce([Unit], '') + '; ' Item
    From InventoryProperty Inner Join Property
    On InventoryProperty.PropertyId = Property.PropertyId
    Where InventoryProperty.InventoryId = @intInventoryId

Open curItems

Exec util.ap_Cursor2Varchar @chvProperties OUTPUT, @debug

Close curItems
Deallocate curItems

Return 0
Go
```

The second stored procedure is generic and converts information from a cursor
into a single variable:

```
ALTER Procedure util.ap_Cursor2Varchar
-- Process information from cursor initiated in calling sp.
-- Convert records into a single varchar.
    (
        @chvResult varchar(max) OUTPUT,
        @debug int = 0
    )
```

```
As


Declare    @chvItem varchar(255)

set @chvResult = ''

Fetch Next From curItems
Into @chvItem


While (@@FETCH_STATUS = 0)
Begin

     If @debug <> 0
         Select @chvItem Item

     -- assemble list
     Set @chvResult = @chvResult + @chvItem

     If @debug <> 0
         Select @chvResult chvResult

     Fetch Next From curItems
     Into @chvItem

End

Return
```

You can execute the outer stored procedure from Management Studio:

```
declare @chvResult varchar(max)
exec dbo.ap_InventoryProperties_Get_wNestedCursor 5, @chvResult OUTPUT, 1
select @chvResult
```

How to Process the Result Set of a Stored Procedure

From time to time, you will encounter stored procedures that return result sets that you need to process. This is not as simple as it sounds.

One option is to receive the result set in a client application or middleware component and process it from there. Sometimes this option is not acceptable, for a variety of reasons. For example, the result set might be too big, in which case network traffic could be considerably increased. Since the result set needs to be transferred to the middleware server before it is processed, the performance of the system could be degraded. There might be security implications—for example, you may determine that a user should have access only to a segment of a result set and not to the complete result set.

An alternative option is to copy the source code of the stored procedure into your stored procedure. This could be illegal, depending on the source of the original stored procedure. It also reduces the maintainability of your code, since you have two copies to maintain; if the other stored procedure is a system stored procedure, Microsoft can change its internals with the release of each new version of SQL Server. Your stored procedure will then need to be changed.

It is possible to collect the result set of a stored procedure in Transact-SQL code. You need to create a (temporary) table, the structure of which matches the structure of the result set exactly, and then redirect (insert) the result set into it. Then you can do whatever you want with it.

The following stored procedure uses the sp_dboption system stored procedure to obtain a list of all database options and to obtain a list of database options that are set on the Asset5 database. Records that have a structure identical to that of the result set as returned by the stored procedure are collected in temporary tables. The Insert statement can then store the result set in the temporary table. The contents of the temporary tables are later compared and a list of database options not currently set is returned to the caller.

```
Create Procedure util.ap_NonSelectedDBOption_List
-- return list of non-selected database options
-- test: exec util.ap_NonSelectedDBOption_List 'Asset5'
(
      @chvDBName sysname
)
As


Set Nocount On

Create Table #setable (name nvarchar(35))
Create Table #current (name nvarchar(35))

-- collect all options
Insert Into #setable
    Exec sp_dboption

-- collect current options
Insert Into #current
    Exec sp_dboption @dbname = @chvDBName
```

```
-- return non-selected
Select name non_selected
From #setable
Where name not in (Select name From #current)

Drop Table #setable
Drop Table #current


Return 0
```

The only trouble with this method is that you need to know the structure of the result set of the stored procedure in advance in order to create a table with the same structure, although this is not a problem for user-defined stored procedures. It used to be a problem for system stored procedures, but SQL Server Books OnLine now provides information regarding the result sets generated by these stored procedures.

NOTE

Unfortunately, it is not possible to capture the contents of a result set if a stored procedure returns more than one result set.

This technique also works with the Exec statement. For example, if you try to collect a result set from the DBCC command in this way, SQL Server will return an error. But you can encapsulate the DBCC statement in a string and execute it from Exec.

The following stored procedure returns the percentage of log space used in a specified database:

```
Create Procedure util.ap_LogSpacePercentUsed_Get
/*
-- Return percent of space used in transaction log for
-- the specified database.

--test:
declare @fltUsed float
exec util.ap_LogSpacePercentUsed_Get 'Asset5', @fltUsed OUTPUT
select @fltUsed Used
*/      (
            @chvDbName sysname,
            @fltPercentUsed float OUTPUT
    )
```

```
As
Set Nocount On


    Create Table #DBLogSpace
        (    dbname sysname,
             LogSizeInMB float,
             LogPercentUsed float,
             Status int
        )

-- get log space info. for all databases
    Insert Into #DBLogSpace
        Exec ('DBCC SQLPERF (LogSpace)')

-- get percent for specified database
    select @fltPercentUsed = LogPercentUsed
    from #DBLogSpace
    where dbname = @chvDbName


drop table #DBLogSpace

return
```

You can test this stored procedure from Management Studio, as shown on Figure 15-3.

These techniques were extremely important before SQL Server 2000. In the last two versions it is now possible to use the `table` data type as a return value for user-defined functions. You learned how to use table-valued user-defined functions in Chapter 10. Unfortunately, it is still not possible to use a `table` variable as the output parameter of a stored procedure.

You have another option available when you want to pass a result set (or multiple result sets) to a calling stored procedure—you can use the `cursor` data type as the output parameter of a stored procedure. In the following example, ap_InventoryProperties_Get_wCursor creates and opens a cursor. The content of the cursor is then returned to the calling procedure.

```
Create Procedure dbo.ap_InventoryProperties_Get_wCursor
-- Return Cursor that contains properties
-- that are describing selected asset.

    (
        @intInventoryId int,
        @curProperties Cursor Varying Output
    )
```

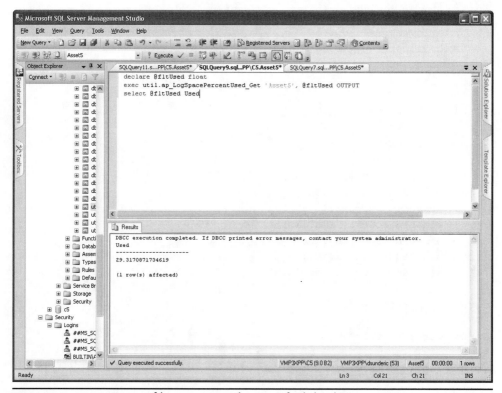

Figure 15-3   *Percentage of log space used in specified database*

```
As

Set @curProperties = Cursor Forward_Only Static For
   Select Property, Value, Unit
   From InventoryProperty inner join Property
   On InventoryProperty.PropertyId = Property.PropertyId
   Where InventoryProperty.InventoryId = @intInventoryId

Open @curProperties

Return
```

The preceding stored procedure will be called from the following stored procedure:

```
Create Procedure dbo.ap_InventoryProperties_Get_UseNestedCursor
-- return comma-delimited list of properties
-- that are describing asset.
-- i.e.: Property = Value unit;Property = Value unit;
-- Property = Value unit;Property = Value unit;...
```

```
    (
        @intInventoryId int,
        @chvProperties varchar(max) OUTPUT,
        @debug int = 0
    )

As

Declare @intCountProperties int,
        @intCounter int,
        @chvProperty varchar(50),
        @chvValue varchar(50),
        @chvUnit varchar(50),
        @insLenProperty smallint,
        @insLenValue smallint,
        @insLenUnit smallint,
        @insLenProperties smallint

Set @chvProperties = ''

Declare @CrsrVar Cursor

Exec dbo.ap_InventoryProperties_Get_wCursor @intInventoryId,
                                            @CrsrVar Output

Fetch Next From @CrsrVar
Into @chvProperty, @chvValue, @chvUnit

While (@@FETCH_STATUS = 0)
Begin

    Set @chvUnit = Coalesce(@chvUnit, '')

    If @debug <> 0
        Select @chvProperty Property,
               @chvValue [Value],
               @chvUnit [Unit]

    -- assemble list
    Set @chvProperties = @chvProperties
                        + @chvProperty + '='
                        + @chvValue + ' '
                        + @chvUnit + '; '
    If @debug <> 0
        Select @chvProperties chvProperties
```

```
Fetch Next From @CrsrVar
Into @chvProperty, @chvValue, @chvUnit

End

Close @CrsrVar
Deallocate @CrsrVar

Return
```

It is the responsibility of the caller to properly close and deallocate the cursor at the end.

TIP

You should not use a cursor as an output parameter of a stored procedure unless you have to. Such a solution is inferior because procedures are coupled and prone to errors. You should use table-valued user-defined functions as part of your Select statements instead.

Using Identity Values

In previous chapters, I introduced the function of identity values in a table. They are used to generate surrogate keys—unique identifiers based on sequential numbers.

A Standard Problem and Solution

Identity values are similar to the `autonumber` data type in Access tables, but there is one difference that generates many questions in Usenet newsgroups among developers who are used to Access/ADO behavior. When you insert a record into a table, the value of the `autonumber` field is immediately available in Access. Unfortunately, due to the nature of the client/server environment, this is not the case in SQL Server.

The best way to insert a record into a SQL Server table and obtain an identity key is to use a stored procedure. The following stored procedure, ap_Inventory_Insert, presents such a solution. A new record is inserted into a table and the key is read using the Scope_Indentity() function.

```
Create Procedure dbo.ap_Inventory_Insert
-- insert inventory record and return Id
    @intEquipmentId int,
    @intLocationId int,
    @inyStatusId tinyint,
    @intLeaseId int,
```

```
        @intLeaseScheduleId int,
        @intOwnerId int,
        @mnsRent smallmoney,
        @mnsLease smallmoney,
        @mnsCost smallmoney,
        @inyAcquisitionTypeID int,
        @intInventoryId int OUTPUT

As
Set Nocount On

Insert into dbo.Inventory (EquipmentId, LocationId, StatusId,
            LeaseId, LeaseScheduleId, OwnerId,
            Rent, Lease, Cost,
            AcquisitionTypeID)
  Values (     @intEquipmentId, @intLocationId, @inyStatusId,
            @intLeaseId, @intLeaseScheduleId, @intOwnerId,
            @mnsRent, @mnsLease, @mnsCost,
            @inyAcquisitionTypeID)

Select @intInventoryId = Scope_Indentity()

Return
```

Identity Values and Triggers

The @@identity function/global variable is a traditional alternative to the Scope_Identity() function. However, there is one significant difference. @@identity returns the last identity value set in the current connection, while Scope_Identity() returns the last identity value that was set in the current scope (for example, in a stored procedure). If the table in which the record was inserted (in this case, Inventory) has a trigger that inserts a record into some other table with an identity key, the value of that key will be recorded in @@identity.

You can reproduce this behavior using the following script. It must be executed against the *tempdb* database.

```
Create Table a (a_id int identity(1,1),
            a_desc varchar(20),
            b_desc varchar(20))
Go
```

```
Create Table b (b_id int identity(1,1),
                b_desc varchar(20))
Go

Create Trigger tr_a_I
On dbo.a
After Insert     -- For Insert
As

If @@Rowcount = 0
    Return

Insert Into b (b_desc)
    Select b_desc from inserted
Go
```

Now execute this batch:

```
Insert into b (b_desc)
Values ('1')

Insert into a (a_desc, b_desc)
Values ('aaa', 'bbb')

Select @@identity [IdentityValue]
```

SQL Server returns the following result:

```
 (1 row(s) affected)


 (1 row(s) affected)


IdentityValue
----------------------------------------
2

(1 row(s) affected)
```

The first Insert statement adds the first record to table b. The second Insert statement adds the first record in a table. Because there is a trigger on the table, another record (the second one) will be inserted into table b, and the value of @@identity will be set to 2. If there was no trigger, the Select statement would return a value of 1.

This is not a problem if you use the Scope_Identity() function. It returns the last identity value generated in the current scope of the current process. The following example adds this function to the code executed earlier against the *tempdb* database:

```
Insert into b (b_desc)
Values ('1')

Insert into a (a_desc, b_desc)
Values ('aaa', 'bbb')


Select @@identity [@@Identity], SCOPE_IDENTITY() [SCOPE_IDENTITY()]
```

When you execute it, notice that the Scope_Identity() function returns the proper result:

```
(1 row(s) affected)

(1 row(s) affected)

@@Identity                                      SCOPE_IDENTITY()
------------------------------------            -----------------------------
4                                               2

(1 row(s) affected)
```

TIP

You should always use Scope_Identity() instead of the @@identity function.

GUIDs

Distributed environments have different requirements for the generation of unique keys. A typical example is a database of sales representatives who are carrying notebook computers with local databases installed on them. These users do not have to be connected to a central database. They do the majority of their work locally and then replicate the information in their local database to the central database once in a while. The use of identity fields as a unique key will lead to unique key violations, unless the key is composite and consists of an identity field and another field that is unique to the user. Another solution could be to divide key ranges between users (for example, by setting an identity seed differently in each database). Each of these solutions has different limitations.

One way to generate unique keys is to use GUIDs (globally unique identifiers). You can find more details about the `uniqueidentifier` data type in Appendix A. When a column in a table is assigned this data type, it does not mean that its (unique) value will be generated automatically. The unique value must be generated using the NewID() function.

Typically, a GUID value is generated as a default value of a table, as shown in the following code:

```
Create Table Location(
 LocationId uniqueidentifier NOT NULL DEFAULT newid(),
 Location varchar(50) not null,
 CompanyId int NOT NULL,
 PrimaryContactName varchar(60) NOT NULL,
 Address varchar(30) NOT NULL,
 City varchar(30) NOT NULL,
 ProvinceId varchar(3) NULL,
 PostalCode varchar(10) NOT NULL,
 Country varchar(20) NOT NULL,
 Phone varchar(15) NOT NULL,
 Fax varchar(15) NULL
)
Go
```

You can also generate a GUID in a stored procedure:

```
Create Procedure dbo.ap_Location_Insert
 @Location varchar(50),
 @CompanyId int,
 @PrimaryContactName varchar(60),
 @Address varchar(30) ,
 @City varchar(30) ,
 @ProvinceId varchar(3) ,
 @PostalCode varchar(10),
 @Country varchar(20) ,
 @Phone varchar(15),
 @Fax varchar(15),
 @LocationGUID uniqueidentifier OUTPUT

AS
Set @LocationGUID  = NewId()

Insert Into dbo.Location (Location_id, Location, CompanyId,
                          PrimaryContactName, Address, City,
                          ProvinceId, PostalCode, Country,
                          Phone, Fax)
```

```
values (@LocationGUID, @Location, @CompanyId,
        @PrimaryContactName, @Address, @City,
        @ProvinceId, @PostalCode, @Country,
        @Phone, @Fax)
Return @@error
```

The stored procedure will return the GUID value to the caller.

A While Loop with Min() or Max() Functions

It is possible to iterate through a table or recordset using a While statement with the aggregate() function, which returns extreme values: Min() and Max(). Take a look at the following batch:

```
declare Value int
-- get first value
Select @Value = MIN(Value)
From aTable

-- loop
While @Value is not null
Begin
    -- do something instead of just displaying a value
    Select @Value value

    -- get next value
    Select @Value = MIN(Value)
    From aTable
    Where Value > @Value
End
```

The first Select statement with the Min() function obtains a first value from the set (table):

```
Select @Value = MIN(Value)
From aTable
```

The next value is obtained in a loop as a minimal value bigger than the previous one:

```
Select @Value = MIN(Value)
From aTable
Where Value > @Value
```

If no records qualify as members of the set, an aggregate() function will return null. You can then use null as a criterion to exit the loop:

```
While @Value is not null
```

To demonstrate this method, the following rewrites prSpaceUsedByTables, which displays the space used by each user-defined table in the current database:

```
Create Procedure util.ap_SpaceUsedByTables_4
-- loop through table names in current database
     -- display info about amount of space used by each table

-- demonstration of while loop

As
Set nocount on
Declare @TableName sysname

-- get first table name
Select @TableName = Min(name)
From sys.sysobjects
Where xtype = 'U'

While @TableName is not null
Begin

    -- display space used
    Exec sp_spaceused  @TableName

    -- get next table
    Select @TableName = Min(name)
    From sysobjects
    Where xtype = 'U'
    And name > @TableName
End

Return 0
```

This was just an academic example. Naturally, the proper solution includes a temporary table to collect all results and display them at the end in one recordset. Note that I am not talking about a temporary table such as the one used in Chapter 3 for looping using a While statement.

You can step backward through the recordset if you use the Max() function and if you compare the old record and the remainder of the set using the < operator.

TIP

This method may be a quick solution for problems that require iteration. However, solutions based on set operations usually provide superior performance.

Looping with sp_MSForEachTable and sp_MSForEachDb

You can find and review the sp_MSForEachTable and sp_MSForEachDb system stored procedures in the *master* database, but they are not documented in SQL Server Books OnLine. Microsoft has designed them to support writing a single statement that can perform the same activity on all databases on the current server or on all tables in the current database.

To demonstrate this, set Query Analyzer to Result In Text and execute the following:

```
exec sp_MSforEachDb
@Command1 = "Print '?'",
@Command2 = "select count(name) from ?.dbo.sysobjects where xtype = 'U'"
```

SQL Server returns a count of user-defined tables from each database on the current server:

```
Asset5
----------
36

DEPLOY
----------
0

master
----------
10

...
```

The @Command1 and @Command2 parameters are used to specify the actions that the stored procedure will execute against each database. The database name was replaced with a question mark. It is possible to specify up to three commands (using @Command3). Behind the scenes, the stored procedure will open a cursor for the records in the sysdatabases table (which contains a list of existing databases) and dynamically assemble a batch that will be executed against each record in a loop.

The following command creates a report about space usage of each database:

```
exec sp_MSforEachDb @Command1 = "use ? exec sp_Spaceused"
```

It is even more interesting to run sp_spaceused against all tables in the current database:

```
exec sp_MSforEachTable @Command1 = "sp_spaceused '?'"
```

Unfortunately, the result is not nicely aligned in either text or grid mode.

You can also get a number of records in each table:

```
exec sp_MSforEachTable
    @Command1 = "Print '?'",
    @Command2 = "select Count(*) from ?"
```

In the last two queries, the result is not ordered as you might expect. It simply follows the order of records in systables (in other words, the order of creation). If you want to order it by table name, you must use the @whereand parameter:

```
exec sp_MSforEachTable
    @command1 = "exec sp_spaceused '?'",
    @whereand = "order by 1"
```

This parameter was originally designed to allow you to add a Where clause, but since the query is dynamically assembled, you can sneak an Order By clause into it as well.

You can use the @replacechar parameter to specify a different placeholder for database and table names. This parameter is useful when your commands require the use of a question mark—for example, as a wild card in the Like clause.

If a command should be executed only once before or after the loop, you should use the @precommand and @postcommand parameters.

Property Management

One of the features that I wanted to see in SQL Server for a long time is the capability to add descriptions to database objects. Microsoft Access had that feature from the start. Naturally, you could be even more ambitious. It would be helpful on some projects to be able to store additional attributes such as field formats, input masks, captions, and the location and size of screen fields in the database. The more things you manage centrally, the fewer maintenance and deployment issues you will have later in production.

Microsoft introduced *extended properties* in SQL Server 2000 to address this. You can define extended properties, store them in the database, and associate them with database objects. Each database object can have any number of extended properties, and an extended property can store a sql_variant value up to 7,500 bytes long.

SQL Server has three stored procedures and one function for managing extended properties. The sp_addextendedproperty, sp_updateextendedproperty, and sp_dropextendedproperty stored procedures are used to create, change, or delete extended properties, respectively. They all have very unusual syntax. The following example examines this syntax in sp_addextendedproperty:

```
sp_addextendedproperty
    [@name =]{'property_name'}
    [, [@value =]{'extended_property_value'}
        [, [@level0type =]{'level0_object_type'}
        , [@level0name =]{'level0_object_name'}
            [, [@level1type =]{'level1_object_type'}
            , [@level1name =]{'level1_object_name'}
                    [, [@level2type =]{'level2_object_type'}
                    , [@level2name =]{'level2_object_name'}
                    ]
            ]
        ]
    ]
```

Here, @name and @value are the name and value of the extended property. Other parameters define the name and type of the object with which the extended property will be associated. For this reason, database objects are divided into three levels:

1. User, user-defined type
2. Table, view, stored procedure, function, rule, default
3. Column, index, constraint, trigger, parameter

If you want to assign an extended property to an object of the second level, you must also specify an object of the first level. If you want to assign an extended property to an object of the third level, you must also specify an object of the second level. For example, to specify an extended property Format to be associated with the column Phone in the table Contact, you must specify the owner of the table:

```
Exec sp_addextendedproperty 'Format', '(999)999-9999',
                    'schema', dbo,
                            'table', Contact,
                                    'column', Phone
```

To update the description of an object such as a stored procedure, you need to define the extended property named MS_Description on an object:

```
EXEC sys.sp_addextendedproperty @name=N'MS_Description',
        @value=N'List records in Eq table.' ,
        @level0type=N'SCHEMA', @level0name=N'dbo',
        @level1type=N'PROCEDURE', @level1name=N'ap_Eq_List'
```

The fn_ListExtendedProperty() function is designed to list the extended properties of an object. It requires that you specify objects in the same manner as the stored procedures do. If you want, you can use fn_ListExtendedProperty() to test for the presence of an extended property to determine if you need to add or update it:

```
declare @v      sysname
declare @table  sysname
declare @col    sysname

set @table = N'Contact'
SET @v     = N'persons that are in relationships in Asset'

if not exists(
    SELECT objtype, objname, name, value
    FROM fn_listextendedproperty (NULL, 'schema', 'dbo',
                                    'table', 'Contact',
                                    default, default)
)
    EXECUTE sp_addextendedproperty N'MS_Description', @v,
                                    N'SCHEMA', N'dbo',
                                    N'TABLE', @table,
                                    NULL, NULL
else
    EXECUTE sp_updateextendedproperty N'MS_Description', @v,
                                    N'SCHEMA', N'dbo',
                                    N'TABLE', @table,
                                    NULL, NULL

set @table = N'Contact'
SET @v     = N'surrogate identifier'
set @col   = N'ContactID'
```

```
if not exists(SELECT objtype, objname, name, value
        FROM fn_listextendedproperty (NULL, 'schema', 'dbo',
                                            'table', @table,
                                            'column', @col))
    EXECUTE sp_addextendedproperty N'MS_Description', @v,
                                N'SCHEMA', N'dbo',
                                N'TABLE', @table,
                                N'COLUMN', @col
else
    EXECUTE sp_updateextendedproperty N'MS_Description', @v,
                                N'SCHEMA', N'dbo',
                                N'TABLE', @table,
                                N'COLUMN', @col
GO
```

CHAPTER 16

Debugging

D ebugging and error handling seem like such negative topics. By admitting debugging as a necessary phase of development and error handling as a required practice, we seem to admit to weakness in our abilities as developers. But we are not the computers themselves: we cannot account for all contingencies when we write code. So, to find the error of our ways after the fact, we need a coherent approach to the identification and resolution of defects in our code and a coherent strategy for handling errors in our code as they occur. The process of debugging, therefore, is an integral part of both the development and stabilization phases of software production.

What Is a "Bug"?

You have probably heard errors and defects found in software referred to as "bugs." This word has found its way into our everyday language and reality so that we now seem to regard the bug as normal and inevitable—like death and taxes. However, not many people know how this term actually entered the language.

It happened in the dim, distant technological past when computers occupied whole rooms (if not buildings). On one occasion, technicians were investigating a malfunction on such a computer. Much to their surprise, they found the cause of the circuit malfunction to be a large moth that had been attracted by the heat and glow of the machine's vacuum tubes. Over time, all computer-related errors (particularly the ones that were difficult to explain) came to be known as bugs.

Sometimes we anthropomorphize bugs—give them human attributes. They can seem in turn capricious and malicious, but the bugs we experience in application and database development are not related to mythological folk such as gremlins. Bugs are very real, but their causes are inevitably human. Computers bear no malice toward users or developers, compilers do not play practical jokes, and operating systems are not being stubborn when they refuse to operate as expected. No, when you encounter an error, you can be sure that it was you or another programmer who caused it. What you need to do is find the offending code and fix it, but to find bugs efficiently and painlessly, you need to establish a debugging process—a formal routine with well-defined steps and rules.

The Debugging Process

The objectives of the debugging process are to identify and resolve the defects present in a software product. This process consists of two phases:

▶ Identification

▶ Resolution

Identification

The identification phase consists of two primary activities:

▶ Stabilize the error.

▶ Find the source of the error.

Stabilize the Error

In most cases, identifying the error consumes 95 percent of your debugging time, whereas fixing it often requires just a few minutes. The first step in identifying an error is to stabilize (or isolate) the error. You must make the error repeatable. What this means is that you must find a test case that causes the error to recur predictably. If you are not able to reproduce the error, you will not be able to identify its cause nor will you be able to fix it.

But we need to qualify the test case in another way. It is not enough to create a test case that will cause the error to occur predictably. You must also strive to simplify the test case in order to identify the minimum circumstances under which the error will occur. Refining the test case is certainly the most difficult aspect of debugging, and cultivating this skill will greatly enhance your debugging efficiency, while removing a large part of the frustration. Stabilizing the error answers the question, "What is the error?" With this knowledge in hand, you can go on to answer the question, "Why does the error occur?"

Find the Source of the Error

After you identify the minimum circumstances under which the error will occur, you can proceed to find the source of the error. If your code is properly structured and well written, this search should not be a difficult task. You can apply a variety of tools at this point:

▶ **Your brain**   The most important debugging tool at your disposal is your brain. If you can follow the program's execution and understand its logic, you will be able to understand the problem as well. When you have learned everything your test cases can teach you, you can create a hypothesis, and then prove it through further testing.

▶ **SQL Server**   Some errors will be clearly reported by SQL Server. Be sure that your client application picks up and displays all error messages reported by the server. Also, try using the Query editor window to execute your stored procedures without the client application. Naturally, you should take care to use the same parameters that were passed from the client application when you produced the error.

▶ **SQL Profiler**   Some errors will occur only when the application is executing stored procedures and queries in SQL Server. Too often, the application does not properly collect all error information, and then application and database developers play ping-pong, blaming each other for the reported defect. SQL Profiler can resolve such disputes. It can be configured to collect information about events such as stored procedures, transactions, and server, database, and session events. When you analyze the collected data, you will be able to determine which of the stored procedure's calls and parameters are responsible for the individual errors.

▶ **Transact-SQL Debugger**   An integral part of Visual Studio 2005 is the Transact-SQL Debugger. It enables you to set breakpoints in your code and pause execution to investigate and change the contents of local variables, functions, and input and output parameters. The Transact-SQL Debugger lets you step through the code of your stored procedures and triggers. It is unfortunate, however, that Management Studio does not contain a debugger, as Query Analyzer did.

Resolution

Resolving defects in code is usually much easier than finding those defects, but do not take this phase too lightly. At this point in the development cycle, when the product shipping date is looming large, you may be tempted by the "quick fix." Resist this temptation: it often causes developers to introduce new errors while fixing the old ones. It is seldom an issue of carelessness or incompetence, but rather of increased pressure to fix and ship a product.

The resolution phase consists of two primary activities:

▶ Develop the solution in a test environment.

▶ Implement the solution in the production environment.

Develop the Solution in a Test Environment

To consistently resolve defects in your code, you need to assemble two critical ingredients—a test environment and source code control.

▶ **Test environment**   SQL Server is especially susceptible to errors generated in haste to solve a problem because a stored procedure is compiled and saved as a single action.

If you are trying to resolve defects on the production system, you are performing brain surgery *in vivo*. Although it is possible to perform fixes in a production environment, it is always much better to step back, spend adequate time understanding the problem, and then attempt to solve the problem outside of the production environment.

If a test environment does not exist or if the existing test environment is outdated, you may be tempted to save time with a "quick and dirty" fix. Before you go down this path, however, you should consider the resources that would be required to reverse the changes made if you happen to make a mistake. Anything you do, you should be able to undo quickly and easily.

Let it be understood, loud and clear: you need a test environment!

▶ **Source code control**   Keep source code of your procedures and database objects. Source code control gives you a snapshot of your application at critical points in the development cycle and allows you to "turn back the clock." It gives you the ability to reverse changes if you find they have introduced new problems or failed to solve the existing one. Visual SourceSafe, which is examined in Chapter 17, is a perfect tool for this function.

Source code control works best if you take a patient approach to debugging. You should save versions often to help you identify the source of errors when they occur. It is a poor practice to make multiple changes per version. Old and new errors tend to overlap and lead you to incorrect conclusions.

Implement the Solution in the Production Environment

Once you are satisfied with the change, you should implement it in the production environment. Then test. Then test again. You should not assume that it will work in the production environment because it worked in the test environment. If, after stringent testing, everything is still functioning properly, you should then look for other places in the code and database structure where similar errors may exist.

Debugging Tools and Techniques

Modern development environments contain sophisticated tools to help you debug your applications. The Transact-SQL Debugger in Visual Studio will help you to identify and fix problems in your code. However, even if your development environment does not support the Transact-SQL Debugger (if you do not have Visual Studio 2005), there are techniques you can employ to achieve the same results. I will discuss these techniques in "Poor Man's Debugger" later in this chapter.

Transact-SQL Debugger in Visual Studio 2005

This section demonstrates the use of the Transact-SQL Debugger from Visual Studio 2005. The major difference between debugging stored procedures and debugging within other programming languages is that you do not need to run the application to debug a single procedure.

The process for starting the debugger is to point to the stored procedure and invoke the Step Into Stored Procedure command:

1. Open Visual Studio.
2. Select View | Server Explorer.
3. In Server Explorer, right-click to open the context-sensitive menu and choose Add Connection.
4. In the Choose Data Source window, select Microsoft SQL Server and verify that .NET Data Provider for SQL Server is also selected. Click Continue.
5. In the Add Connection window, specify server name, authentication, and database name (as usual, use Asset5).
6. Test the connection and if everything is working, click OK to close each window.
7. Server Explorer now contains a node showing the connection that you have described. It functions like nodes in the Object Browser of Management Studio. Expand the nodes until you find Stored Procedures.
8. Right-click dbo.ap_InventoryProperties_Get_TempTblOuter to display the context-sensitive menu.
9. Choose Step Into Stored Procedure (instead of the usual Execute) and the program will initiate the debugging session.
10. Fill in the input parameters in the Run Stored Procedure window:

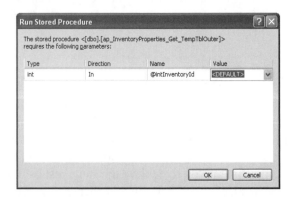

11. When you click OK, the program will display a window with the stored procedure in Debugging mode (see Figure 16-1).

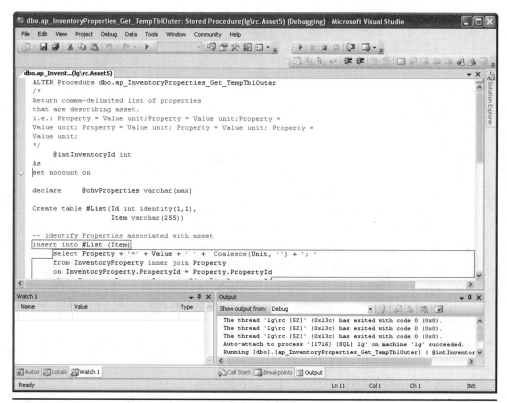

Figure 16-1   *A stored procedure in Debugging mode*

The Transact-SQL Debugger opens the source code of the procedure and pauses on the first executable statement. A small yellow arrow on the left border marks the position of the statement to be executed next.

Debug Windows

The commands in the Debug menu become enabled, as do several more docked windows displayed as tabbed panes, described here, that enable you to examine the state of the environment.

▶   **Locals window**   Allows you to scroll through the local variables and parameters of the stored procedure and to see its current contents and data type:

As the stored procedure's code is executed, the values of variables change. To help you follow the execution, the Transact-SQL Debugger colors the values of variables that were changed in the previous statement. The Locals window allows you to change values of variables interactively during execution of the code (through the context-sensitive menu for the Value column).

▶ **Watch window**   Has a similar function to the Locals window. You can type, or drag from the code, a Transact-SQL expression to be evaluated in this window. This feature is useful when you want to investigate the values of expressions in If, While, Case, and other similar statements. It is possible to work with up to four Watch windows.

▶ **Output window**   Displays result sets returned by the Select statement and messages sent from the Print statement (see Figure 16-1).

▶ **Breakpoints window**   Allows the user to define code locations (lines) and conditions for pausing execution. However, you can also associate it with some additional conditions. For example, you may want to create a breakpoint that pauses execution when a specified location is reached a specified number of times:

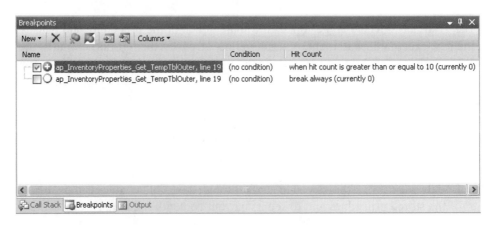

These panes have more than four tabs, but only these mean anything for the Transact-SQL Debugger. The other tabs are used to debug client applications.

Breakpoints

Breakpoints are markers in code that serve to stop execution when certain conditions are met. In the Transact-SQL Debugger, you can use only a very limited set of conditions. Typically, you can only specify a condition in which the execution has reached the position of the breakpoint or in which a breakpoint has been reached a selected number of times. In other .NET languages such as C# and Visual Basic, the condition can apply when a variable changes value, when a Boolean expression is true, or even when execution starts a specified process or thread.

Breakpoints can be set three ways:

▶ Using the toolbar in the Breakpoints window

▶ Clicking the left edge of the code window

▶ Pressing F9 when the cursor is on the line in which you want to place a breakpoint

Visual Studio marks the breakpoint with a big red dot at the beginning of the line. If the dot contains a plus (+), the breakpoint contains additional criteria.

The toolbar and the Debug menu can contain additional commands for managing breakpoints. You can temporarily enable or disable all breakpoints and permanently remove them. A single breakpoint can be removed by clicking the dot or by pressing F9 when the cursor is on the line containing the breakpoint.

Stepping Through Execution

The majority of commands available on the Debug menu target execution control. Most of the time, you will use the Step Into or Step Over command to step through a stored procedure. These commands execute one Transact-SQL statement at a time. The difference between them is in the way they behave when they encounter a nested stored procedure:

▶ **Step Into** (F11)   Opens the code of the nested stored procedure and lets you step through it.

▶ **Step Over** (F10)   The nested stored procedure is treated as any other Transact-SQL statement and is executed in a single step.

▶ **Step Out** (SHIFT-F11)   Enables you to execute the rest of the nested stored procedures without pause and halts only when the stored procedure is completed in the calling stored procedure.

▶ **Run To Cursor** (CTRL-F10)   Enables you to position the cursor somewhere in the code and to execute everything to that point in a single step. In essence, this command lets you set a temporary breakpoint.

- ▶ **Continue** (F5)   Resumes execution of the code until the (original entry) procedure is completed or until the next breakpoint is reached.

- ▶ **Stop Debugging** (SHIFT-F5)   Discontinues execution.

NOTE

Visual Studio menus can be customized to contain different sets of options. If your configuration does not contain options that are mentioned in this section, go to Tools | Customize, open the Commands tab, click the Debug category, and drag commands from the list to the Debug menu. Additionally, you can access these options using keyboard shortcuts even when the commands are not on the menu.

One of my favorite features in the Visual Studio debugger is the ability to continue execution from the position of the cursor. Unfortunately, due to the architecture of the Transact-SQL Debugger, the Set Next Step command is not available. Another cool feature that was originally available in Visual Basic and then missing in early versions of Visual Studio .NET was the ability to modify code on the fly (during debugging).

Debugging CLR Database Objects

You must also use Visual Studio 2005 if you want to use the debugger against CLR database objects. You can use the standard set of debugger features:

- ▶ Use Step In, Step Over, Step Out, and Run To Cursor to control execution of code.

- ▶ Step in from the CLR database object code into Transact-SQL code and vice versa.

- ▶ Investigate or modify values of variables.

- ▶ Investigate results and messages that are returned to the caller.

- ▶ Use breakpoints to pause execution of the CLR code.

SQL Server projects (in Visual Studio 2005) contain a Test Scripts node (see Solution Explorer). Scripts in this node are entry points into the debugger. By default, the node contains just the Test.sql script. Everything in this script is initially commented out. You can enable a segment or simply add new lines to execute the target database objects. The batch in this script should work similarly to batches executed from the Query window in Management Studio.

NOTE

Alternatively, you can create a new script under the Test Scripts node. In this case, you can select which test script you want to use by choosing Set As Default Debug Script in the context-sensitive menu for the script.

To start debugging you should follow these steps:

1. Set the breakpoint in the CLR object (or Transact-SQL code) where you want to start debugging.
2. Choose Debug | Start Debugging (or press F5).

Let's walk through debugging a simple managed stored procedure:

1. Create a new database project, for example, in C#.
2. Add a stored procedure (template) to it.
3. Change the code of the stored procedure template to be something like this:

```csharp
using System;
using System.Data;
using System.Data.SqlClient;
using System.Data.SqlTypes;
using Microsoft.SqlServer.Server;

public partial class StoredProcedures
{
    [Microsoft.SqlServer.Server.SqlProcedure]
    public static void cp_DebugTest()
    {
        int count = 1;
        SqlContext.Pipe.Send("Hello world 1!\n");
        count++;
        SqlContext.Pipe.Send("Hello world 2!\n");

        using (SqlConnection conn =
            new SqlConnection("Context Connection=true"))
        {
            string EqType = "";

            // Set up the command object used to execute the stored proc
            SqlCommand cmd = new SqlCommand("dbo.ap_EqType_List", conn);
            cmd.CommandType = CommandType.StoredProcedure;

            //execute sp
            conn.Open();

            using (SqlDataReader reader = cmd.ExecuteReader())
            {
                while (reader.Read()) // Advance one row, until you can
```

```
                        {
                            // Return output parameters from returned data stream
                            //id = reader.GetInt32(0); // do not need first column
                            EqType = EqType + reader.GetString(1) + ", ";
                        }
                    }
                }

            }
        };
```

4. Position the cursor on the first line in the method and press F9 to set the breakpoint.

5. Open Test.sql from the Test Scripts node of Solution Explorer and add the following code to it:

```
Exec dbo.cp_DebugTest
```

6. Choose Debug | Start Debugging from the menu (or press F5). The program will spend some time hooking the debugger to the connection that is being executed. You can see its progress in the Output pane of Visual Studio.

7. Finally, the debugger will stop on the breakpoint (see Figure 16-2). The yellow error will point to the line that needs to be executed next.

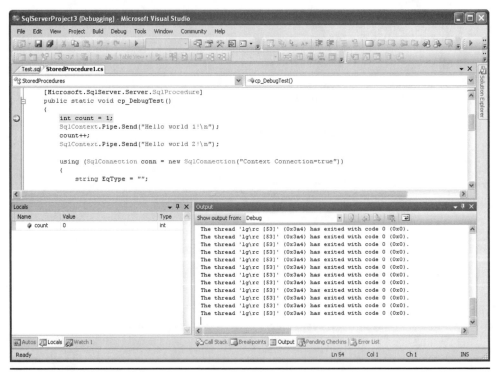

Figure 16-2   *SQLCLR debugging*

8. This is the point where you can take control of the execution (using comments as in Debug | Step Into) or investigate and set the values of variables. Start pressing F11 (Step Into) and the debugger will eventually step into the Transact-SQL stored procedure (see Figure 16-3).

9. Continue executing Step Into and the program will step out of the Transact-SQL procedure and go back to the CLR stored procedure.

During all of these steps, all result sets and string messages (such as strings in the Print statement or Raiserror) will be collected in the Output window, and you can scroll up and down to review them.

The Visual Studio debugger can only hook to connections initiated by these scripts, not to existing connections initiated from some other client such as Management Studio. It is possible to debug multiple Transact-SQL sessions on one server at one time, but this practice could lead to locking issues on the server. On the other hand, it is possible to debug only a single session at a time for any CLR database object.

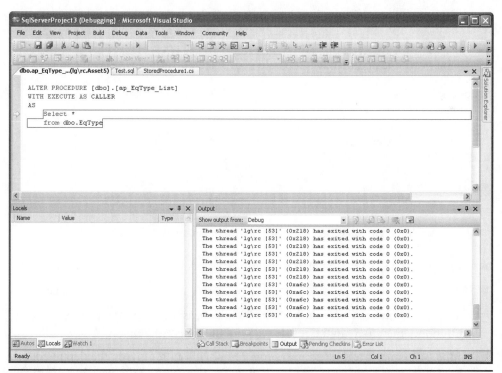

Figure 16-3 *Stepping into a procedure written in a different language*

NOTE

Only members of the sysadmin server role are allowed to debug code on SQL Server.

Poor Man's Debugger

You can debug your stored procedures even if you do not have Visual Studio. Before debuggers became part of the programming environment, developers used simple techniques to print the contents of variables and follow the execution of code. Some programming languages include commands (for instance, Assert in Visual Basic 6.0) that are active only during debugging. In others, you simply add print commands during the development stage and comment them out before releasing the code into production.

In Transact-SQL, I use a very simple technique that allows me to view the contents of the variables and recordsets when I am testing a stored procedure from the Query window. I add one additional parameter with the default set to 0 to the stored procedure:

```
@debug int = 0
```

At all important points in the stored procedure, I add code that tests the value of the @debug variable and displays the values of selected variables or result sets:

```
if @debug <> 0
    select    @chvProperty Property,
              @chvValue [Value],
              @chvUnit [Unit]
. . .

if @debug <> 0
    select * from #Properties
```

I do not use the Print statement for this purpose because

▶ It does not support the display of result sets.

▶ In older versions, it was impossible to concatenate a string inside a Print statement.

▶ Some client utilities and applications handle messages from the Print statement differently than they do the result set from the Select statement.

▶ If the procedure was moved into production without removing the debug code, the debug code would not be executed due to the value of the variable. If Print statements were inadvertently left in procedures when they were moved into production, this would present a problem for the application.

In the following example, you can see a stored procedure that is designed to support this kind of testing:

```
ALTER Procedure [dbo].[ap_InventoryProperties_Get]
/***************************************************************
Return comma-delimited list of properties that are describing asset.
i.e.: Property = Value Unit;Property = Value Unit;Property = Value
 Unit;Property = Value Unit;Property = Value Unit;...

test:
declare @p varchar(max)
exec ap_InventoryProperties_Get 5, @p OUTPUT, 1
select @p
***************************************************************/
    (
         @intInventoryId int,
         @chvProperties varchar(max) OUTPUT,
         @debug int = 0
    )

As

declare @intCountProperties int,
        @intCounter int,
        @chvProperty varchar(50),
        @chvValue varchar(50),
        @chvUnit varchar(50) ,
     @chvProcedure sysname

set @chvProcedure = 'ap_InventoryProperties_Get'

if @debug <> 0
    select '**** '+ @chvProcedure + 'START ****'


Create table #Properties(
        Id int identity(1,1),
        Property varchar(50),
        Value varchar(50),
        Unit varchar(50))

-- identify Properties associated with asset
insert into #Properties (Property, Value, Unit)
    select Property, Value, Unit
    from dbo.InventoryProperty InventoryProperty
      inner join dbo.Property Property
```

```
            on InventoryProperty.PropertyId = Property.PropertyId
         where InventoryProperty.InventoryId = @intInventoryId

if @debug = 1
   select * from #Properties

-- set loop
select @intCountProperties = Count(*),
       @intCounter = 1,
       @chvProperties = ''
from #Properties

-- loop through list of properties
while @intCounter <= @intCountProperties
begin
     -- get one property
     select @chvProperty = Property,
          @chvValue = Value,
          @chvUnit = Unit
     from #Properties
     where Id = @intCounter

     if @debug <> 0
          select    @chvProperty Property,
                    @chvValue [Value],
                    @chvUnit [Unit]

     -- assemble list
     set @chvProperties = @chvProperties + '; '
                       + @chvProperty + '='
                       + @chvValue + ' ' +  ISNULL(@chvUnit, '')

if @debug = 1
   select @chvProperties [@chvProperties], @intCounter [@intCounter]

     -- let's go another round and get another property
     set @intCounter = @intCounter + 1
end

if Substring(@chvProperties, 0, 2) = '; '
   set @chvProperties = Right(@chvProperties, Len(@chvProperties) - 2)

drop table #Properties

if @debug <> 0
     select '**** '+ @chvProcedure + 'END ****'
return 0
```

To debug or test a stored procedure, I execute the stored procedure from the Query window with the @debug parameter set to 1:

```
declare @chvResult varchar(max)
exec dbo.ap_InventoryProperties_Get'
    @intInventoryId = 5,
    @chvProperties = @chvResult OUTPUT,
    @debug = 1

select @chvResult Result
```

Remember that you can pass parameters either by name or by position. The result of the execution will be an elaborate printout like the one shown in Figure 16-4.

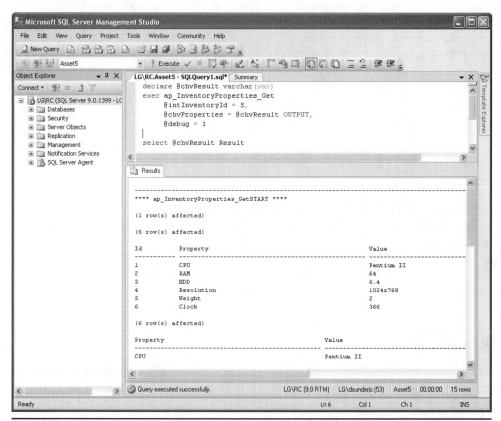

Figure 16-4   *Result of execution of a stored procedure in "poor man's debugger mode"*

Execution in the Production Environment

In production, the stored procedure is called without a reference to the @debug parameter. Here, SQL Server assigns a default value to the parameter (0), and the stored procedure is executed without debug statements:

```
exec dbo.ap_InventoryProperties_Get'
        @intInventoryId = 5,
        @chvProperties = @chvResult OUTPUT
```

Nested Stored Procedures

Two tricks can help you debug a set of nested stored procedures (that is, when a stored procedure calls another stored procedure). It is a useful practice to display the name of the stored procedure at the beginning and end of the stored procedure:

```
declare @chvProcedure sysname
set @chvProcedure = 'ap_InventoryProperties_Get''

if @debug <> 0
    select '**** '+ @chvProcedure + 'START ****'
...
if @debug <> 0
    select '**** '+ @chvProcedure + 'END ****'

return 0
```

When you call a nested stored procedure, you need to pass the value of the @debug parameter to it as well. In this way, you will be able to see its debugging information.

```
exec dbo.ap_InventoryProperties_Get' @intInventoryId,
                        @chvProperties OUTPUT,
                        @debug
```

Output Clause

A new feature of SQL Server 2005 is the Output clause of DML statements. It gives access to the set of affected records. Similar to triggers, it is based on the usage of Inserted and Deleted tables. In its simplest form, it is used to return records that were altered to the caller. If you execute the following statement, you will return records that were modified (in their original state) as a result:

```
Update dbo.EquipmentBC
Set  EqBC = '111'
    OUTPUT DELETED.*
Where EqID = 1
```

Naturally, you could reference the Inserted table to return records in a transformed state.

The following example demonstrates an interesting effect. The Output clause can access fields that are being generated (such as an identify field):

```
INSERT dbo.Equipment2(EqTypeID, Make, Model)
    Output Inserted.EqId, Inserted.EqTypeID,
           Inserted.Make + ' - ' + Inserted.Model
VALUES (22, N'Alfa', '2000X');
```

It is possible to do this because the Output clause works like the After trigger at the end of the statement's execution. You can also show the result of computed columns or include expressions based on columns in the Output clause.

NOTE

The Output clause cannot return the result to the console on tables that have enabled triggers. I guess that the problem has something to do with the fact that both the Output clause and trigger use Inserted and Deleted virtual tables. Theoretically, you can set the trigger to return something to the console, but that is not recommended practice. It is better to use table variables (described in the following text).

From time to time it is useful to return original (deleted) or transformed (inserted) records along with some other data. You cannot use the Join clause within the Output clause, but there is a workaround. The Output clause can send the result to the table variable, temporary table, or static table, instead of to the console:

```
begin tran
declare @tbl table (EqId int,
                    EqTypeID int,
                    Eq varchar(100));

delete dbo.Equipment2
   OUTPUT Deleted.EqId, Deleted.EqTypeID,
          Deleted.Make + ' - ' + Deleted.Model
   into @tbl
where Make like  'C%';
```

```
select t.*, EqType.EqType
from @tbl t inner join EqType
on t.EqTypeID = EqType.EqTypeID
```

The biggest disadvantage of this method is that you have to know the schema of the table variable in advance.

SQL Profiler

SQL Profiler allows you to monitor and capture events on an instance of SQL Server. You can configure it to capture all events or just a subset that you need to monitor. It lets you do the following:

▶ Capture Transact-SQL statements that are causing errors.

▶ Debug individual stored procedures or Transact-SQL statements.

▶ Monitor system performance.

▶ Collect the complete Transact-SQL load of a production system and replay it in your test environment.

SQL Profiler can collect external events initiated by end users (such as batch starts or login attempts), as well as internal events initiated by the system (such as individual Transact-SQL statements from within a stored procedure, table or index scans, objects locks, and transactions).

Using SQL Profiler

SQL Profiler is an MDI application that contains one or more trace windows. A *trace window* allows you to first configure events, filters, and data columns, and then to collect data from the server that is being audited.

After you start SQL Profiler, the first thing you should do is open a new trace window (File | New Trace) and select the server instance to be audited and the connection parameters. You will be prompted to specify the name of the trace, configure trace properties by choosing a predefined template (in the Use the Template list box), decide on a location of collected data, and predefine when tracing should be stopped:

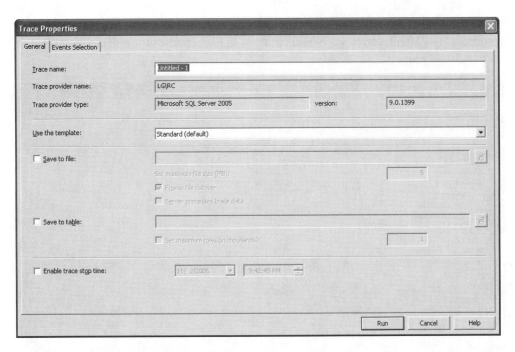

There are numerous templates available, some of the most useful of which are the following:

▶ **Standard (default)**   Collects information about connections, stored procedures, and batches that are executed against the server

▶ **T-SQL_SPs**   Collects information about individual stored procedures and all Transact-SQL statements initiated within the stored procedure

▶ **SP_Counts**   Displays stored procedures and the number of times they have been executed

▶ **T-SQL_Replay**   Collects all Transact-SQL statements that have been executed against the server to allow you to play them later (against the same or some other server)

By default, data is collected on the screen, but it can also be stored in a file or in a database table. The latter two options allow you to preserve the data for future use and further analysis. Storing in a file is particularly useful for replaying the data, while storing in a table is useful for analyzing data using SQL queries.

On the Events Selection tab, you can specify events and data columns to be recorded. By default, only events and columns that are part of the selected template will be displayed:

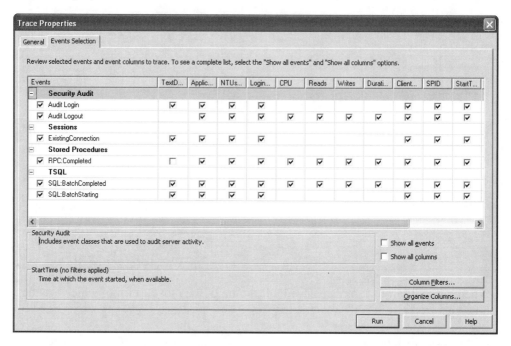

Some data columns are not applicable for some events, and SQL Server will leave them empty. You can set the Show All Events and/or Show All Columns checkboxes to see the complete matrix. Two panes in the lower-left corner display explanations of the selected event and column. It takes a little time and experimentation to learn which are the most useful. I recommend you analyze some of the templates and see how they are built.

Filters provide you with a way to avoid information overload. For example, you can decide to monitor only those activities performed just by a particular user, only activities with a duration longer than specified, or all activities except those initiated by SQL Profiler in a specific database.

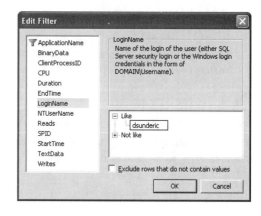

EventClass	TextData	ApplicationName	NTUserName	LoginName	CPU	Reads	W
Trace Start							
ExistingConnection	-- network protocol: LPC set quote...	.Net SqlClie...	dsunderic	LG\dsu...			
ExistingConnection	-- network protocol: LPC set quote...	Microsoft SQ...	dsunderic	LG\dsu...			
ExistingConnection	-- network protocol: LPC set quote...	Microsoft SQ...	dsunderic	LG\dsu...			
SQL:BatchStarting	declare @chvResult varchar(max) ex...	Microsoft SQ...	dsunderic	LG\dsu...			
SQL:BatchCompleted	declare @chvResult varchar(max) ex...	Microsoft SQ...	dsunderic	LG\dsu...	0	74	
SQL:BatchStarting	declare @chvResult varchar(max) ex...	Microsoft SQ...	dsunderic	LG\dsu...			
SQL:BatchCompleted	declare @chvResult varchar(max) ex...	Microsoft SQ...	dsunderic	LG\dsu...	0	74	
SQL:BatchStarting	declare @chvResult varchar(max) ex...	Microsoft SQ...	dsunderic	LG\dsu...			
SQL:BatchCompleted	declare @chvResult varchar(max) ex...	Microsoft SQ...	dsunderic	LG\dsu...	0	72	
SQL:BatchStarting	declare @chvResult varchar(max) ex...	Microsoft SQ...	dsunderic	LG\dsu...			
SQL:BatchCompleted	declare @chvResult varchar(max) ex...	Microsoft SQ...	dsunderic	LG\dsu...	0	72	
SQL:BatchStarting	declare @chvResult varchar(max) ex...	Microsoft SQ...	dsunderic	LG\dsu...			
SQL:BatchCompleted	declare @chvResult varchar(max) ex...	Microsoft SQ...	dsunderic	LG\dsu...	0	72	

```
declare @chvResult varchar(max)
exec ap_InventoryProperties_Get
    @intInventoryId = 5,
    @chvProperties = @chvResult OUTPUT,
    @debug = 1

select @chvResult Result
```

Trace is running.   Ln 11, Col 2   Rows: 14

Figure 16-5   *Trace window*

When you have finished modifying the trace properties, you should run the trace. Profiler starts to collect data and display it on the screen (see Figure 16-5).

When you have gathered enough data, you can pause or stop data collection without closing the window. The top pane displays all specified data columns. In the bottom pane, SQL Profiler displays the complete content of the TextData column for the selected event. In the case of batches and stored procedures in the TextData column, you can find (and copy, for example, to the Query window of Management Studio for further analysis) the command that caused an error or that took too long.

SQL Profiler may consume substantial resources if you just run it without careful planning. For example, gathering too many different events and too many data columns without filtering might reduce the performance of the monitored server; and the trace itself might overwhelm the machine with the amount of data gathered. Some database departments have therefore introduced very rigid limitations on the use of SQL Profiler in production environments. It is unfortunate to lose such a valuable tool, but there are ways to reduce resource contention:

▶ Do not run SQL Profiler on the server that you are monitoring.

▶ If the volume of the gathered data is an issue, save it to a file (not to the screen or a database table). Storing trace data in a database table allows you to analyze it with the full power of SQL Server tools, but it might also introduce a performance problem. Ideally, gather data in a file and then periodically load it to a database table.

▶ To reduce network contention on a busy production server, add a new network connection dedicated to SQL Profiler (in other words, an additional NIC and additional network).

▶ Use PerfMon to track the impact of SQL Profiler on the production system.

NOTE

SQL Server has a set of system stored procedures for creating traces, running them, and collecting data. Their usage might be the preferred solution if you are facing a great quantity of data, or if you want to design a custom application for monitoring SQL Server that introduces new features not covered by SQL Profiler.

Typical Errors

You should keep the following issues in mind when you are writing your code and testing Transact-SQL programs:

▶ Handling null

▶ Assignment of variable from the result set

▶ No records affected

▶ Wrong size or data type

▶ Default length

▶ Rollback of triggers

▶ Warnings and lower-priority errors

▶ Return codes vs. Raiserror

▶ Nested comments

▶ Deferred name resolution

▶ Cursors

▶ Overconfidence

Handling Null

Many errors are a result of the inadequate treatment of null values in Transact-SQL code. Developers often forget that local variables or table columns might contain null. If such a value becomes part of any expression, the result will also be null.

The proper way to test the value of an expression for null is to use the Is Null or Is Not Null clause. Microsoft SQL Server treats the use of = Null as another way to type Is Null (when Set Ansi_Nulls is set to Off), but <> Null is not the equivalent of Is Not Null. The result of such an expression is always simply null. It will never be true, and stored procedures will always skip statements after the If statement when you use the <> Null clause:

```
If @intInventoryId IS NULL
...
If @intInventoryId = NULL
...
If @intInventoryId IS NOT NULL
...
If @intInventoryId <> NULL   -- WRONG!!!
...
```

Assignment of Variable from the Result Set

Earlier, I discussed assigning the value for a variable using the result set of the Select statement. This technique is fine when the result set returns only one record. However, if the result set returns more than one record, the variable is assigned using the value from the last record in the recordset—not perfect, but in some cases, you can live with it. It is sometimes difficult to predict which record will be returned last in the recordset. It depends on both the query and the index that SQL Server has used.

A more serious problem occurs when the recordset is empty. The values of the variables are changed in this case and the code is vulnerable to several mistakes. If you do not expect the result set to be empty, your stored procedure will fail. If you expect the values of the variables to be null, your stored procedure will function correctly only immediately after it is started (that is, in the first iteration of the process). In such a case, the local variables are not yet initialized and will contain null. Later, when variables are initialized, their values will remain unchanged. If you are testing the contents of the variables for null to find out if the record was selected, you will just process the previous record again.

No Records Affected

Developers sometimes assume that SQL Server will return errors if a Transact-SQL statement affects no records. Unfortunately, this error is semantic rather than syntactic and SQL Server will not detect it.

To identify this type of error, use the @@rowCount function rather than the @@error function:

```
declare @intRowCount int
declare @intErrorCode int

update Inventory
Set StatusId = 3
where InventoryID = -11

select @intRowCount = @@rowCount,
       @intErrorCode = @@error

if @intRowCount = 0
begin
     select 'Record was not updated!'
     return 50001
end
```

Wrong Size or Data Type

I can recall one occasion when a colleague of mine spent two days going through a complicated data conversion process to find out why his process was consistently failing. In one of the nested stored procedures, I had declared the variable as tinyint instead of int. During the testing phase of the project, everything worked perfectly because the variable was never set to a value higher than 255. However, a couple of months later in production, the process started to fail as values climbed higher.

Similar problems can occur if you do not fully understand the differences between similar formats (for example, char and varchar or money and smallmoney), or if you fail to synchronize the sizes of data types (for instance, char, varchar, numeric, and other data types of variable size).

Default Length

A similar problem can occur when a developer does not supply the length of the variable data type and SQL Server assigns a default length.

For example, the default length of the `varchar` data type is 30. Most of the time, SQL Server reports an error if the length is omitted, but not always. In the Convert() function, for example, the user needs only to specify the data type:

```
Convert(varchar, @intPropertyId)
```

If the resulting string is short enough, you will not have any problems. I recall a colleague who employed this method for years without any problems, and then….

Unfortunately, other statements and functions behave as expected. If you declare a variable and assign it like so:

```
Declare @test varchar
Set @test = '12345678901234567890123456789'
Select datalength(@test), @test
```

SQL Server will allocate just one byte to the string and return the following:

```
----------- ----
1           1

(1 row(s) affected)
```

Rollback of Triggers

In different versions of SQL Server, triggers react differently in rollback transaction statements. When a trigger is rolled back in SQL Server 2005, 2000, or 7.0, the complete batch that initiated the trigger fails and the execution continues from the first statement of the next batch. Version 4.2 behaves in a similar manner. In version 6.0, processing continues in the trigger but the batch is canceled. In version 6.5, the processing continues in both the trigger and the batch. It was the responsibility of the developer to detect errors and cascade out of the process (in other words, go out of all nested procedures and triggers).

Warnings and Lower-priority Errors

Warnings do not stop the execution of a stored procedure. In fact, you cannot even detect them from within the SQL Server environment.

Low-level errors, which are detectable using the @@error function, do not abort the execution either. Unfortunately, there are also errors that abort processing completely, so that the error handlers in stored procedures do not process the error.

Return Codes vs. Raiserror

I recommend that you decide whether you are going to use return values or Raiserror to notify middleware that something has gone wrong, and then stick to that decision. You do not want your middleware to be expecting Raiserror while you are trying to send it an error code or a status using your return code.

Some people even recommend that you use Raiserror exclusively, since middleware has to be able to handle errors raised directly from the SQL Server engine. In this way, you can be sure that an application developer will not forget to check the return code.

Nested Comments

Only single-line comments (--) can be nested. Nested multiline comments (/* */) may be treated differently by different client tools.

I recommend that you put one or two stars (**) at the beginning of each line that is commented out. In this manner, the problem will be obvious if the comments are nested and SQL Server starts to compile part of the code that you consider to be commented out:

```
/************************************************************
**      select *
**      from #Properties
*************************************************************/
```

Deferred Name Resolution

It is possible (in Microsoft SQL Server 2005, 2000, and 7.0) to create database objects (such as stored procedures and triggers) that refer to other database objects that do not yet exist within the database. In previous versions, this would have been treated as a syntax error. This feature helps tremendously when you need to generate a database structure and objects using script. Unfortunately, this introduces a number of risks. If, as in the following example, you make a typo in the name of the table from which you want to retrieve records, SQL Server will not report a syntax error during compilation but will report a runtime error during execution.

```
Create Procedure dbo.ap_DeferredNameResolution
As
    set nocount on
    select 'Start'
    select * from NonExistingTable
    select 'Will execution be stopped?'
return
```

If you attempt to run this stored procedure, SQL Server will return the following:

```
-----
Start

Server: Msg 208, Level 16, State 1,
Procedure ap_DeferredNameResolution, Line 5
Invalid object name 'NonExistingTable'.
```

The execution will be stopped. Even an error handler written in Transact-SQL will not be able to proceed at this point.

Cursors

Be very cautious when you use cursors: Test the status after each fetch; place error handling after each command; do not forget to close and deallocate the cursor when you do not need it anymore. There are many rules and regulations for using cursors and some of them might seem trivial, but even the smallest mistake can halt the execution of your code.

Overconfidence

The overconfidence that comes with routine may be your worst enemy. If you perform the same or similar tasks over and over again, you can lose focus and skip basic steps. Do not put code into production before it is thoroughly tested; do not place bug fixes directly into production; use error handling even if the code seems straightforward and the chance for error slight.

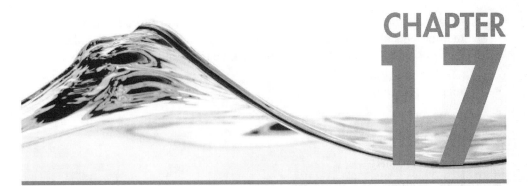

Source Code Management

*S*ource code control (or *version control*) is typically introduced in development environments in which more than one developer needs to work with the same piece of code. It allows development organizations and their members to

▶   Manage code centrally

▶   Manage multiple versions of the same code

▶   Track change history

▶   Compare versions

▶   Prevent or allow developers from modifying the same piece of code at the same time

▶   Synchronize deployment of all modifications needed to implement a single feature or bug fix

In this chapter, I will introduce methods and tools for source code management. I will present solutions using two different approaches. One approach is for developers who have Visual Studio .NET (and who are probably doing both database and application development). The other, more traditional, approach is geared toward SQL Server specialists who are working with traditional database development tools such as Management Studio. I will use the tools that are delivered with SQL Server, as well as tools that I have developed, to automate some processes.

Microsoft provides source code control software as an integral part of its development environment under the name Visual SourceSafe. This application allows developers to control their most valuable asset—source code. You can also use the Visual SourceSafe database to manage other file types such as web content, documentation, and test data, but our focus in this chapter is on how to use Visual SourceSafe to manage database objects.

Introduction to Microsoft Visual SourceSafe

Microsoft's primary purpose in delivering Visual SourceSafe as a part of its Visual Studio .NET suite of development tools is to provide a project-oriented means of storing and organizing code that allows developers to spend more time developing their projects and less time managing them. The emphasis is on ease of use and integration with a wide range of development tools. SQL Server developers can benefit greatly from this ease of use and integration, not only with regard to source code, but also as a means of organizing related files such as project documentation and test data.

As with SQL Server, there are different ways to use Visual SourceSafe. It is essentially a client/server application, but if you are an independent developer, your development workstation will likely also be your application server, database server, and source code server. Of course, if you are an independent developer, you may be wondering why you have a need for source code control at all. I will discuss this issue later in the chapter. For now, you can take my word that source code control is just as important for the solo developer working on a simple project as it is for a large development team working on a complex, component-based project.

If you are a member of a development team, the Visual SourceSafe client will allow you to work with local copies of code while preventing other members of your team from overwriting your changes while you have the code checked out from the Visual SourceSafe database. The benefit of this simple concept is obvious, but you have to work with and become comfortable with Visual SourceSafe before its many other benefits will become just as obvious. After you have posted your source code, you can

- ▶ Get the current version of all files.

- ▶ Check out a copy of a file that needs to be changed. Visual SourceSafe is, by default, configured to prevent all other developers from changing the file until it is returned (checked in) to the Visual SourceSafe database. View differences between a local version of a source code file and the latest version stored in the Visual SourceSafe database.

- ▶ Label versions of files to identify them with a particular release of a software product.

- ▶ Retrieve older versions of a particular file or a complete set of project files.

- ▶ View changes between any two versions of a source code file.

- ▶ Share common files between separate projects.

- ▶ Make a single backup copy of the complete source code and all supporting files.

- ▶ Create branches of source code files to separately manage multiple versions of a software project.

- ▶ Merge code in different branches of the source code file.

Administering the Visual SourceSafe Database

Before you can use Visual SourceSafe, you need to

▶   Create the SourceSafe database.

▶   Create users and assign privileges to them.

You can do these operations via the Visual SourceSafe Administration tool:

1.   Start the tool from Start | Visual SourceSafe | Visual SourceSafe Administration.

2.   To create a new database, start the wizard by selecting File | New Database from the main menu.

3.   Set the path of the VSS database (i.e., D:\VSS).

NOTE

You should set the location of the VSS database on the local drive (to avoid performance problems). If you want to point to some network drive, you should probably use that file server as your VSS server.

4.   Set the name of your VSS database connection (i.e., MyVSS).

5.   Verify that Team Version Control Model is set to Lock-Modify-Unlock Model.

NOTE

The Copy-Modify-Merge model is a new unorthodox source control model that allows multiple users to make modification on the same file at the same time. Unfortunately, the price to pay for such freedom is the potential for conflicting changes to files. Unless you are certain that you want to work in this model and you know how to resolve conflicts and merge changes, I recommend you use the standard Lock-Modify-Unlock model.

When you install Visual SourceSafe, you create just two users: *Admin* and *Guest*. The Admin user has all privileges in the database and can also create other users. The Guest user should be immediately limited to read-only access to source code files. Both users are created with their passwords set to an empty string (that is, blank). Since this state constitutes a threat to your source code, your first step should be to set their passwords using User | Change Password.

When you are done, create a user for yourself (User | Add User) with the appropriate permissions. Note that some versions of Visual SourceSafe create a user for the person that has created VSS database automatically.

TIP

If your Visual SourceSafe username and password match your operating system username and password, you will not have to type them each time you open Visual SourceSafe on the local system. Visual SourceSafe can be configured to use them automatically.

With Visual SourceSafe, you can assign more refined permission levels, such as Add, Rename, Delete, Check In, Check Out, Destroy, and Read. To activate this wide-ranging control, click Tools | Options | Project Rights and check the Enable Project Security option. It is not a bad idea to do that. It is especially useful to prevent your users from permanently deleting source code files (Destroy).

Adding Database Objects to Visual SourceSafe in Visual Studio .NET

To demonstrate the implementation of source code control in a database project, you add code from your sample Asset5 database in Visual Studio .NET:

1. Create the Asset5 database project in Visual Studio .NET.
2. Open Solution Explorer.
3. Make sure that the Asset5 database is one of the Database References. If the reference does not already exist, right-click Database References and select New Database Reference to create one that points to the Asset5 database.
4. In Server Explorer, expand the Data Connections node.
5. Expand the Asset5 node and keep expanding until you get to the list of stored procedures.
6. Open a context-sensitive menu of one stored procedure and choose Generate Create Script to Project. The program will add its script to the Create Scripts folder of the project.
7. Now, navigate Server Explorer until you find a list of tables and then open a context-sensitive menu of a table and choose Generate Create Script to Project. The program will add its script to the project as well.

NOTE

Depending on the version and edition of Visual Studio that you have, the Generate Create Script command may or may not be available in the context-sensitive menu of a data connection node of Server Explorer. If it is available, you may use it to generate Create scripts of all database objects. If it is missing, you have two options—to use the TbDbScript tool described in the "Adding Database Objects to Visual SourceSafe: Traditional Approach" section, or to generate scripts using the Script Wizard of Management Studio (also described later in the chapter).

Now we will add this project and all its files to Visual SourceSafe.

8. Select File | Source Control | Add Project to Source Control. Visual Studio .NET will prompt you to log in to a Visual SourceSafe database:

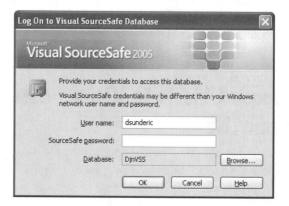

9. Now Visual SourceSafe prompts you to add a project to the Visual SourceSafe database. Name the project (you can also type a comment to describe the project).

Visual SourceSafe creates a project and locks all *Create scripts* (scripts that can be used to drop and create objects from scratch). You can see a small lock icon beside each Create script in Solution Explorer:

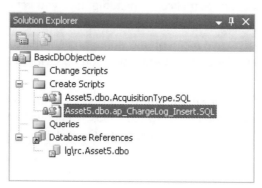

NOTE

From this moment, you must "check out" a Create script before you can change it.

Managing Create Scripts in Visual Studio .NET

When Create scripts are locked, you can open them for viewing in the editor, but Visual Studio .NET will prevent you from changing them until you check them out.

To view a Create script, right-click the script you want to review and select Open. Visual Studio .NET opens a copy of the Create script but marks it "read-only."

The following steps demonstrate how to change a stored procedure:

1. Close the window with the read-only version of the Create script.
2. Right-click the script for a stored procedure and select Check Out from the pop-up menu. The program prompts you for comment:

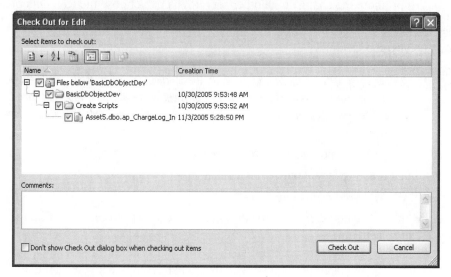

3. Make some trivial change to the stored procedure.
4. Save the changes (File | Save) in the change file.
5. Right-click the file and choose Check In from the menu. The program prompts you for comment again.

TIP

Take the time to describe what changes you made in your comment. This will be incredibly helpful if some detective work is required later.

6. Click Check In. Visual Studio .NET saves the changes in Visual SourceSafe and locks the Create script.

7. Keep in mind that at this point, the stored procedure *does not yet exist in SQL Server!* You must right-click the file and select Run to deploy it to the default database. Visual Studio .NET opens the Database Output pane to show the results (and possibly errors) of the execution; however, it probably makes more sense to deploy the change to the development SQL Server before it is saved to the VSS database.

NOTE

Unfortunately, this solution does not prevent another developer from using some other tool to change a database object directly in the database. You can even open Server Explorer in Visual Studio .NET to change one without source code control. Visual SourceSafe works only through consensus; loose cannons can still wreak havoc on your development ship.

To promote the change to another server, you can choose the Run On option in the context menu of the Change script.

TIP

When I first started to use Visual SourceSafe, the directions implied by the terms "Check Out" and "Check In" sounded inverted to me. Just think of Visual SourceSafe as an actual safe from which you are taking your code and into which you subsequently put back your code after you are done with it.

8. Now, go back and check out the same stored procedure again.

9. Open it and reverse your previous changes.

10. Save the stored procedure.

11. Run the Change script against the server to test it (right-click the Change script and select Run).

Assume that you are not satisfied with these changes and that you want to abandon them. (i.e., that you have tested them and the result is not what you expected.) To reverse changes,

1. Select Undo Check Out from the context menu. The Visual SourceSafe Server locks the file again and uses the previous copy from Visual SourceSafe to reverse the changes in the local file.

2. To reverse changes to the database, you must run the Change script again.

NOTE

Undo Check Out does not actually change any code already deployed but merely reverses the check out process.

Visual SourceSafe Explorer

The full power of Visual SourceSafe can only be realized through one special tool—Visual SourceSafe Explorer. Take a look at this tool by following these steps:

1. Open Visual SourceSafe Explorer from the Windows Start menu (depending on the version that you have: Start | Programs | Microsoft Visual Studio .NET | Microsoft Visual SourceSafe | Visual SourceSafe) or from Visual Studio .NET (File | Source Control | Launch Microsoft Visual SourceSafe).

2. Expand the project and drill down until you reach stored procedures (see Figure 17-1).

The following sections examine some of the most interesting features of Visual SourceSafe Explorer, particularly history, labels, and versions.

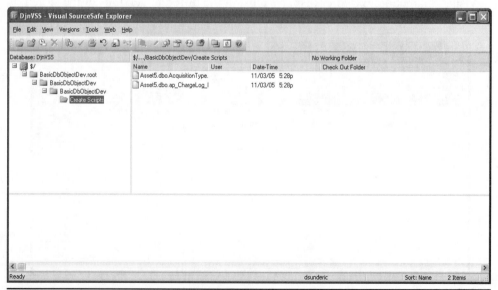

Figure 17-1 *Visual SourceSafe Explorer*

History

Visual SourceSafe keeps an audit trail of changes made to a file. To view this history of changes:

1. Right-click the stored procedure that you edited earlier in this chapter and select Show History from the pop-up menu.

2. Visual SourceSafe prompts you to define the history details you would like to display:

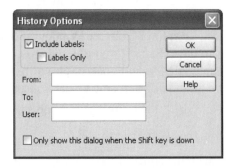

3. In this case, accept the defaults and click OK.

Visual SourceSafe Explorer displays a list of the different versions of the stored procedure, along with the name of the user responsible for each action:

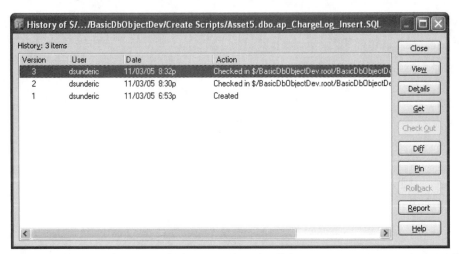

Now you have several options. If you select one version, you can view (click View) the code in an ASCII viewer. You can also see details, such as comments and timestamp, (click Details) of the selected version. The Get button lets you obtain a version of the stored procedure in a text file.

You can also temporarily or permanently set one of the previous versions to be a current one. The Pin option is usually applied as a temporary measure to test the behavior of an older version of a procedure. If you find that changes you made in your code are introducing more problems than they are solving, you can use the Rollback function to return to an earlier version of the code. Note that all newer versions will be deleted.

My favorite option is Diff; it compares two versions of a file. To use it,

1. Select two versions of a stored procedure (for example, version 2 and version 3) in the History window. You can select multiple versions by pressing the CTRL key and then clicking them.

2. Click the Diff button. The Difference Options dialog box appears:

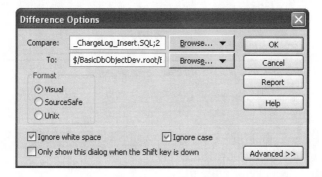

3. This dialog box lets you specify parameters for comparing files. If you wish to ignore case and white space, click OK to accept the defaults; Visual SourceSafe Explorer displays a window in which the differences between the two versions are highlighted (see Figure 17-2).

Labels and Versions

You have probably realized by now that the term "version" in Visual SourceSafe does not actually correspond to the concept of version (or release) that we generally think of when we consider software. A Visual SourceSafe "version" actually corresponds to a change in the source code. You should use labels in Visual SourceSafe to implement the equivalent of a release.

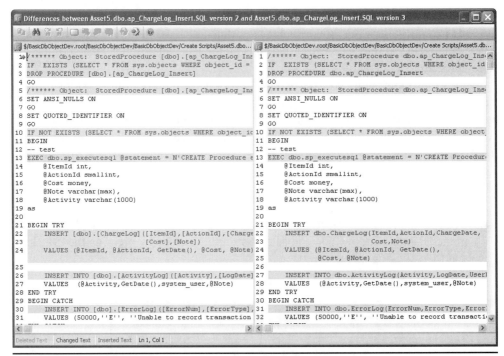

Figure 17-2 *File differences in Visual SourceSafe Explorer*

You can apply the Label option from the main window of Visual SourceSafe Explorer. You can select one or more files and/or one or more projects (folders). When you apply the Label option (File | Label), the Label dialog box appears and prompts you to specify the text of the label (your official release number, for example).

The current versions of all selected files will be labeled. Later, you can use these labels to collect the code that belongs to a particular version. This feature can be very important for supporting or testing the product.

Even more exciting is the opportunity to view the complete history of a project (right-click the project folder and select Show History from the pop-up menu) and determine many historical facts about the project, such as which changes were performed on it after a particular release.

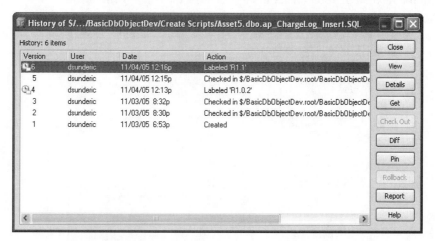

Adding Database Objects to Visual SourceSafe: Traditional Approach

Unfortunately, if you do not have Visual Studio .NET, it is not easy enough to manage the code of individual database objects with only the tools built into SQL Server and Visual SourceSafe. The process involves two steps:

1. Generate scripts from SQL Server.
2. Check in files to Visual SourceSafe.

Creating Scripts Using Script Wizard

You can use Management Studio to generate Create scripts of all objects in a database:

1. In Object Explorer, navigate to a database.
2. Open the context-sensitive menu and choose Tasks | Generate Scripts (not Script Database As | Create To).
3. The program will open the Generate SQL Server Script Wizard.

4. In the second step, select a database.

5. In the next step, you can set the options for the script generation:

6. On the next screen, you need to select the object types to be generated:

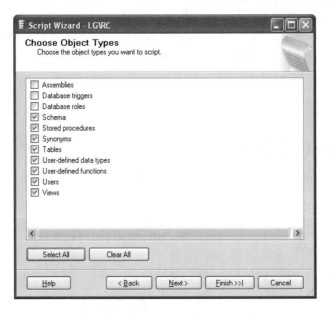

7. The program will then prompt you to select individual objects of every type that you have selected on the previous screen:

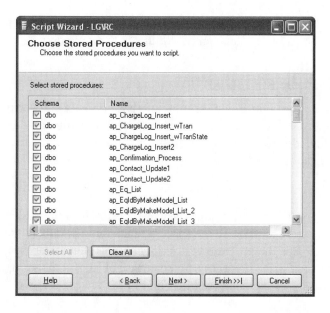

NOTE

The Script Wizard in SQL Server 2005 supports CLR database objects as well. It will create code for attaching assemblies to the database and prompt you to select managed database objects that are based on them.

8. Finally, the program will prompt you for the destination of the script:

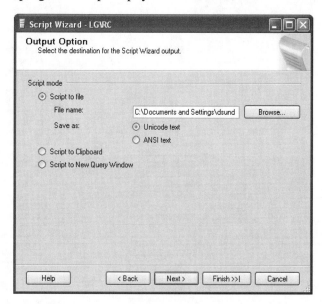

Based on your choice the Script Wizard will store script in a Unicode file, an ANSI file, on the Clipboard, or in Management Studio's Query window.

Creating Scripts Using TbDbScript

I've also created a tool that loops through database objects and scripts them into separate files—TbDbScript. It's written in VBScript and you can download it from www.TrigonBlue.com/tsql.net/download.htm. To run it, you must use Windows Script Host and cscript.exe. Execute the following from the command prompt:

```
cscript TbDbScript.vbs .\ss2k5 sa password c:\sql\ Asset5
```

The parameters are the server, login, password, destination of database files, and, optionally, the database name. Use the space character as a parameter delimiter. If you omit the last parameter, the program will script all nonsystem databases on the server.

When scripting is finished, you will find database objects in the set of Create scripts in the folder named after the database (see Figure 17-3).

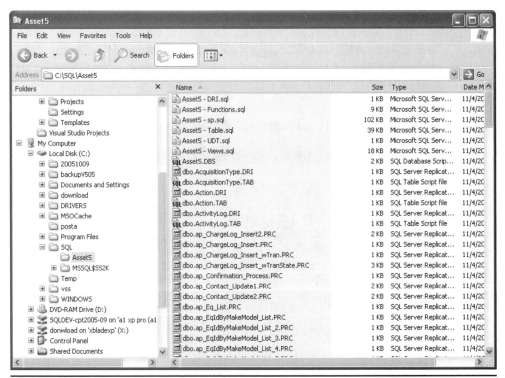

Figure 17-3 *Database object scripts generated by TbDbScript*

The tool also creates *deployment scripts*. They contain Create scripts grouped by type. You will read more about them in the "Deployment Scripts: Traditional Approach" section, in the next chapter.

It is true that the Script Wizard will perform similar actions, but there are several significant differences:

▶ The script generates individual database object Create scripts and deployment scripts at the same time.

▶ You can also schedule usage of TbDbScript, which may be very useful when the development team is not using Visual SourceSafe religiously—as when the team is making changes live to the development database.

▶ Generation does not require user intervention and therefore is less prone to errors. The resulting files are always the same.

▶ Every deployment script file begins with a Use *database_name* statement and they can even be deployed manually using Management Studio.

Putting Scripts to Visual SourceSafe Using TbDir2Vss.vbs

Now that Create scripts and deployment scripts are created, all you need to do is check them into the Visual SourceSafe database. You can do this manually with Visual SourceSafe Explorer. Simply add the working folder in or do it automatically with a little VBScript tool—TbDir2Vss.vbs. You can download the tool from:

```
www.TrigonBlue.com/tsql.net/download.htm.
```

To run it, you must use Windows Script Host and cscript.exe. You need to specify the location of the srcsafe.ini file, username, password, Visual SourceSafe project folder, and local folder:

```
cscript TbDir2Vss.vbs "C:\Program Files\Microsoft Visual
Studio\Common\VSS\srcsafe.ini" admin password $/Asset/ c:\dbscripter\Asset\
```

TIP

The TbDir2Vss.vbs tool can also be scheduled along with TbDbScript.vbs to script databases and put them in Visual SourceSafe.

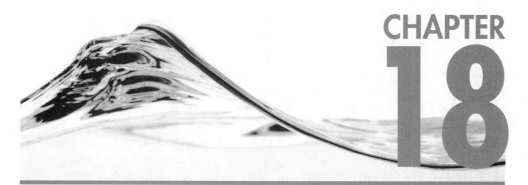

CHAPTER
18

Database Deployment

IN THIS CHAPTER

The problem that you will face relatively often is that, while you develop your database (and application) in a development environment, you must deploy the database first in a test environment and then in a production environment. Initially, you need to deploy the complete database, but later you will have to update the database with design changes and hot fixes.

I will present solutions using two different approaches. One approach is for developers who have Visual Studio .NET (and who are probably doing both database and application development). The other, more traditional approach is geared toward SQL Server specialists who are working with traditional database development tools. I will use the tools that are delivered with SQL Server, as well as tools that I have developed, to automate some processes.

Traditionally, RDBMS installation is perceived as complicated, and your customer will understand that you need to send a database administrator (or a couple of them) to set up the environment. When you work with a file-based database system such as Access, database deployment is not a big issue. You usually create a setup program for your client application, and your database (*.mdb*) file is just one more file that must be installed on the computer. When you are working in a client/server environment with SQL Server, you first have to install and configure the database server and then install databases.

Fortunately, installation of SQL Server has been simplified significantly. Almost anyone can perform it and there are usually no problems. In fact, SQL Server can be configured to be installed unattended. Microsoft SQL Server 2005 Express Edition is designed to be deployed on client computers using a special set of setup files that can be included in your setup program.

Some early versions of SQL Server required that all dependent objects be present on the server before a new object could be created. Administrators had to use many tricks to transfer a database from one server to another. The introduction of Deferred Name Resolution has reduced the complexity of database deployment in the SQL Server environment. For example, a stored procedure can be created even if it references a stored procedure that is not yet on the server. Unfortunately, it is not perfect yet. For example, it is not possible to create a foreign key that references a table that is not yet in the database.

The methods for database deployment can be divided into two groups:

▶ Deployment of a complete database

▶ Deployment of individual objects

Deployment of a Complete Database: Traditional Approach

The idea behind this method is to use some means of moving the complete database so that relationships between individual database objects do not have to be managed once they are established. There are several options:

▶ Detach and reattach the database in Transact-SQL

▶ Attach and detach the database in Management Studio

▶ Backup and restore

Detach and Reattach the Database in Transact-SQL

The idea behind this option is to detach the database from the server, copy the database files to the production server, and then attach the database files to the new server (and reattach the database files to the original server, if applicable). To detach the Asset5 database manually, you can use the following script:

```
EXEC sp_detach_db 'Asset5'
```

SQL Server checks the integrity of the database, flushes everything that is in memory to disk, stops further changes to the database, and releases database files.

NOTE

You must have exclusive use of the database to perform this function.

You can then copy the files (in this case, Asset5.mdf and Asset5_log.ldf) from the ...\mssql\data folder to a data folder on the target server. To attach the Asset5 database, you can use

```
EXEC sp_attach_db @dbname = 'Asset5',
            @filename1 = 'c:\Program Files\Microsoft SQL ',
                  + 'Server\MSSQL.1\mssql\data\Asset5.mdf'
            @filename2 = 'c:\Program Files\Microsoft SQL '
                  + 'Server\MSSQL.1\mssql\data\Asset5_log.ldf'
```

If your database consists of more files, simply add them to the list of parameters. But if your database contains just one data file, you can use an alternative command:

```
EXEC sp_attach_single_file_db
            @dbname = 'Asset5',
```

```
@physname = 'c:\Program Files\Microsoft SQL ',
            + 'Server\MSSQL.1\mssql\data\Asset5.mdf'
```

TIP

There is no harm in dropping the transaction log file and attaching just the data file (as long as you do not have some special reason, such as replication, to preserve the log).

You can execute these Transact-SQL statements manually in the Query window of Management Studio, from SQLCMD or from the setup program. The setup program can use the command-prompt utility SQLCMD to run a script file or use ADO.NET to execute the script.

NOTE

I have chosen this method for deployment of the sample database to your computer.

Attach and Detach in Management Studio

The previous operations are possible through Management Studio commands and windows. To detach a database:

1. Open the context-sensitive menu of the database and select Tasks | Detach.
2. The program will open the Detach Database window that shows if the database is ready for the operation. For example, it is possible that some users are still connected to the database (see Figure 18-1).
3. You can decide to wait and e-mail users to exit or you can use the Drop Connections option.

To attach a database on another server, you need to

1. Copy data and log files to a data folder on the target server.
2. Open the context-sensitive menu of the Databases node in the Object Browser and choose Attach.
3. The program will open the Attach window. Click the Add button and browse for the data file (.mdf) of your database. This will automatically load all the remaining files that are part of the database (see Figure 18-2).

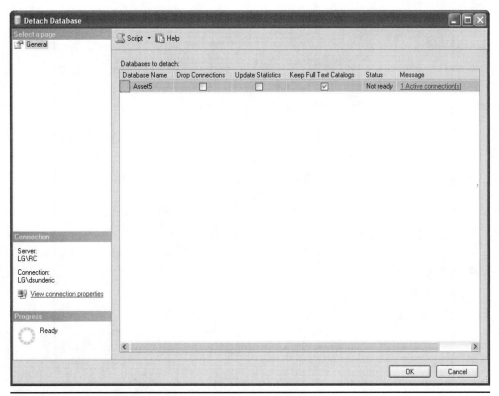

Figure 18-1   *Detach Database in Management Studio*

Backup and Restore

Another solution is based on creating a backup of the database on a development
server and then restoring the database on a test or a production server. Again, this
can be performed manually or it can be scripted and included in the setup program.

Potential Problems

Unfortunately, these techniques will not restore the links between server logins and
database users. Server logins are stored in the *master* database; on different servers,
different logins will have different IDs. Database users are stored in each user database.
One of the parameters for a database user is the ID of the login to which it is attached.

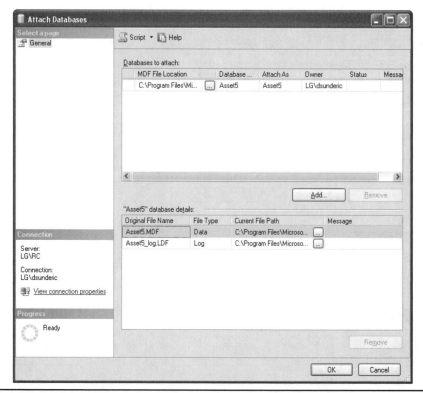

Figure 18-2   *Attach Databases window in Management Studio*

However, that ID is likely to refer to a different login on the production server. The simplest way to handle this problem is either to create all users again using Management Studio or a script that you have prepared in advance, or to use roles instead of users as the foundation of your security solution. See Chapter 19 for more information. SQL Server offers another solution to this problem—see "Synchronization of Login and Usernames" in Chapter 19.

Another disadvantage to these methods is that you have to maintain a "clean" database—a database that contains just database objects and seed data. Such a database can be delivered to a customer, but it cannot be used for development and testing. In both development and test environments, you need to add test data in order to test all features. You need to develop either scripts for adding test data or, alternatively, scripts for removing test data from a development database.

Deployment of Individual Objects

Some organizations choose to manage the code for individual objects and to deploy the database piecemeal by executing the code on the production server. This provides more flexibility, but requires more effort.

Deployment Scripts: Traditional Approach

Individual object scripts can be grouped in files with all objects of a particular type or even with all objects in a database. Such files can be created using the Generate Script command in Management Studio. It is also possible to use a custom tool to aggregate individual database object files from the Visual SourceSafe database. Most ERD modeling tools can also produce such scripts (but their scripts often require manual intervention). You can also use TbDbScript, described in the previous chapter.

To have better control, I like to use the TbDbScript tool to create one deployment script for each type of database object. When the system contains more than one database, I find it very useful that TbDbScript names deployment script files using the *Database - DbObjectType*.sql convention (see Figure 18-3).

Scripting Data: Traditional Approach

Some tables contain data (seed, static, or lookup data) that needs to be deployed along with the database schema. To assist in deployment and to facilitate storing the data with the source code, use the util.ap_DataGenerator stored procedure, described in Chapter 15.

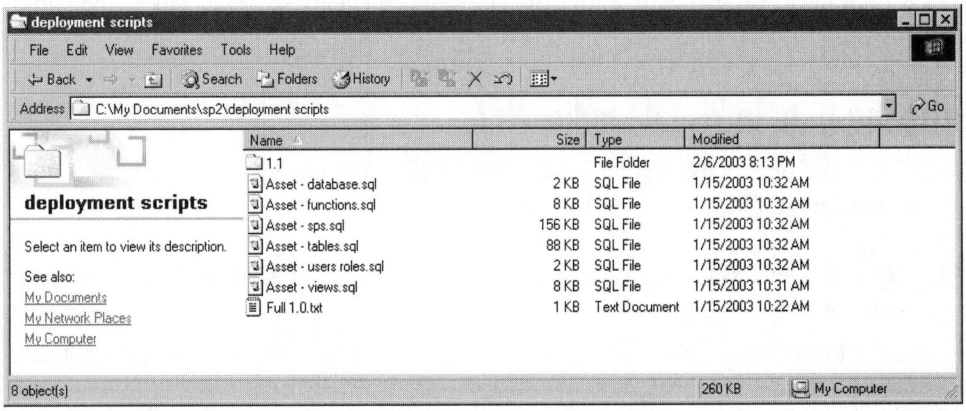

Figure 18-3   *Deployment scripts*

Use the util.ap_DataGenerator procedure on all tables with data that need to be scripted:

```
set nocount on
exec util.ap_DataGenerator 'AcquisitionType'
exec util.ap_DataGenerator 'EqType'
exec util.ap_DataGenerator 'Location'
exec util.ap_DataGenerator 'OrderStatus'
exec util.ap_DataGenerator 'OrderType'
exec util.ap_DataGenerator 'Status'
exec util.ap_DataGenerator 'Province'
```

The result will be a script that consists of Insert statements (which had to be cropped to fit the page):

```
------------------------------------------------------------------
Insert into AcquisitionType(AcquisitionTypeId,AcquisitionType) values
Insert into AcquisitionType(AcquisitionTypeId,AcquisitionType) values
Insert into AcquisitionType(AcquisitionTypeId,AcquisitionType) values
Insert into AcquisitionType(AcquisitionTypeId,AcquisitionType) values
Insert into AcquisitionType(AcquisitionTypeId,AcquisitionType) values


------------------------------------------------------------------
Insert into EqType(EqTypeId,EqType) values (1,'Desktop')
Insert into EqType(EqTypeId,EqType) values (2,'Notebook')
Insert into EqType(EqTypeId,EqType) values (3,'Monitor')
Insert into EqType(EqTypeId,EqType) values (4,'Ink Jet Printer')
...
```

Save the resulting scripts in a text file (I often use Database - Data.sql as the name of this file).

Scripting Data in Visual Studio .NET

Alternatively, you can use Visual Studio 2003 .NET (but not Visual Studio 2005) to script data and add it to Visual SourceSafe:

1. Open Server Explorer, navigate through the nodes, and expand the Tables node in the Asset5 database.
2. Select the tables with seed data (such as AcquisitionType, EqType, OrderStatus, and OrderType).
3. Right-click the selection and select Export Data from the menu.

4. The program prompts you for Locations For Exported Data File and to confirm that you want to export the selected data. The default location will be the folder that contains the Create scripts you generated earlier.

5. When you confirm the export operation, the program generates a set of DAT files. You typically need to select the files in Solution Explorer and Check (them) In.

These files are not SQL Server scripts but simple binary files (see the content of a file in Figure 18-4).

Deploying Scripts: Traditional Approach

The deployment scripts can then be executed manually one by one in the Query window of Management Studio, but I have created one program and a couple of stored procedures that allow me to automate execution of a set of scripts.

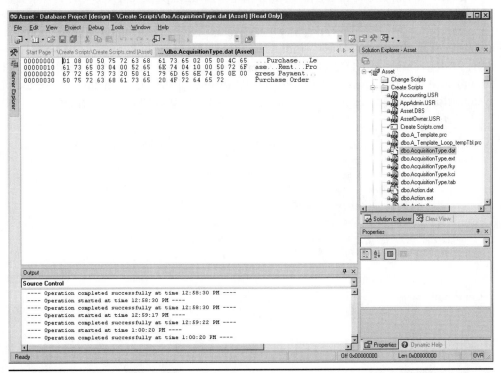

Figure 18-4 *Content of DAT file*

To prepare for deployment, I need to create a list of scripts and save it in a text file. The procedure executes the scripts in the order in which they are listed in the text file:

```
-- list of deployment scripts for Asset5 database
Asset5 - database.DBS
Asset5 - UDT.sql
Asset5 - Table.sql
Asset5 - DRI.sql
Asset5 - Functions.sql
Asset5 - sp.sql
Asset5 - Views.sql
```

Although Deferred Name Resolution allows you to ignore the order of creation of stored procedures, there are still some dependencies that must be followed. For example, indexes must be created after tables, tables after user-defined data types, and all of them after the database has been initiated.

With this in mind, one of the main advantages of util.ap_BatchExec_OA is that it preserves the order of execution of files. No human intervention is required and the opportunity for error is reduced. The procedure uses SQL Distributed Management Objects (SQL-DMO) to execute individual scripts against the database server. SQL-DMO is a set of COM objects that encapsulate the functionality needed for administering SQL Server. To use SQL-DMO from SQL Server, you have to use the system stored procedures for OLE Automation (COM), described in Chapter 21:

```
alter proc util.ap_BatchExec_OA
-- Execute all sql files in the specified folder using the alphabetical order.
-- Demonstration of use of OLE Automation.
    @ServerName sysname = '(local)\rc',
    @UserId sysname = 'sa',
    @PWD sysname = 'my,password',
    @DirName varchar(400)='C:\sql\test',
    @File varchar(400) = 'list.txt',
    @UseTransaction int = 0
as

set nocount on

declare @FileSystemObject int,
        @objSQL int,
        @hr int,
        @property varchar(255),
        @return varchar(255),
        @TextStream int,
```

```
          @BatchText varchar(max),
          @FilePath varchar(500),
          @ScriptId varchar(200),
          @Cmd varchar(1000)

--- Get list of files
create table #FileList (ScriptId int identity(1,1),
                        FileName varchar(500))

select  @Cmd = 'cd ' + @DirName + ' & type ' + @File

insert #FileList (FileName)
exec master.sys.xp_cmdshell @Cmd

-- remove empty rows and comments
delete #FileList where FileName is null
delete #FileList where FileName like '--%'

-- prepare COM to connect to SQL Server
EXEC @hr = sp_OACreate 'SQLDMO.SQLServer', @objSQL OUTPUT
IF @hr < 0
BEGIN
   print 'error create SQLDMO.SQLServer'
   exec sys.sp_OAGetErrorInfo @objSQL, @hr
   RETURN
END

EXEC @hr = sp_OAMethod @objSQL, 'Connect', NULL, @ServerName, @UserId, @PWD
IF @hr < 0
BEGIN
   print 'error Connecting'
   exec sys.sp_OAGetErrorInfo @objSQL, @hr
   RETURN
END

EXEC @hr = sp_OAMethod @objSQL, 'VerifyConnection', @return OUTPUT
IF @hr < 0
BEGIN
   print 'error verifying connection'
   exec sys.sp_OAGetErrorInfo @objSQL, @hr
   RETURN
END

-- prepare file system object
EXEC @hr = sp_OACreate 'Scripting.FileSystemObject', @FileSystemObject OUTPUT
IF @hr < 0
```

```
BEGIN
   print 'error create FileSystemObject'
   exec sp_OAGetErrorInfo @FileSystemObject, @hr
   RETURN
END


-- begin transaction
if @UseTransaction <> 0
BEGIN
   EXEC @hr = sp_OAMethod @objSQL, 'BeginTransaction '
   IF @hr < 0
   BEGIN
      print 'error BeginTransaction'
      exec sp_OAGetErrorInfo @objSQL, @hr
      RETURN
   END
END


-- iterate through the temp table to get actual file names
select @ScriptId = Min (ScriptId) from #FileList

WHILE @ScriptId is not null
BEGIN
   select @FilePath = @DirName + '\' + FileName
   from #FileList where ScriptId = @ScriptId
    if @FilePath <> ''
    BEGIN
      print 'Executing ' + @FilePath

      EXEC @hr = sp_OAMethod @FileSystemObject, 'OpenTextFile',
                             @TextStream output, @FilePath
      IF @hr < 0
      BEGIN
         print 'Error opening TextFile ' + @FilePath
         exec sp_OAGetErrorInfo @FileSystemObject, @hr
         RETURN
      END

      EXEC @hr = sp_OAMethod @TextStream, 'ReadAll', @BatchText output
      IF @hr < 0
      BEGIN
          print 'Error using ReadAll method.'
          exec sp_OAGetErrorInfo @TextStream, @hr
         RETURN
      END
```

```
    -- print @BatchText
    -- run it.
    EXEC @hr = sp_OAMethod @objSQL, 'ExecuteImmediate', Null , @BatchText
    IF @hr <> 0
    BEGIN
        if @UseTransaction <> 0
        BEGIN
            EXEC @hr = sp_OAMethod @objSQL, 'RollbackTransaction '
            IF @hr < 0
                BEGIN
                    print 'error RollbackTransaction'
                    exec sp_OAGetErrorInfo @objSQL, @hr
                RETURN
            END
        END
        print 'Error ExecuteImmediate.' --Transaction will be rolled back.
        exec sp_OAGetErrorInfo @objSQL, @hr
        RETURN
    END


    EXECUTE sp_OADestroy @TextStream
  END

  print 'Finished executing ' + @FilePath

  select @ScriptId = Min(ScriptId) from #FileList where ScriptId > @ScriptId
end

print 'Finished executing all files.'
drop table #FileList
EXECUTE sp_OADestroy @FileSystemObject

if @UseTransaction <> 0
BEGIN
    EXEC @hr = sp_OAMethod @objSQL, 'CommitTransaction '
    IF @hr < 0
    BEGIN
        print 'error CommitTransaction'
        exec sp_OAGetErrorInfo @objSQL, @hr
        RETURN
    END
END

RETURN
```

To execute the util.ap_BatchExec_OA procedure, you need to specify values for the parameters for the SQL Server instance, login, password, and folder that contains your deployment scripts, and the name of the file containing the list of deployment scripts. You also need to decide whether deployment is to be performed as a transaction. Transactions cannot be used for initial deployment because database creation cannot be performed by a transaction. However, using transactions is very useful for incremental builds.

The util.ap_BatchExec_OA procedure has one limitation. It can process only short (up to 8,000 characters) scripts. Automation stored procedures, such as sp_OAMethod, were designed before SQL Server got `varchar(max)` data types, so they are limited to 8,000 characters. I have decided to include it in this the book for two reasons. First, 8,000 characters is probably enough for running an incremental build. Second, it's educational—it demonstrates the use of COM objects from Transact-SQL.

Alternatively, on SQL Server 2005, you can use an updated version that utilizes the `varchar(max)` data type— util.ap_BatchExec8. The procedure can be used to run larger scripts:

```
create proc util.ap_BatchExec8
-- Execute specified sql files.
    @ServerName sysname = '.\rc',
    @UserId sysname = 'sa',
    @PWD sysname = 'my,password',
    @DirName varchar(400)='C:\sql\test',
    @File varchar(400) = 'list.txt',
    @UseTransaction int = 0,
    @debug int = 0
as

set nocount on

declare @FilePath varchar(500),
        @FileId int,
        @MaxFileID int,
        @OldFileId int,
        @Cmd varchar(1000),
        @i int,
        @iOld int,
        @max int,
        @s varchar(max),
        @line varchar(max)
```

```
--- Get list of files
create table #FileList (FileId int identity(1,1),
                        FileName varchar(500))

select  @Cmd = 'cd ' + @DirName + ' & type ' + @File

insert #FileList (FileName)
exec master.sys.xp_cmdshell @Cmd

-- remove empty rows and comments
delete #FileList where FileName is null
delete #FileList where FileName like '--%'

if @debug <> 0
   select * from #FileList

create table #script (SQL    varchar(max),
                      LineId int identity)

select @FileId = Min (FileId),
       @MaxFileID = Max(FileId)
from #FileList

-- loop through files
WHILE @FileId <= @MaxFileID
BEGIN
   -- get name of the file to be processed
   select @FilePath = @DirName + '\' + FileName
   from #FileList
   where FileId = @FileId

   if @FilePath <> ''
   BEGIN
      if @debug <> 0
         print 'Reading ' + @FilePath

      set @cmd = 'Type "' + @FilePath + '"'

      insert #script (SQL)
      exec master.sys.xp_cmdshell @Cmd
```

```
Select  @i = Min (LineId),
        @max = Max(LineId),
        @s = ''
from #script

while @i <= @max
begin

    Select @line = Coalesce(SQL, ' ')
    from #script
    where LineId = @i

    if @debug <> 0
        select 'read line =', @i i, @line line

    if Left(@line, 2) <> 'GO'
    begin
        -- the line and go another round
        select @s = @s + char(13) + char(10) + @line
        if @debug <> 0
            select @s [@s]
    end
    else
    begin
        begin try
            if @debug = 0
                exec sp_sqlexec @s
            else
                select @s
        end try
        begin catch
            print Error_message()
            print 'Process stopped.'
            return
        end catch
        set @s = ''
    end
    -- continue line by line
    set @iOld = @i
    select @i = Min(LineId)
    from #script
    where LineId > @iOld
end
```

```
        END
        -- get next file
        set @FileID = @FileId + 1
        select @fileID FileId

        truncate table #script
END
return
```

You may find it strange that this stored procedure does not have a transaction inside. You can easily make it run under a transaction if you do something like this:

```
Set xact_abort on
Begin tran
Exec util.ap_BatchExec8 "(local)\ss2k5", "sa", "my,password", "c:\script\test
list.txt"
Commit tran
```

You should carefully consider the pros and cons of executing deployment scripts in transaction. It is nice to promise your IT management that you will roll back everything if there is any unforeseen problem, but operations will be slower if you run them in transaction; complete rollback may take much more time than you expected and some operations cannot be rolled back.

The third method for deploying database scripts is the BatchExec.exe program that you can download from www.Trigonblue.com/tsql.net/download.htm. This is a console C# application and you can run it on computers that have the .NET Framework installed using:

```
BatchExec (local)\ss2k5 sa my,password c:\script\test list.txt
```

Deploying Create Scripts in Visual Studio .NET

Create scripts generated in Visual Studio 2003 .NET (but unfortunately not in Visual Studio 2005) can also be "glued" together and deployed on other servers:

1. Select the Create Scripts folder in Solution Explorer, and then select Project | Create Command File.
2. Set the Name Of Command File and move all or just some of the scripts in the Available Scripts list to the list of Scripts To Be Added To The Command File.

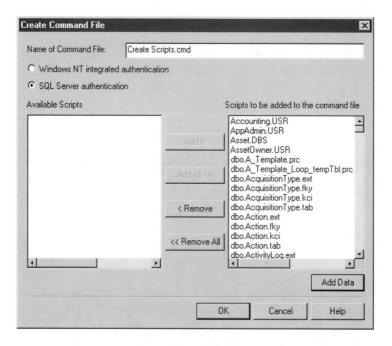

3. If you have moved some of the table files (TAB) that have data files (DAT) associated with them, the Add Data button becomes available. Click the button and the program prompts you to confirm associations between files.

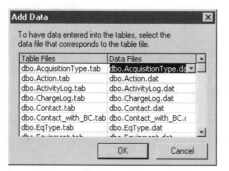

4. You probably do not need to change anything, so just click OK and the program returns you to the previous screen.

5. Click OK again and the program generates a command file (or batch file) that can be used to execute all Create scripts on any server (see Figure 18-5).

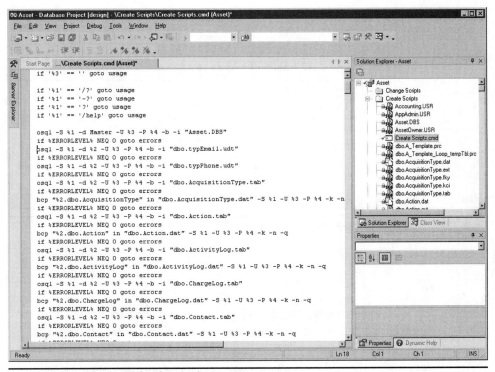

Figure 18-5   *Command file for deploying Create scripts*

Incremental Build: Traditional Approach

Whichever method you choose for performing a full build of the database, you will eventually need to deploy design changes and hot fixes while preserving data in the database. Such changes can even accumulate over time. Typically, code changes for procedures can simply be executed in their latest form against the production database, but changes to the database structure (tables) must be implemented in such a way that they preserve data.

util.ap_BatchExec8 is very useful for deploying incremental changes on the database server. Individual changes to database objects can be grouped by defect number or version number (see Figure 18-6).

It is especially useful to run the process as a transaction in this case. If an unexpected error occurs during the deployment, it is preferable to roll back all the changes, leaving the production system intact. If changes are not very big, it may not take too much time.

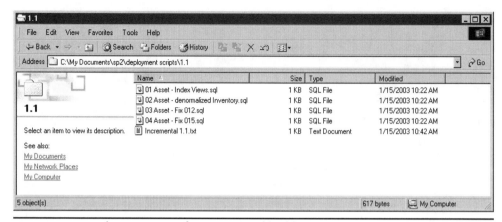

Figure 18-6   *Deployment script for incremental build*

TIP

Once you assemble deployment scripts, it is critical to perform sufficient unit testing. You can run the scripts against a new server or a new instance on the existing server and test the changes.

You should repeat the deployment, fixing issues that you find, until it runs without a glitch. The ultimate test is whether the application can work with the database system without additional intervention.

Incremental Build in Visual Studio .NET

Alternatively, you can create incremental scripts in Visual Studio .NET. In this case, you create Change scripts and manage them in the folder of the same name (in Solution Explorer). You should again create a command file, but you should probably name it differently. You will use the same techniques and methods that have already been described regarding the full build in the earlier section "Scripting Data in Visual Studio .NET."

TIP

You should pay special attention to avoid mixing versions of files and to execute database changes in the right order. It is a good idea to add sequential numbers or the date and time at the beginning of filenames. You can store different releases in different folders, or you can have different command files if you keep all Change scripts in the same folder. When you are done, test, test, and test again.

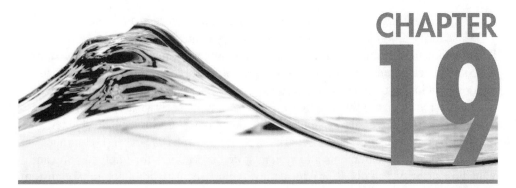

CHAPTER
19

Security

SQL Server 2005 is much more secure than earlier versions. The whole security architecture has been dramatically changed and many new features added. For example, permissions are more granular, more objects are securable, more sophisticated encryption has been added, SQL Server logins are as secure as Windows logins, and new schema objects have replaced object owners, but we will have a different focus in this chapter. I will describe the security architecture of the data layer and not cover all possible security details of SQL Server. The chapter starts with an introduction to the security architecture of SQL Server. It continues with an overview of statements and system stored procedures for implementing and managing security. Finally, it provides a few typical security architectures for custom applications.

Security Architecture

Implementing security on SQL Server is not difficult, but you need to have a good understanding of its security architecture before you can define and implement an effective and manageable security solution. Let's start by describing basic concepts and terminology.

Authentication and Authorization

Authentication is the process of identifying a user or process. *Authorization* is the process of granting an authenticated user or process specific rights to access or modify resources.

Principals

Principals are users, groups, and processes that can ask for access to SQL Server resources. Principals have several common characteristics. Each principal has its own security identification number (SID). Principals could be sets of principals (such as Windows groups or database roles) or indivisible principals (such as local or domain logins). Each principal has a scope, and scopes are based on the level at which the principal is defined (see Table 19-1).

In the following sections, I will try to make these abstract principals easier to envision by referring often to them as "users". Just remember that a *user,* in this sense, can represent any of the principals shown in Table 19-1.

Windows-level Principals	SQL Server–level Principals	Database-level Principals
Local logins	Native SQL Server login	Database role
Domain logins	SQL Server login linked with Windows login or group	Application role
Local groups	SQL Server login linked with asymmetric key	Database user
Domain groups	SQL Server login linked with certificate	Database user linked with Windows user or group
		Database user linked with asymmetric key
		Database user linked with certificate

Table 19-1 *Principals by Level*

Securables

Securables are server or database objects that can be secured with permissions. They are divided by scope into three groups (see Table 19-2).

Server Scope Securables	Database Scope Securables	Schema Scope Securables
Logins	Users	Tables
Databases	Database roles	Views
Endpoints	Application roles	Stored procedures
	Schemas	Functions
	Certificates	Types
	Services	Synonyms
	Assemblies	Aggregates
	Message types	XML schema collections
	Routes	Queues
	Remote service binding	
	Full-text catalogs	
	Asymmetric keys	
	Symmetric keys	
	Contracts	

Table 19-2 *Securables by Scope*

Access Levels

A user (a person or application) has to go through four levels of security before performing an action on a database object:

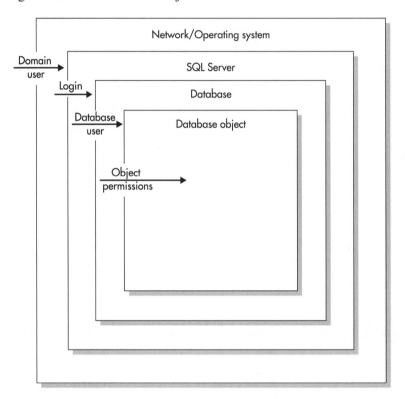

Network/OS Access

A user needs access to the client computer, operating system, and network on which the server is located. Usually, granting this access is the responsibility of technical support specialists or network administrators. However, in smaller environments, this responsibility may fall to a DBA or a developer instead.

Server Access

This is the first level of security that pertains strictly to SQL Server. It allows a client to access a server. This security level is always the responsibility of database administrators.

The client has to authenticate itself (verify its identity) to the server before it is allowed to request additional resources. SQL Server supports Windows or SQL Server authentication to verify the identity of the client.

SQL Server authentication is based on logins and passwords that SQL Server stores in its master database. The client must supply them or it will be prompted for a login and password.

Windows authentication is based on Windows (network) domain or local logins. A client's connection to a server is associated with its Windows login. The client will not be prompted for logins and password. A behind-the-scenes process authenticates the client using its Windows login and SID.

Windows authentication is usually considered more secure and easier to maintain, partly because of the infrastructure work that Microsoft has done in Windows, and partly because of the availability of tools on the Internet that can read passwords from SQL Server logins. Windows authentication is easier to manage for both the user (who has to remember only one login and password combination and to type them just once to log in to the network) and the administrator (who can manage all logins and passwords centrally).

NOTE

Microsoft has made some improvements on SQL Server authentication in SQL Server 2005. For example, a SQL Server 2005 instance can be set to require strong passwords and to require password updates after a specified period of time. However, Microsoft still recommends using Windows authentication, saying that SQL Server authentication should be used only for legacy applications.

SQL Server can be installed or configured in two *authentication modes*:

▶ **Windows Authentication Mode** allows clients to authenticate themselves using only Windows authentication. Before SQL Server 7.0, it was called *integrated security.*

▶ **Mixed Authentication Mode** supports both SQL Server and Windows authentication. Some users can log in with their network account while others (who may or may not have a Windows account) can log in using their SQL Server login.

NOTE

Early versions of SQL Server (before 7.0) could be installed in Standard security/mode, which supported only SQL Server authentication.

Database Access

Access to a server does not automatically provide a user with access to a database. An administrator has to assign a database to a login in one of the following manners:

▶ The administrator creates a *database user* that corresponds to the login in each database to which the user needs access.

▶ The administrator configures a database to treat a login/database user as a member of a *database role.* Such a user inherits all permissions from the role.

▶ The administrator sets a login to use one of the *default user accounts*: guest or database owner (dbo).

Once access to a database has been granted, the user can see all database objects because the object definitions are stored in system tables to which every user has read access.

Permissions

Permissions are the final level of SQL Server security. To have access to securables (resources) on SQL Server, a principal has to have permissions to perform actions on them.

SQL Server 2005 has a new object model with more granular permissions (than earlier versions) that are organized in a hierarchy. You can see a complete list if you execute the sys.fn_builtin_permissions function (see Figure 19-1). The result contains almost 200 individual permissions.

Principals can be given *Select, Update, Insert*, and *Delete* permissions to schema-contained securables (such as tables and views), to schemas, and to databases. This access level means that the user can read, write, delete, or change data. *Reference* permission allows a principal to use a foreign key constraint to validate an entry using an object such as a column or a table. *Execute* permission is given on programmatic objects (such as stored procedures).

View Definition will allow a principal to get scripts for server and database object creation, while *Alter* permission will allow principals to modify (change, drop, or create) server or database objects. Database users that create objects become their owners (unless they are also already owners of the schema). *Take Ownership* permission allows other users to acquire them instead. *Control* includes all permissions (contained in Alter and Take Ownership permissions) and permission to grant others permissions on the object.

Alter Any permission applies to a collection of objects of a particular class. For example, Alter Any Database allows a user to alter all databases on the server.

The key to the table in Figure 19-1 is a combination of permission_name + class_descr (the name of the class of objects that the permission applies to).

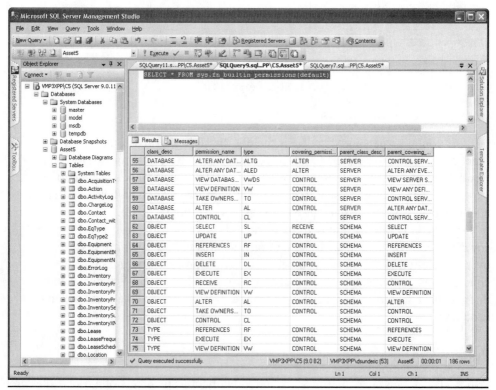

Figure 19-1   *List of built-in permissions*

Some permissions have parents and a combination of fields; covering_permission_
name + class_descr points to them. For example, if a principal (user) has the Control
permission over the Database class of objects, that permission also implies all (child)
permissions such as View Definition and Alter for all Database class objects. You can
see the complete hierarchy if you execute the following common table expression:

```
WITH Perms(class_desc, covering_permission_name, permission_name, level) AS
(
    -- anchor member (for first iteration)
    SELECT class_desc, covering_permission_name, permission_name, 0 level
    FROM sys.fn_builtin_permissions(default)
    WHERE covering_permission_name = ''
        UNION ALL
    -- recursive member (for later iterations)
    SELECT o.class_desc, o.covering_permission_name, o.permission_name, p.level +
1 level
    FROM sys.fn_builtin_permissions(default) o
        INNER JOIN Perms p
        ON o.covering_permission_name = p.permission_name
```

```
        and o.class_desc = p.class_desc
)
SELECT s.class_desc, s.permission_name, s.covering_permission_name, s.level
FROM Perms s
INNER JOIN sys.fn_builtin_permissions(default) o
ON o.permission_name = s.permission_name
and o.class_desc = s.class_desc
ORDER BY s.class_desc, s.level;
```

BOL contains the source code for the dbo.ImplyingPermissions user-defined function, which can be used to reveal covering permissions—permissions that "imply" the specified permission. For example, after you compile the function in the master database, you can use it to get a list of permissions of a higher level that can alter database objects such as stored procedures (see Figure 19-2).

There is one more hierarchy implemented through parent_class_descr + parent_covering_permission_name. This hierarchy ensures that, if you have permissions over a higher class of objects, you will also have appropriate permissions over their child objects. For example, if you have Control permission over Schema, it implies that you have Control permission over other objects in the schema (such as tables and views).

Roles

Principals can be granted permissions individually or as members of a *role*. Roles are the SQL Server equivalent to groups in a Windows domain.

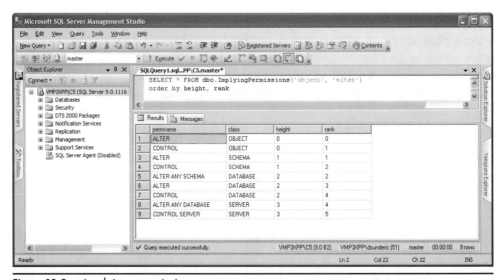

Figure 19-2   *Implying permissions*

In early versions of SQL Server, a user could belong to only one role (group). This restriction led to some pretty unrefined security solutions. A user can now be a member of many roles. Instead of managing large groups of users and their permissions, the idea is to grant permissions to a role and then assign users to it. Therefore, roles can be used to provide an efficient and sophisticated security model, managing access to the required securables (functionality and objects).

Fixed Server Roles

Server-level principals can become members of server roles to control server-scope securables (or lower). Server roles are fixed—it is not possible to change the permissions granted to them and it is not possible to create new server roles. The set of server roles is

- ► sysadmin
- ► securityadmin
- ► serveradmin
- ► setupadmin
- ► processadmin
- ► diskadmin
- ► dbcreator
- ► bulkadmin

In earlier versions of SQL Server, you could use the following stored procedures to get the list of permissions that is granted to the role:

```
exec sp_srvrolepermission 'processadmin'
```

Unfortunately, this stored procedure is not supported in SQL Server 2005. You can find a list of permissions granted to server roles in BOL in the "Permissions of Fixed Server Roles" section.

Fixed Database Roles

Database-level principals can become members of fixed database roles to manage database-scoped securables:

- ► db_accessadmin
- ► db_backupoperator
- ► db_datareader

► db_datawriter

► db_ddladmin

► db_denydatareader

► db_denydatawriter

► db_owner

► db_securityadmin

► public

You can get the list of permissions assigned to each of these roles in BOL in the "Permissions of Fixed Database Roles" section.

The public role is special. Every user that is granted access to the database is automatically a member of the public role (and inherits the permissions granted to it).

Custom Database Roles

You can create database roles and assign permissions to database- and schema-scoped securables. One user can be a member of zero, one, or more database roles (fixed or custom).

Microsoft recommends that you create database roles when there is no Windows group that can be used to manage permissions, or when you do not have permission to manage Windows groups. I believe that you should always have database roles. A Windows group or user to which you have assigned appropriate permissions could be deleted or used for something else, and that would require you to reassign individual permissions. If you have assigned them all to a single role (permissions are also grouped this way), it is much simpler to reassign them to the new user or group.

Application Roles

Sometimes you want to force your users to access a database only through a custom application. This scenario is quite typical when you are building business logic into middleware components. If your users (or their roles) have permissions to underlying objects, they can use generic tools such as Management Studio to access them directly. Microsoft has created application roles to prevent users from accessing underlying objects directly.

Application roles are custom roles defined on the database level that do not have members (principals), and that require a password to become active. When a connection string specifies an application role and provides the password, SQL Server disregards all user privileges and assigns the user only the privileges assigned to the application role.

NOTE

Application roles have a serious limitation in performing cross-database or cross-server operations. They are designed as database-level principals and they cannot have explicit permissions outside of the database in which they are created. An application role will get the permissions assigned to the guest user account (which is typically not much).

Ownership Chains

Database objects such as stored procedures, views, and functions can reference other database objects such as tables, as well as other stored procedures, views, and functions. Underlying objects can also reference other database objects. You can envision the structure of objects linked this way as a tree, but SQL Server documentation refers to it (in the context of security) as a *chain*. SQL Server has to evaluate permissions that users have on each object individually and sequentially (that's why it's called a *chain*), before it allows the user to access them. This could be very complex and time-consuming, but fortunately there is a shortcut called an *ownership chain* that SQL Server uses. If all constituent objects belong to the same schema as the object that references them, SQL Server will not evaluate the permissions of the user to access individual (constituent) objects. However, if even one of them does not belong to the schema of the top object (that is, if the chain is broken), SQL Server will evaluate the user's permissions to access all underlying objects.

In SQL Server 2005, database objects are owned by schemas. Before SQL Server 2005, database objects were owned by owners such as dbo, and therefore, these chains were given the name *ownership chains*.

The main purpose of ownership chains is to simplify security management of database objects. It is typically sufficient to give users access to only top-level objects (such as stored procedures).

Cross-database Ownership Chains

Database objects can also reference objects in other databases. In that case, ownership chains span multiple databases and they are called *cross-database ownership chains*. By default, cross-database ownership chains are not enabled on SQL Server. However, during the installation of the server, you can enable them for all databases on the server. Alternatively, you can enable cross-database ownership chains between specific databases.

CAUTION

Cross-database ownership chains are potentially dangerous and you should not enable them unless you need them. For example, say that there is a user John in a database Asset5 that has Select permission on the vInventory view that belongs to dbo schema. The user also exists in database Finance but he is not given permissions to select data from table dbo.Transactions. If the user can modify the vInventory view to read data from Finanace.dbo.Transactions, SQL Server will just verify that the schema of the view matches the schemas of all underlying objects and automatically give access to data in the table in the Finance database without checking permissions.

Switching of Execution Context

I have demonstrated in earlier chapters how you can use the Execute As clause of stored procedures, user-defined functions (except inline table-valued UDFs), and triggers to control execution context. Basically, you can define procedures so that they are executed as if they were authenticated as a different user.

The Execute As Caller option is the default that is compatible with the behavior of earlier versions of SQL Server. The user needs to have permissions on the procedure and all objects it references.

The Execute As User = 'user' option is useful when a caller does not have permissions on underlying objects, and when those permissions are required (for example, when a procedure is dynamically assembling a batch, it is not sufficient to rely on permission to the procedure and the compatibility of schemas). The procedure will be executed in the context of 'user' (if he or she has adequate permissions).

The Execute As Self option will execute a procedure using the name of the user that has created or altered the procedure.

The Execute As Owner option specifies that the procedure will be executed as the owner of the object, or if the owner is not defined, in the context of the schema owner. The owner must be a singleton account—it cannot be a group or a role.

The Execute As statement (we described the Execute As clause in the previous section) changes execution context on the level of the session. It is possible to specify a different user or login to be impersonated on the level of a database or server respectively. In this case, permissions will be checked based on the security context of the specified user or login and all permissions of the original login will be ignored.

NOTE

If a session is set to impersonate a database user, any attempt to access objects outside of the database will fail (even distributed queries and the Use statement).

Once set, the context of the session will be in effect until it is set again, until connection is dropped, or until the user invokes the Revert statement (which returns the execution context to the original login).

Implementing Security

You can implement a security solution with Management Studio or Transact-SQL statements, using system and extended stored procedures. Security stored procedures can also be used to manage security or implement some additional security features from a client application.

Selection of Authentication Mode

You select an authentication mode during installation of the server or in the Server Properties dialog box.

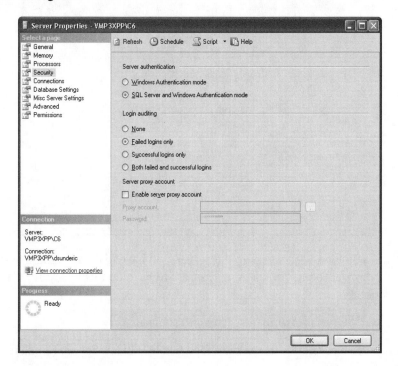

To open the Security page, right-click the server in the Object Browser, select Properties, and then select Security page.

Managing Logins

To allow a person to access SQL Server, you must first define his or her (server) login account. To create a login, expand the Security branch of Management Studio, right-click Logins, and select New Login from the pop-up menu. To manage an existing login, right-click the login in the List pane and select Properties. Management Studio opens the Login window to enable you to manage login properties. On the General page, you can select a name and type of login, password, default database, and language. You can switch to other pages of the window to specify membership in server roles, permissions on server securables, and access to databases.

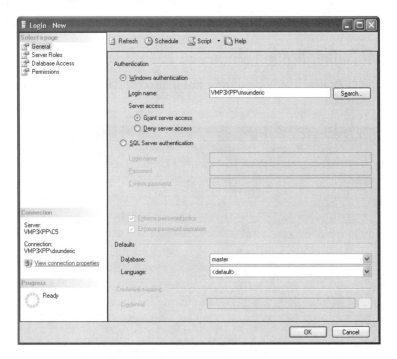

To allow a Windows user access to the server, you have to create a login associated with the Windows account. You can use Transact-SQL to do this in several ways, but the basic option is

```
Create Login [MyDomain\NikolaS] FROM WINDOWS;
```

Alternatively, you can create a server login for a whole Windows group (domain or local) that the user belongs to:

```
CREATE LOGIN [MyDomain\MyGroup] FROM WINDOWS;
```

You can use Create Login to create a SQL Server login as well:

```
Create Login nsunderic WITH PASSWORD = 'my,password326'
```

In this case, a person will need to use a password when authenticating to SQL Server.

NOTE

In previous versions of SQL Server, you had to use system stored procedures such as sp_addlogin to achieve the same goals. They are still supported to preserve compatibility.

The set of Login statements is orthogonal—there are Drop Login and Alter Login statements as well. You can get a list of server principals from the sys.server_principals catalog view.

```
if exists(select * from sys.server_principals where name = 'nsunderic')
  Drop Login nsunderic
```

You can get more information about specified login using the sp_HelpLogin system stored procedure. It will return the list of matching logins and the list of associated database users.

The Database Access page of the Login window manages the databases the user can access and the user's membership in database roles.

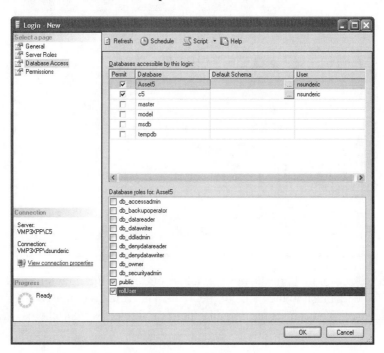

You can also grant logins using stored procedures. You can use sp_grantlogin to create a login on SQL Server. To give a Windows user access to a SQL server, only the name of the user is required as a parameter:

```
exec sp_grantlogin @login = 'Accounting\TomB'
```

Granting Database Access

As you have seen, database access can be granted to a login during the login's creation. There is also a way to approach user creation from the database side and create a user by specifying the login or granting access to additional database objects after the user has been created. Database users can be managed from the *server* | Databases | *database* | Security | Users node of a database in the Object Browser. From the context-sensitive menu, you can choose to create a new user or edit an existing one. Management Studio will open the Database User window:

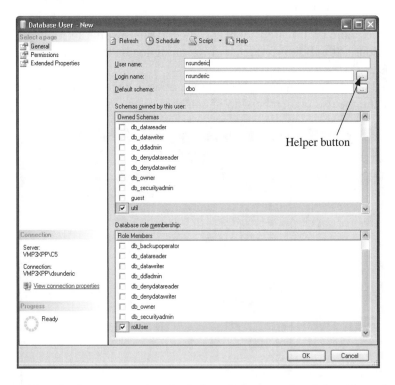

It is best to select login names using the helper button on the right side and to set a username to be identical to the name of the login. This is not required, but it simplifies user management. You can set the default schema and select which schemas are owned by the user. In the Database Role Membership section, you check all database roles to which you want to grant the user membership. You can perform the same operations from Transact-SQL.

To grant access to the database, use the Create User statement:

```
USE [Asset5]
GO
CREATE USER [nsunderic] FOR LOGIN [nsunderic]
GO
```

In this case, login nsunderic will become associated with the new nsunderic user in the current database. If you omit the For Login clause, SQL Server will attempt to associate the user with a login that has the same name.

You can review access using sp_HelpUsers. You can delete users using the Drop User statement and you can change them using the Alter User statement. The sys.database principals catalog view can be used to list database users (and other principals).

```
if exists(select * from sys.database_principals where name = 'nsunderic')
   DROP USER nsunderic
```

Granting Role Membership

To assign a user to a user-defined database role, you issue a command such as:

```
exec sp_addrolemember @rolename='rolUser', @membername='nsunderic'
```

The @membername parameter can be a database user, another database role, a server login based on a Windows user, or a server login based on a Windows group.

You can review membership using sp_helprolemember and revoke it using sp_droprolemember.

You can create roles using sp_addrole:

```
Create Role 'rolBcmManagement'
```

You can remove roles using Drop Role or change their names using Alter Role. To view a list of roles, use sp_helpfixeddbroles and sp_helproles.

Granting Schema Ownership

To give a user ownership of a schema, use

```
ALTER AUTHORIZATION ON SCHEMA::[util] TO [nsunderic]
```

Assigning Permissions

The system of permissions controls user and role access to database objects and statements. Permissions can exist in one of following two states:

▶ **Granted**   Means that a user has permission to use an object, feature, or statement.

▶ **Denied**   Means that a user is not allowed to use a statement, feature, or object, even if the user has previously inherited permission (that is, the user is a member of a role that has permission granted).

Physically, a record is stored in either the sys.database_permissions or the sys .server_permissions catalog views for each user (or role) and object (or statement) for which permission has been granted or denied.

Because of their physical implementation, permissions are cumulative. For example, a user can receive permissions from one role and other permissions from some other role. Or, the user can be denied permissions that have been granted to all other members of a role.

You can control permissions from the Permissions page of the Database User window:

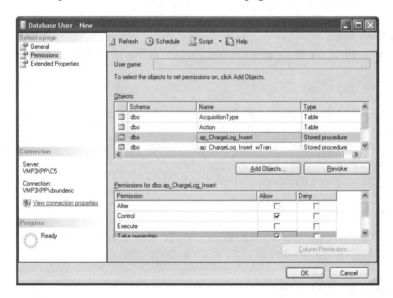

The bottom list contains permissions for the object specified in the top window. You can use the Add Objects and Revoke (remove from the list) buttons to manage the Objects list, and you can grant or deny individual permissions on specified objects using checkboxes.

Grant Statement

There are many forms of the Grant statement (and the Deny and Revoke statements), because there are many forms of securables. I will try to give you an idea how to use them and to cover the most important.

The following statement allows JohnS (SQL Server login) and TomB from the Accounting domain (Windows domain user) to create a database on the current server:

```
Grant Create Database
To JohnS, [Accounting\TomB]
```

You can also combine several permissions in one statement:

```
GRANT   ADMINISTER BULK OPERATIONS,
      ALTER ANY LINKED SERVER,
      CREATE ANY DATABASE,
      VIEW ANY DATABASE
TO JohnS
```

The following statement grants rolUser members rights to execute the stored procedure, view its definition, or change it:

```
GRANT EXECUTE, VIEW DEFINITION, ALTER
ON dbo.ap_ChargeLog_Insert
TO rolUser
GO
```

The following statement allows members of the rolUser role to view, add, delete, change, and reference (in a foreign key) records in the Inventory table:

```
Grant Select, Insert, Update, Delete, REFERENCES
On dbo.Inventory
To rolUser
```

Deny Statement

The Deny statement is used to negate permissions explicitly. Its syntax is basically the same as the syntax of the Grant statement (except that the keyword Deny is used).

The following statement prevents TomB of the Accounting domain from creating a database:

```
Deny Create Database
To [Accounting\TomB]
```

The following statement prevents JohnS from deleting and changing records from the Inventory table, even though he has inherited rights to view, store, delete, and change records as a member of the AssetOwners role:

```
Deny Update, Delete
On dbo.Inventory
To JohnS
```

A Deny statement, even at the user level, will supersede all Grant permissions, whether at the user or role level.

Revoke Statement

The Revoke statement is used to deactivate statements that have granted or denied permissions. It has the same syntax as the Grant and Deny statements (except that the keyword Revoke is used).

It is easy to understand that permission can be removed using the Revoke statement. It is a little more challenging to understand how a permission can be granted by revoking it. To help you understand this concept, consider the following example in which a user, JohnS, is a member of the AssetOwner role, which has permission to insert, update, select, and delete records from the Inventory table:

```
exec sp_addrolemember 'AssetOwner', 'JohnS',
```

The administrator then decides to deny JohnS permission to delete and update records from Inventory:

```
Deny Update, Delete
On dbo.Inventory
To JohnS
```

After a while, the administrator issues the following statement:

```
Revoke Update, Delete
On dbo.Inventory
To JohnS
```

In effect, this command has granted Update and Delete permission on the Inventory table to JohnS.

Since the Revoke statement removes records from the sys.database_protects table in the current database, the effect of the Revoke statement is to return permissions to their original state. Naturally, this means that the user will not have access to the object (or statement). In that respect, its effect is similar to the Deny statement. However, there are two major differences between revoked and denied permissions: the Revoke statement does not prevent permissions from being granted in the *future*; and the Revoke statement doesn't supersede any other granted permissions provided by membership in other roles, whereas Deny does supersede those permissions.

Synchronization of Login and Usernames

Chapter 18 discusses in detail deploying/moving databases from one server to another. The problem you will encounter in this situation is a mismatch between users and logins. This problem is a result of the fact that records in the sys.database_principals catalog view of the copied database point to the records in the sys.server_principals catalog view with matching sid fields. Unfortunately, the same sid value might be used by different logins on two different servers. It is also possible that a login with a specific sid value does not yet exist on a new server. These database users are sometimes referred to as *orphaned users*. One solution is to create and manage a script that re-creates logins and users on the new server before or after a database is copied.

Another solution is to assemble a script dynamically to create logins on the target server before the database is copied:

```
SET NOCOUNT ON
SELECT 'CREATE LOGIN [' + name + '] '
+ 'with password = ''My1.Password'',
DEFAULT_DATABASE = tempdb,
sid ='
' sid
--select *
FROM sys.server_principals
WHERE principal_id > 256
and type_desc = 'SQL_LOGIN'

SELECT 'CREATE LOGIN [' + name + '] FROM WINDOWS; '
FROM sys.server_principals
WHERE principal_id > 256
and type_desc = 'WINDOWS_LOGIN'
and name not in ('NT AUTHORITY\SYSTEM', 'BUILTIN\Administrators')


select 'EXEC sp_addsrvrolemember '''+loginname+''', ''sysadmin'''
from syslogins
where sysadmin = 1
union
select 'EXEC sp_addsrvrolemember '''+loginname+''', ''securityadmin'''
from syslogins
```

```
where securityadmin = 1
union
select 'EXEC sp_addsrvrolemember '''+loginname+''', ''serveradmin'''
from syslogins
where serveradmin = 1
union
select 'EXEC sp_addsrvrolemember '''+loginname+''', ''setupadmin'''
from syslogins
where setupadmin = 1
union
select 'EXEC sp_addsrvrolemember '''+loginname+''', ''processadmin'''
from syslogins
where processadmin = 1
union
select 'EXEC sp_addsrvrolemember '''+loginname+''', ''diskadmin'''
from syslogins
where diskadmin = 1
union
select 'EXEC sp_addsrvrolemember '''+loginname+''', ''dbcreator'''
from syslogins
where dbcreator = 1
union
select 'EXEC sp_addsrvrolemember '''+loginname+''', ''bulkadmin'''
from syslogins
where bulkadmin = 1


-----------------------------------------
-----------------------------------------
select 'Run these after dbs are created:'

select ' EXEC sp_defaultdb @loginame = ''' + name + ''''
,', @defdb = ''' + Coalesce(default_database_name, 'tempdb') + ''''
FROM sys.server_principals
WHERE principal_id > 256
and type_desc = 'SQL_LOGIN'


-----------------------------------------

select ' EXEC sp_defaultdb @loginame = ''' + name + ''''
,', @defdb = ''' + Coalesce(default_database_name, 'tempdb') + ''''
FROM sys.server_principals
WHERE principal_id > 256
and type_desc = 'WINDOWS_LOGIN'
and name not in ('NT AUTHORITY\SYSTEM', 'BUILTIN\Administrators')
```

When executed on the source server, the script generates one group of commands to be executed before database deployment, and one group to be executed after the databases are deployed on the target server. The first group re-creates logins and preserves their IDs but not passwords, and then renews their membership in server roles. The second group sets their default databases.

NOTE

This method does not preserve passwords for SQL Server logins. You must ask the people to whom these logins are assigned to modify them as soon as possible (using the sp_password stored procedure).

SQL Server also offers the sp_change_users_login procedure. It is designed to manage orphaned users of SQL Server logins. It cannot be used to manage Windows logins. You can use it to display the database users without mapping to server logins:

```
exec sp_change_users_login @Action = 'Report'
```

NOTE

sp_change_users_login, when used with @Action='Report', does not accept parameters for user or login names.

You can set a SQL Server login manually for a single orphaned user:

```
exec sp_change_users_login @Action = 'Update_one',
                           @UserNamePattern = 'TomB',
                           @LoginName = 'TomB'
```

SQL Server can also match all orphaned database users to SQL Server logins with the same name:

```
exec sp_change_users_login @Action = 'Auto_Fix',
                           @UserNamePattern = '%',
                           @password = 'my1.password'
```

For each user, SQL Server tries to find a SQL Server login with the same name and to set the corresponding `sid`. If the login already exists, the stored procedure will leave its original password intact. If the matching login does not exist, SQL Server will create it and set its password. The password cannot be left unset or set to null. The person who is actually using the login can later change the password using the sp_password stored procedure.

TIP

sp_change_users_login with 'Auto_Fix' does a decent job, but the cautious DBA should inspect the results of this operation.

Managing Application Security Using Stored Procedures, User-defined Functions, and Views

When permissions are granted on complex objects such as stored procedures, user-defined functions, or views, the user does not need to have permissions on the underlying objects within or referenced by it. This characteristic is illustrated in the following example:

```
Create Database TestCOC
Go
create login AnnS WITH PASSWORD = 'My,password', DEFAULT_DATABASE = TestCOC
GO
Use TestCOC
GO
CREATE USER AnnS
Go

Create Table dbo.aTable(
     Id int identity(1,1),
     Description Varchar(20)
     )
Go

Create Procedure dbo.ap_aTable_List
as
     Select * from dbo.aTable
go

Create Procedure dbo.ap_aTable_Insert
     @Desc varchar(20)
as
     Insert Into dbo.aTable (Description)
     Values (@Desc)
Go
```

```
Deny Select, Insert, Update, Delete
On dbo.aTable
To Public

Grant Execute
On dbo.ap_aTable_Insert
To Public

Grant Execute
On dbo.ap_aTable_List
To Public
Go
```

A table is created along with two stored procedures for viewing and inserting records into it. All database users are prevented from using the table directly but are granted permission to use the stored procedures.

NOTE

All database users are automatically members of the Public role. Whatever permissions are granted or denied to the Public role are automatically granted or denied to all database users.

After this script is executed, you can log in as AnnS in Query Analyzer and try to access the table both directly and through stored procedures. Figure 19-3 illustrates such attempts.

There are some exceptions to the rule I have just described:

▶ If the schema of the stored procedure is not the schema of all the database objects in the stored procedure, SQL Server will check the object's permissions on each underlying database object. This is not an issue when all objects belong to the default dbo schema. However, you will have to do some careful planning when you decide to use database schemas.

▶ If you are executing a character string batch in a stored procedure, you still need to set permissions on all underlying objects. SQL Server will consider this string to be a separate batch and therefore it will check the permissions of underlying objects. For more details, refer to the "Ownership Chains" section, earlier in this chapter.

▶ If a stored procedure references objects in some other database, behavior will depend on whether cross-database ownership chains are enabled or not. For more details, refer to the "Cross-database Ownership Chains" section, earlier in this chapter.

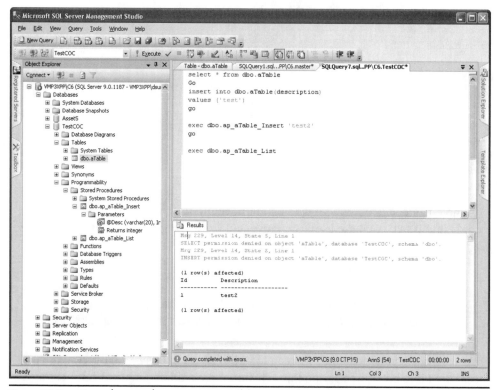

Figure 19-3   *Stored procedures are accessible even when underlying objects are not.*

Stored procedures, user-defined functions, and views are important tools for implementing sophisticated security solutions in a database. Each user should have permissions to perform activities tied to the business functions for which he or she is responsible and to view only related information. It is also easier to manage security in a database on a functional level than on the data level. Therefore, client applications should not be able to issue ad hoc queries against tables in a database. Instead, they should execute stored procedures.

Users should be grouped in roles by the functionality they require, and roles should be granted with execute permissions on related stored procedures. Since roles are stored only in the current database, using them helps you avoid problems that occur during the transfer of the database from the development to the production environment.

Managing Application Security Using a Proxy User

Security does not have to be implemented on SQL Server. If the application is developed using three-tier architecture, objects can use roles, users, and other security features of Component Services (in Windows 2003 and 2000 Server) or Microsoft Transaction Server (on Windows NT) to implement security. Security is sometimes also implemented inside the client application.

In both cases, database access is often accomplished through a single database login and user. Such a user is often called a *proxy user.*

NOTE

The worst such solution occurs when the client application developer completely ignores SQL Server security and achieves database access using the sa login. I have seen two variants on this solution.

One occurs when the developer hard-codes the sa password inside an application. The administrator is then prevented from changing the password (or the application will stop functioning) and the security of the entire SQL Server is exposed.

The other occurs when a developer stores login information in a file or registry so that it can be changed later. Unfortunately, it can also be read by unauthorized people, and again, SQL Server security is compromised.

Managing Application Security Using Application Roles

Application roles are designed to implement security for particular applications. They are different from standard database roles in that

► Application roles require passwords to be activated.

► They do not have members. Users access a database via an application. The application contains the name of the role and its password.

► SQL Server ignores all other user permissions when the application role is activated.

To create an application role, administrators should use sp_addapprole:

```
Exec sp_addapprole @rolename = 'Accounting', @password = 'password'
```

Permissions are managed using the Grant, Deny, and Revoke statements in the usual manner.

A client application (or a middle-tier object) should first log in to SQL Server in the usual manner and then activate the application role using sp_setapprole:

```
Exec sp_setapprole @rolename = 'Accounting', @password = 'password'
```

Now the application will not be able to use permissions granted to its original login/user, but only the permissions granted to the application role.

The biggest disadvantage to application roles is that they can access objects in other databases only as guest users, which may not be sufficient. For more information, refer to the "Application Roles" section earlier in this chapter.

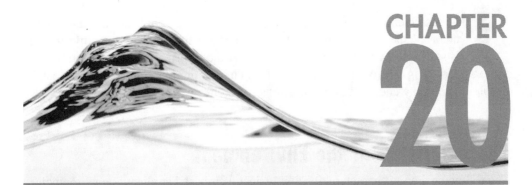

Stored Procedures for Web Search Engines

The search engine is a standard element of every web application. Many tools are available to help web developers create a search engine when information is stored in the form of web pages, but if the information is on a database server, everything has to be customized. This chapter demonstrates some typical problems you may encounter and solutions for them.

Characteristics of the Environment

The following are the characteristics of a typical web-based application environment:

▶ The system has impatient users. Pages must be served quickly or users will leave and go to another web site.

▶ A three-tier architecture is typically used to make the system more scalable.

▶ To be scalable, the system may be deployed on a farm of web and/or middleware servers. If more users need to be processed, you can simply add more servers.

▶ Since it may be deployed on a farm of servers, the application must use stateless connections to the database.

▶ The database server cannot be scaled in the same manner as web and middleware servers. Federated servers allow users to split a database among several servers, but one record will be stored on only one server. It is also not such a trivial matter to add another database server. Tables that are vertically split between servers have to be reorganized so that a new server gets its share of the table. Therefore, the database server is a more precious resource than the web and middleware servers.

▶ Network traffic could be an issue—both internally (between servers) and externally (users could be linked by modem).

A Simple Solution...

Typically, web search engines have two types of web pages—one type for entering criteria and another type for displaying results. The criteria page can sometimes be very simple—a single text box feeding a single table in the database. Sometimes, you may have a web page with a number of objects (such as text boxes, list boxes, and checkboxes) that correspond to different fields in different tables. Potentially, all recordset (table) fields could be exposed as criteria fields. A user can use a single field or multiple fields to specify the criteria. I call such pages and corresponding queries *quick* and *full* (or *advanced*), respectively.

The quick criteria page is naturally implemented in SQL Server as a stored procedure with one parameter. In the case of full criteria, the fact that users can specify values for an unknown number of fields, unsurprisingly, leads developers to implement it as a dynamically assembled ad hoc query joining a large number of normalized tables. To illustrate this in the Asset5 database, I have created a query against Inventory and other associated tables:

```
SELECT Inventoryid, Make,          Model,
       EqType,      Location,       FirstName,
       LastName,    AcquisitionType, Address,
       City,        ProvinceId,     Country,
       Phone,       Fax,            Email,
       UserName,    OrgUnit
from dbo.Inventory Inventory
  inner join dbo.Contact Contact
  on Inventory.OwnerId = Contact.ContactId
    inner join dbo.Location Location
    on Inventory.LocationId = Location.LocationId
      inner join dbo.AcquisitionType AcquisitionType
      on AcquisitionType.AcquisitionTypeId = Inventory.AcquisitionTypeId
        inner join dbo.Equipment Equipment
        on Equipment.EqId = Inventory.EqId
          inner join dbo.EqType EqType
          on Equipment.EqTypeId = EqType.EqTypeId
            inner join dbo.OrgUnit OrgUnit
            on Contact.OrgUnitId = OrgUnit.OrgUnitId
where Make = 'Compaq'
  And EqType = 'Storage Array'
order by  Country, ProvinceId, City, Location
```

In the real world, such a query may be designed to run against more tables—I have seen solutions with 20 or more joined tables. Such a design might look elegant during development if it is tested by only a couple of users using only a small number of records per table. Unfortunately, in production, an application will work against tables with thousands (or millions) of records and will have to serve dozens (or hundreds) of concurrent users.

NOTE

One such system that I've encountered in the past had difficulty supporting even ten users. The simplest queries took five to ten seconds. Regular queries often timed out after 60 seconds. Users were so frustrated that they would issue a query without criteria, and then copy the complete result set to Excel or Access to query it on their local machines.

... and Its Disadvantages

The following are the standard problems with a "simple" solution based on a single query:

▶ **The query joins many tables** Specifying a number of tables that is acceptable is difficult, but 15 or 20, and sometimes even 10, is too many. SQL Server has to do a considerable amount of work to join them all. A normalized set of tables is optimal for modifying data, but for querying, designers should explore denormalization of the model.

▶ **(B)locking** If users are accessing the same set of tables for both updating and querying, they will block each other. SQL Server puts a shared lock on records that qualify as a result of a query while the query is in progress. Other queries are not blocked by it and can be executed at the same time. However, those locks will prevent modifications of the records until the query is done. On the other hand, when a transaction is modifying a record, users will have to wait for the transaction to be completed to have the results to their queries returned.

▶ **The complete result set is sent to the client** Too often, users specify criteria that are not selective enough and may return hundreds (or thousands) of records. Such a recordset is seldom required and users will not browse through it. Typically, they will modify the original criteria and make the query more selective to get a subset of the original recordset.

▶ **Sorting** Users expect the result set to be sorted and they also expect to be able to change the sort order on-the-fly. These actions require processing power.

▶ **Table scans** Some queries may contain criteria that are not optimizable (SARG-able). A common example occurs when a user requests all records for which the Name field contains a specified string. The query is implemented using the Like operator with wild cards (%) at the beginning and the end of the string, such as

```
Where name Like '%str%'
```

SQL Server will not be able to use the index on the name field to process such a query.

▶ **Ad hoc queries**   Since the user has the freedom to specify an unknown number and combination of criteria, queries are typically assembled dynamically. The disadvantage to this flexibility is that you do not have control over these queries, which opens up code management, optimization, and security issues. On the other hand, a dynamically created query allows an experienced user to restrict the query to only those elements that are really needed. You can drop unnecessary tables and segments of criteria.

▶ **Improper indexes**   You should review indexes that are created on tables. Keep in mind that indexes are optimal for querying but not optimal for modifying data. They become overhead on transactions.

Available Solutions

You can do many things to improve this kind of system:

▶ **Denormalization**   This is probably the most effective way to improve the system. SQL Server will have to query a smaller number of tables. You can create a redundant set of tables (one or more, depending on the subject) and periodically (for example, every hour or every day) transfer data from the normalized tables to it. An additional benefit is that "readers" and "writers" will not block each other.

▶ **Limit the result set**   Most search engines on the Web limit the number of results that the user can return (for example, 200 or 500 records).

▶ **Split results rather than limit result sets**   Users should be able to access records in batches (of, for example, 25 or 50 records). Chances are that the user will browse through only the first couple of pages. There is no need to serve the user with 5,000 records that he or she will not review.

▶ **Index**   An additional benefit of splitting tables to provide one table for data modification and another for querying is that the indexes you would need to create on the denormalized tables will not slow down data modification transactions.

▶ **Stored procedures vs. ad hoc queries**   Because of the many performance and management reasons discussed in the "Reuse of Stored Procedure Execution Plans" in Appendix B, you should use precompiled objects such as stored procedures as much as you can. Often, you can significantly simplify a query by dynamically assembling it. When you reduce the number of tables and parameters, the query optimizer creates a better execution plan.

▶ **Search types**   Good results can sometimes be achieved by using a little psychology. For example, users do not always need to do a "Contains" search on a string (like *'%string%'*). Most of the time, "Begins with" (like *'string%'*) and "Match" (=*'string'*) searches are sufficient. For the latter two, SQL Server does not ignore the index. If you add a list box with "Search types" to the text box and make "Begins With" the default option, users will use it probably 90 percent of the time. SQL Server does a table scan only when users really need to scan the whole field.

I will review in detail some of these options in an Asset5 database scenario.

Result Splitting

There are three options for achieving result splitting:

▶ On a web server

▶ Using a temporary table on the database server

▶ Using a static denormalized table on the database server

Page Splitting on a Web Server

Some web sites split the result set on a web server. The complete result set is transferred to the web server and components on it create HTML pages with links between them. There are several good reasons to use this technique. A farm of web servers can efficiently balance the load. There are solutions on the market that can be purchased and implemented rapidly. Unfortunately, network traffic between servers is not reduced and SQL Server has to grab and transfer much more than it should. I will not go into the details of how to implement such a solution (you'll need a different book for that).

Page Splitting Using a Temporary Table on the Database Server

The idea of this solution is to collect the complete recordset in a temporary table and then to send to the caller only a subset of records (for example, 25 records) to be displayed on the current page.

In the following example, the query creates a temporary table that has an additional identity field. The second query returns records with identity values between the specified numbers. Initially, these numbers might be 1 and 25. The next time it is called, the client increases the values of the first and the last records to be displayed.

```
CREATE PROCEDURE ap_InventoryByMakeModel_Quick_TempTbl
-- Return a batch (of specified size) of records which satisfy the criteria
-- Demonstration of use of temporary table to perform record set splitting.
  @Make varchar(50) = '%',
  @Model varchar(50) = '%',
  @FirstRec int = 1,
  @LastRec int = 25,
  @RowCount int = null output
AS
/* test:
declare @rc int
exec ap_InventoryByMakeModel_Quick_TempTbl @RowCount = @rc output
select @rc
exec ap_InventoryByMakeModel_Quick_TempTbl @FirstRec = 26,
                                @LastRec = 50,
                                @RowCount = @rc output
*/
SET NOCOUNT ON

Create table #Inv(ID int identity,
                Inventoryid int,
                Make varchar(50),
                Model varchar(50),
                Location varchar(50),
                FirstName varchar(30),
                LastName varchar(30),
                AcquisitionType varchar(12),
                Address varchar(50),
                City varchar(50),
                ProvinceId char(3),
                Country varchar(50),
                EqType varchar(50),
                Phone varchar(20),
                Fax varchar(20),
                Email varchar(128),
                UserName varchar(50))

insert into #Inv(InventoryId,     Make,      Model,
                Location,        FirstName, LastName,
                AcquisitionType, Address,   City,
                ProvinceId,      Country,   EqType,
                Phone,           Fax,       Email,
                UserName)
```

```
SELECT
  Inventory.Inventoryid, Equipment.Make, Equipment.Model,
  Location.Location, Contact.FirstName,  Contact.LastName,
  AcquisitionType.AcquisitionType, Location.Address, Location.City,
  Location.ProvinceId, Location.Country, EqType.EqType,
  Contact.Phone, Contact.Fax, Contact.Email,
  Contact.UserName
 FROM  dbo.EqType EqType
  RIGHT OUTER JOIN dbo.Equipment Equipment
  ON EqType.EqTypeId = Equipment.EqTypeId
    RIGHT OUTER JOIN dbo.Inventory Inventory
    ON Equipment.EqId = Inventory.EqId
      INNER JOIN dbo.Status Status
      ON Inventory.StatusId = Status.StatusId
        LEFT OUTER JOIN dbo.AcquisitionType AcquisitionType
        ON Inventory.AcquisitionTypeID = AcquisitionType.AcquisitionTypeId
          LEFT OUTER JOIN dbo.Location Location
          ON Inventory.LocationId = Location.LocationId
            LEFT OUTER JOIN dbo.Contact Contact
            ON Inventory.OwnerId = Contact.ContactId
where Make Like @Make
and Model Like @Model
order by Location, LastName, FirstName

select @RowCount = @@rowcount

SELECT *
FROM #Inv
WHERE ID >= @FirstRec AND ID <= @LastRec
order by ID
return
```

The stored procedure should be used the first time in the following manner to get the first batch of records and the number of records:

```
declare @rc int
exec ap_InventoryByMakeModel_Quick_TempTbl @RowCount = @rc output
select @rc
```

The next time, the user must specify the first and last record that he wants to see:

```
declare @rc int
exec ap_InventoryByMakeModel_Quick_TempTbl @FirstRec = 26,
                                            @LastRec  = 50,
                                            @RowCount = @rc output
```

There are, however, several problems with this solution. You are still executing the query against a large set of normalized tables. You are also creating a large temporary table every time you execute the stored procedure. Because you are working in a stateless environment, you cannot keep the temporary table on the server. Therefore, SQL Server works much harder than it should. The advantage to this technique is that network traffic is significantly reduced.

Page Splitting Using Denormalized Tables on the Database Server

To reduce the number of tables that need to be joined every time, you can create a new table that contains all the fields that you typically need in the query. The InventorySum table has such a role in the Asset5 database.

InventorySum		
Column Name	Condensed Type	Nullable
ID	int	Yes
InventoryId	int	Yes
Make	varchar(50)	Yes
Model	varchar(50)	Yes
Location	varchar(50)	Yes
FirstName	varchar(30)	Yes
LastName	varchar(30)	Yes
AcquisitionT...	varchar(12)	Yes
Address	varchar(50)	Yes
City	varchar(50)	Yes
ProvinceId	char(3)	Yes
Country	varchar(50)	Yes
EqType	varchar(50)	Yes
Phone	varchar(20)	Yes
Fax	varchar(20)	Yes
Email	varchar(128)	Yes
UserName	varchar(50)	Yes
MakeModel...	int	Yes
LFNameSIdx	int	Yes
CountrySIdx	int	Yes

Most of the fields are just copied from normalized tables. ID is an identity field, which you will use to request a subset of records and to sort records on. Several records have a SIdx suffix. I call them *surrogate indexes*. They store the position of the record in a set when it is sorted in a particular order. For example, LFNameSIdx is the surrogate index that is used when a recordset is returned sorted by first and last name (see Figure 20-1).

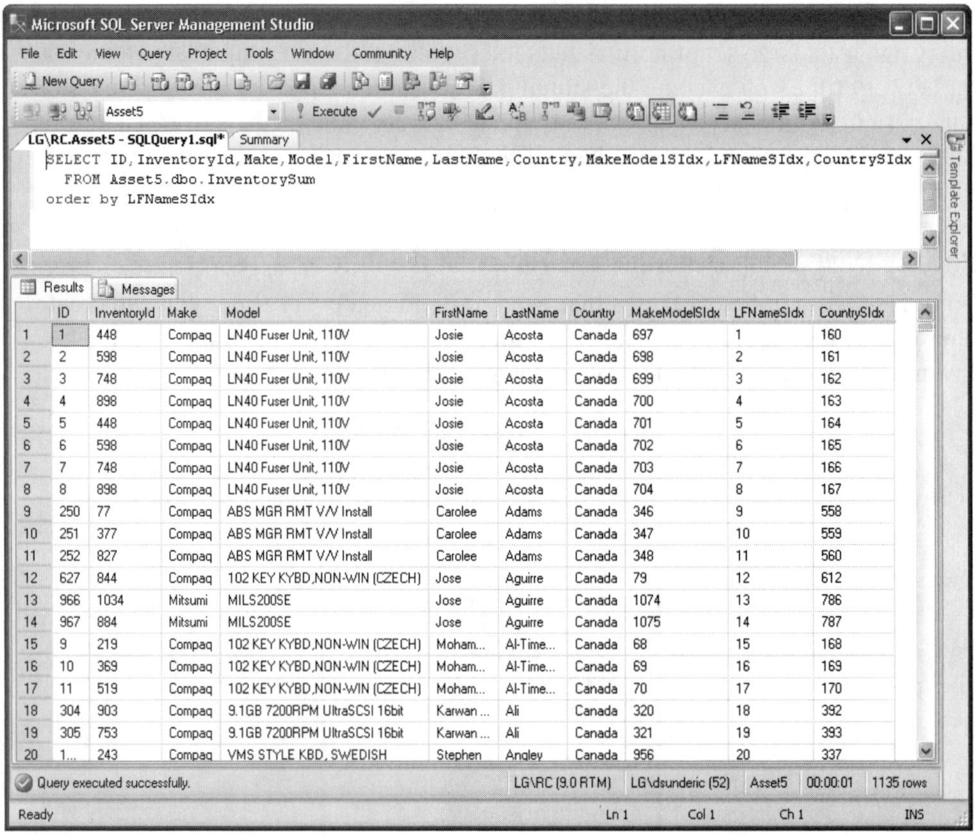

Figure 20-1 *Surrogate index*

I have created a stored procedure to be executed periodically from a job to populate the denormalized table:

```
Alter Procedure ap_InvSum_Generate
-- Generate denormalized table that will speed-up the querying.
      @debug int = 0
As

SET NOCOUNT ON
SET XACT_ABORT ON

declare @intTransactionCountOnEntry int
```

```
create table #Inv(ID int identity(1,1),
                  Inventoryid int,
                  Make varchar(50),
                  Model varchar(50),
                  Location varchar(50),
                  Status varchar(15),
                  FirstName varchar(30),
                  LastName varchar(30),
                  AcquisitionType varchar(12),
                  Address varchar(50),
                  City varchar(50),
                  ProvinceId char(3),
                  Country varchar(50),
                  EqType varchar(50),
                  Phone varchar(20),
                  Fax varchar(20),
                  Email varchar(128),
                  UserName varchar(50),
                  MakeModelSIdx int,
                  LFNameSIdx int,
                  CountrySIdx int)

-- get result set
insert into #Inv(InventoryId,   Make, Model,
                 Location, FirstName, LastName,
                 AcquisitionType, Address,
                 City, ProvinceId, Country,
                 EqType,Phone, Fax,
                 Email, UserName
)
SELECT Inventory.Inventoryid, Equipment.Make, Equipment.Model,
       Location.Location, Contact.FirstName,
       Contact.LastName, AcquisitionType.AcquisitionType, Location.Address,
       Location.City, Location.ProvinceId, Location.Country,
       EqType.EqType, Contact.Phone, Contact.Fax,
       Contact.Email, Contact.UserName
FROM   dbo.EqType EqType
RIGHT OUTER JOIN dbo.Equipment Equipment
ON EqType.EqTypeId = Equipment.EqTypeId
    RIGHT OUTER JOIN dbo.Inventory Inventory
    ON Equipment.EqId = Inventory.EqId
        LEFT OUTER JOIN dbo.AcquisitionType AcquisitionType
```

```
        ON Inventory.AcquisitionTypeID = AcquisitionType.AcquisitionTypeId
          LEFT OUTER JOIN dbo.Location Location
          ON Inventory.LocationId = Location.LocationId
            LEFT OUTER JOIN dbo.Contact Contact
            ON Inventory.OwnerId = Contact.ContactId
order by Location, LastName, FirstName


-- now, let's do record sorting


---- Make, Model -------------------
create table #tmp (SID int identity(1,1),
                    ID int)
insert into #tmp(ID)
select ID
from #inv
order by Make, Model


update #inv
set MakeModelSIdx = #tmp.SId
from #inv inner join #tmp
on #inv.ID = #tmp.id


drop table #tmp


-----------------------------------------
---- CountrySIdx: Country, Province, City, Location -------------------
create table #tmp2 (SID int identity(1,1),
                     ID int)
insert into #tmp2(ID)
select ID
from #inv
order by Country, ProvinceId, City, Location


update #inv
set CountrySIdx = #tmp2.SId
from #inv inner join #tmp2
on #inv.ID = #tmp2.id


drop table #tmp2
-----------------------------------------
---- LFNameSIdx: LName, FName -------------------
create table #tmp3 (SID int identity(1,1),
                     ID int)
```

```
insert into #tmp3(ID)
select ID
from #inv
order by LastName, FirstName

update #inv
set LFNameSIdx = #tmp3.SId
from #inv inner join #tmp3
on #inv.ID = #tmp3.id

drop table #tmp3
----------------------------------------

-- use transaction to hide operation from users
Select @intTransactionCountOnEntry = @@TranCount
BEGIN TRANSACTION

-- recreate table
if exists (select * from dbo.sysobjects
            where id = object_id(N'[InventorySum]')
            and OBJECTPROPERTY(id, N'IsUserTable') = 1)
    drop table dbo.[InventorySum]

create table dbo.InventorySum(ID int,
            InventoryId int,
            Make varchar(50),
            Model varchar(50),
            Location varchar(50),
            FirstName varchar(30),
            LastName varchar(30),
            AcquisitionType varchar(12),
            Address varchar(50),
            City varchar(50),
            ProvinceId char(3),
            Country varchar(50),
            EqType varchar(50),
            Phone varchar(20),
            Fax varchar(20),
            Email varchar(128),
            UserName varchar(50),
            MakeModelSIdx  int,
            LFNameSIdx int,
            CountrySIdx int)
```

```
-- populate table
insert into dbo.InventorySum (ID,
            InventoryId, Make, Model,
            Location, FirstName, LastName,
            AcquisitionType, Address, City,
            ProvinceId, Country, EqType,
            Phone, Fax, Email,
            UserName, MakeModelSIdx, LFNameSIdx,
            CountrySIdx)
select  ID, InventoryId, Make, Model,
        Location, FirstName, LastName,
        AcquisitionType, Address, City,
        ProvinceId, Country, EqType,
        Phone, Fax, Email,
        UserName, MakeModelSIdx, LFNameSIdx,
        CountrySIdx
from #inv

-- create indexes
CREATE UNIQUE CLUSTERED INDEX [idx_InvSum_Id]
ON [dbo].[InventorySum] ([ID])

CREATE INDEX [idx_InvSum_LFName]
ON [dbo].[InventorySum] (LastName, FirstName)

CREATE INDEX [idx_InvSum_Location]
ON [dbo].[InventorySum] (Location)

CREATE INDEX [idx_InvSum_ModelMakeEqType]
ON [dbo].[InventorySum] (Model, Make, EqType)

-- complete transaction - give access to users
If @@TranCount > @intTransactionCountOnEntry
    COMMIT TRANSACTION

return
```

At first sight, the stored procedure might look a bit unusual to you. I first collect all data in a temporary table and then, within a transaction, drop the denormalized table, re-create it, and copy the collected data from the temporary table into it. I wrote the stored procedure in this way for performance reasons. It is critical for users to be able to query the table without interruption. The whole process typically takes a couple of minutes, and queries will time-out if not completed after 30 seconds (or the limit that is specified on the server, in the ADO connection, or MTS). Therefore, it is critical to shorten the interruption. The process of copying collected data is much shorter than the process of collecting it.

On one project where I applied this solution, the complete process took about three minutes. The transaction that re-creates the table and copies data into it took about 20 seconds.

NOTE

It is certainly possible to perform the loading transaction in other ways. Creating an additional static table and renaming it comes to mind.

Quick Queries

This section walks you through the process of gradually adding the following features to a stored procedure, implementing a quick query:

▶ Result splitting

▶ Sorting

▶ Search type

▶ Counting

I will build a stored procedure that returns a list of equipment with a specified make and model:

```
alter proc ap_InventoryByMakeModel_Quick1
   @Make varchar(50) = null,   -- criteria
   @Model varchar(50) = null   -- criteria
/* test:
exec ap_InventoryByMakeModel_Quick1 'Compaq', 'D%'
*/
as

select Inventoryid ,    Make ,        Model,
       Location ,       FirstName ,   LastName ,
       AcquisitionType, Address ,     City ,
       ProvinceId ,     Country ,     EqType ,
       Phone ,          Fax ,         Email ,
       UserName
from dbo.InventorySum
where Make LIKE @Make
and Model LIKE @Model
```

The preceding is a simple stored procedure that uses the Like operator, and therefore enables the caller to add a wild card (%) to the string.

Now I'll add sorting to the stored procedure. I can sort only by sort orders for which I have defined surrogate indexes:

```
create proc ap_InventoryByMakeModel_Quick2
  @Make varchar(50) = null,  -- criteria
  @Model varchar(50) = null,  -- criteria
  @SortOrderId smallint = 0

/* test:
exec ap_InventoryByMakeModel_Quick2 'Compaq', 'D%', 1
*/
as

  select Id = Case @SortOrderId
           when 1 then MakeModelSIdx
           when 2 then CountrySIdx
           when 3 then LFNameSIdx
         End,
       Inventoryid ,    Make ,       Model,
       Location ,       FirstName , LastName ,
       AcquisitionType, Address ,    City ,
       ProvinceId ,     Country ,    EqType ,
       Phone ,          Fax ,        Email ,
       UserName
  from dbo.InventorySum
  where Make like @Make
  and Model like @Model
  order by case @SortOrderId
       when 1 then MakeModelSIdx
       when 2 then CountrySIdx
       when 3 then LFNameSIdx
      end
  return
```

I have also added an ID column to the recordset. I use a Case statement to set it with one of the surrogate indexes. The second instance of the Case statement is a little bit unusual. Note that I am using it inside an Order By clause.

Now I will add code that will return the result set in batches of 25 records:

```
create proc ap_InventoryByMakeModel_Quick3
  @Make varchar(50) = null,  -- criteria
  @Model varchar(50) = null,  -- criteria
```

```
  @PreviousID int = 0,            -- last record from the previous batch
  @SortOrderId smallint = 0


/* test:
exec ap_InventoryByMakeModel_Quick3 'Compaq', 'D%', 444, 1
*/
as

  select    top 25 Id = Case @SortOrderId
                when 1 then MakeModelSIdx
                when 2 then CountrySIdx
                when 3 then LFNameSIdx
              End,
          Inventoryid ,     Make ,         Model,
          Location ,        FirstName ,    LastName ,
          AcquisitionType,  Address ,      City ,
          ProvinceId ,      Country ,      EqType ,
          Phone ,           Fax ,          Email ,
          UserName
  from dbo.InventorySum
  where Case @SortOrderId
     when 1 then MakeModelSIdx
     when 2 then CountrySIdx
     when 3 then LFNameSIdx
    End > @PreviousID
  and Make like @Make
  and Model like @Model
  order by case @SortOrderId
        when 1 then MakeModelSIdx
        when 2 then CountrySIdx
        when 3 then LFNameSIdx
      end
  return
```

I have added Top 25 to the Select statement. I added a parameter that will be used to pass the identifier of the last record seen in the previous batch. I also added a Case function in the Where clause that allows me to return records that were not previously seen by the user.

Next I will add code to support Begins With, Contains, and Match search types. I will simply add different combinations of wild cards to the search parameters:

```
create proc ap_InventoryByMakeModel_Quick
  @Make varchar(50) = null,  -- criteria
  @Model varchar(50) = null,  -- criteria
  @PreviousID int = 0,     -- last record from the previous batch
```

```
    @SortOrderId smallint = 0,
    @SearchTypeid tinyint = 0  -- 0: Begins With, 1: Match, 2: Contains
/* test:
exec ap_InventoryByMakeModel_Quick 'Compaq', 'D', 50, 2, 2
*/
as

if @SearchTypeId = 0
begin
  set @Make = @Make + '%'
  set @Model = @Model + '%'
end

if @SearchTypeid = 2
begin
  set @Make  = '%' + @Make  + '%'
  set @Model = '%' + @Model + '%'
end

select top 25 Id = Case @SortOrderId
            when 1 then MakeModelSIdx
            when 2 then CountrySIdx
            when 3 then LFNameSIdx
         End,
      Inventoryid ,    Make ,       Model,
      Location ,         FirstName , LastName ,
      AcquisitionType, Address ,   City ,
      ProvinceId ,      Country ,   EqType ,
      Phone ,          Fax ,        Email ,
      UserName
from dbo.InventorySum
where Case @SortOrderId
    when 1 then MakeModelSIdx
    when 2 then CountrySIdx
    when 3 then LFNameSIdx
  End > @PreviousID
and Make like @Make
and Model like @Model
order by case @SortOrderId
      when 1 then MakeModelSIdx
      when 2 then CountrySIdx
      when 3 then LFNameSIdx
    end
return
```

Since it is important to display the total number of records that satisfy specified criteria, I will create a stored procedure to return the count to the user. I have two options: I could add the code to the stored procedure that does the search, but the better option is to make code more readable and create a separate procedure:

```
create proc ap_InventoryByMakeModel_Count
  @Make varchar(50) = null,  -- criteria
  @Model varchar(50) = null,  -- criteria
  @SearchTypeid tinyint = 0,  -- 0: Begins With, 1: Match, 2: Contains
  @Count int output
/* test:
declare @count int
exec ap_InventoryByMakeModel_Count 'Compaq', 'D', 2, @count output
select @count count
*/
as

if @SearchTypeId = 0
begin
  set @Make = @Make + '%'
  set @Model = @Model + '%'
end

if @SearchTypeid = 2
begin
  set @Make  = '%' + @Make  + '%'
  set @Model = '%' + @Model + '%'
end

select @Count = count(*)
from dbo.InventorySum
where Make like @Make
and Model like @Model

return
```

Advanced Queries

An advanced query allows users to specify criteria using any combination of input parameters. Therefore, all parameters have default values specified so that they will never become part of the criteria (I can agree with web developers that null means that the user didn't specify a value for the parameter on the web page):

```
alter procedure ap_InventorySearchAdvFull_ListPage
-- display a batch of 25 assets that specify the criteria

-- Example of use of dynamically assembled query
-- and denormalized table with surrogate index fields
-- to return result in batches of 25 records.

    @Make varchar(50) = null,
    @Model varchar(50) = null,
    @Location varchar(50) = null,
    @FirstName varchar(30) = null,
    @LastName varchar(30) = null,
    @AcquisitionType varchar(20) = null,
    @ProvinceId char(3) = null,
    @Country varchar(50) = null,
    @EqType varchar(30) = null,
    @City varchar(50) = null,
    @UserName varchar(50) = null,
    @email varchar(50) = null,
    @SortOrderId smallint = 0,   -- 1: Make and model;
                                 -- 2: Country, Prov, City, Loc;
                                 -- 4: LName; FName
    @PreviousID int = 0,       -- last record from the previous batch
    @BatchSize int = 25,
    @debug int = 0
/* test:
exec ap_InventorySearchAdvFull_ListPage
    @Make = 'Compaq',
    @Model= null,
    @Location = null,
    @FirstName = 'Michael',
    @LastName = null,
    @AcquisitionType = null,
    @ProvinceId  = null,
    @Country = null,
    @EqType = null,
    @City = null,
    @UserName = null,
    @email = null,
    @SortOrderId = 2,    -- 2: Make and model
    @PreviousID = 25,    -- last record from the previous batch
    @BatchSize = 25,
    @debug = 0
```

```
*/
as
SET CONCAT_NULL_YIELDS_NULL OFF
SET NOCOUNT ON

declare @chvSelect varchar(max),
        @chvFrom varchar(max),
        @chvWhere varchar(max),
        @chvOrderby varchar(max),
        @chvSQL varchar(max)


-- order records
set @chvSelect = 'SELECT top ' + Convert(varchar, @BatchSize)
            + '    Inventoryid ,       Make ,            Model,
                Location ,          FirstName ,
                LastName ,          AcquisitionType, Address ,
                City ,              ProvinceId ,     Country ,
                EqType ,            Phone ,          Fax ,
                Email ,             UserName, '
          + Case @SortOrderId
                when 1 then ' MakeModelSIdx '
                when 2 then ' CountrySIdx '
                when 3 then ' LFNameSIdx '
             End
          + ' as ID '

set @chvFrom = ' FROM   dbo.InventorySum '

set @chvWhere = ' where '
            + Case @SortOrderId
                when 1 then ' MakeModelSIdx'
                when 2 then ' CountrySIdx '
                when 3 then ' LFNameSIdx '
              End + '> '
            + Convert(varchar, @PreviousID)

if   @Make is not null
    set @chvWhere = @chvWhere + ' AND Make = ''' + @Make + ''' '
if   @Model is not null
    set @chvWhere = @chvWhere + ' AND Model = ''' + @Model + ''' '
if   @Location is not null
    set @chvWhere = @chvWhere + ' AND Location = ''' + @Location + ''' '
if   @FirstName is not null
    set @chvWhere = @chvWhere + ' AND FirstName = ''' + @FirstName + ''' '
```

```
if   @LastName is not null
    set @chvWhere = @chvWhere + ' AND lastName = ''' + @lastName + ''' '
if   @AcquisitionType is not null
    set @chvWhere = @chvWhere + ' AND AcquisitionType = '''
                    + @AcquisitionType + ''' '
if   @ProvinceId  is not null
    set @chvWhere = @chvWhere + ' AND ProvinceId = ''' + @ProvinceId + ''' '
if   @Country is not null
    set @chvWhere = @chvWhere + ' AND Country = ''' + @Country + ''' '
if   @EqType is not null
    set @chvWhere = @chvWhere + ' AND EqType = ''' + @EqType + ''' '
if   @City is not null
    set @chvWhere = @chvWhere + ' AND City = ''' + @City + ''' '
if   @UserName is not null
    set @chvWhere = @chvWhere + ' AND UserName = ''' + @UserName + ''' '
if   @email is not null
    set @chvWhere = @chvWhere + ' AND email = ''' + @email + ''' '

set @chvOrderBy = ' order by '
            + Case @SortOrderId
              when 1 then ' MakeModelSIdx'
              when 2 then ' CountrySIdx '
              when 3 then ' LFNameSIdx '
              End

set @chvSQL = @chvSelect + @chvFrom + @chvWhere + @chvOrderby

if @debug = 0
    exec (@chvSQL)
else
    select @chvSQL
```

The stored procedure dynamically assembles the query using just the Where clause for input parameters that were specified. This technique allows SQL Server to optimize the query and use the appropriate indexes. Similarly, Order By and Select clauses are assembled based on the specified sort order. The Top clause is added dynamically to the Select clause based on the number of records that the user wants to see in the batch.

NOTE

Something that I didn't demonstrate here, but that could also be very useful for joining tables on demand, is the following: if some tables are joined just to support some additional search criteria, they might be added to the rest of the From clause only when their values are specified. The query will perform better if the number of joined tables is smaller.

Fancy New Solution: Row Versioning

All the solutions we have explored so far are applicable to all versions of SQL Server. Row versioning is a new feature in SQL Server 2005 that you can use to address the reader and writer (b)locking problem.

When the ALLOW_SNAPSHOT_ISOLATION or READ_COMMITTED_ SNAPSHOT database option is set to ON, the SQL Server 2005 Database Engine starts tracking versions of all rows that are modified. When an application or a Transact-SQL batch modifies a row in that database, the Database Engine stores the original version of the row in the tempdb database. If an application or a query using compatible isolation levels (Snapshot or Read Committed Snapshot) needs to read the record before the transaction is completed, the Database Engine provides the version from tempdb. It does not need to wait for the transaction to be completed, nor to read the changed record before it is committed.

If more than one application or batch is modifying the record concurrently, multiple versions of the record are stored in tempdb in the form of a linked list. Naturally, as transactions are committed, the Database Engine records the changes in the database and deletes the old row versions in tempdb.

This row versioning feature isolates readers from the effects of record modifications. There is no need to handle this issue using shared locks. Therefore, when the database is set in this mode, readers do not acquire shared locks, which leads to a significant reduction in the number of locks. Locks are needed only for transactions that are modifying records.

In the following sections, I will demonstrate how to set a database to perform row versioning, and what needs to be done on the client to exploit this feature.

How to Set Databases

Administrators can set the database option to allow snapshot isolation using the Alter Database statement:

```
ALTER DATABASE Asset5
  SET ALLOW_SNAPSHOT_ISOLATION ON;
```

From this point, the database will track row versions of all (new) transactions in tempdb.

NOTE

This database option can be set while users are connected to the database. Administrators do not need to disconnect them (to kill connections). However, if users are running transactions, those transactions must be completed before row versioning can be set. The database is in the PENDING_ON state until the transactions are finished. If someone tries to run snapshot transactions before the regular transactions are finished, an error will be raised.

Alternatively, an administrator can set the READ_COMMITTED_SNAPSHOT database option to ON:

```
ALTER DATABASE Asset5
  SET READ_COMMITTED_SNAPSHOT ON;
```

From this point, the Database Engine will use row versioning instead of locking for transactions, using the READ_COMMITTED_SNAPSHOT isolation level.

NOTE

READ_COMMITTED_SNAPSHOT can be set to ON only when the database is set to single-user mode. However, the advantage to this option is that the database is switched to this mode immediately. There is no possibility of a pending state as in the case of snapshot isolation.

How to Set Connections/Clients

When the ALLOW_SNAPSHOT_ISOLATION database option is set to ON, queries must set the Transaction Isolation Level to Snapshot in order to access original rows and avoid being blocked by transactions:

```
SET TRANSACTION ISOLATION LEVEL SNAPSHOT;
GO
exec ap_InventoryByMakeModel_Quick 'Nec', 'V', 50, 2, 2
```

Naturally, if a query is executed with a noncompatible isolation level, results will be as usual. For example, if you use the default (Read Committed) or higher isolation level, the query waits for the transaction to complete; if you use Read Uncommitted, the query immediately returns the changed record (even if it is not committed).

After the database is set to support snapshot isolation level, transactions do not have to be run with isolation level set to Snapshot. However, you may choose to do so if your transaction is also reading records:

```
SET TRANSACTION ISOLATION LEVEL SNAPSHOT;
GO
declare @EqId int

select @EqId = EqId
from dbo.Inventory
where InventoryID = 117
```

```
begin tran
update dbo.Eq
Set Model = 'V91'
where EqId = @EqId

update dbo.Eq
Set Model = 'V90'
where EqId = (select EqId
             from Inventory
             where InventoryID = 118)

commit tran
```

Managed applications that are using the System.Data.SQLClient namespace should set the isolation level using the SQLConnection.BeginTransaction method:

```
SqlConnection conn = new (string myConnString);
...
SqlTransaction trans = conn.BeginTransaction(IsolationLevel.Snapshot);
...
```

Older systems such as ADO applications can set the *Autocommit Isolation Levels* property. OLEDB applications should set the DBPROPSET_SESSION property to DBPROP_SESS_AUTOCOMMITISOLEVELS, and ODBC applications should set the SQL_ATTR_TXN_ISOLATION attribute using the SQLSetConnectAttr.

Clients could be set to use Read Committed Snapshot isolation level when the READ_COMMITTED_SNAPSHOT database option is set to ON:

```
SET TRANSACTION ISOLATION LEVEL READ_COMMITTED_SNAPSHOT;
GO
exec ap_InventoryByMakeModel_Quick 'Nec', 'V', 50, 2, 2
```

Using Row Versioning

Figure 20-2 demonstrates how data can be available for reading during a long-running transaction. The first connection modifies a record, but it does not finish the transaction. I didn't execute Commit Tran to simulate execution of the long query. The second query can access a copy of the record before the change. By using snapshot isolation, the second connection is able to overcome this limitation in the default Database Engine's behavior (that is, it does not have to wait for the transaction to finish and the lock to be released).

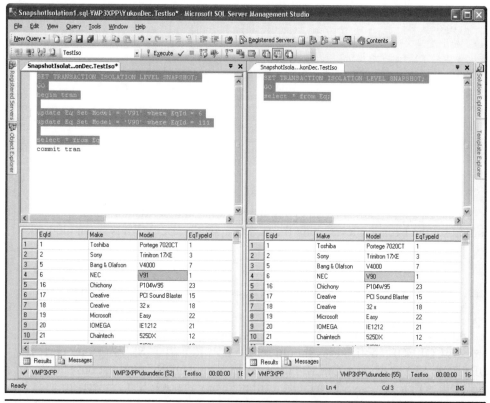

Figure 20-2 *Connections using snapshot isolation level before transaction completion*

Naturally, after the transaction is committed, the second query can see the modified record (see Figure 20-3).

NOTE

The tempdb database has to have enough space to store all row versions of all changed records. However, if tempdb becomes full, transactions will continue to work without problem, but queries that require missing row versions will fail.

The example in Figure 20-4 demonstrates the concurrency conflict that arises when two transactions read and update the same record. I opened their code in two windows and I executed them part by part (you can use "-- pause" comments to identify the parts). I initially executed the batches to *pause 1* and *pause 2,* respectively. Since they both use snapshot isolation, they both initially read the original values of rows

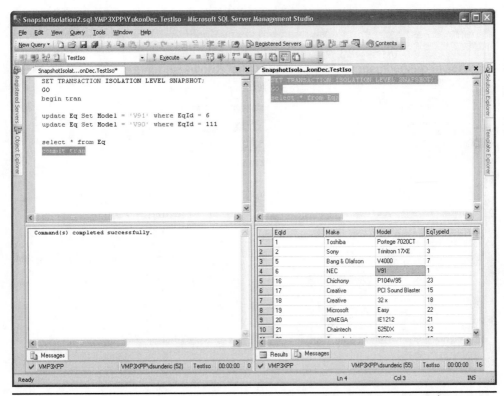

Figure 20-3   *Connections using snapshot isolation level after transaction completion*

that will be updated later. Then I executed the *pause 1* to *pause 3* section of the first transaction. It updated the rows, but the transaction was not completed. Then I executed the *pause 2* to *pause 4* section in the second batch. Since the first transaction was not committed, the second batch had to wait for the exclusive lock to be cleared. As soon as I executed the remainder of the first transaction, the Database Engine attempted to update the records. It detected that the row had been changed in the meantime and returned error 3960.

NOTE

There is one more thing that you should worry about. If transactions are using global temporary tables, you must set tempdb to support Snapshot or Read Committed Snapshot isolation levels (since global temporary tables are stored in the tempdb database). You do not have to do so if your transactions are using (regular) temporary tables or table variables, since they are not shared.

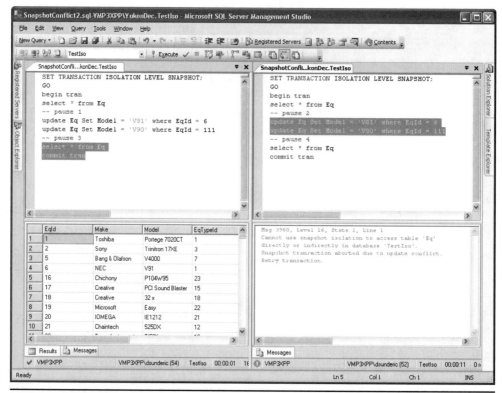

Figure 20-4   *Conflict of concurrent snapshot transactions*

Its Disadvantages...

Snapshot and Read Committed Snapshot isolation levels are not the Holy Grail of database programming. They have significant advantages and disadvantages. First, the disadvantages:

▶ Storing row versions in tempdb leads to increased space requirements and an increase in tempdb IOs.

▶ Setting a database to support the Snapshot or Read Committed Snapshot isolation level will increase the required CPU cycles and use more memory.

▶ Transactions need to maintain row versions even if there are no readers that require original rows using a row versioning isolation level. Therefore, updates are generally slower. How efficient this method is depends on the ratio of update to read operations.

▶ Readers are also slowed down because they have to go across the linked list of row versions to get the data.

▶ Some DDL operations are prohibited in snapshot transactions (Alter Index, Alter Partition Function, Alter Table, Create Index, Create Xml Index, Dbcc DbReindex, Drop Index).

▶ New concurrency issues may occur when a database is set to support snapshot isolation. If two snapshot isolation transactions are trying to update the same record, the later transaction will fail with a 3960 error (see Figure 20-4). The engine will prevent the second transaction from updating the record that was already updated without reading it first. However, this problem does not occur in the case of the Read Committed Snapshot isolation level.

▶ Distributed transactions and queries are not supported.

▶ I think the biggest limitation of snapshot isolation is the fact that you have to change both database and application (queries) to support it. It would be nicer if all you needed to do was to adjust your database.

... and Its Advantages

The most important advantages of row versioning are

▶ Writers do not block readers, since readers can get the last committed version of the row from tempdb.

▶ Readers do not block writers, since they do not issue shared locks.

▶ Readers receive transactionally consistent content—row values that were valid and consistent before the transaction started.

▶ The number of deadlocks is reduced.

TIP

You can also combine row versioning and denormalized tables. Users will not be blocked during table re-creation.

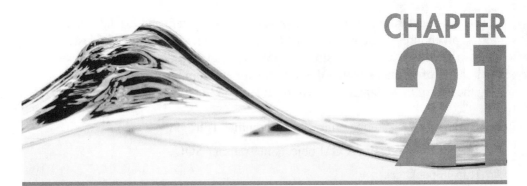

Interaction with the SQL Server Environment

T his chapter focuses on the ways you can use system and extended stored procedures to interact with the SQL Server environment. It also discusses the ways user-defined stored procedures can help you leverage the existing functionality of elements within the SQL Server environment.

By the end of this chapter, you will be able to do the following:

▶ Run programs and operating system commands from the command shell

▶ Use OLE Automation/COM objects in Transact-SQL

▶ Run IS packages

▶ Execute DTS packages

▶ Implement looping in DTS packages

▶ Manage jobs in Job Scheduler

▶ Perform administration tasks with stored procedures

▶ Read and write Registry entries

▶ Use the e-mail capabilities of SQL Server to notify users of events on the server

▶ Use the e-mail capabilities of SQL Server to send query results

▶ Expose stored procedures as web services

Running Programs

Before Microsoft included support for .NET framework, OLE Automation, and COM in SQL Server, administrators ran command-prompt programs and commands using the xp_cmdshell extended stored procedure:

```
xp_cmdshell {'command'} [, no_output]
```

When xp_cmdshell is executed, a *command* string is passed to the command shell of the operating system to be executed. Any rows of text that are normally displayed by the command shell are returned by the extended stored procedure as a result set. There is also an option to ignore the output.

The status of the execution is returned as an output parameter of the extended stored procedure. Its value is set to 0 if execution was successful and 1 if execution failed.

Figure 21-1 shows the use of the command-prompt instruction to list files in the Backup folder. This output can be received in a temporary table and further processed in Transact-SQL code.

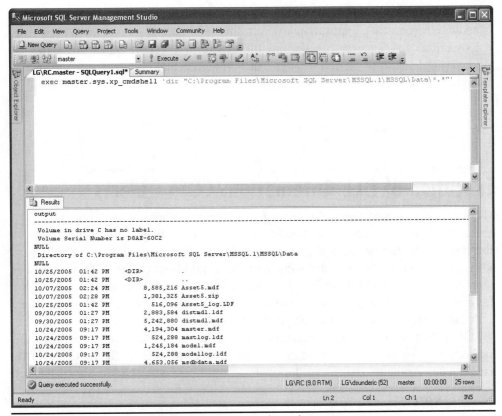

Figure 21-1 *Using xp_cmdshell to run commands and programs*

The following batch-copies files from the Backup folder to another drive:

```
exec master..xp_cmdshell 'copy e:\w2kPro~1\Micros~1\'
                   + 'MSSQL\BACKUP\*.* m:', no_output
```

Running Windows Script Files

The Windows Script Host enables users to write and execute scripts in VBScript, JavaScript, and other languages compatible with the Windows environment. It was initially developed as an additional component, but since Windows 98 it is integrated into all new editions of Windows operating system.

Script files usually have .vbs and .js extensions. They are executed from the Windows environment using wscript.exe or from the command prompt using csript.exe.

Execution of script files can also be initiated from Transact-SQL code. The following statement runs a demo script that starts Excel and populates a worksheet with information:

```
exec xp_cmdshell 'c:\windows\command\cscript.exe '
    + 'c:\windows\samples\wsh\Excel.vbs', NO_OUTPUT
```

Execution of OLE Automation/COM Objects

Microsoft has developed several *unmanaged* technologies that enable developers to encapsulate unmanaged code and custom objects into executable components. These components can then be invoked by other applications developed in the same (or any other) programming language that supports these kinds of components. This is an older alternative to achieving the same task using managed (.NET) components. Through the years, this technology has been known by different names: OLE, OLE Automation, COM, DCOM, Automation, ActiveX, and COM+.

SQL Server can initiate managed code components and access the properties and methods exposed by them. A set of system stored procedures (with the prefix sp_OA) has been designed and implemented in SQL Server to help you accomplish such tasks.

NOTE
When Microsoft first unveiled this feature in SQL Server, code components were known as "OLE Automation objects." For this reason, Microsoft attached the OA prefix to these stored procedure names, and I used OLE Automation Objects in the title of the section.

By default, usage of OLE Automation/COM objects is disabled in SQL Server 2005. It can be enabled using the Surface Area Configuration tool at the end or after the installation. Alternatively, you can enable it using the following script:

```
Exec sp_configure 'Ole Automation Procedures', 1
GO
RECONFIGURE
GO
```

To demonstrate the use of OLE Automation on a simple Visual Basic function in Visual Basic 6:

1. Create the DjnToolkit ActiveX DLL project in Visual Basic 6 and then create a DjnTools class.

2. Create a method called SpellNumber, which ignores the input value (currency amount) and returns a constant string (see Figure 21-2).

NOTE

Even if you run the object from the Visual Basic IDE (instead of compiling and installing it), you will still be able to access it from Transact-SQL code. This is an important feature for debugging the object.

The stored procedure shown in the code on the following page first initiates the COM object using the sp_OACreate system stored procedure. It obtains a token @intObject, which is used from that point to access the class.

The sp_OAMethod stored procedure is used to execute class methods. The return value and input parameter of the method are placed at the end of the stored procedure's parameter list.

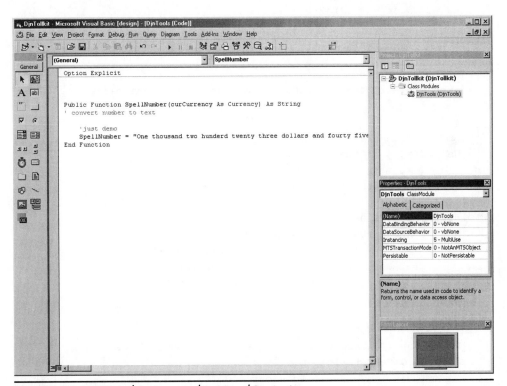

Figure 21-2 *A COM object created in Visual Basic 6*

Before the stored procedure is complete, the COM object must be destroyed using sp_OADestroy.

If an automation error occurs at any point, sp_OAGetErrorInfo can be used to obtain the source and description of the most recent error:

```
Alter Procedure dbo.ap_SpellNumber
-- demo of use of Automation objects
    @mnsAmount money,
    @chvAmount varchar(500) output,
    @debug int = 0


As
set nocount on

Declare @intErrorCode int,
        @intObject int,  -- hold object token
        @bitObjectCreated bit,
        @chvSource varchar(255),
        @chvDesc varchar(255)


Select @intErrorCode = @@Error

If @intErrorCode = 0
    exec @intErrorCode = sp_OACreate 'DjnToolkit.DjnTools',
                                     @intObject OUTPUT

If @intErrorCode = 0
    Set @bitObjectCreated = 1
else
    Set @bitObjectCreated = 0

If @intErrorCode = 0
    exec @intErrorCode = sp_OAMethod @intObject,
                                     'SpellNumber',
                                     @chvAmount OUTPUT,
                                     @mnsAmount

If @intErrorCode <> 0
begin
    Raiserror ('Unable to obtain spelling of number', 16, 1)
    exec sp_OAGetErrorInfo @intObject,
                           @chvSource OUTPUT,
                           @chvDesc OUTPUT
```

```
        Set @chvDesc = 'Error ('
                    + Convert(varchar, @intErrorCode)
                    + ', ' + @chvSource  + ') : ' + @chvDesc
        Raiserror (@chvDesc, 16, 1)
end

if @bitObjectCreated = 1
    exec  sp_OADestroy @intObject

return @intErrorCode
```

Once you are sure that communication between Transact-SQL and Visual Basic code is working, you can write code in Visual Basic that converts numbers to text. Since this is not a book about Visual Basic, I will not go into detail on that subject.

There is an even better example on how to use these stored procedures in Chapter 18.

NOTE

You should avoid using OLE Automation/COM objects if possible. Managed components developed in .NET are much more stable and secure.

Data Type Conversion

Keep in mind that COM code components and Transact-SQL code use different data types. You have to set compatible data types on both sides to allow the OLE Automation system stored procedures to automatically convert data between them. You can identify most of the compatible data types using common sense (for example, `varchar`, `char`, and `text` types in SQL Server translate to the `String` data type in Visual Basic, and the `int` SQL Server data type translates to the `Long` data type). However, some data types deserve special attention.

When values are passed from SQL Server to Visual Basic, `binary`, `varbinary`, and `image` are converted to a one-dimensional `Byte` array. Any Transact-SQL value set to null is converted to a `Variant` set to null. `Decimal` and `numeric` are converted to `String` (not `currency`).

When values are passed from Visual Basic to SQL Server, `Long`, `Integer`, `Byte`, `Boolean`, and `Object` are converted to the `int` data type. Both `Double` and `Single` data types are converted to `float`. Strings shorter than 255 characters are converted to `varchar`, and strings longer than 255 characters are converted to the `text` data type. One-dimensional `Byte()` arrays shorter than 255 characters become `varbinary` values, and those longer than 255 become `image` values.

Running SQL Server 2005 Integration Services (SSIS) Packages

Integration Services is a new component of SQL Server 2005. It is created as a platform for developers to create solutions for extraction, transformation, and load of data (in data warehouse and other scenarios). This technology is a successor of Data Transformation Services that was introduced in SQL Server 7.0. Solutions created with it are wrapped and stored as SSIS packages. Naturally, their design and management are beyond the scope of this book, but I will show you how to run an SSIS package from a stored procedure.

SQL Server 2005 includes the dtexec.exe utility, which allows you to execute SSIS packages from the command prompt. We can simply call it using xp_cmdshell. To execute an SSIS package stored as DW_ETL.dtsx file, use

```
exec xp_cmdshell ' dtexec /f "c:\SSIS\DW_ETL.dtsx"', NO_OUTPUT
```

To execute an SSIS package that is stored in SQL Server and uses Windows authentication, use something like this:

```
exec xp_cmdshell ' dtexec /sq DW_ETL /ser myServer', NO_OUTPUT
```

Running DTS Packages

Data Transformation Services (DTS) is an older SQL Server platform for the visual design and execution of data transformation routines. It is still supported in SQL Server 2005. The old engine is also present on the installation disk and you can decide to install it on your server if you have some old DTS packages. I will show you how to run a DTS package from a stored procedure.

SQL Server 2005 includes the dtsrun.exe utility, which allows you to execute DTS packages from the command prompt. Again we can simply call it using xp_cmdshell:

```
exec xp_cmdshell 'dtsrun /SmyServer /Udbo /E /NDW_ETL '
            + '/ADatabase:8=Asset5 /AServer:8=myServer', NO_OUTPUT
```

Running/Looping Through DTS Packages

One of the features that every DTS developer wants to use but that is missing is looping. The tool simply does not allow you to create tasks to be executed in a loop. The solution is to use a scripting language (such as T-SQL or VBScript) to launch a group of tasks (organized into a single DTS package) in a loop. The following procedure loops through a list of databases and executes a DTS package with a database name as an input parameter (a global variable in DTS terminology):

```
ALTER PROCEDURE  util.ap_DTS_Loop
-- Loop through Asset databases
    -- run the DTS package for each of them

-- test:     exec util.ap_DTS_Loop 1
   @debug int = 0
As
set nocount on
declare @intCount int,
        @intCounter int,
        @chvDOS varchar(2000),
        @chvDB sysname,
        @chvServer sysname

Declare @intErrorCode int,
        @chvProcedure sysname

set xact_abort on
set nocount on

set @chvProcedure = 'util.ap_DTS_Loop'
if @debug <> 0
   select '**** '+ @chvProcedure + ' START ****'
   Create table #db(Id int identity(1,1),
                    Name sysname)

   insert into #db (Name)
      select Name from master.dbo.sysdatabases
      where name like 'Asset%'

   -- set loop
   select @intCount = Count(*),
          @intCounter = 1,
          @chvServer = @@SERVERNAME
   from #db


-- loop through list of databases
while @intCounter <= @intCount
```

```
begin
   -- get db
      select @chvDB = Name
      from #db
      where Id = @intCounter


      SELECT    @chvDOS = 'dtsrun /S' + @chvServer
                   + ' /Udbo /E /NDW_ETL'
                   + ' /ADatabase:8=' + @chvDB
                   + ' /AServer:8=' + @chvServer

      if @debug = 0
         EXEC master.dbo.xp_cmdshell @chvDOS, no_output
      else
         select @chvDOS

   -- let's go another round and get another property
      set @intCounter = @intCounter + 1
end

drop table #db

if @debug <> 0
   select '**** '+ @chvProcedure + ' END ****'
return
```

If you run the procedure, it will generate and execute the following set of commands:

```
dtsrun /SA1000 /Udbo /E /NDW_ETL /ADatabase:8=Asset     /AServer:8=A1000
dtsrun /SA1000 /Udbo /E /NDW_ETL /ADatabase:8=Asset7    /AServer:8=A1000
dtsrun /SA1000 /Udbo /E /NDW_ETL /ADatabase:8=Asset2000 /AServer:8=A1000
dtsrun /SA1000 /Udbo /E /NDW_ETL /ADatabase:8=Asset2000_2 /AServer:8=A1000
dtsrun /SA1000 /Udbo /E /NDW_ETL /ADatabase:8=Asset5    /AServer:8=A1000
```

Interacting with the NT Registry

Developers of client applications in a 32-bit environment often use the Registry as a repository for application configuration data and defaults. The Registry is a database (but not an RDBMS) that stores configuration information centrally.

SQL Server exposes the following extended stored procedures for manipulating the Registry:

Extended Stored Procedure	Purpose
xp_regread	Reads a Registry value
xp_regwrite	Writes to the Registry
xp_regdeletekey	Deletes a key
xp_regdeletevalue	Deletes a key's value
xp_regenumvalues	Lists names of value entries
xp_regaddmultistring	Adds a multistring (zero-delimited string)
xp_regremovemultistring	Removes a multistring (zero-delimited string)

xp_regread

This stored procedure enables you to read the value of the Registry key located on the specified path of the specified subtree:

```
xp_regread subtree,
         path,
         key,
         @value   OUTPUT
```

In the following example, this extended stored procedure reads the default folder for storing SQL Server database data files:

```
declare @chvSQLPath varchar(8000)

exec master.dbo.xp_regread

    'HKEY_LOCAL_MACHINE'

    ,'SOFTWARE\Microsoft\Microsoft SQL Server\MSSQL.2\MSSQLServer'

    ,'DefaultData',@chvSQLPath   OUTPUT

select   @chvSQLPath SQLPath

go
```

xp_regwrite

This stored procedure enables you to write a new value to the Registry key located on the specified path of the specified subtree:

```
xp_regwrite subtree,
            path,
            key,
            datatype,
            newvalue
```

In the following example, this extended stored procedure adds one value to the Setup key:

```
exec master..xp_regwrite
     'HKEY_LOCAL_MACHINE'
    ,'SOFTWARE\Microsoft\Microsoft SQL Server\MSSQL.2\MSSQLServer'
    ,'Test'
    ,'REG_SZ'
    ,'Test'
go
```

TIP

You should be very careful when writing and deleting Registry keys using Transact-SQL. It is often a better idea (performance-wise) to store most of your configuration parameters in a special table in the application database.

Jobs

One valuable administrative feature of SQL Server is the capability to launch the execution of custom jobs at specified times. Each job has properties such as name, description, schedule, and a list of operators to be notified in case of success, completion, or failure, as well as a list of steps that will be performed as part of the job and actions to be taken after completion of a job. These steps can be defined as Transact-SQL code, Active Script code, or operating system commands.

Administration of Jobs

This section looks at the basics of job creation from Management Studio to show the potential of this feature, but it will not go into too much detail. The following exercise creates a job that performs a backup of the transaction log if it is more than 95 percent full. It is based on the util.ap_LogBackupIfAlmostFull stored procedure.

You can create a job using a wizard or directly from the Management Studio tree:

1. Open Management Studio and expand the local server in Object Explorer.

2. Expand SQL Server Agent. Make sure that it is running (you'll see a green arrow on the icon or you can open Properties on the context-sensitive menu).

3. Right-click Jobs and choose New Job. Management Studio displays a New Job window.

4. Fill in the General tab with the information shown in the following illustration:

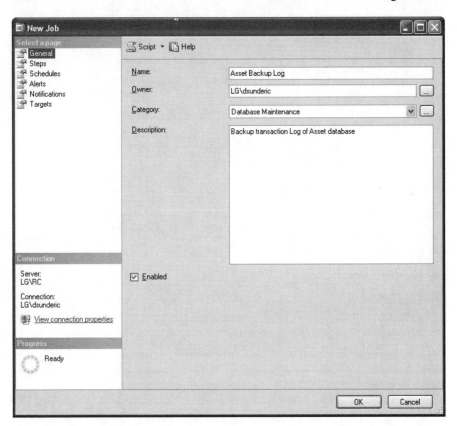

5. Open the Steps page.

6. Click New to start creating the first step. The application displays the New Job Step dialog box.

7. In the Step Name field, type **do backup**.

8. Make sure that Transact-SQL Script (T-SQL) is selected in the Type list.

9. Specify Asset5 as the working database.

10. You can either populate the Command text box with script from the file (using the Open button) or, as in this case, enter code manually for the execution of a stored procedure:

```
exec util.ap_LogBackupIfAlmostFull 'Asset5', 95
```

11. The dialog box should look like this:

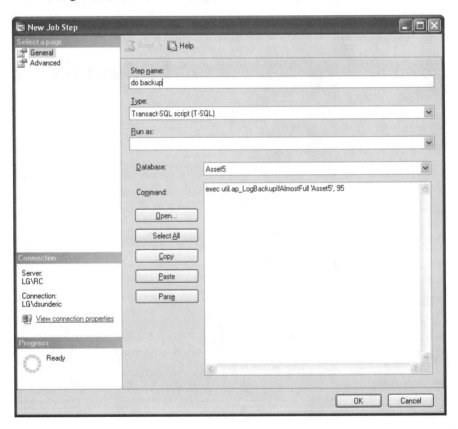

12. Click the Advanced page to see other options. You can specify behavior in the case of successful or unsuccessful completion, the log file to record the output of the script, and retry options. For this exercise, accept the default values and close the dialog box. SQL Server returns you to the Steps tab of the New Job window.

13. You will create only one step for this job, so now you can click the Schedules option to set a schedule.

14. Click the New button to display the New Job Schedule dialog box.

15. Name the schedule **Every 5 min**. The Schedule Type is set to Recurring, but the default frequency is not what you want.

16. Select Daily in Occurs under the Frequency group.

17. Set Daily Frequency to Occurs Every 5 Minute(s), as shown here:

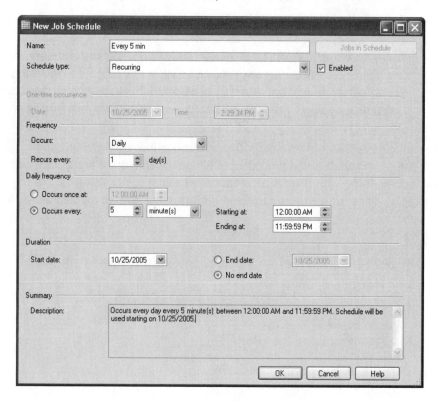

18. Click OK to close the dialog box. The application returns you to the New Job window.

19. You can use the Notifications page to set activities that will occur when the job completes. It is possible to page operators or to send e-mail to operators, write the status to the Windows NT application event log, or automatically delete the job. You can also set Alerts and alternate Target server, but for this example leave the default values and press OK.

NOTE

SQL Server will execute this job every five minutes from now on. If you want to disable it, you can edit the job or just right-click the job in Management Studio and select Disable Job from the pop-up menu.

All of the functionality in this job is actually provided by the util.ap_ LogBackupIfAlmostFull stored procedure.

NOTE

The only requirement that such a stored procedure must comply with is that it must return a success status (0 in the case of success; any other number represents an error code). SQL Server Agent uses this value to determine the completion status of the job and potentially execute subsequent steps. Returning a success status is a highly recommended practice when the stored procedure works inside the job.

The util.ap_LogBackupIfAlmostFull stored procedure calls the util.ap_ LogBackupIfAlmostFull stored procedure to obtain the amount of log space available in the database. If the limit is reached, it creates a backup device using the sys.sp_ addumpdevice system stored procedure and performs a backup of the transaction log:

```
alter Procedure util.ap_LogBackupIfAlmostFull
-- Do backup of transaction log
-- if percent of space used is bigger than @fltPercentLimit.

-- test: exec util.ap_LogBackupIfAlmostFull 'Asset5', 0, 1
    (
        @chvDbName sysname,
        @fltPercentLimit float,
        @debug int = 0
    )
As
set nocount on
set xact_abort on

declare    @intErrorCode int,
           @fltPercentUsed float,
           @chvDeviceName sysname,
           @chvFileName sysname,
           @chvSQLPath varchar(8000)

-- how much of log space is used at the moment
exec util.ap_LogSpacePercentUsed_Get @chvDbName,
                                    @fltPercentUsed OUTPUT
```

```
-- if limit is not reached, just go out
if @fltPercentUsed < @fltPercentLimit
    return

exec master.dbo.xp_regread
      'HKEY_LOCAL_MACHINE'
    ,'SOFTWARE\Microsoft\Microsoft SQL Server\MSSQL.2\MSSQLServer'
    ,'BackupDirectory',@chvSQLPath    OUTPUT



Select @chvDeviceName = @chvDbName
                      + Convert(Varchar, GetDate(), 112),
       @chvFileName   = @chvSQLPath + '\'
                      + @chvDeviceName
                      + '.bkp'

if @debug <> 0
    select @chvDeviceName chvDeviceName,
           @chvFileName chvFileName

set xact_abort off
begin try
   EXEC sys.sp_addumpdevice 'disk', @chvDeviceName, @chvFileName
end try
begin catch
   SELECT @intErrorCode = ERROR_NUMBER();
end catch
set xact_abort on

-- 15026 - it is OK if dump device already exists
if @intErrorCode = 0 or @intErrorCode = 15026
    BACKUP LOG @chvDbName TO @chvDeviceName

return
```

TIP

Some might argue that such a stored procedure and job are not needed in the last couple of versions of SQL Server because it can increase the size of a transaction log automatically if it approaches its specified limit and that this is an academic example. This is true, but it's valid only if you can afford unlimited storage. If your disk resources are limited, it is a much better solution to clear the log. Alternatively, you can increase the frequency of scheduled transaction log backups.

An Alternative to Job Scheduler

Microsoft has developed Job Scheduler into a relatively sophisticated tool, with these features:

- ▶ Steps are included as components of jobs to allow better control.

- ▶ You can continue or even stop execution from different points, depending on the success or failure of each step.

- ▶ Operators can be notified according to predefined criteria.

- ▶ Each step can be coded in a different language (including Transact-SQL, ActiveX Scripts, operating system commands, or commands that call replication and maintenance services and utilities).

In the past, the only way to create a complex job was to code everything in Transact-SQL. Now, simpler jobs can be implemented using steps. If you really need a sophisticated solution, you still need the power of Transact-SQL or ActiveX Script.

SQL Server includes a set of stored procedures and extended stored procedures that can achieve everything that you can do within Job Scheduler. They reside in the *master* and *msdb* databases. (The database is used by SQL Server Agent to hold information about jobs, schedules, and operators.)

The following paragraphs will quickly review some of these stored procedures.

Stored Procedures for Maintaining Jobs

The sp_help_job stored procedure returns information about jobs. If no parameters are specified, the stored procedure returns a result set with a list of jobs and their attributes. If the job name (or ID) is specified, the stored procedure returns an additional result set that describes the job's steps, schedules, and target servers.

The sp_add_job, sp_delete_job, and sp_update_job stored procedures are used to create, delete, and change existing jobs, respectively.

The sp_add_jobschedule and sp_add_jobstep stored procedures are designed to associate a schedule and steps with an existing job. Naturally, there are corresponding stored procedures that allow you to delete or update schedules and steps and obtain information about them.

The following example creates a single-step job to perform a backup of the transaction log and assigns a nightly schedule to it:

```
USE msdb
EXEC sp_add_job @job_name = 'Asset Backup Log',
    @enabled = 1,
    @description = 'Backup transaction Log of Asset database',
    @owner_login_name = 'sa'

EXEC sp_add_jobserver @job_name = 'Asset Backup Log',
   @server_name = 'DSUNDERIC\ss2k'

EXEC sp_add_jobstep @job_name = 'Asset Backup Log',
    @step_name = 'Backup Log',
    @subsystem = 'TSQL',
    @server =  'DSUNDERIC\ss2k5',
    @command = ' BACKUP LOG Asset TO bkpAssetLog',
    @retry_attempts = 5,
    @retry_interval = 5

EXEC sp_add_jobschedule @job_name = 'Asset Backup Log ',
    @name = 'Nightly Backup',
    @freq_type = 4,      -- daily
    @freq_interval = 1, -- every 1 day
    @active_start_time = '000000' - midnight
```

It is much easier to create jobs, schedules, and steps from Management Studio, but
the previous script might be useful for deploying a job from a development or test
environment into a production environment. Therefore, Microsoft has created a way
for you to generate scripts that correspond to your jobs. Just open the context-sensitive
menu of a job in Management Studio and choose Script Job | Create To | Query Editor
Window. The following script is Management Studio's interpretation of the job that we
created two sections ago for managing transaction logs:

```
USE [msdb]
GO
/****** Object:  Job [do backups]  ******/
BEGIN TRANSACTION
DECLARE @ReturnCode INT
SELECT @ReturnCode = 0
/****** Object:  JobCategory [Database Maintenance]  ******/
IF NOT EXISTS (SELECT name FROM msdb.dbo.syscategories
     WHERE name=N'Database Maintenance' AND category_class=1)
```

```
BEGIN
EXEC @ReturnCode = msdb.dbo.sp_add_category
          @class=N'JOB',
          @type=N'LOCAL',
          @name=N'Database Maintenance'
IF (@@ERROR <> 0 OR @ReturnCode <> 0) GOTO QuitWithRollback

END

DECLARE @jobId BINARY(16)
EXEC @ReturnCode =  msdb.dbo.sp_add_job @job_name=N'do backups',
      @enabled=1,
      @notify_level_eventlog=0,
      @notify_level_email=0,
      @notify_level_netsend=0,
      @notify_level_page=0,
      @delete_level=0,
      @description=N'No description available.',
      @category_name=N'Database Maintenance',
      @owner_login_name=N'sa', @job_id = @jobId OUTPUT
IF (@@ERROR <> 0 OR @ReturnCode <> 0) GOTO QuitWithRollback

/****** Object:  Step [Backup if log is 95% full]  ******/
EXEC @ReturnCode = msdb.dbo.sp_add_jobstep
      @job_id=@jobId,
      @step_name=N'Backup if log is 95% full',
      @step_id=1,
      @cmdexec_success_code=0,
      @on_success_action=1,
      @on_success_step_id=0,
      @on_fail_action=2,
      @on_fail_step_id=0,
      @retry_attempts=0,
      @retry_interval=0,
      @os_run_priority=0, @subsystem=N'TSQL',
      @command=N'exec util.ap_LogBackupIfAlmostFull ''Asset5'', 95',
      @database_name=N'Asset5',
      @flags=0
IF (@@ERROR <> 0 OR @ReturnCode <> 0) GOTO QuitWithRollback
EXEC @ReturnCode = msdb.dbo.sp_update_job @job_id = @jobId,
                                          @start_step_id = 1
```

```
IF (@@ERROR <> 0 OR @ReturnCode <> 0) GOTO QuitWithRollback
EXEC @ReturnCode = msdb.dbo.sp_add_jobschedule
        @job_id=@jobId,
        @name=N'Every 5 min',
        @enabled=1,
        @freq_type=4,
        @freq_interval=1,
        @freq_subday_type=4,
        @freq_subday_interval=5,
        @freq_relative_interval=0,
        @freq_recurrence_factor=0,
        @active_start_date=20051017,
        @active_end_date=99991231,
        @active_start_time=0,
        @active_end_time=235959
IF (@@ERROR <> 0 OR @ReturnCode <> 0) GOTO QuitWithRollback
EXEC @ReturnCode = msdb.dbo.sp_add_jobserver
        @job_id = @jobId,
        @server_name = N'(local)'
IF (@@ERROR <> 0 OR @ReturnCode <> 0) GOTO QuitWithRollback
COMMIT TRANSACTION
GOTO EndSave
QuitWithRollback:
   IF (@@TRANCOUNT > 0) ROLLBACK TRANSACTION
EndSave:
```

You can use sp_start_job to instruct SQL Server Agent to run the job immediately, as in the following example:

```
USE msdb
EXEC sp_start_job @job_name = 'Asset Backup Log'
```

There is also an orthogonal stored procedure, sp_stop_job, which is designed to stop execution of a job that is in progress.

Once a job is completed, SQL Server Agent will record its completion status in the job history. You can view the history of a job using sp_help_jobhistory, and you can delete old records from the history using sp_purge_jobhistory.

Operators and Alerts

SQL Server Agent also maintains a list of operators and a list of alerts.

Operators are administrators who should be notified of predefined events configured in SQL Server. The system keeps track of the operator's network, e-mail, and pager addresses, as well as a timetable indicating when the operator is available during the week (and weekends).

Alerts are events that can occur in SQL Server, such as specific errors, errors of a certain severity, and conditions that can occur in a database, as well as the actions that need to be taken to handle the event (such as sending a message to the operator or executing a job).

There is also a third type of object that serves as a link between alerts and operators. *Notifications* are used to assign and send a message to operator(s) to handle alerts.

Naturally, there are stored procedures to manage these lists of operators and alerts:

► sp_help_operator, sp_add_operator, sp_delete_operator, sp_update_operator

► sp_help_alert, sp_add_alert, sp_delete_alert, sp_update_alert

► sp_help_notification, sp_add_notification, sp_delete_notification, sp_update_ notification

E-mail

SQL Server has the capability to interact with administrators and users via e-mail. Usually, operators are notified by SQL Server when specific events occur. You can use the Alert and Operator mechanisms to implement and define this behavior.

This feature is an alternative to standard methods of processing errors, such as recording critical errors in the error log. If SQL Server is in critical need of attention and your operators do not possess pagers, SQL Server can send e-mail to them. This approach is also practical for notifying administrators of successfully completed jobs.

Another common use is to process e-mail that contains database queries. Remote users can send queries to SQL Server and have it return result sets to them.

SQL Server can also send messages that include result sets in the form of a report to one or more users. Although these result sets are rather crude (just ASCII text), it is possible to envision and create an application that uses this capability to notify management when some change occurs in the database (however, it probably makes more sense to create such applications using Reporting Services or Service Broker).

SQL Server contains several services that handle e-mail. I will not go into detail on the implementation and configuration of these services. Refer to SQL Server Books OnLine and the Microsoft Support web site for more details. We will just explore usage of the service called Database Mail.

Database Mail

This is a new feature introduced in SQL Server 2005. It is a robust and high-performance service designed to provide enterprise-level capability for sending and managing e-mails (through external SMTP servers). It is designed to be

▶ **Scalable** It provides background asynchronous delivery implemented through Service Broker.

▶ **Reliable** It is implemented as a process isolated from the rest of SQL Server that supports server clustering and failover of SMTP servers, and one that does not require Outlook or Extended MAPI as alternate technologies, as in previous versions of SQL Server.

▶ **Secure** It is turned off by default and is fully manageable when in use. For example, only members of the msdb role DatabaseMailUserRole (or its parents) are allowed to send e-mails; it is possible to limit the type and size of attachments.

▶ **Supportable** It is integrated in SQL Server Database Engine and manageable from Management Studio or Transact-SQL. It is possible to log all events and audit all messages.

Configuring Database Mail

Before you can use Database Mail, you must install it and enable it:

1. Enable Database Mail from the SQL Server Surface Area configuration (Start | Programs | SQL Server 2005 | Configuration Tools). Alternatively, you can use

```
Exec sp_configure 'show advanced options', 1;
GO
RECONFIGURE;
GO
Exec sp_configure 'Database Mail XPs', 1;
GO
RECONFIGURE
GO
```

2. Now configure it using the Database Mail Configuration Wizard:

   a. Open the context menu of Management Studio | Server | Management | Database Mail.

   b. Press Next on the first page.

   c. Make sure that Setup Database Mail is selected on the next page and press Next.

d. On the New Profile page, set the Profile Name:

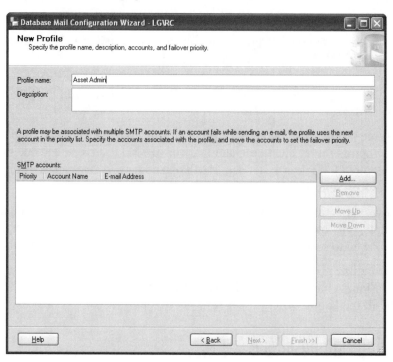

3. Click Add and fill the parameters of the mail account:

4. You can create more than one (failover) SMTP account. Click OK.

5. On the Manage Profile Security page, define which profiles are public and which user accounts have access to which private profiles, and then click Next.

6. On the next page, set the rest of the system configuration parameters:

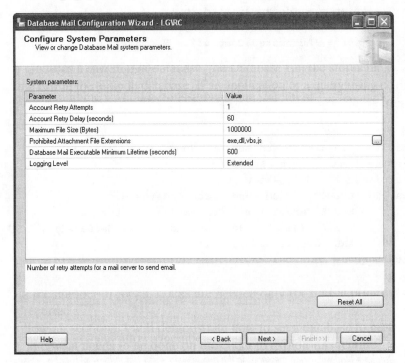

7. When you click Next on the following page, Management Studio will get Database Mail ready for you to dispatch e-mails.

NOTE

If you never tried to set mail features of earlier versions of SQL Server, you may consider this simple and straightforward. If you did, you will appreciate the work that Microsoft has invested in this version to simplify configuration.

Sending E-mails

The stored procedure msdb.dbo.sp_send_dbmail places specified e-mail in the Database Mail queue and returns an ID of the message in the queue to the caller. Service Broker manages the queue, reads messages one by one, and processes them.

The following batch sends a simple text message:

```
Declare @mailitem_id int
EXEC @mailitem_id = msdb.dbo.sp_send_dbmail
        @profile_name = 'Asset Admin',
        @recipients = 'dejan@asset.co.yu',
        @body = 'The ETL procedure completed successfully.',
        @subject = 'Automated Completion Message';
select @mailitem_id [@mailitem_id]
```

The following batch sends a message that contains a result of a query as an attachment:

```
Declare @mailitem_id int
EXEC @mailitem_id = msdb.dbo.sp_send_dbmail
    @profile_name = 'Asset Admin',
    @recipients = 'admin@asset.co.yu',
    @query = 'SELECT * FROM Asset5.dbo.OrderHeader
            WHERE TargetDate > Convert(smalldatetime,
            Convert(varchar(30), DateAdd(d, 1, GetDate()), 101))
            AND  OrderStatusId = 1',
    @attach_query_result_as_file = 1 ;

select @mailitem_id [@mailitem_id]
```

NOTE

Database Mail will accept messages in the queue even when Database Mail is not processing messages. You can start Database Mail using the msdb.dbo.sysmail_start_sp stored procedure or stop it using msdb.dbo.sysmail_stop_sp.

Check Status

You can examine the status of the message that was placed in the queue by running a query with mailitem_id, which was returned by msdb.dbo.sp_send_dbmail:

```
select * from msdb.dbo.sysmail_allitems
where mailitem_id = 123
```

Exposing Stored Procedures As Web Services

SQL Server 2005 supports HTTP/SOAP endpoints that allow developers to expose database objects as web services.

NOTE

Similar functionality existed in SQL Server 2000 with SQLXML 3.0. The major difference is that the earlier SQL Server version required the services of an external web server—IIS. That's not the case anymore. SQL Server 2005 uses the Windows Server 2003 kernel listener—HTTP.sys. However, you should not think of endpoints as a replacement for SQLXML; they have different and complementary features.

Endpoints

Only stored procedures or user-defined functions can be exposed through endpoints. They support two types of protocols—TCP and HTTP. They can also support different types of payload—database mirroring, Service Broker, T-SQL, and SOAP.

I will create an endpoint on a set of stored procedures for querying inventory in the Asset5 database:

```
CREATE ENDPOINT ept_AssetInventory
      STATE = STARTED
   AS HTTP
   (
      PATH = '/AssetInventory',
      AUTHENTICATION = (INTEGRATED),
      PORTS = (CLEAR),
      SITE = 'Asset5'
   )
   FOR SOAP
   (
      WEBMETHOD 'AssetInventoryQuickByMakeModel'
         (NAME='Asset5.dbo.ap_InventoryByMakeModel_Quick3'),
      WEBMETHOD 'AssetPhoto'
       (NAME='Asset5.dbo.ap_InventoryById_GetPhoto),
      WEBMETHOD 'AssetProperties'
       (NAME='Asset5.dbo.ap_InventoryProperties_Get'),
      BATCHES = DISABLED,
      WSDL = DEFAULT,
      DATABASE = 'Asset5',
      NAMESPACE = 'http://Asset5/AssetInventory'
   )
```

The endpoint will listen to the HTTP or TCP port described in the As clause. The Site parameter is the name of your server and Path is the virtual folder that will be associated with the endpoint. The For clause defines a type of payload for the endpoint (for web services, put SOAP). It lists web methods and associated stored procedures and/or functions. The Batches parameter should be set to Disabled unless you want to allow users to send any type of query.

A client application can reference this endpoint on a URL that contains the Site and Path parameters (in this example, http://Asset5/AssetInventory). However, inside the .NET client application, the endpoint should be referenced using its name (in this example, ept_AssetInventory).

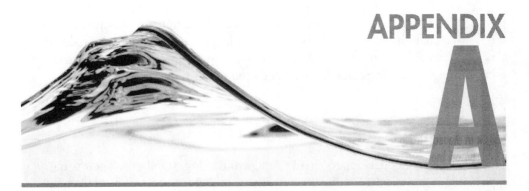

Naming Conventions

O ne of the most important things you can do to improve the quality and readability of your code is to use standards to name variables, procedures, and objects in your database. We will now go through the importance of using naming conventions and describe one used in this book.

Why Bother?

Unfortunately, many developers dislike, and avoid using, standards. Their usual explanation is that standards stifle their creativity, or that the constant need to comply with standards distracts them from what they are really being paid to do. While there may be some truth in these claims, compliance with reasonable standards is another one of those habits that differentiates the professional from the amateur (not to mention the prima donna). Often, however, the problem lies not in the presence or content of a standard but in the spirit of its enforcement. Frequently, organizations (or the people in them) get carried away. They forget the reasons for enforcing standards and the standards become an end in themselves.

There are several valid reasons for introducing naming conventions:

▶   The main reason for the existence of naming conventions is to make code readable, understandable, and easy to remember.

▶   A standard allows developers to speak a common "language" that will help the team to communicate more efficiently.

▶   Team members will be able to understand and learn parts of the code with which they are not familiar.

▶   New team members will have to learn only one standard way of coding instead of having to learn the distinct coding habits of individual team members.

▶   Time will be saved and confusion avoided, since it will be easier to define and identify unique names for objects and variables.

If you are developing a project on your own, you might go through it without implementing a standard (or without being aware that you actually have a standard). However, in most cases, the introduction of a standard becomes critical, such as when the following conditions exist:

- More than one developer is working on the project.

- The code or project will be maintained or reviewed by other developers who are not currently members of the team.

- The application under development is too complex for one person to analyze all aspects at once and requires different components to be designed and implemented separately.

Conventions do not have to be complicated. To demonstrate this point, consider this simple example. If you name a variable @OrderNum, you will become confused about its contents because the name does not convey its purpose clearly. Does it contain the total number of orders or the index of a particular order? To resolve this confusion, you could establish a convention that indexes are named with "Id" and totals with "Count" at the end of the name. In this case, the variable becomes @OrderId or @OrderCount.

Naming Objects and Variables

The naming of objects should take into account the following details:

- Entity description
- Name length
- Abbreviations
- Name formatting

Entity Description

It is common knowledge that variables, procedures, and objects should be named after the entities or processes that they represent. Therefore, just to type a full description is a good start. The advantages of this approach are

- Nobody will be confused about the purpose or contents.

- It makes for easy-to-read code, since no cryptic abbreviations are used.

- It makes the entity name easy to understand and memorize, since the description closely matches the entity.

Just compare the names in the following table:

Good	Bad
@CurrentDate	@D
@ActivityCount	@ActNum
@EquipmentType	@ET
CalculateOrderTotal	RunCalc

NOTE

Such descriptions are usually just the basis for a name. Standards generally prescribe the use of different prefixes or suffixes to further describe other attributes such as the type of object, the data type of a variable, and the scope.

A very common mistake is to use computer-oriented terminology instead of business-oriented terminology. For example, ProcessRecord is a confusing name for a procedure. It should be replaced with a business description of the process, such as CompleteOrder.

Name Length

Unfortunately, if you are too literal in naming procedures according to their business descriptions, you end up with names like:

▶ PickupReconciliationInventoryIdentifier

▶ TotalAmountOfMonthlyPayments

▶ GetParentOrganizationalUnitName

Although SQL Server supports the use of identifiers up to 128 characters long, research has shown that code in which most variable names are between 8 and 15 characters in length is easiest to develop, read, debug, and maintain. This fact does not imply that all of your variables must have lengths in that range, but you can use it as a rule of thumb.

Another rule of thumb is to try to limit names to three words. Otherwise, names become too long and thus more difficult to use and maintain.

You could go to an extreme in the other direction, as well. If you are using a variable as a temporary counter in a loop, you could name it @I. But even in such a case, it might be easier to understand your code if you name it @OrderItem.

Abbreviations

A simple way to reduce the length of a name is to abbreviate it. If you can find an abbreviation in a thesaurus or dictionary, you should use it. You will avoid potential confusion. If not, you can simply remove vowels (except at the beginning of the word) and duplicate letters from each word, as in these examples:

▶ Current = Crnt

▶ Address = Adr

▶ Error = Err

▶ Average = Avg

You could also use the first letters of words or the first few letters of a word, but make sure that the names you create will not be confused with other, more common abbreviations. For example, you could abbreviate Complete Order Management to COM, but Visual Basic programmers might assume it stands for "component."

If you do not want to confuse readers of your code (such as the fellow programmers trying to maintain it months after you have taken early retirement and moved to a remote tropical island), you should *avoid* using phonetic abbreviations like

▶ 4tran (Fortran)

▶ xqt (execute)

▶ b4 (before)

Abbreviations are great, but you should be careful not to confuse your colleagues. Try to be consistent. If you start abbreviating one word, you should do the same in all occurrences (variables, procedures, objects). It is potentially confusing to abbreviate the word Equipment as Eq in one case and leave the full word in another case. You will cause confusion as to which to use and whether they are equivalent.

To avoid confusion, you can write a description (using full words) in comments beside the declaration of a variable, in the definition of an object, or in the header of a procedure; for example:

```
declare @ErrCd int  -- Error Code
```

Ideally, the use of abbreviations should be defined, documented, and enforced as a naming convention and therefore applied consistently by everyone on the team.

Name Formatting

I have heard endless debates about formatting identifiers. To underscore or not to underscore—that is the question:

▶   LeaseScheduleId

▶   lease_schedule_id

The truth is it does not matter. You should avoid mixing these two conventions because developers will never know what they have used for which variable. Unfortunately, you can catch even Microsoft developers mixing them. They are just human beings, after all.

In some rare cases, I believe it is justifiable to mix these two conventions in one identifier. For example, I like to note modification statements at the end of the name of a trigger (Insert and Update trigger on OrderItem table):

```
trOrderItem_IU
```

I also use an underscore to divide table names joined with a foreign key (such as a foreign key between Order and OrderItem tables):

```
fk_Order_OrderItem
```

Suggested Convention

In computer science theory, you can find several well-documented formal conventions. The most famous one is the Hungarian convention:

http://msdn.microsoft.com/isapi/ msdnlib.idc?theURL=/library/techart/hunganotat.htm

I will present a convention that is rather informal and tailored for use in Transact-SQL. You do not have to follow it literally, but you should have a good reason to break any rule.

TIP

Rules are made to be broken but only if the solution is thereby improved.

Variables

Variable identifiers should consist of two parts:

▶ The *base part*, which describes the content of the variable

▶ The *prefix*, which describes the data type of the variable

Table A-1 shows data type abbreviations that should be used as prefixes.

Data Type	Prefix	Example
char	chr	@chrFirstName
varchar	chv	@chvActivity
nchar	chrn	@chrnLastName
nvarchar	chvn	@chvnLastName
text	txt	@txtNote
ntext	txtn	@txtnComment
datetime	dtm	@dtmTargetDate
smalldatetime	dts	@dtsCompletionDate
tinyint	iny	@inyActivityId
smallint	ins	@insEquipmentTypeId
integer	int	@intAsset
bigint	inb	@inbGTIN
numeric or decimal	dec	@decProfit
real	rea	@reaVelocity
float	flt	@fltLength
smallmoney	mns	@mnsCost
money	mny	@mnyPrice
binary	bin	@binPath
varbinary	biv	@bivContract
image	img	@imgLogo
bit	bit	@bitOperational
timestamp	tsp	@tspCurrent
uniqueidentifier	guid	@guidOrderId
xml	xml	@xmlPart
sql_variant	var	@varPrice
cursor	cur	@curInventory
table	tbl	@tblLease

Table A-1   *Variable Prefixes*

Database Objects

Names of database objects should consist of two parts:

▶ The *base part,* which describes the content of the object

▶ The *prefix,* which describes the type of database object

Table A-2 shows database object abbreviations that should be used as prefixes.

NOTE

Tables, synonyms, and columns should not have prefixes describing the object type.

Database Object	Prefix	Example
Table	(no prefix)	Equipment
Column	(no prefix)	ActivityId
Synonym	(no prefix)	Eq
View	v	vActivities
Stored procedure	pr	prCompleteOrder
Trigger	tr	trOrder_IU
Instead-of trigger	itr	trOrder_IU
DDL trigger	dtr	trdShemaChangesLog
Default	df	dfToday
Rule	rul	rulCheckZIP
Index	ix	idxLastName
Primary key	pk	pk_ContactId
Foreign key	fk	fk_Order_OrderType
Primary XML index	pidx	pidxEquipment
Secondary XML index	sidx	sidxEquipment_Path
User-defined data type	udt	udtPhone
User-defined functions	fn	fnLastBusDay
Table-valued functions	fnt	fntDueDates

Table A-2   *Prefixes of Database Objects*

Triggers

Names of triggers should consist of three parts:

► The *prefix*, which implies the database object type

► The *base part,* which describes the table to which the trigger is attached

► The *suffix,* which shows modification statements (Insert, Update, and Delete)

The following is an example of a trigger name:

► **trOrder_IU**   Insert and Update After trigger on Order table

If more than one trigger per modification statement is attached to the table, the base part should contain the name of the table and a reference to a business rule implemented by a trigger:

► **trOrderCascadingDelete_D**   Delete trigger on Order table that implements cascading deletes of order items

► **trOrderItemTotal_D**   Delete trigger on Order table that maintains a total of order item prices

To differentiate *Instead-of* triggers from standard triggers (*After* triggers), you should use a different naming convention for them. For example, you could use "itr" as a prefix:

► **itrOrder_D**   *Instead-of* Delete trigger on the Order table

To differentiate DDL triggers from DML triggers, you can use the prefix "trd". Typical DDL operations are Create, Drop, and Alter, so we should use C, D, and A, respectively, as operation suffixes:

► **trdLoginChanges_CA**   Server-level DDL trigger that logs Create and Alter statements on server logins

► **trdTableView_DA**   Database-level trigger that logs statements that Drop or Alter tables and views

Stored Procedures

The base name of a stored procedure should usually be created from a noun followed by a verb to describe the process the stored procedure performs on an object, as in these examples:

► ap_Inventory_List

► ap_Lease_Close

I think that the noun-verb order is much more useful for grouping similar objects than verb-object order. In the case of noun-verb order, you will end up with manageable, topic-oriented groups of stored procedures. In the latter case, you will end up with much larger groups of procedures, sorted by operation (which is not very useful).

NOTE

Some developers use the sp_ prefix in front of the base name of a stored procedure. This prefix should be reserved for system stored procedures that reside in the master database and that are accessible from all databases.

You should also *avoid* computer-oriented or fuzzy names like these:

► ap_Data_Process

► ap_FeedData_Load

Names such as these are often a symptom of a poorly designed stored procedure.

If the procedure performs several tasks, all of those tasks should become part of the procedure name. It is okay to make procedure names longer than variable names. You should be able to pack a name into 20 to 40 characters.

Often, you need several stored procedures that query the same table but with different sets of input parameters. Since SQL Server does not support operator overloading, you must give them separate names. I often use By to delimit object name and search criteria:

► **ap_InventoryByStatusId_List**   Lists records from the Inventory table with a specified StatusId

► **ap_InventoryByEqTypeId_List**   Returns Inventory table records of a specified EqTypeId

► **ap_InventoryByLocationByOwner_List**   Returns Inventory records with a specified location, owned by a specified user

In earlier versions of SQL Server, I often grouped stored procedures relating to the same module, application, or functional area using an application or module moniker in front of the object name. Monikers were typically short abbreviations (two to four, ideally three, characters), managed in a separate list:

- ► ap_AST_InventoryByEqType_List
- ► ap_AST_InventoryByLocationByOwner_List
- ► ap_RPT_InventoryByStatus_List

So the template for stored procedure names will be something like this:

```
ap_MON_ObjectByCriteria_Operation
```

TIP

Since SQL Server 2005 has separated schemas from database objects, it makes more sense to group related stored procedures using schemas. Schemas allow you to group other database objects as well.

Stored Procedure Compilation, Storage, and Reuse

ransact-SQL is not a standard programming language, nor is Microsoft SQL Server a standard environment for program execution. However, the process of compiling the source code for a stored procedure and its execution bear some resemblance to the compilation and execution of programs in standard programming languages.

The Compilation and Execution Process

When a developer executes any batch of T-SQL statements, SQL Server performs the following four steps:

1. Parse the batch.
2. Get statistics.
3. Compile the batch.
4. Execute the batch.

Parsing

Parsing is a process during which the Microsoft SQL Server's *Command Parser module* first verifies the syntax of a batch. If no errors are found, the Command Parser breaks the source code into logical units such as keywords, identifiers, and operators. The parser then builds an internal structure that describes the series of steps needed to perform the requested operation or to extract the requested result set from the source data. If the batch contains a query, this internal structure is called a *query tree,* and if the batch contains a procedure, it is called a *sequence tree.*

Get Statistics

Statistics are database objects that describe distribution of data in indexes and columns. Based on them, the engine knows how useful the index for processing of a statement is. By default, databases are set in Auto Create Statistics and Auto Update Statistics modes, and SQL Server automatically maintains them as records that are added, deleted, or modified in tables.

   At this point in the process, SQL Server will load all relevant statistics into memory. If some of the statistics are not up-to-date, SQL Server will initiate a process to updating them. One major difference between SQL Server 2005 and the earlier versions is that statistics can now be updated asynchronously. The compilation will not be blocked by statistics updates. SQL Server can decide to continue the process using "stale" statistics.

Compilation

In this step, a sequence tree is used to generate an execution plan. The *optimizer module* analyzes the ways that information can be retrieved from the source tables. It attempts to find the fastest way that uses the smallest amount of resources (that is, processing time, IOs and memory). It also complements the list of tasks that need to be performed (for instance, it checks security, it verifies that constraints are enforced, and it includes triggers if they need to be incorporated in processing). The result is an internal structure called an *execution plan* (or *query plan*).

Execution

The execution plan is then stored in the *procedure cache* or *plan cache,* from which it is executed, and then associated with *execution context*—a set of parameters used in execution plans. Different steps in the execution plan will be posted to different modules of the relational engine to be executed: DML manager, DDL manager, stored procedure manager, transaction manager, or utility manager. Results are collected in the form of a result set and sent to the caller.

Reuse of Execution Plans

Execution plans remain in the procedure cache for a while. If the same or some other user issues a similar batch, the relational engine first attempts to find a matching execution plan in the procedure cache. If it exists, it will be reused and, therefore, compilation cost will be avoided. If it does not exist, SQL Server parses and compiles a batch.

If SQL Server requires more memory than is available, it might remove some execution plans from memory. There is a sophisticated "aging" algorithm that takes into account how long ago and how many times an execution plan was used. If there is an abundance of memory, it is possible that execution plans will remain in the cache indefinitely.

Execution contexts are also cached and could be reused, but unlike execution plans, they are single-threaded; they can be used by one process at the time. A process first looks for a matching execution plan and when it finds it, it looks for suitable execution context. "Suitable" here means that it is not required that execution context matches exactly.

NOTE

A plan does not have to be in the plan cache to be executed. In fact, there are some plans that will never go into plan cache. For example, batches that contain literals (constants) that are more than 8KB large or batches that contain bulk insert statements will never be cached. However, a plan has to be cached for a process to find it and reuse it.

Levels of Execution Plans

Execution plans can be based on different types of objects:

- ▶ Batch
- ▶ Stored procedure
- ▶ Query
- ▶ Trigger
- ▶ Prepared statement
- ▶ Ad hoc query
- ▶ Statement (!!!)

NOTE

Statement-level execution plans and the possibility of their recompilation (I'll discuss recompilation in the following sections) are a SQL Server feature with very important performance implications. In SQL Server 2000 and earlier versions, it was advised to reduce the size of stored procedures that a system will often recompile. This is not so important in SQL Server 2005, which can recompile just the statement that has caused the recompilation, instead of recompiling a whole stored procedure or a batch.

Caching Levels

The following types of batches are cached separately even when they are created as part of a larger batch:

- ▶ Stored procedures
- ▶ Autoparameterized queries
- ▶ Batches executed using the Exec command

Every level provides additional opportunities for matching and reuse. The only exception occurs when the outer batch is actually a stored procedure and it is executing a nested stored procedure. In this case, the nested stored procedure cannot be reused by another stored procedure that is referencing it.

Reuse of Query Execution Plans

A simple query can be reused only in two scenarios. First, the query text of the second query must be identical to the text of the query described by the execution plan in the cache. Everything has to match—spaces, line breaks, indentation—even case on case-sensitive servers.

The second scenario may occur when the query contains fully qualified database objects to reuse execution plans:

```
Select *
from Asset5.dbo.Inventory
```

Parameterized Queries

The designers of SQL Server have created two methods to improve the reuse of queries that are not designed as stored procedures:

▶ Autoparameterization

▶ The sp_executesql stored procedure

The first of these methods is covered in the following section and the second one in Chapter 15.

Autoparameterization

When a Transact-SQL statement is sent to SQL Server, it attempts to determine whether any of its constants can be replaced with parameters. Subsequent queries that use the same template will reuse the same execution plan.

For example, let's say that SQL Server receives the following ad hoc query:

```
SELECT FirstName, LastName, Phone, Fax, Email, OrgUnitId, UserName
FROM Asset5.dbo.Contact
where ContactId = 3
```

It will try to parameterize it in the following manner and create an execution plan:

```
SELECT FirstName, LastName, Phone, Fax, Email, OrgUnitId, UserName
FROM Asset5.dbo.Contact
where ContactId = @P1
```

After this, all similar queries will reuse the execution plan:

```
SELECT FirstName, LastName, Phone, Fax, Email, OrgUnitId, UserName
FROM Asset5.dbo.Contact
where ContactId = 11
```

SQL Server applies autoparameterization only when a query's template is "safe"—that is, when the execution plan will not be changed and the performance of SQL Server will not be degraded if parameters are changed.

> **NOTE**
>
> *SQL Server might decide to create and use a different execution plan even if the query is based on the same field. For example, imagine that you are querying a table with contact information using the Country field. If your company is operating predominantly in North America, SQL Server might carry out a query for Denmark contacts based on the index on the Country field, and a query for USA contacts as a table scan.*

SQL Server attempts autoparameterization on Insert, Update, and Delete statements, too. First, I'll review the conditions for autoparameterization in SQL Server 2000, and then for those in SQL Server 2005.

The query must match a set of four templates in order for SQL Server 2000 to attempt autoparameterization:

```
Select {* | column-list}
From table
Where column-expression
[Order by column-list]

Insert table
Values ({constant | NULL | Default} [, ...n])

Update table
set column-name = constant
where column-expression

Delete table
Where column-expression
```

Note that *column-expression* is an expression that involves only column names, constants, the And operator, and the comparison operators: <, >, =, >=, <=, and <>.

SQL Server 2000 is more forgiving about formatting the query when autoparameterization is used, but it still does not allow changes in capitalization or changes in the way an object is qualified.

On SQL Server 2005, Microsoft defines conditions for autoparameterization in the opposite way—by listing cases that will *not* be considered as candidates for autoparameterization:

- ▶ Update and Delete statements that contain a From clause with any of following:
  - ▶ More than one table
  - ▶ Table-valued variable or function
  - ▶ Table or index hints
  - ▶ Tablesample clause
  - ▶ Full-text table
  - ▶ OpenRowSet() function
  - ▶ OpenQuery() function
  - ▶ OpenDataSource() function
  - ▶ OpenXml() function
  - ▶ XmlUnnext() function
  - ▶ IRowSet() function
- ▶ Update statements with an Order By clause
- ▶ Any statement with the Top clause
- ▶ WaitFor statements
- ▶ Bulk Insert statements
- ▶ Insert…Exec statements
- ▶ Select statements with an In operator in a Where clause
- ▶ Select statements with Distinct
- ▶ Select or Update statements with a For Browse clause
- ▶ Select statements with query hints with an Option clause
- ▶ Select statements with a subquery
- ▶ Select statements with a Group By, Having, Compute By, Grouping, Union, Into. or For Update clause
- ▶ Select statements with CTE (Common Table Expressions)
- ▶ Statements with a Where clause with expressions joined by Or
- ▶ Statements with a Where clause with expressions that use a <> comparison with constants

- ▶ Statements with a Where clause with expressions that compare two constants
- ▶ Update statements with Set statements that reference variables
- ▶ Full-text predicates
- ▶ Statements in a string submitted through an Exec statement
- ▶ If 1,000 or more parameters are identified by autoparameterization

Reuse of Stored Procedure Execution Plans

Stored procedures do not have the limitations associated with ad hoc queries, and that is the main reason stored procedures are reused more often than queries.

The reuse of execution plans is one of the main reasons why the use of stored procedures is a better solution than the use of ad hoc queries. For example, if you execute a query three times, SQL Server will have to parse, recompile, and execute it three times. A stored procedure will most likely be parsed and recompiled only once—just before the first execution.

NOTE
Someone might argue that the time needed to compile is insignificant compared with the time needed to execute a query. That is sometimes true. But the SQL Server query engine in later versions compares dozens of new processing techniques in order to select the best one to process the query or stored procedure. Therefore, the time needed to recompile a stored procedure is greater in later versions than it is in earlier versions. Fortunately, the introduction of statement-level compilation in SQL Server 2005 will reduce the amount of time needed to recompile a batch or a stored procedure to a time needed to recompile a statement that has led to recompilation.

The execution plan with multiple execution contexts is cached in plan cache. The execution plan will be removed from the procedure cache when a process called *lazywriter* concludes that the execution plan has not been used for a while and that SQL Server needs more memory, or when the execution plan's dependent database objects are changed in any of the following ways:

- ▶ The amount of data is significantly changed.
- ▶ Indexes are created or dropped.
- ▶ Constraints are added or changed.
- ▶ Distribution statistics of indexes are changed.
- ▶ sp_recompile was explicitly called to recompile the stored procedure or trigger.

I was impressed with the way that lazywriter determines which execution plans are obsolete. Microsoft SQL Server 2000 contains a sophisticated emulation of the aging process. When SQL Server creates an execution plan, it assigns it a *compilation cost factor*. The value of this factor depends on the expense required to create the execution plan in terms of system resources. For example, a large execution plan might be assigned a compilation cost factor of 8, while a smaller one might be assigned a factor of 2. Each time the execution plan is referenced by a connection, its age is incremented by the value of the compilation cost factor. Thus, if the compilation cost factor of the execution plan is 8, each reference to the execution plan adds 8 to its "age."

SQL Server uses the lazywriter process to decrement the age of the execution plan. The lazywriter process periodically loops through the execution plans in the procedure cache and decrements the age of each execution plan by 1. When the age of an execution plan reaches 0, SQL Server deallocates it, provided that the system is in need of the resources and no connection is currently referencing the execution plan.

SQL Server 2005 works a little differently. A *query cost* is calculated as the sum of IO cost, CPU cost, and memory cost. Its unit is *tick* (number of ticks) and the maximum value of a query is 31 ticks.

IO cost is calculated as 1 tick for each 2 IOs, with a limit of 19 ticks. Two context switches of CPU are considered as 1 tick of *CPU cost*. Its maximum is set to 8 ticks. A query execution that uses up to 16 memory pages (128 KB) has a memory cost of 1 tick. The maximum of memory cost is 4 ticks.

SQL Server 2005 does not use lazywriter to periodically age execution plans. Its behavior is much simpler. When the plan cache reaches 50 percent of the buffer pool size, the next plan access decrements all existing execution plans by 1. When it reaches 75 percent, a dedicated resource monitoring thread is reactivated and it decrements tick counts of all existing execution plans by 1. When the plan is reused, its cost is returned to the original value. When the age of an execution plan reaches 0, SQL Server deallocates it (only if nothing is using it at that moment).

If a dependent database object is deleted, the stored procedure will fail during execution. If it is replaced with a new object (new object identification number) with the same name, the execution plan does not have to be recompiled and will run flawlessly. Naturally, if the structure of the dependent object is changed so that objects that the stored procedure is referencing are not present or not compatible anymore, the stored procedure will fail, resulting in a runtime error.

In some cases, an execution plan cannot be reused:

▶   When an instance of a stored procedure is executed against one database, the execution plan cannot be reused when another instance of the stored procedure is executed against a different database.

NOTE

Ad hoc queries, batches, and dynamic queries from the Exec statement can be reused even in this case.

▶ Batches with unqualified object names (such as select * from MyTable).

TIP

This is why it is critical to prefix everything with a schema name.

▶ Batches with constants longer than 8KB.

▶ Batches with bulk insert statements.

▶ Batches from CLR cannot reuse execution plans of Transact-SQL batches, and vice versa.

▶ Notification queries cannot reuse non-notification queries, and vice versa.

▶ Batches flagged with the For Replication flag cannot reuse batches that are not flagged, and vice versa.

▶ Stored procedures that were created or executed using the With Recompilation clause.

Recompiling Stored Procedures

SQL Server automatically recompiles some or all statements in a stored procedure when

▶ Data in referenced tables is changed significantly,

▶ A Set statement that can change a query result is in the middle of the stored procedure (or batch), or

▶ Schemas of referenced objects (such as tables, functions, and stored procedures) have been changed since the stored procedure was last recompiled.

SQL Server is intelligent enough to recompile a stored procedure when a table referenced by that stored procedure changes. Unfortunately, SQL Server might or might not recompile when you add an index that might help execution of the stored procedure. It all depends on SQL Server's ability to identify and store dependent objects. To force compilation of a stored procedure, a DBA can use sp_recompile:

```
Exec sp_recompile dbo.ap_OrdersByCountry_List
```

This task can be very tedious if many stored procedures and/or triggers depend on a table for which an index was added. Fortunately, it is possible to name the table for which dependent objects should be recompiled:

```
Exec sp_recompile Orders
```

This statement will recompile all triggers and stored procedures that depend on the Orders table. When a stored procedure or a trigger is specified as a parameter, only that stored procedure or trigger will be recompiled. If you use a table or a view as a parameter, all dependent objects will be recompiled.

TIP

Do not forget to recompile dependent objects after you add an index to a table. Otherwise, SQL Server may not be able to use them.

A developer might also decide to recompile a stored procedure each time it is used. A typical example is when a stored procedure is based on a query, the execution and performance of which depend on the value used as a criterion. I discussed such an example earlier, in the "Autoparameterization" section.

In that example, when a user requests orders from the USA, the selectivity of the index might be such that it is better for the query to do a table scan. If a user requests orders from a country that rarely appears in the particular database, the query engine might decide to use the index. To force SQL Server to evaluate these options every time, the developer should use the With Recompile option when designing the stored procedure:

```
Create Procedure dbo.ap_OrdersByCountry_List
      @Country char(3)
With Recompile
as
      Select *
      from dbo.Orders
      where Country =  @Country
```

The execution plan of a stored procedure created in this manner will not be cached on SQL Server.

It is also possible to force recompilation of a stored procedure during execution using the With Recompile option:

```
Exec dbo.ap_OrdersByCountry_List 'USA' With Recompile
```

The *recompilation threshold* is a number of changed rows in a table that will trigger the recompilation of a stored procedure (or a batch). It depends on the number of rows in a table and a table type. For temporary tables with up to six rows, the recompilation threshold is six; for temporary and static tables with up to 500 rows, it is 500; for larger temporary and static tables, it is 500 + 20 percent of the number of rows.

Table variables do not have a recompilation threshold, so their changes will not lead to recompilation. That is another reason to use table variables instead of temporary tables whenever possible.

Storing Stored Procedures

Stored procedures are persistent database objects, and Microsoft SQL Server stores them in virtual objects (that Microsoft used to call *system tables* and now calls *system views* or *catalog views*) to preserve them when their execution plan is removed from the procedure cache or when SQL Server is shut down.

When the Create Procedure statement is executed, SQL Server creates a new record in the sys.objects catalog view (and its equivalent sys.sysobjects) of the current database (see Figure B-1).

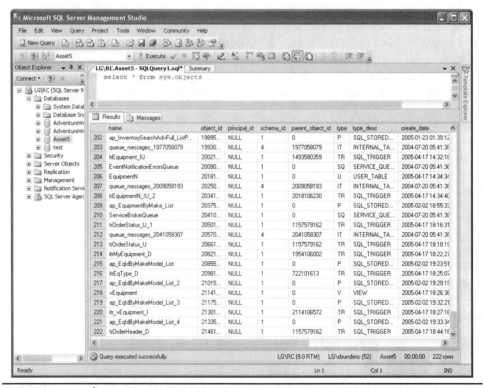

Figure B-1   *sys.objects*

This catalog view contains all schema-bound types of database objects (everything except DDL triggers, which are not schema-bound). Therefore, it is sometimes useful to filter it by object type (using the *type* field).

The source code of the stored procedure is recorded in the sys.syscomments system table (unless the stored procedure is encrypted). To see the source code, execute sp_helptext or query the sys.syscomments system table directly (see Figure B-2).

The source code is stored in a field named *text*. The data type of this field is `nvarchar(4000)`. Fortunately, this does not mean that stored procedures are limited to 4,000 characters. If the stored procedure is larger than 4,000 characters, SQL Server allocates additional records with an incremented *colid* field. Since this field is declared as `smallint`, a stored procedure can be 32KB × 4,000 bytes = 125MB large. In SQL Server 6.5 and earlier versions, *colid* was of the data type `byte` and the text was `varchar(255)`, so stored procedures were limited to 255 × 255 = 64KB.

You can hide the source code for a stored procedure if you encrypt it during creation. After you create the stored procedure using With Encryption, none of the users (not even the system administrator) will be able to see it on the server. Keep in mind that you can (and should) keep source code in a separate external script file.

Figure B-2   *sys.syscomments*

NOTE

Before this feature was introduced in SQL Server, developers achieved the same effect by setting the sys.syscomments.text file associated with the stored procedure to null. SQL Server was able to run the stored procedure without any problem. Unfortunately, this solution caused problems during SQL Server upgrades, since setup programs expected to use the text of stored procedures in order to recompile the stored procedures in the new environment. The inclusion of the With Encryption clause eliminated this issue.

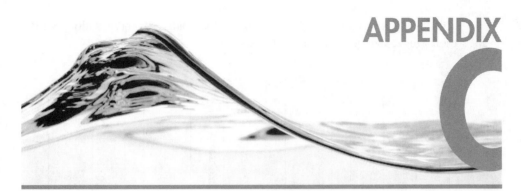

APPENDIX C

Data Types in SQL Server 2005

Table C-1 contains a list of all SQL Server 2005 native data types along with their range, size, and sample constants.

Data Type and Synonym	Description	Range or Length	Storage Size	Sample Constant
Character Strings				
char (character)	Character string	1 to 8,000 chrs	1 to 8,000 bytes	'D12-D13A36'
varchar (character varying)	Variable-length character string	1 to 8,000 chrs	1 to 8,000 bytes	'Toronto'
varchar(max)	New large value variable-length character string	1 to $2^{31} - 1$ chrs	16 bytes + 0 to 2GB	'SQL Server'
text	Large value variable-length character string from earlier versions	1 to $2^{31} - 1$ chrs	16 bytes + 0 to 2GB	'SQL Server'
Unicode Character Strings				
Nchar (national character or national char)	Unicode character string	1 to 4,000 chrs	2 to 8,000 bytes	N'Šunderić'
Nvarchar (national character varying or national char varying)	Variable-length Unicode character string	1 to 4,000 chrs	2 to 8,000 bytes	N'Ω'
Nvarchar(max)	New large value variable-length Unicode character string	1 to $2^{30} - 1$ chrs	16 bytes + 0 to 1GB	N'Никола'
Ntext (national text)	Large value variable-length Unicode character string from earlier versions	1 to $2^{30} - 1$ chrs	16 bytes + 0 to 1GB	
Date and Time				
datetime	Date and time	1-Jan-1753 to 31-Dec-9999; precision: 3 ms	8 bytes	'6/27/1998 10:20:17.31'
smalldatetime	Small date and time	1-Jan-1900 to 6-Jun-2079; precision: 1 min	4 bytes	'Oct 30, 1993 14:30'

Table C-1 SQL Server 2005 Native Data Types

Data Type and Synonym	Description	Range or Length	Storage Size	Sample Constant
Integer Numbers				
tinyint	Tiny integer	0 to 255	1 byte	17
smallint	Small integer	-32,768 to 32,767 (-2^{15} to $2^{15}-1$)	2 bytes	23017
int	Integer	-2,147,483,648 to 2,147,483,647 (-2^{31} to $2^{31}-1$)	4 bytes	343013
bigint	Big integer	-9,223,372,036,854,775,808 to 9,223,372,036,854,775,807 (-2^{63} to $2^{63}-1$)	8 bytes	322121343013
bit	Logical	0, 1, or Null	1 byte (up to 8 bits per byte)	1
Exact Numbers				
numeric (decimal or dec)	Numeric or decimal	$-10^{38}-1$ to $10^{38}-1$ (depends on precision and scale)	5 to 17 bytes	-352.4512
Approximate Numbers				
real	Real (single-precision) number	$-3.40\ 10^{38}$ to $3.40\ 10^{38}$	4 bytes	-232.212E6
float	Float (double-precision) number	$-1.79\ 10^{308}$ to $1.79\ 10^{308}$	8 bytes	34.2131343E-64
Monetary				
smallmoney	Small monetary data type	-214,768.3648 to 214,748.3647	4 bytes	$120.34
money	Monetary data type	-922,337,203,685,477.5808 to 922,337,203,685,477.5807	8 bytes	$120000000

Table C-1   SQL Server 2005 Native Data Types (continued)

Data Type and Synonym	Description	Range or Length	Storage Size	Sample Constant
Binary				
binary	Fixed-length binary string	1 to 8,000 bytes	1 to 8,000 bytes	0xa5d1
varbinary	Variable-length binary string	1 to 8,000 bytes	1 to 8,000 bytes	0xA5F2
varbinary(max)	New large value variable-length binary string	1 to 2^{31}–1 bytes	16 + 0 to 2GB	0xA5F22362F282
image	Large value variable-length binary string from earlier versions	1 to 2^{31}–1 bytes	16 + 0 to 2GB	0xA5F22362F282
timestamp	Database-wide unique number	n/a	8 bytes	n/a
uniqueidentifier	Globally unique identifier (GUID)	n/a	16 bytes	6F9619FF-8B86-D011-B42D-00C04FC964FF
Special				
cursor	Cursor reference	n/a	n/a	n/a
sql_variant	Variant	n/a	n/a	n/a
table	Table	n/a	n/a	n/a
xml	XML string	1 to 2^{31} – 1 chrs	16 bytes + 0 to 2GB	<PartID> 23151-123123123 </PartID>

Table C-1 SQL Server 2005 Native Data Types (continued)

Index